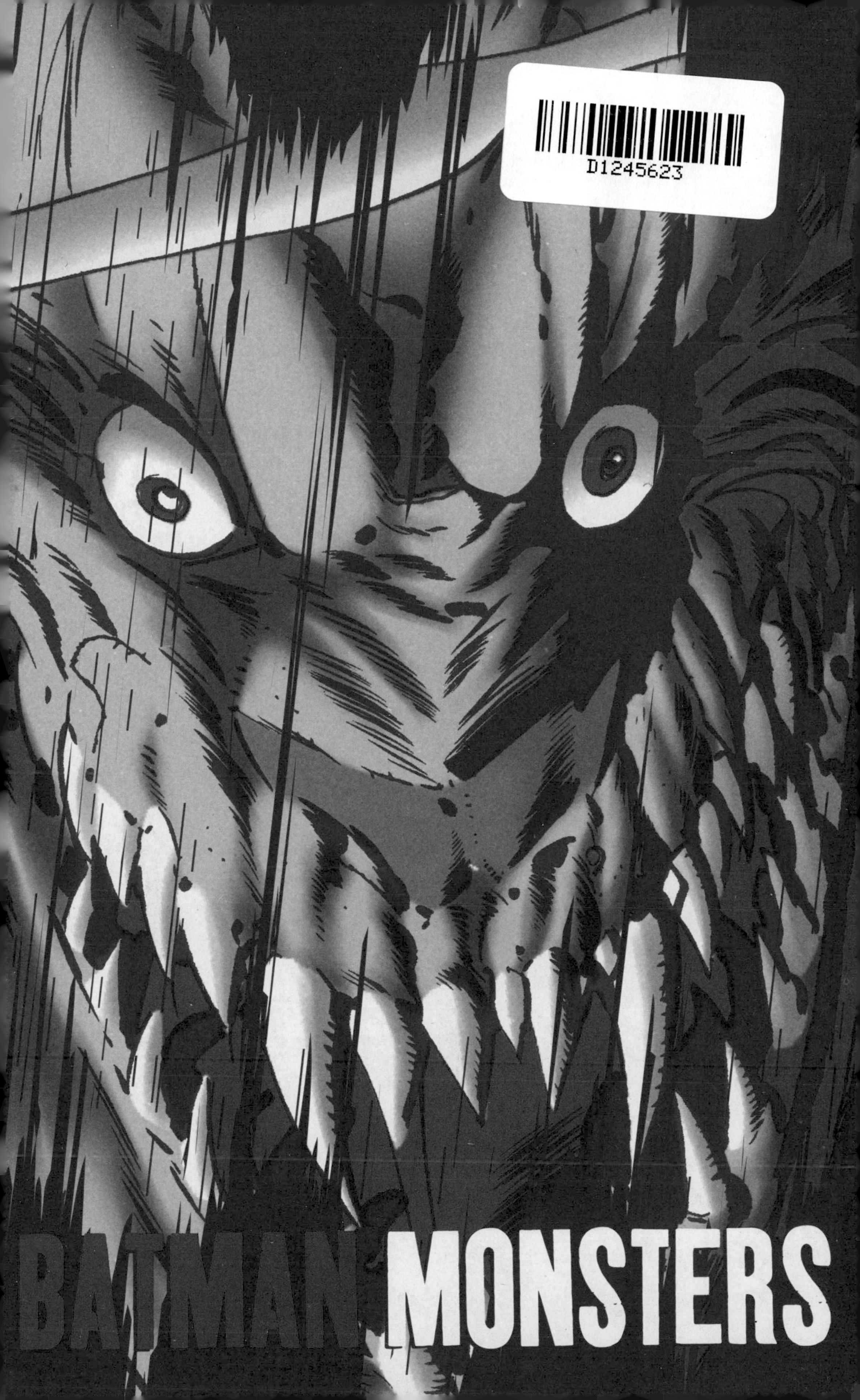
BATMAN MONSTERS

WEREWOLF

JAMES ROBINSON writer
JOHN WATKISS artist
DIGITAL CHAMELEON colorist

INFECTED

WARREN ELLIS writer
JOHN MCCREA artist
DIGITAL CHAMELEON colorist

CLAY

ALAN GRANT writer
QUIQUE ALCATENA artist
JESSICA KINDZIERSKI colorist

WILLIE SCHUBERT letterer

BATMAN created by **BOB KANE**

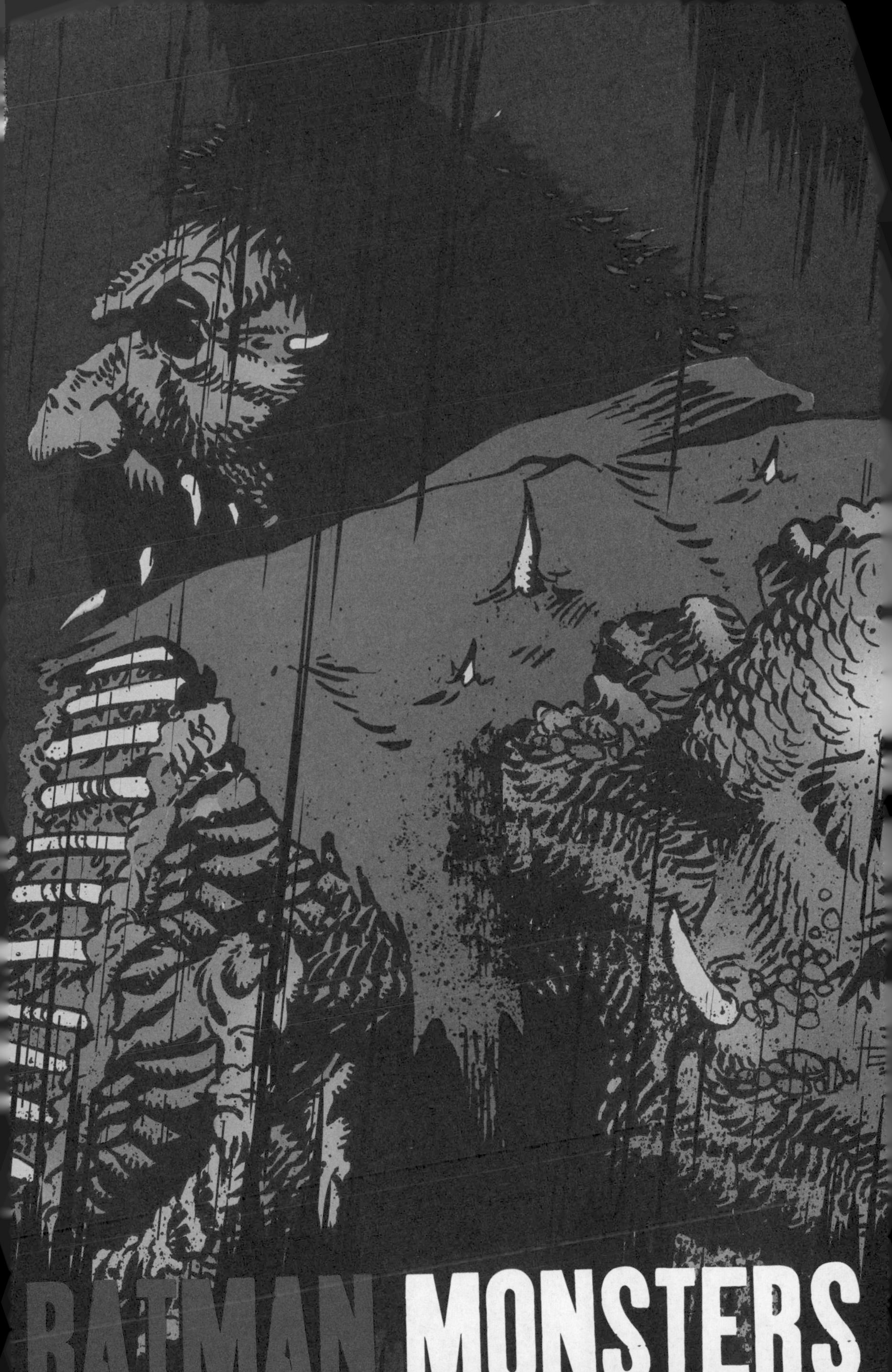

BATMAN MONSTERS

Dan DiDio SVP-Executive Editor
Archie Goodwin Editor-original series
Georg Brewer VP-Design & DC Direct Creative
Bob Harras Group Editor-Collected Editions
Sean Mackiewicz Editor
Robbin Brosterman Design Director-Books

DC COMICS
Paul Levitz President & Publisher
Richard Bruning SVP-Creative Director
Patrick Caldon EVP-Finance & Operations
Amy Genkins SVP-Business & Legal Affairs
Jim Lee Editorial Director-WildStorm
Gregory Noveck SVP-Creative Affairs
Steve Rotterdam SVP-Sales & Marketing
Cheryl Rubin SVP-Brand Management

Cover by John Watkiss

DC Comics, 1700 Broadway, New York, NY 10019
A Warner Bros. Entertainment Company
Printed by World Color Press, Inc.
St-Romuald, QC, Canada 9/30/09.
First Printing.
ISBN: 978-1-4012-2494-3

SUSTAINABLE FORESTRY INITIATIVE
Certified Fiber Sourcing
www.sfiprogram.org
Fiber used in this product line meets the sourcing requirements of the SFI program. www.sfiprogram.org PWC-SFICOC-260

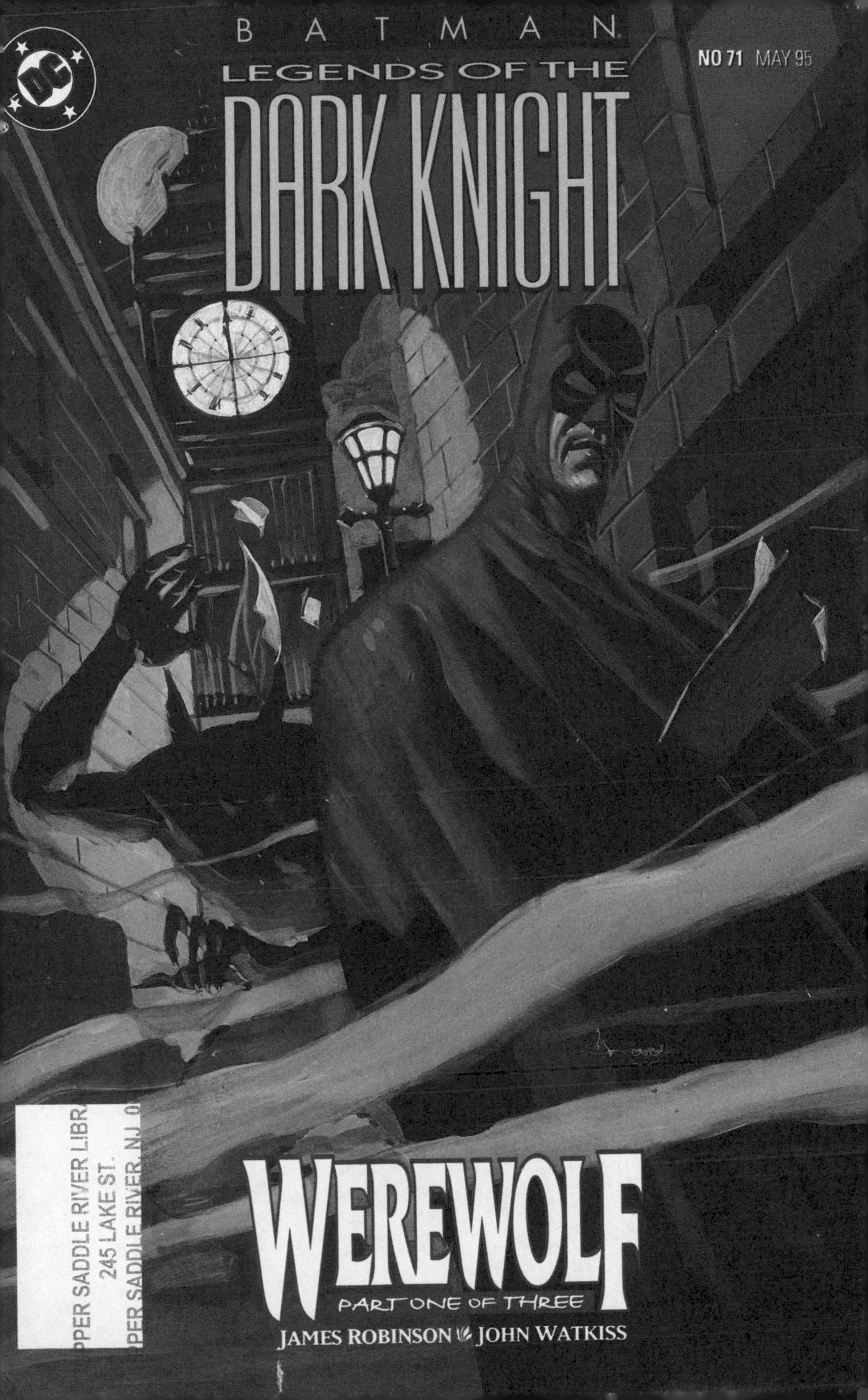
BATMAN
LEGENDS OF THE
DARK KNIGHT
NO 71 MAY 95
WEREWOLF
PART ONE OF THREE
JAMES ROBINSON JOHN WATKISS

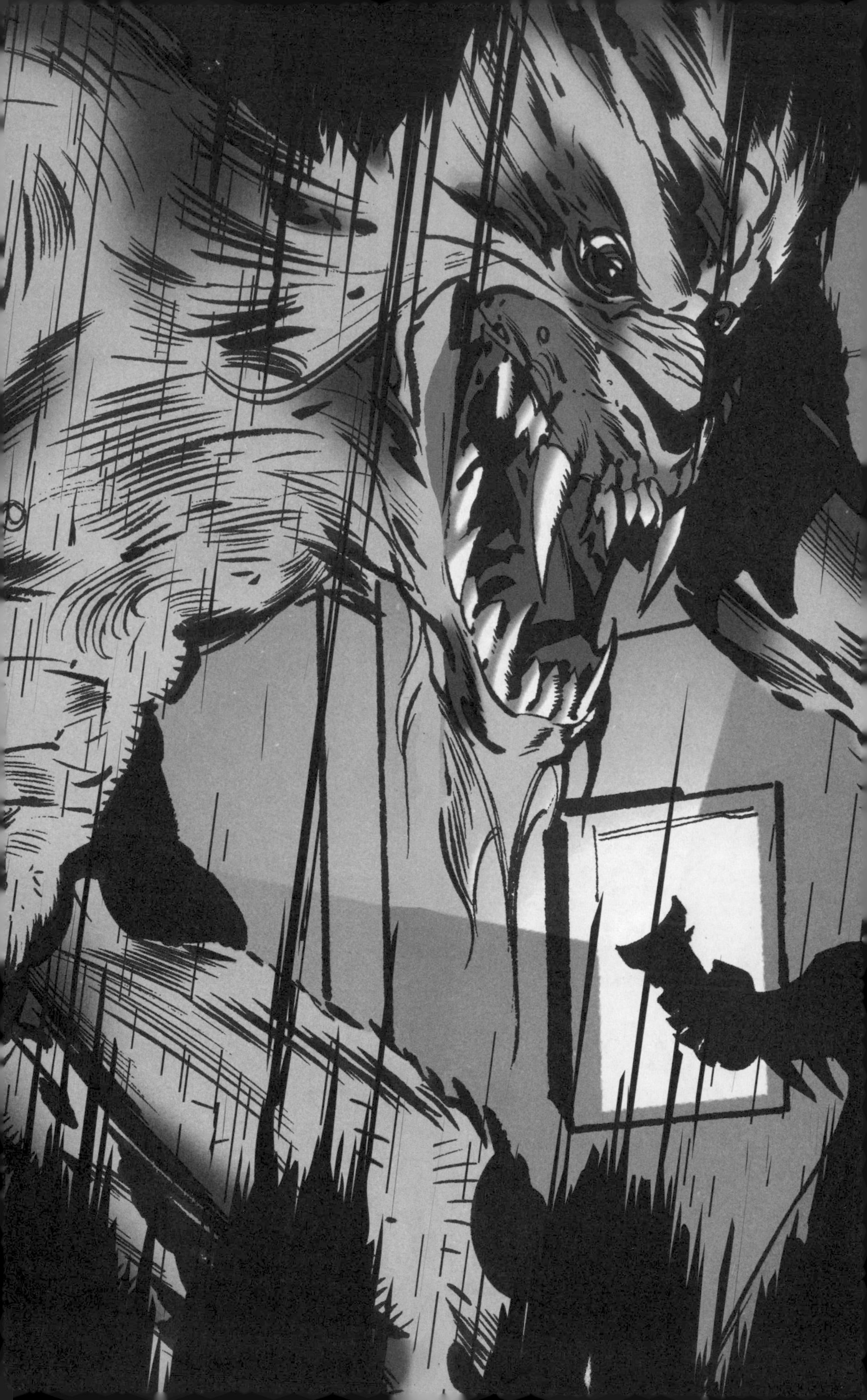

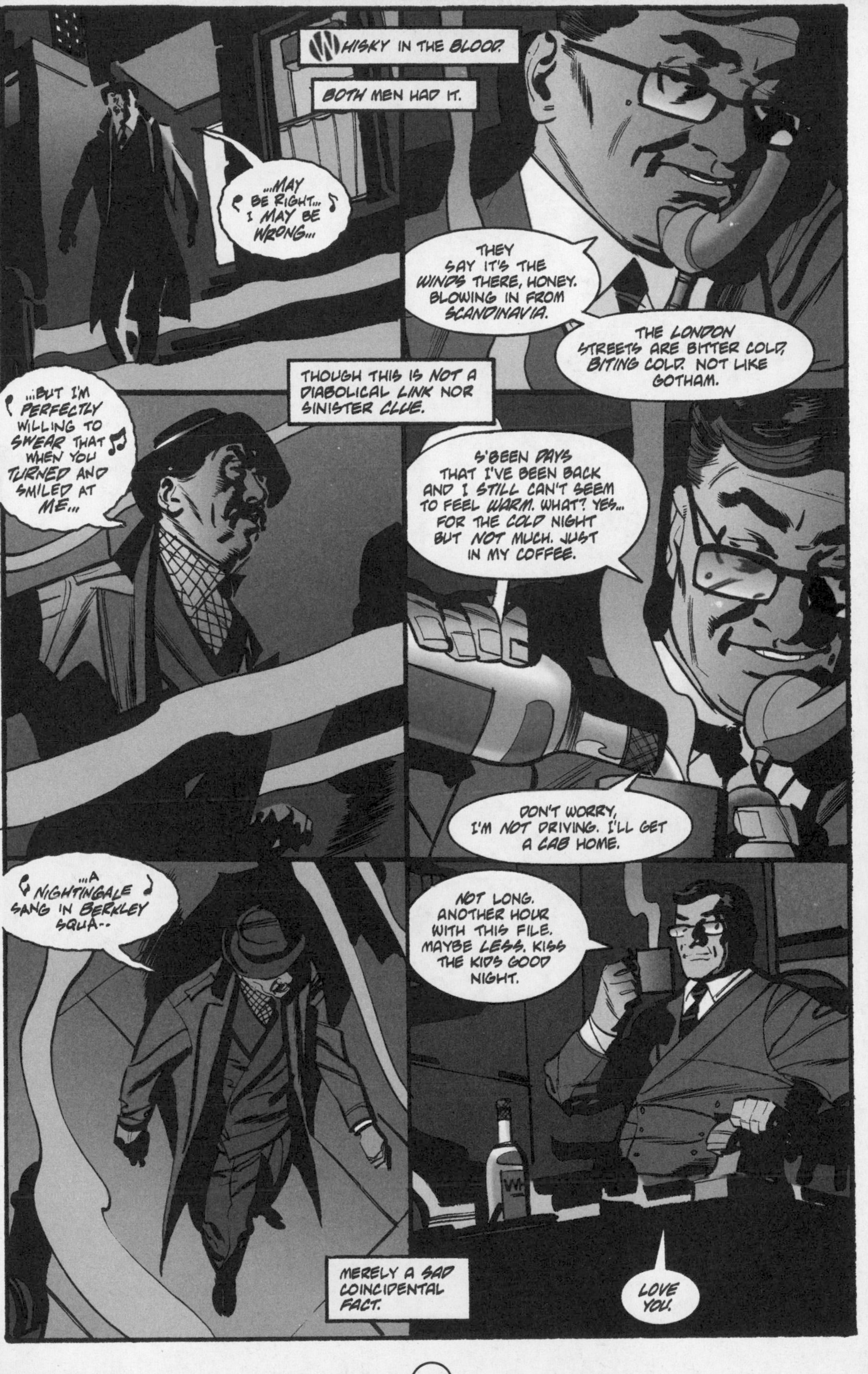
WHISKY IN THE BLOOD.
BOTH MEN HAD IT.
...MAY BE RIGHT... I MAY BE WRONG...
THEY SAY IT'S THE WINDS THERE, HONEY. BLOWING IN FROM SCANDINAVIA.
THE LONDON STREETS ARE BITTER COLD, BITING COLD. NOT LIKE GOTHAM.
THOUGH THIS IS NOT A DIABOLICAL LINK NOR SINISTER CLUE.
...BUT I'M PERFECTLY WILLING TO SWEAR THAT WHEN YOU TURNED AND SMILED AT ME...
S'BEEN DAYS THAT I'VE BEEN BACK AND I STILL CAN'T SEEM TO FEEL WARM. WHAT? YES... FOR THE COLD NIGHT BUT NOT MUCH. JUST IN MY COFFEE.
DON'T WORRY, I'M NOT DRIVING. I'LL GET A CAB HOME.
...A NIGHTINGALE SANG IN BERKLEY SQUA--
NOT LONG. ANOTHER HOUR WITH THIS FILE. MAYBE LESS. KISS THE KIDS GOOD NIGHT.
MERELY A SAD COINCIDENTAL FACT.
LOVE YOU.

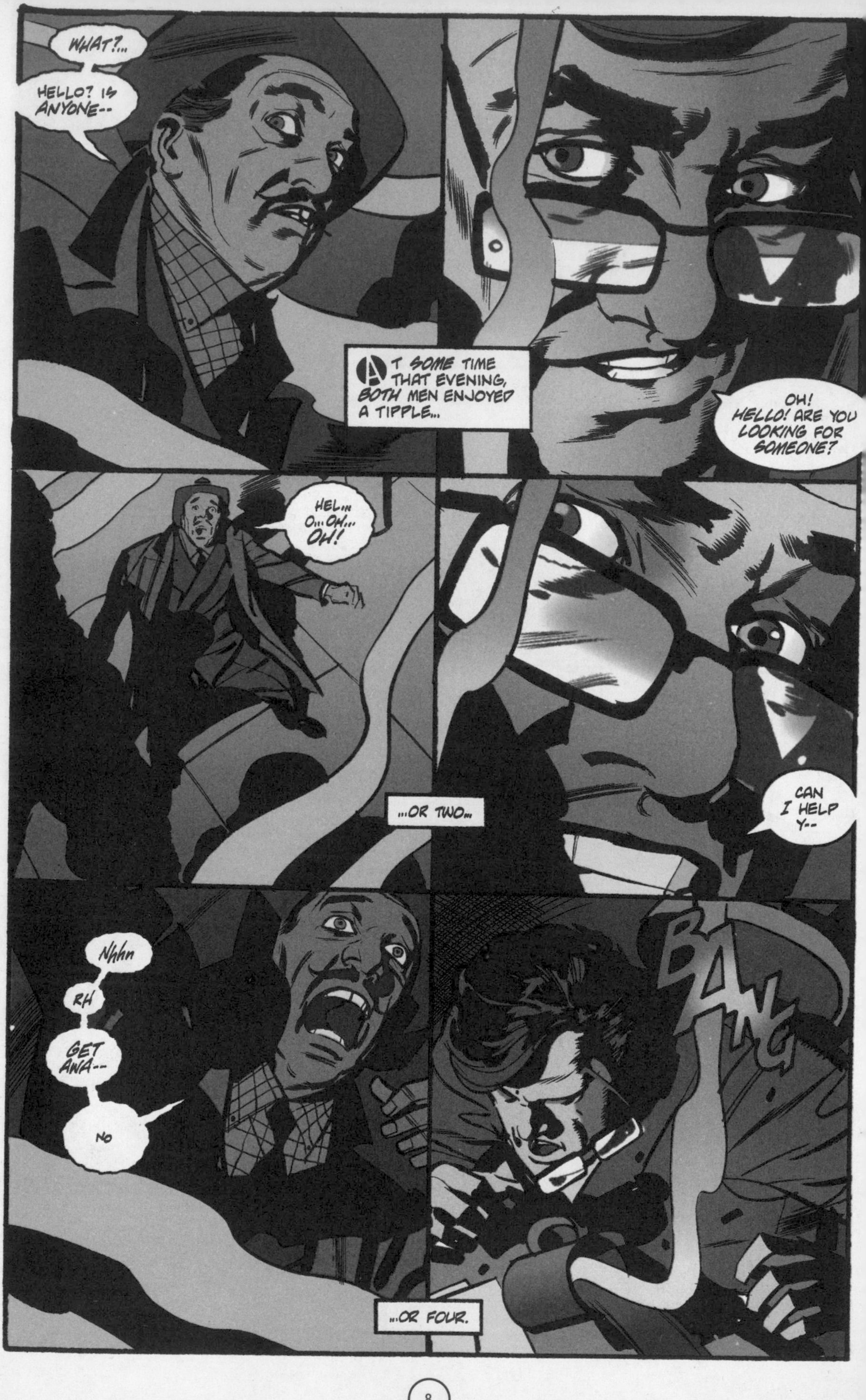
WHAT?...
HELLO? IS ANYONE--
AT SOME TIME THAT EVENING, BOTH MEN ENJOYED A TIPPLE...
OH! HELLO! ARE YOU LOOKING FOR SOMEONE?
HEL... O...OH... OH!
...OR TWO...
CAN I HELP Y--
Nhhn
RH
GET AWA--
NO
BANG
...OR FOUR.

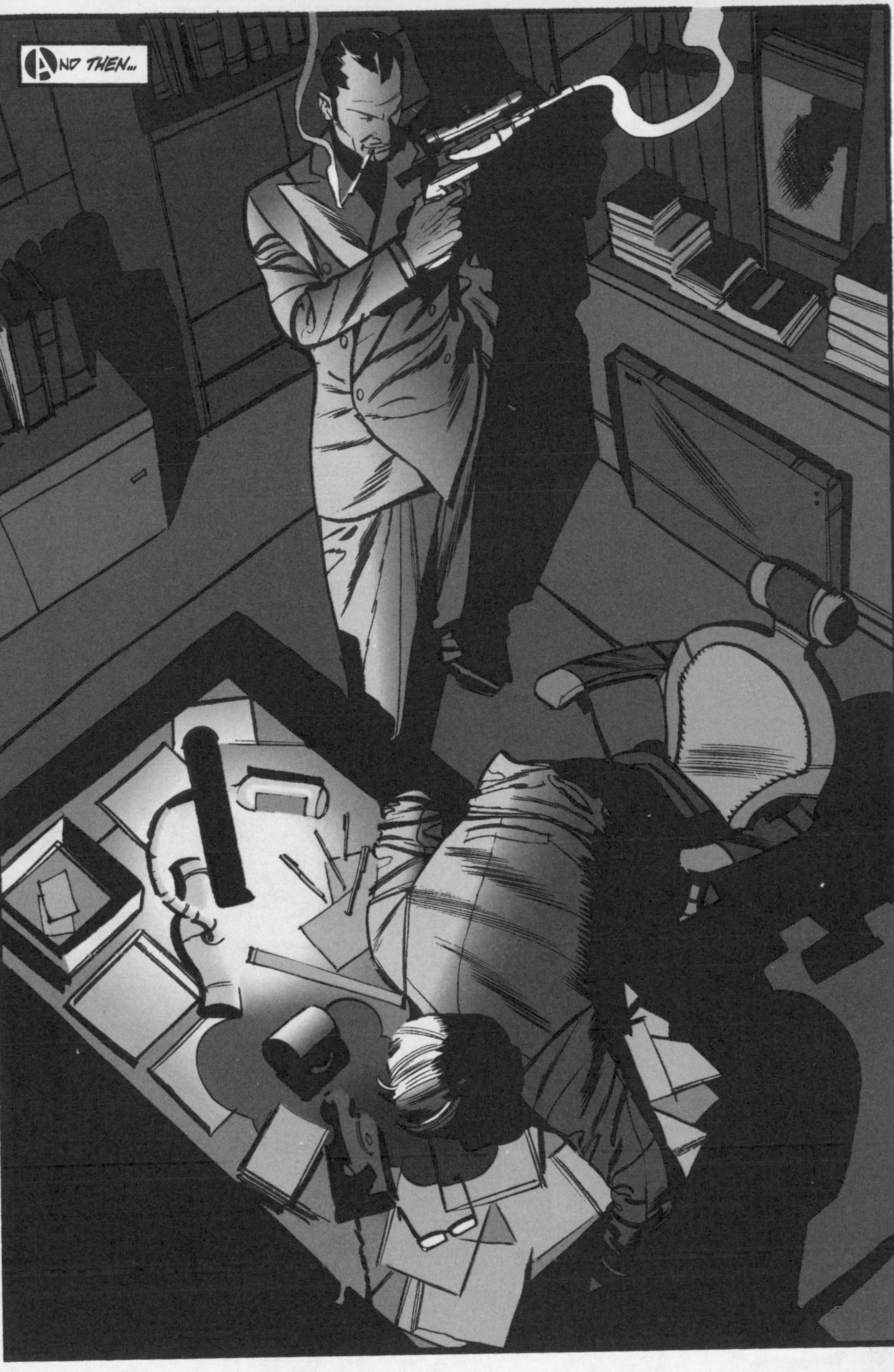
AND THEN...

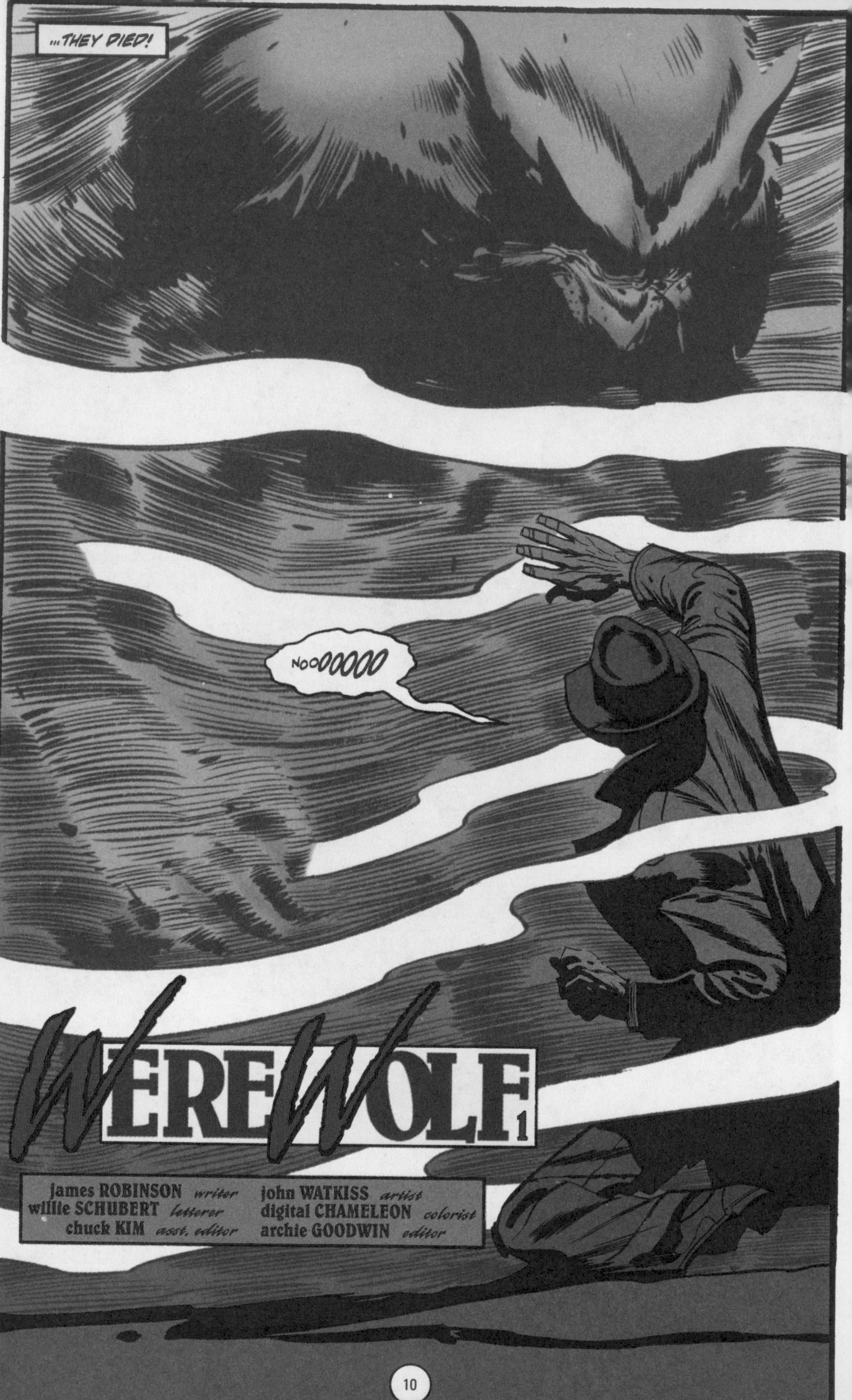
...THEY DIED!
NoooOOOO
WEREWOLF 1
james ROBINSON writer
john WATKISS artist
willie SCHUBERT letterer
digital CHAMELEON colorist
chuck KIM asst. editor
archie GOODWIN editor

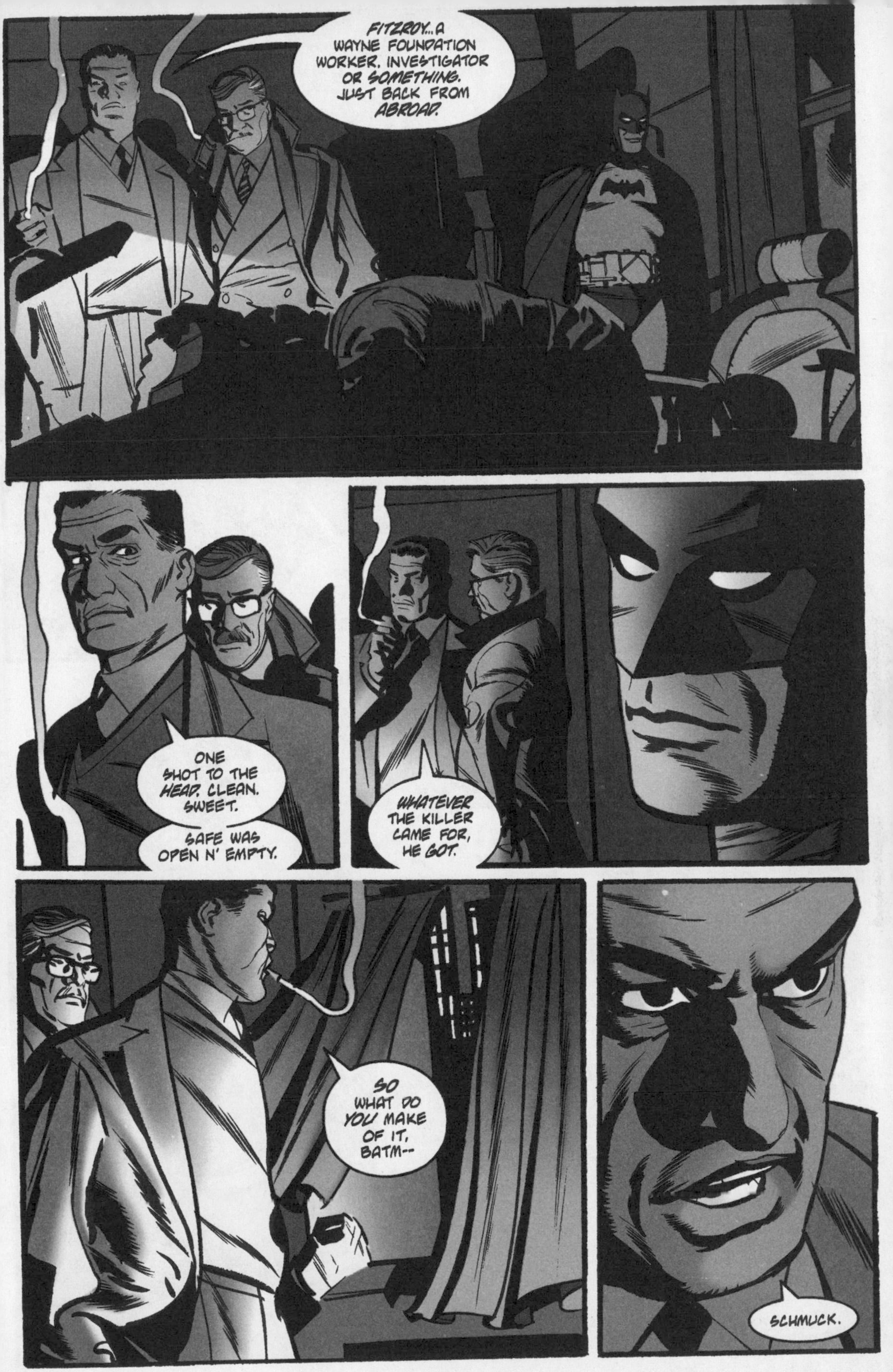
FITZROY...A WAYNE FOUNDATION WORKER. INVESTIGATOR OR SOMETHING. JUST BACK FROM ABROAD.
ONE SHOT TO THE HEAD. CLEAN. SWEET.
SAFE WAS OPEN N' EMPTY.
WHATEVER THE KILLER CAME FOR, HE GOT.
SO WHAT DO YOU MAKE OF IT, BATM--
SCHMUCK.

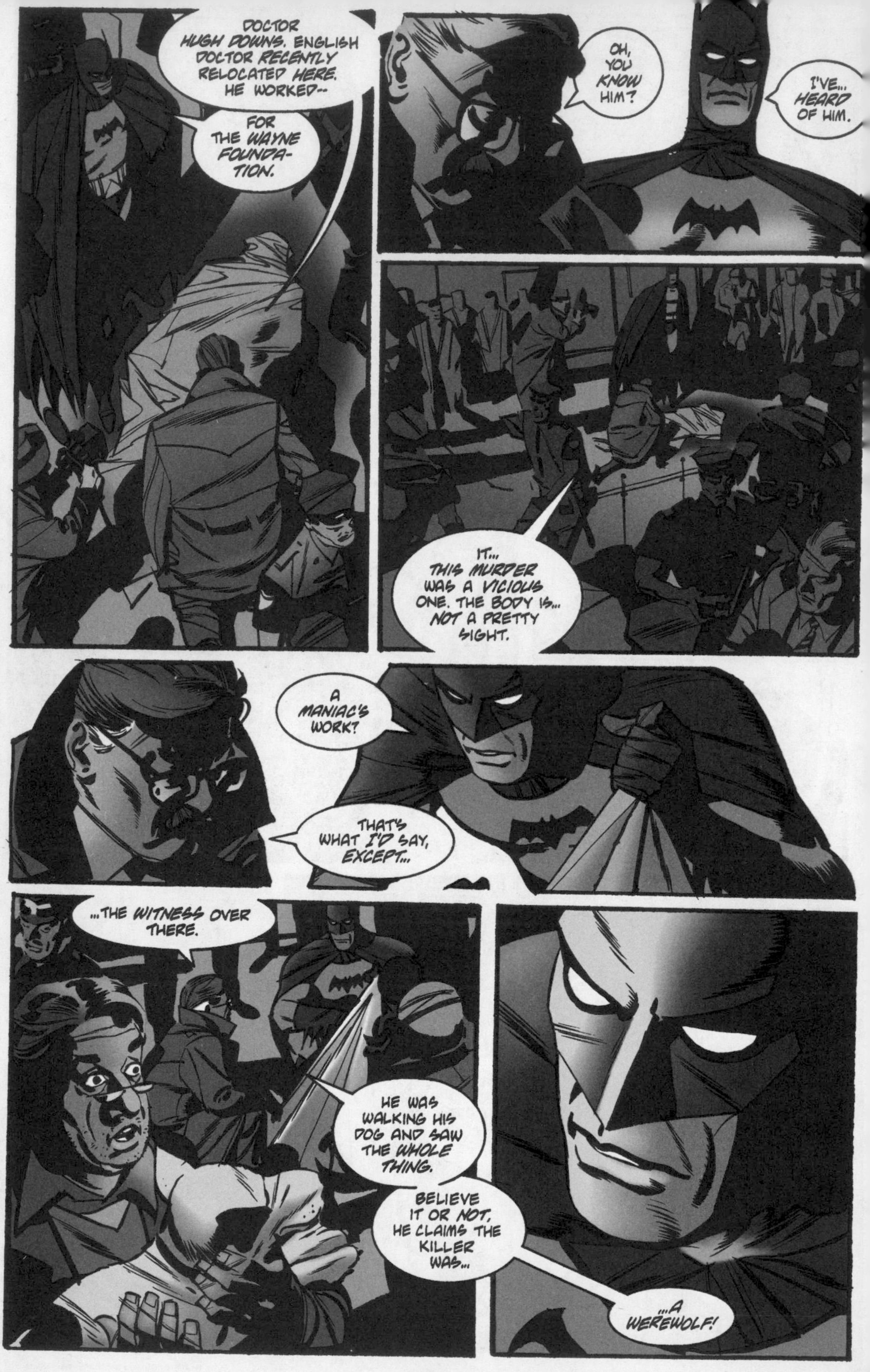
DOCTOR HUGH DOWNS. ENGLISH DOCTOR RECENTLY RELOCATED HERE. HE WORKED--
FOR THE WAYNE FOUNDATION.
OH, YOU KNOW HIM?
I'VE... HEARD OF HIM.
IT... THIS MURDER WAS A VICIOUS ONE. THE BODY IS... NOT A PRETTY SIGHT.
A MANIAC'S WORK?
THAT'S WHAT I'D SAY, EXCEPT...
...THE WITNESS OVER THERE.
HE WAS WALKING HIS DOG AND SAW THE WHOLE THING.
BELIEVE IT OR NOT, HE CLAIMS THE KILLER WAS...
...A WEREWOLF!

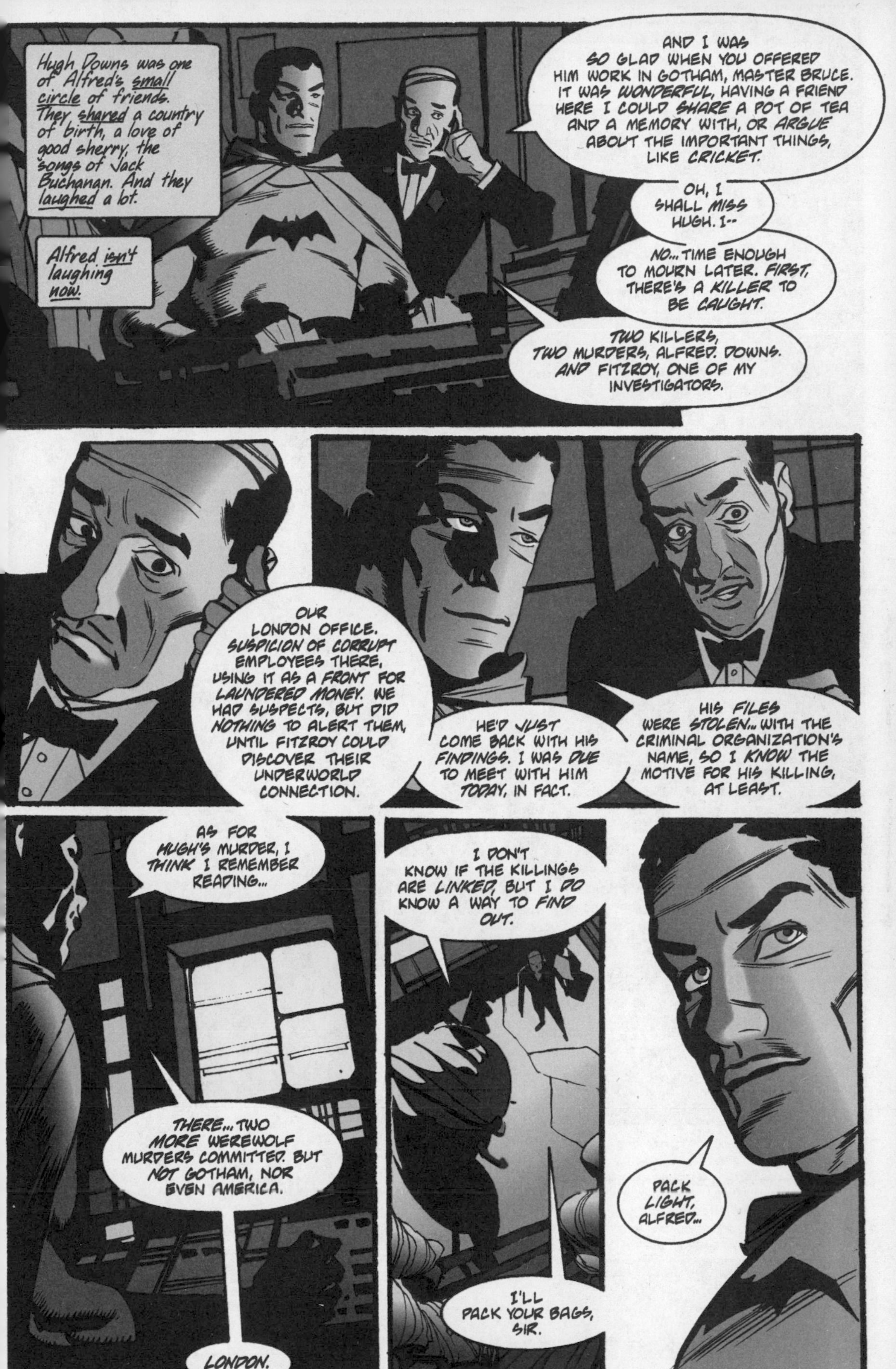
Hugh Downs was one of Alfred's small circle of friends. They shared a country of birth, a love of good sherry, the songs of Jack Buchanan. And they laughed a lot.
AND I WAS SO GLAD WHEN YOU OFFERED HIM WORK IN GOTHAM, MASTER BRUCE. IT WAS WONDERFUL, HAVING A FRIEND HERE I COULD SHARE A POT OF TEA AND A MEMORY WITH, OR ARGUE ABOUT THE IMPORTANT THINGS, LIKE CRICKET.
OH, I SHALL MISS HUGH. I--
Alfred isn't laughing now.
NO... TIME ENOUGH TO MOURN LATER. FIRST, THERE'S A KILLER TO BE CAUGHT.
TWO KILLERS, TWO MURDERS, ALFRED. DOWNS. AND FITZROY, ONE OF MY INVESTIGATORS.
OUR LONDON OFFICE. SUSPICION OF CORRUPT EMPLOYEES THERE, USING IT AS A FRONT FOR LAUNDERED MONEY. WE HAD SUSPECTS, BUT DID NOTHING TO ALERT THEM, UNTIL FITZROY COULD DISCOVER THEIR UNDERWORLD CONNECTION.
HE'D JUST COME BACK WITH HIS FINDINGS. I WAS DUE TO MEET WITH HIM TODAY, IN FACT.
HIS FILES WERE STOLEN... WITH THE CRIMINAL ORGANIZATION'S NAME, SO I KNOW THE MOTIVE FOR HIS KILLING, AT LEAST.
AS FOR HUGH'S MURDER, I THINK I REMEMBER READING...
THERE... TWO MORE WEREWOLF MURDERS COMMITTED. BUT NOT GOTHAM, NOR EVEN AMERICA.
LONDON.
I DON'T KNOW IF THE KILLINGS ARE LINKED, BUT I DO KNOW A WAY TO FIND OUT.
I'LL PACK YOUR BAGS, SIR.
PACK LIGHT, ALFRED...

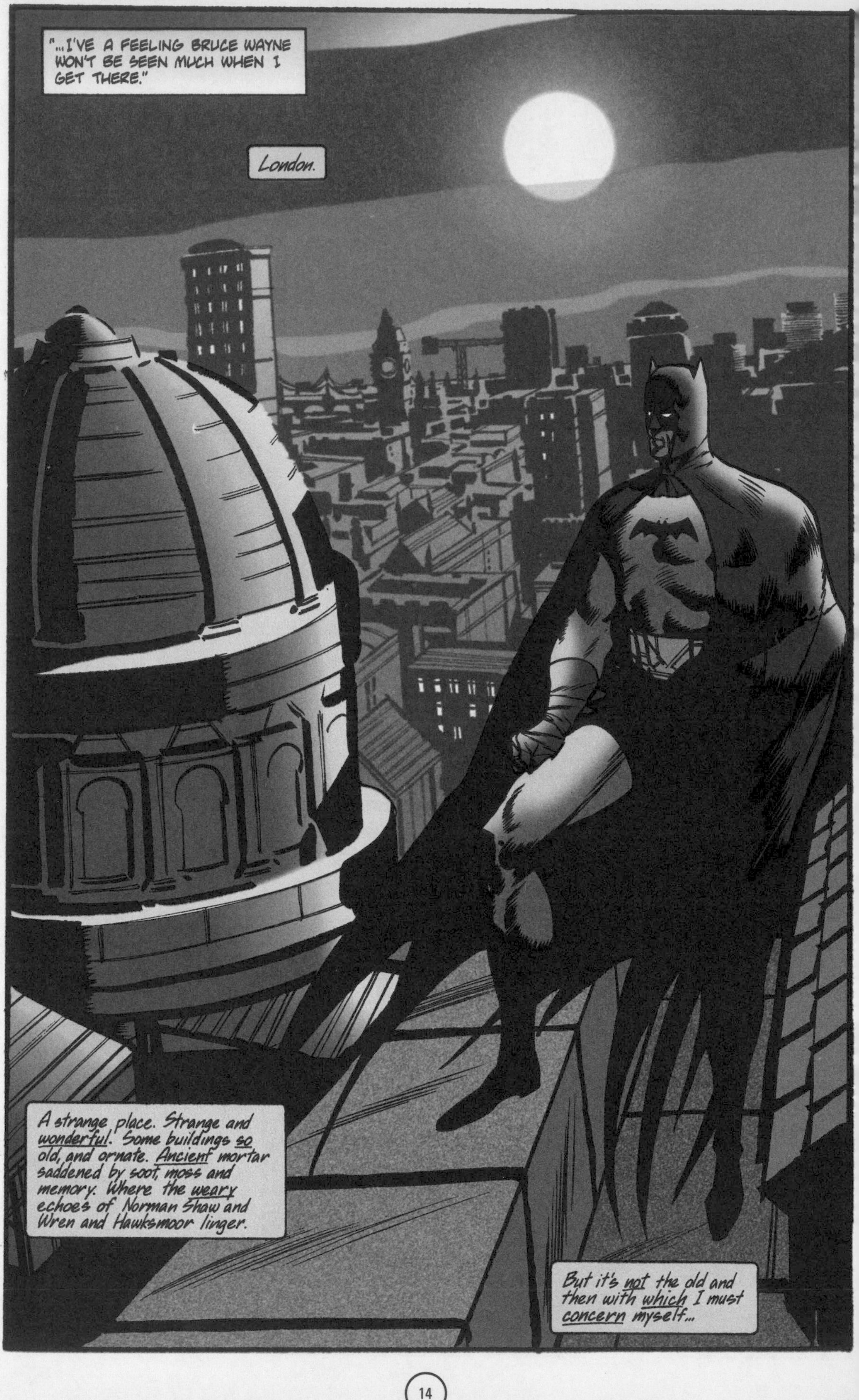
"...I'VE A FEELING BRUCE WAYNE WON'T BE SEEN MUCH WHEN I GET THERE."
London.
A strange place. Strange and wonderful. Some buildings so old, and ornate. Ancient mortar saddened by soot, moss and memory. Where the weary echoes of Norman Shaw and Wren and Hawksmoor linger.
But it's not the old and then with which I must concern myself...

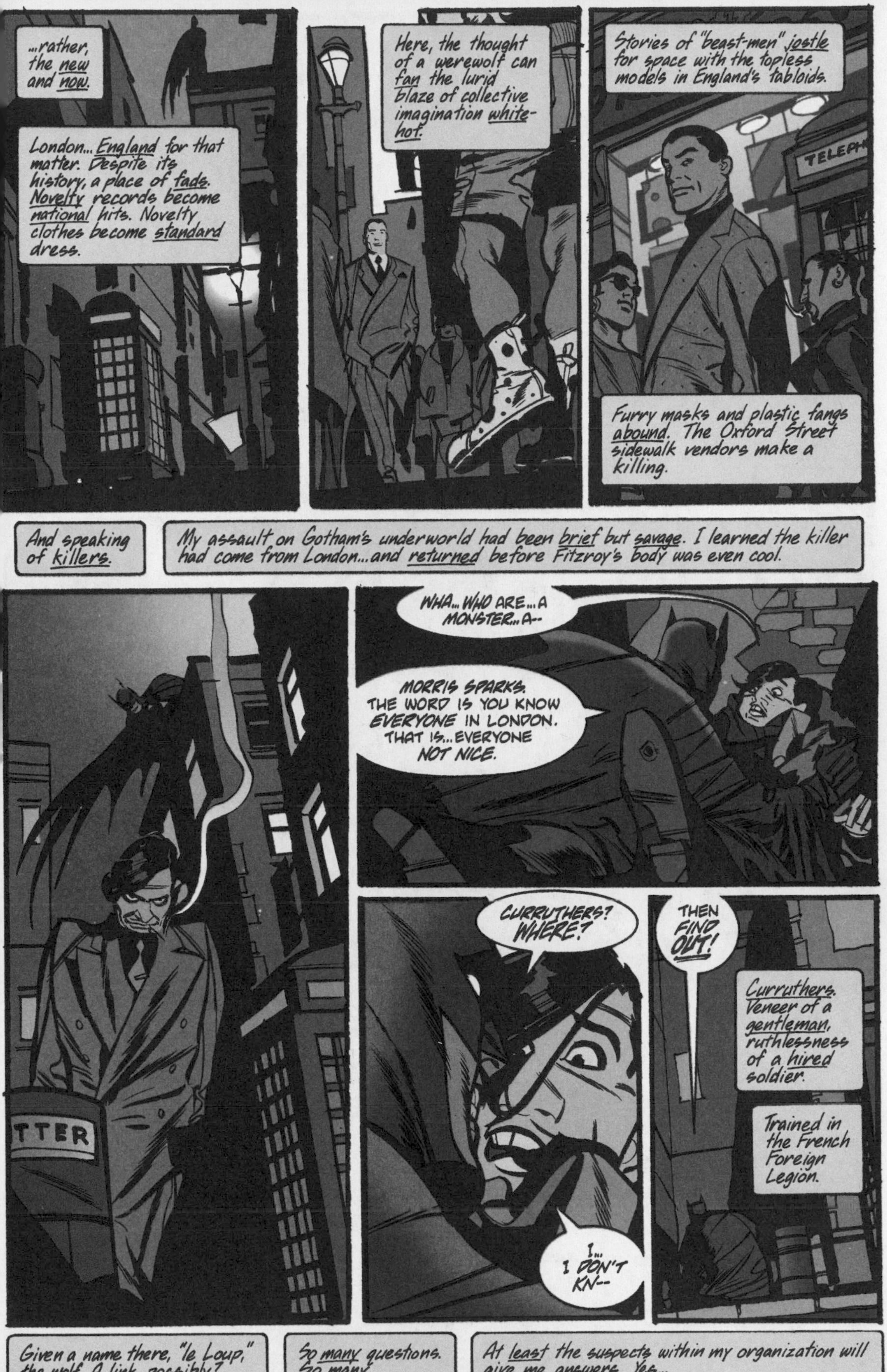

...rather, the new and now.
London... England for that matter. Despite its history, a place of fads. Novelty records become national hits. Novelty clothes become standard dress.
Here, the thought of a werewolf can fan the lurid blaze of collective imagination white-hot.
Stories of "beast-men" jostle for space with the topless models in England's tabloids.
TELEPH
Furry masks and plastic fangs abound. The Oxford Street sidewalk vendors make a killing.
And speaking of killers.
My assault on Gotham's underworld had been brief but savage. I learned the killer had come from London...and returned before Fitzroy's body was even cool.
TTER
WHA... WHO ARE... A MONSTER... A--
MORRIS SPARKS. THE WORD IS YOU KNOW EVERYONE IN LONDON. THAT IS...EVERYONE NOT NICE.
CURRUTHERS? WHERE?
I... I DON'T KN--
THEN FIND OUT!
Curruthers. Veneer of a gentleman, ruthlessness of a hired soldier.
Trained in the French Foreign Legion.
Given a name there, "le Loup," the wolf. A link, possibly?
So many questions. So many.
At least the suspects within my organization will give me answers. Yes...

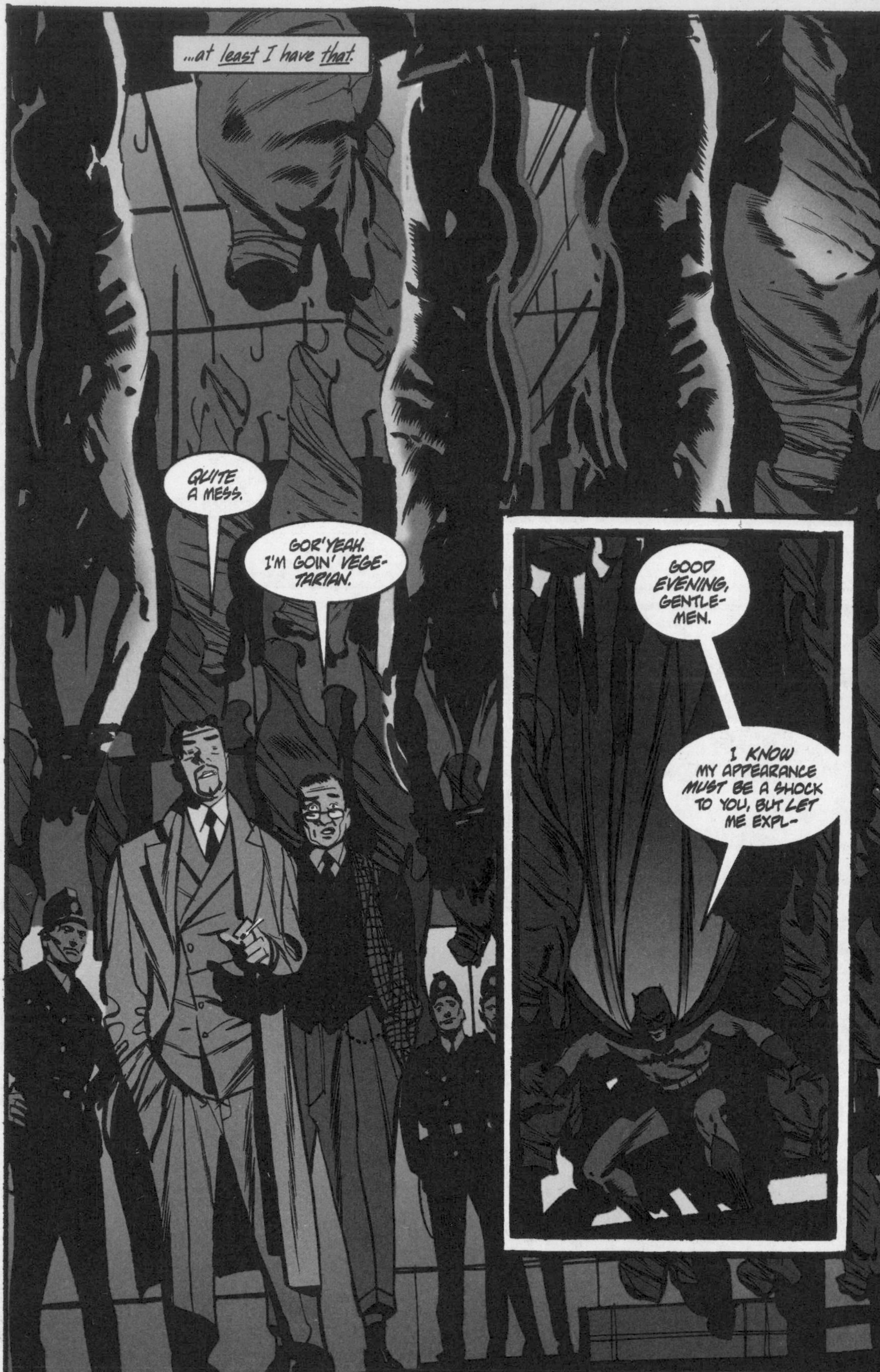
...at least I have that.
QUITE A MESS.
GOR'YEAH. I'M GOIN' VEGE-TARIAN.
GOOD EVENING, GENTLE-MEN.
I KNOW MY APPEARANCE MUST BE A SHOCK TO YOU, BUT LET ME EXPL-

WHAT... WH...

GET HIM.

GRAB.

HANG ON, YOU LOT.

'SCUSE KOJAK, STARSKY AND BLEEDIN' HUTCH HERE. I RECOGNIZE YOU EVEN IF THEY DON'T.

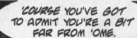

'COURSE YOU'VE GOT TO ADMIT YOU'RE A BIT FAR FROM 'OME.

ONE OF THE WEREWOLF KILLINGS OCCURRED IN GOTHAM. THE TRAIL BACK TO LONDON WAS A LOGICAL ONE.

THESE TWO MORE, D'YOU THINK? HARD TO TELL, SO MUCH BLOOD 'N ALL.

NOT UNLESS THE WEREWOLF LEFT HIS DENTURES AT HOME AND BROUGHT A CLEAVER ALONG INSTEAD.

THEY'VE BEEN BUTCHERED, NOT MANGLED.

THESE MEN WERE WAYNE INTERNATIONAL EMPLOYEES. UNDER INVESTIGATION. BY ME. ANOTHER CASE. ANOTHER REASON I'M IN YOUR CITY.

LOOK, THERE'S OBVIOUSLY STUFF YOU KNOW I DON'T. WE REALLY SHOULD TALK. NAME'S INSPECTOR NASH... COLMAN NASH. IT'D BE AN HONOR TO WORK WITH YOU...REALLY.

YOU HELP ME. I HELP YOU. OUR CASES GET SOLVED ALL THE QUICKER.

YES. PERHAPS THEY MIGHT. PERHAPS WE WILL...

...TALK.

PERHAPS.

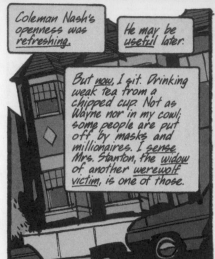

Coleman Nash's openness was refreshing.

He may be useful later.

But now, I sit. Drinking weak tea from a chipped cup. Not as Wayne nor in my cowl; some people are put off by masks and millionaires. I sense Mrs. Stanton, the widow of another werewolf victim, is one of those.

SO MISTER... BLAYLOCK.

YOU'RE A PRIVATE INVESTIGATOR?

FROM AMERICA, YES. A WEREWOLF MURDER THERE. YOUR HUSBAND'S SAD DEATH HERE. I LOOK FOR A LINK.

MY HUSBAND. I...CAN'T HELP FEELING IT'S HIS FAULT.

FOR HIS OWN DEATH?

SORRY, NO... I MEAN MY FIRST HUSBAND, CHARLES BLAKE. HE VANISHED A YEAR AGO FOLLOWING OUR DIVORCE AND HIS BUSINESS GOING BELLY-UP.

THAT WAS HIS FAULT, THOUGH. ALWAYS HIS HEAD FULL OF SOME NEW INVENTION OR GADGET. NEGLECTING ME, AND HIS FIRM.

CHARLIE WAS AN ORPHAN. BOTHERED HIM, THAT. NOT HAVING ROOTS... A FAMILY. HAVING ME AS A WIFE GAVE HIM A SENSE OF SECURITY.

I KNOW HE HATED BARRY, MY...er... MY SECOND HUSBAND FOR "TAKING ME FROM HIM" AS HE PUT IT.

LIKE I SAY, HE VANISHED A YEAR AGO, STRAIGHT AFTER I REMARRIED.

I SENSE CHARLIE HAD SOMETHING TO DO WITH BARRY'S DEATH. I TOLD THE POLICE AS MUCH AND I HOPE THEY'RE...

...OH... YOU'RE EMPTY. MORE TEA?

THANK YOU.

The drink is bitter.

Stirring the cup, a few tea leaves rise to the surface. Spinning in the center. Spinning. Swirling.

Like the questions in my head.

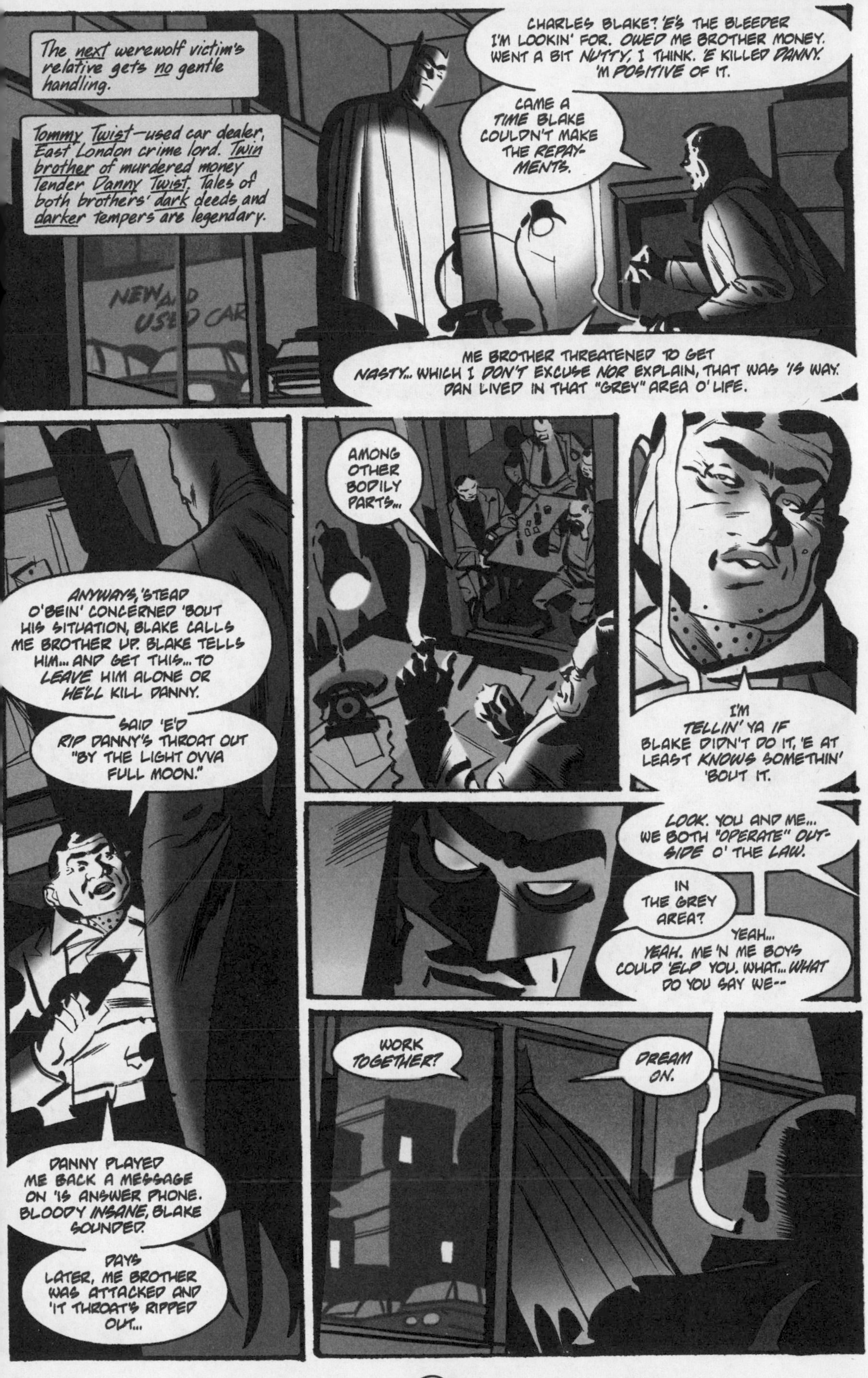
The next werewolf victim's relative gets no gentle handling.
Tommy Twist—used car dealer, East London crime lord. Twin brother of murdered money lender Danny Twist. Tales of both brothers' dark deeds and darker tempers are legendary.
CHARLES BLAKE? 'E'S THE BLEEDER I'M LOOKIN' FOR. OWED ME BROTHER MONEY. WENT A BIT NUTTY, I THINK. 'E KILLED DANNY. 'M POSITIVE OF IT.
CAME A TIME BLAKE COULDN'T MAKE THE REPAY-MENTS.
NEW AND USED CAR
ME BROTHER THREATENED TO GET NASTY... WHICH I DON'T EXCUSE NOR EXPLAIN, THAT WAS 'IS WAY. DAN LIVED IN THAT "GREY" AREA O' LIFE.
AMONG OTHER BODILY PARTS...
ANYWAYS, 'STEAD O'BEIN' CONCERNED 'BOUT HIS SITUATION, BLAKE CALLS ME BROTHER UP. BLAKE TELLS HIM... AND GET THIS... TO LEAVE HIM ALONE OR HE'LL KILL DANNY.
SAID 'E'D RIP DANNY'S THROAT OUT "BY THE LIGHT OVVA FULL MOON."
DANNY PLAYED ME BACK A MESSAGE ON 'IS ANSWER PHONE. BLOODY INSANE, BLAKE SOUNDED.
DAYS LATER, ME BROTHER WAS ATTACKED AND 'IT THROAT'S RIPPED OUT...
I'M TELLIN' YA IF BLAKE DIDN'T DO IT, 'E AT LEAST KNOWS SOMETHIN' 'BOUT IT.
LOOK. YOU AND ME... WE BOTH "OPERATE" OUT-SIDE O' THE LAW.
IN THE GREY AREA?
YEAH... YEAH. ME 'N ME BOYS COULD 'ELP YOU. WHAT... WHAT DO YOU SAY WE--
WORK TOGETHER?
DREAM ON.

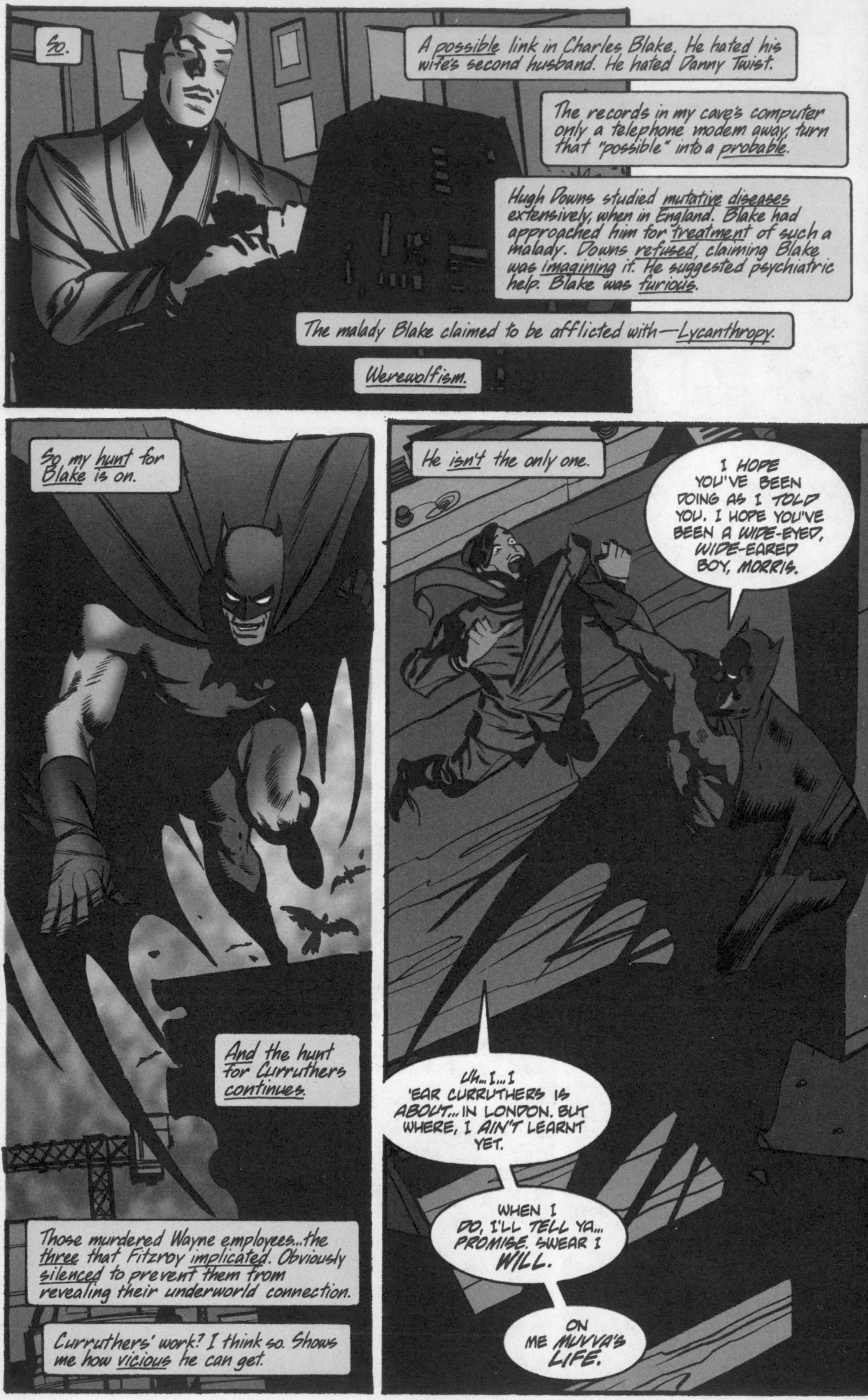
So.
A possible link in Charles Blake. He hated his wife's second husband. He hated Danny Twist.
The records in my cave's computer only a telephone modem away, turn that "possible" into a probable.
Hugh Downs studied mutative diseases extensively, when in England. Blake had approached him for treatment of such a malady. Downs refused, claiming Blake was imagining it. He suggested psychiatric help. Blake was furious.
The malady Blake claimed to be afflicted with—Lycanthropy.
Werewolfism.
So my hunt for Blake is on.
And the hunt for Curruthers continues.
Those murdered Wayne employees...the three that Fitzroy implicated. Obviously silenced to prevent them from revealing their underworld connection.
Curruthers' work? I think so. Shows me how vicious he can get.
He isn't the only one.
I HOPE YOU'VE BEEN DOING AS I TOLD YOU. I HOPE YOU'VE BEEN A WIDE-EYED, WIDE-EARED BOY, MORRIS.
UH... I... I 'EAR CURRUTHERS IS ABOUT... IN LONDON. BUT WHERE, I AIN'T LEARNT YET.
WHEN I DO, I'LL TELL YA... PROMISE. SWEAR I WILL.
ON ME MUVVA'S LIFE.

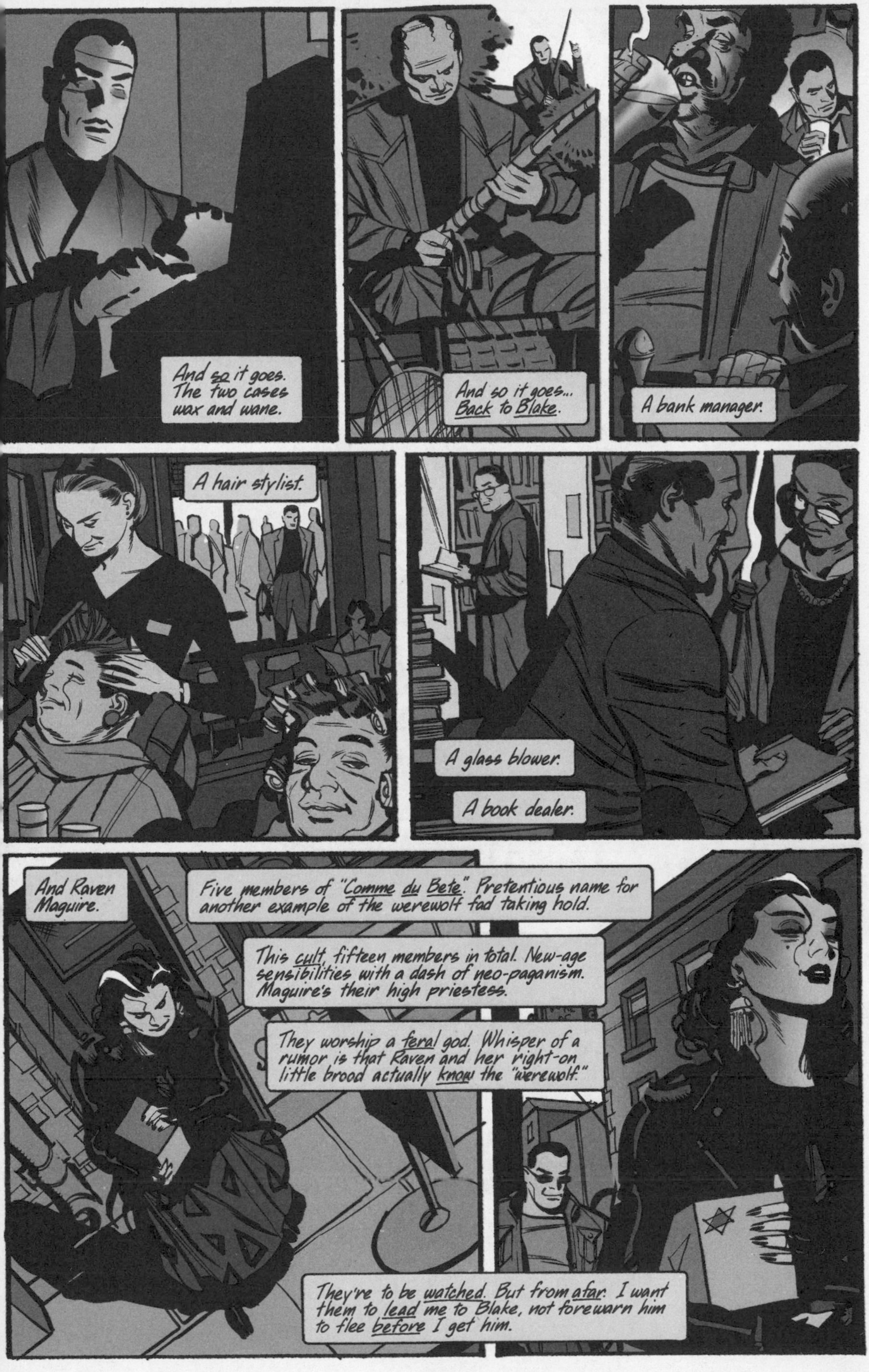

And so it goes. The two cases wax and wane.
And so it goes... Back to Blake.
A bank manager.
A hair stylist.
A glass blower.
A book dealer.
And Raven Maguire.
Five members of "Comme du Bete". Pretentious name for another example of the werewolf fad taking hold.
This cult, fifteen members in total. New-age sensibilities with a dash of neo-paganism. Maguire's their high priestess.
They worship a feral god. Whisper of a rumor is that Raven and her right-on little brood actually know the "werewolf."
They're to be watched. But from afar. I want them to lead me to Blake, not forewarn him to flee before I get him.

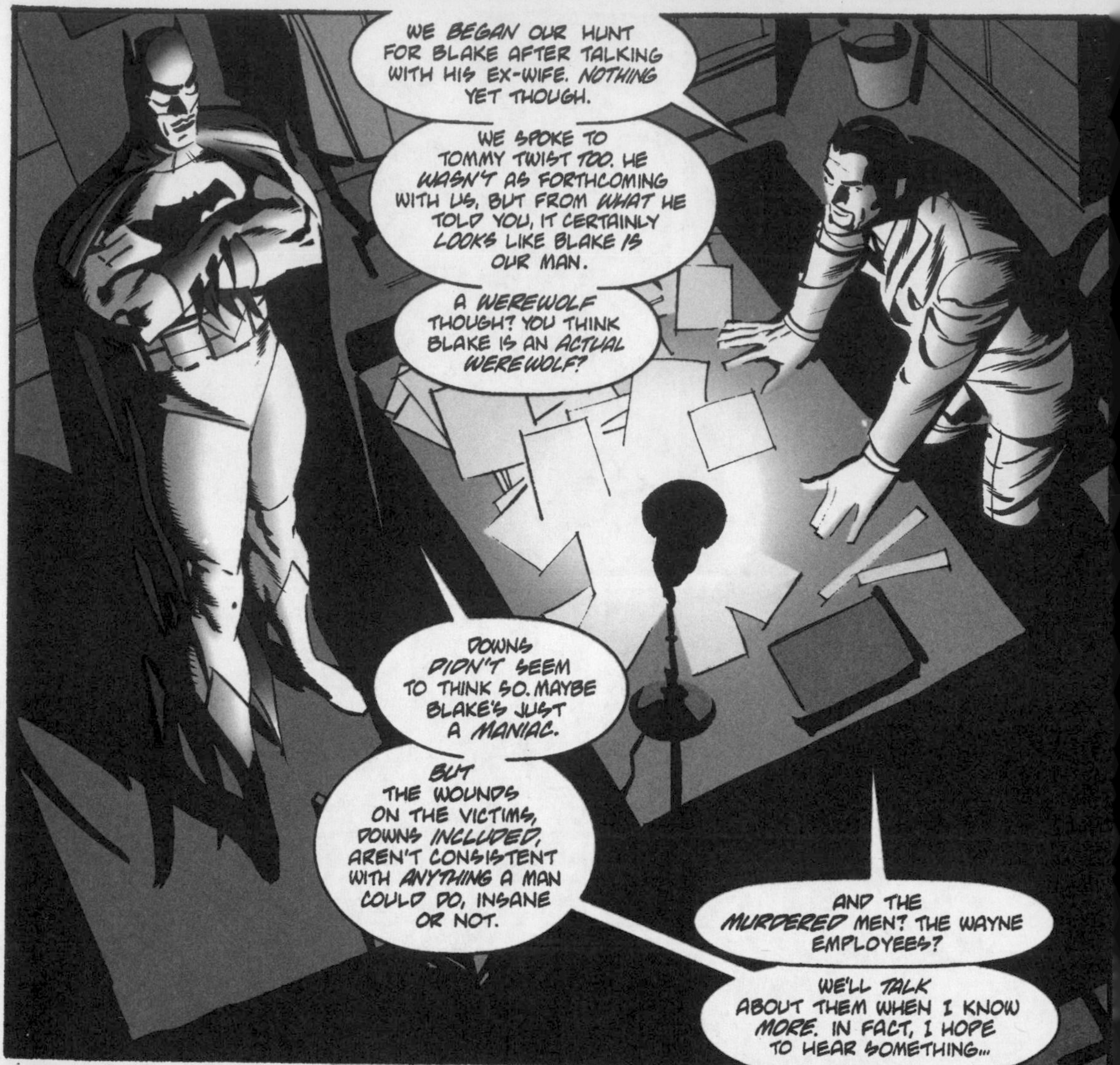
WE BEGAN OUR HUNT FOR BLAKE AFTER TALKING WITH HIS EX-WIFE. NOTHING YET THOUGH.
WE SPOKE TO TOMMY TWIST TOO. HE WASN'T AS FORTHCOMING WITH US, BUT FROM WHAT HE TOLD YOU, IT CERTAINLY LOOKS LIKE BLAKE IS OUR MAN.
A WEREWOLF THOUGH? YOU THINK BLAKE IS AN ACTUAL WEREWOLF?
DOWNS DIDN'T SEEM TO THINK SO. MAYBE BLAKE'S JUST A MANIAC.
BUT THE WOUNDS ON THE VICTIMS, DOWNS INCLUDED, AREN'T CONSISTENT WITH ANYTHING A MAN COULD DO, INSANE OR NOT.
AND THE MURDERED MEN? THE WAYNE EMPLOYEES?
WE'LL TALK ABOUT THEM WHEN I KNOW MORE. IN FACT, I HOPE TO HEAR SOMETHING...

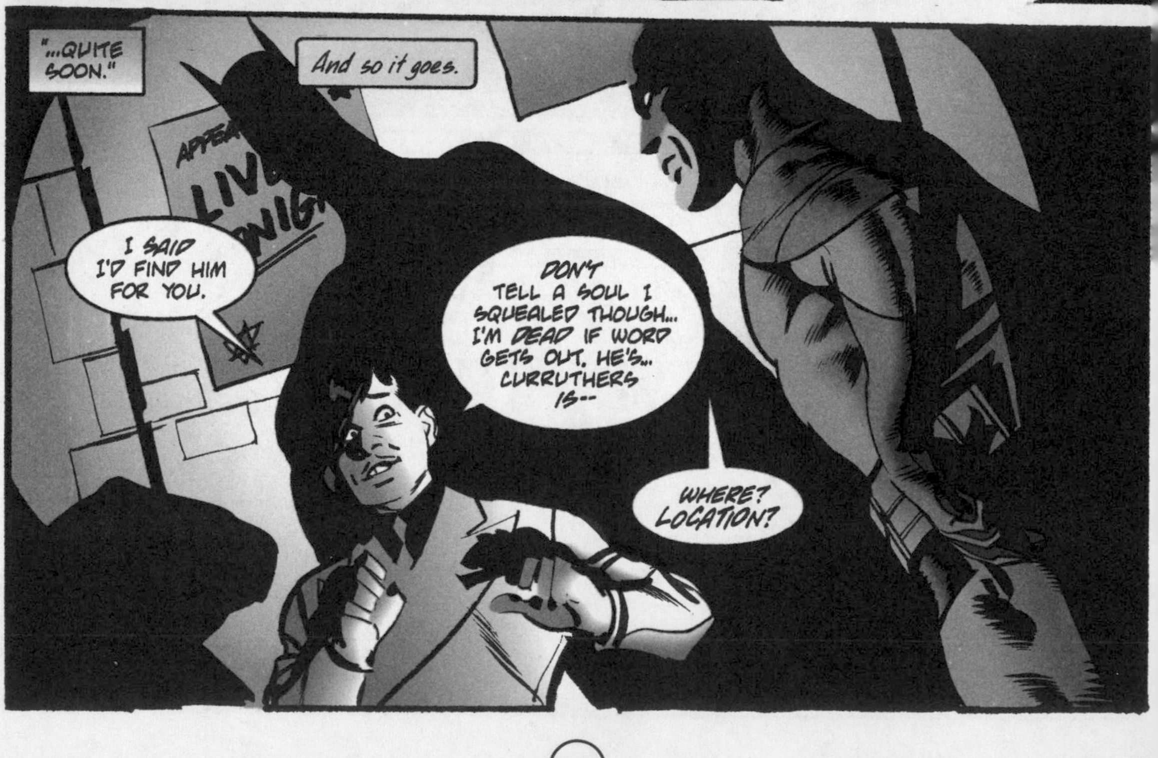
"...QUITE SOON."
And so it goes.
I SAID I'D FIND HIM FOR YOU.
DON'T TELL A SOUL I SQUEALED THOUGH... I'M DEAD IF WORD GETS OUT. HE'S... CURRUTHERS IS--
WHERE? LOCATION?

"DOCKLANDS."

The ships are gone. The cranes and ferries and vermin. The exotic smells of exotic cargos. The bargemen's cries and sailor's curses. _All gone._

Now warehouse facades hide _luxury_ interiors. And the _only_ rats _still_ to be _found_...

...pay _rent._

NO, AUNT DAPHNE, I WON'T BE GONE FOR LONG.

JUST A LITTLE HOLIDAY. I'VE JUST RECEIVED RATHER A BIG ROYALTY.

FROM MY WRITING, YES.

OH, I THOUGHT SWITZERLAND. A LITTLE SKIING, A LITTLE ROMANCE, HOPEFULLY.

DON'T WORRY, I'LL CALL BEFO--

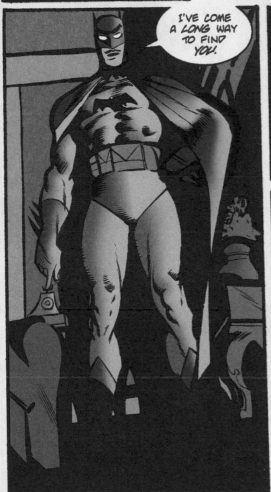

I'VE COME A _LONG WAY_ TO FIND YOU.

YES.

A LONG WAY...

23

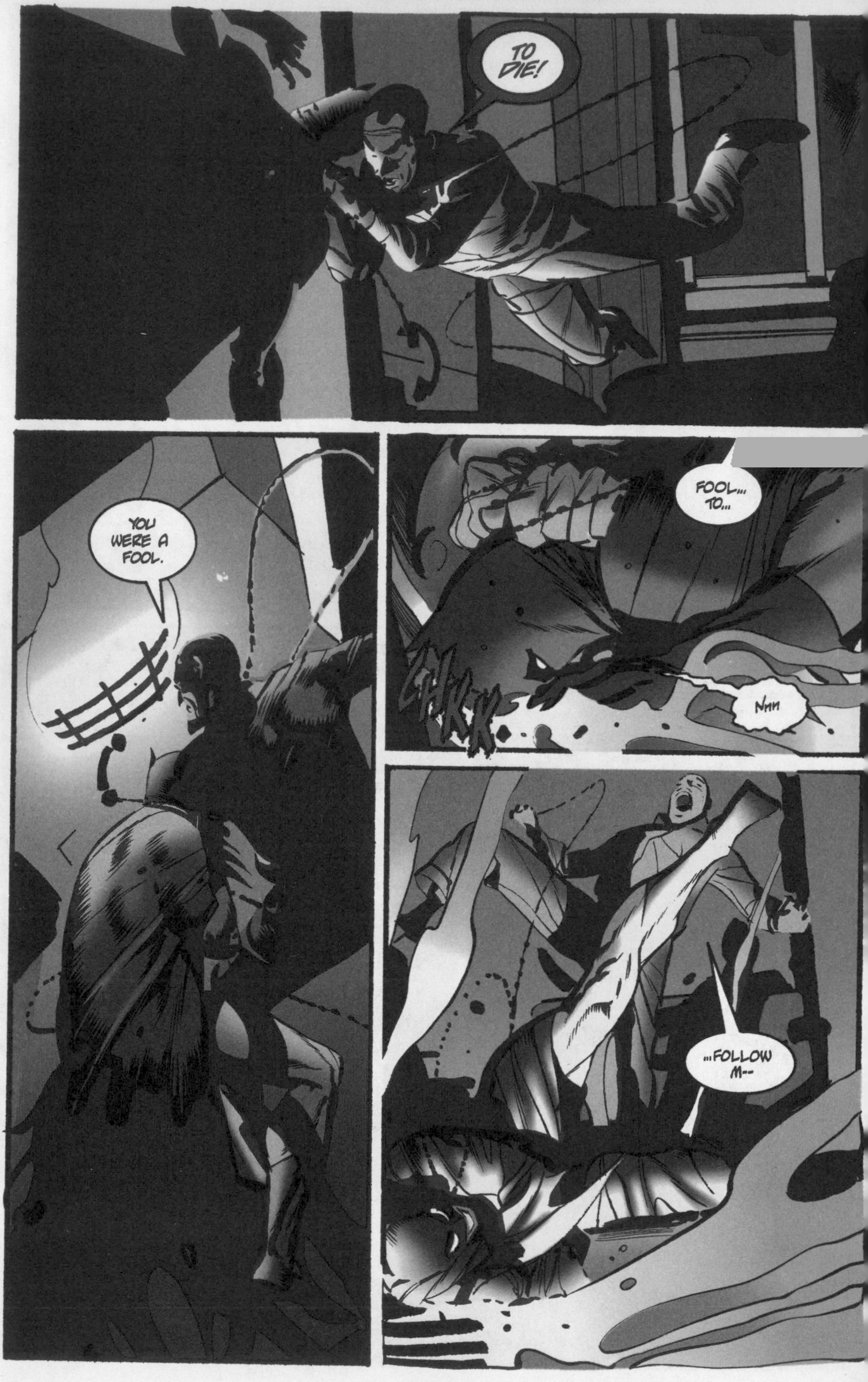

TO DIE!
YOU WERE A FOOL.
FOOL... TO...
CHKK
Nnn
...FOLLOW M--

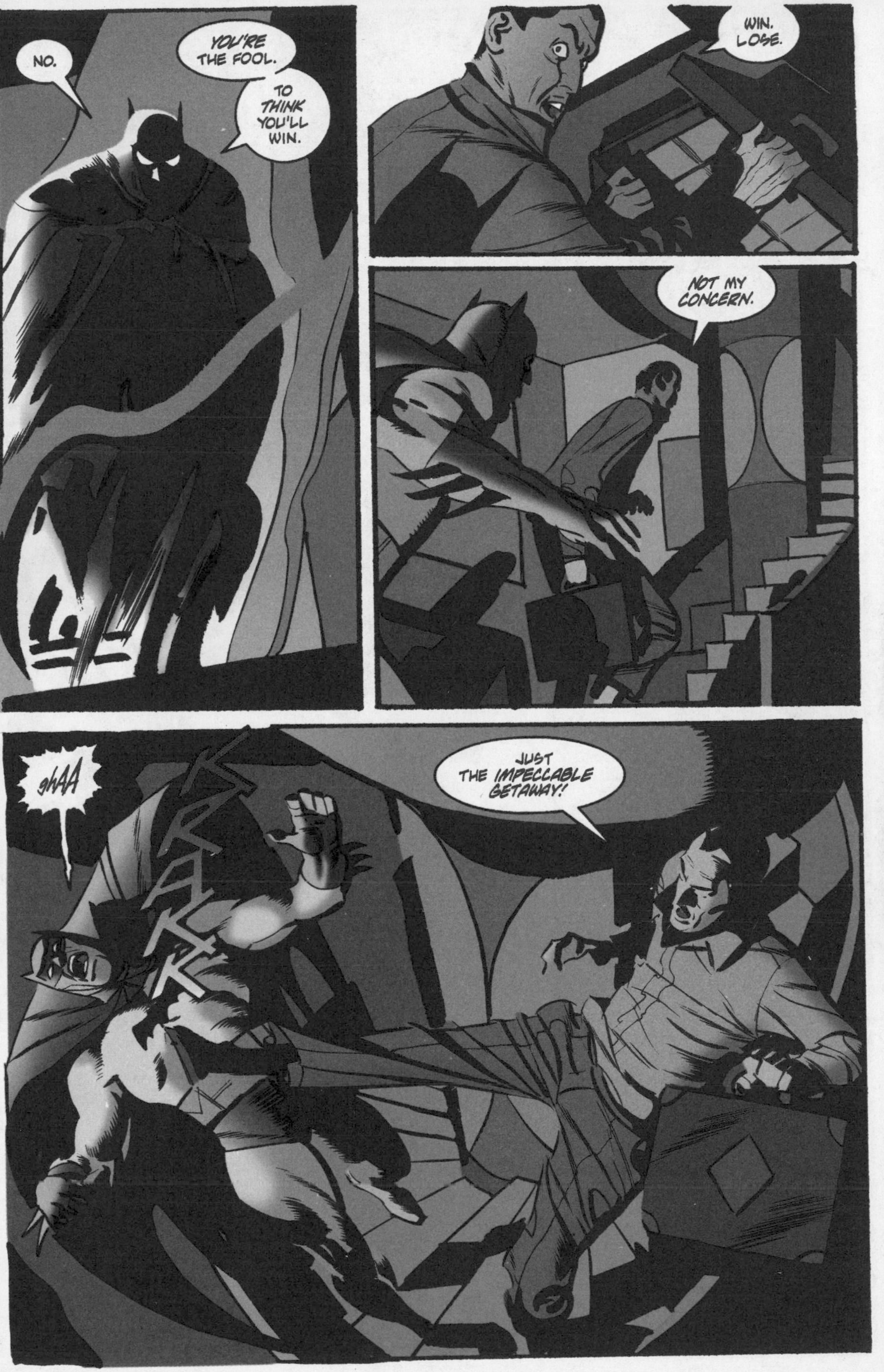
NO.
YOU'RE THE FOOL.
TO THINK YOU'LL WIN.
WIN. LOSE.
NOT MY CONCERN.
gHAA
JUST THE IMPECCABLE GETAWAY!

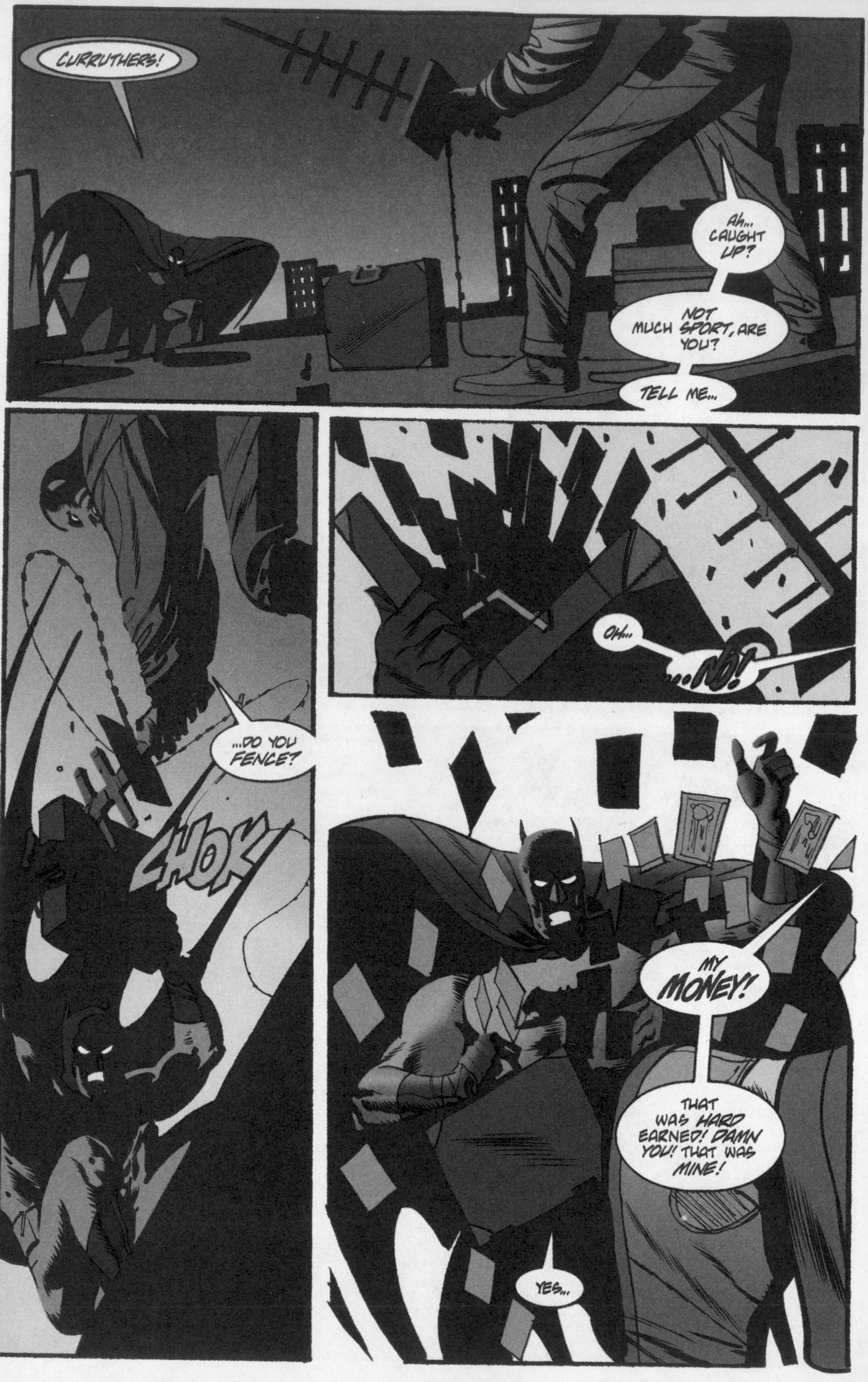
CURRUTHERS!
Ah... CAUGHT UP?
NOT MUCH SPORT, ARE YOU?
TELL ME...
...DO YOU FENCE?
CHOK
OH...
...NO!
MY MONEY!
THAT WAS HARD EARNED! DAMN YOU! THAT WAS MINE!
YES...

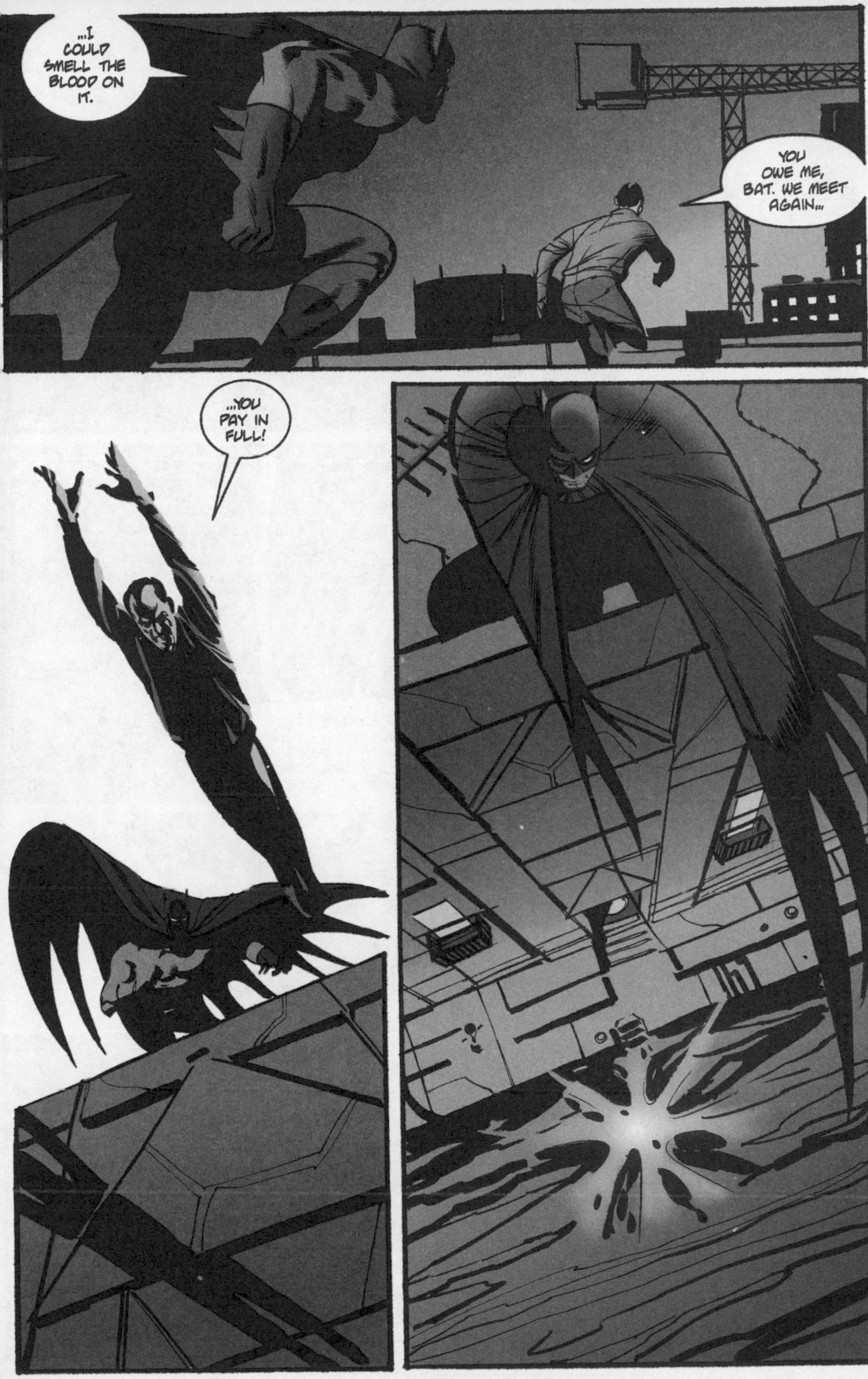
...I COULD SMELL THE BLOOD ON IT.
YOU OWE ME, BAT. WE MEET AGAIN...
...YOU PAY IN FULL!

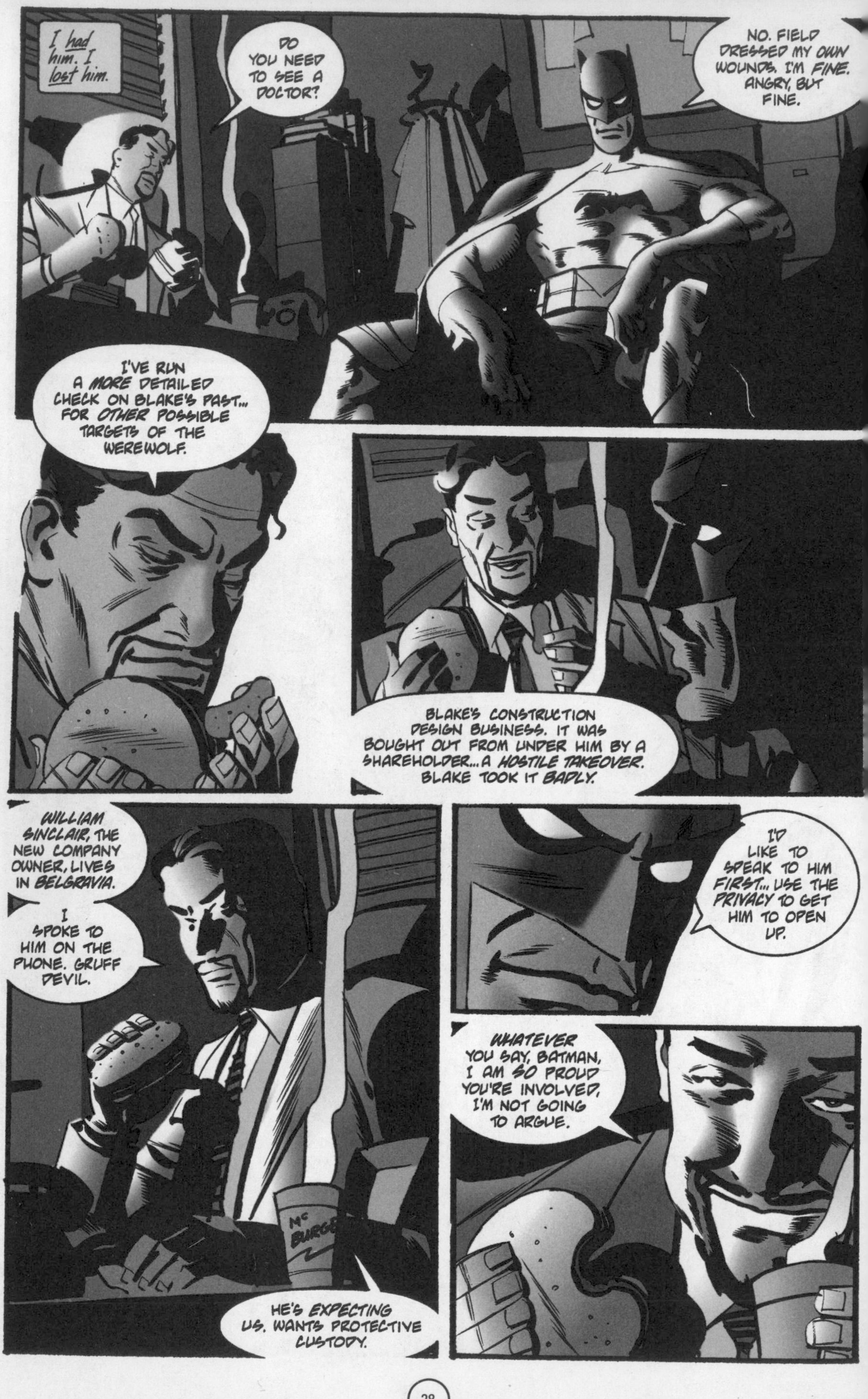

I had him. I lost him.
DO YOU NEED TO SEE A DOCTOR?
NO. FIELD DRESSED MY OWN WOUNDS. I'M FINE. ANGRY, BUT FINE.
I'VE RUN A MORE DETAILED CHECK ON BLAKE'S PAST... FOR OTHER POSSIBLE TARGETS OF THE WEREWOLF.
BLAKE'S CONSTRUCTION DESIGN BUSINESS. IT WAS BOUGHT OUT FROM UNDER HIM BY A SHAREHOLDER... A HOSTILE TAKEOVER. BLAKE TOOK IT BADLY.
WILLIAM SINCLAIR, THE NEW COMPANY OWNER, LIVES IN BELGRAVIA.
I SPOKE TO HIM ON THE PHONE. GRUFF DEVIL.
McBURG
HE'S EXPECTING US. WANTS PROTECTIVE CUSTODY.
I'D LIKE TO SPEAK TO HIM FIRST... USE THE PRIVACY TO GET HIM TO OPEN UP.
WHATEVER YOU SAY, BATMAN, I AM SO PROUD YOU'RE INVOLVED, I'M NOT GOING TO ARGUE.

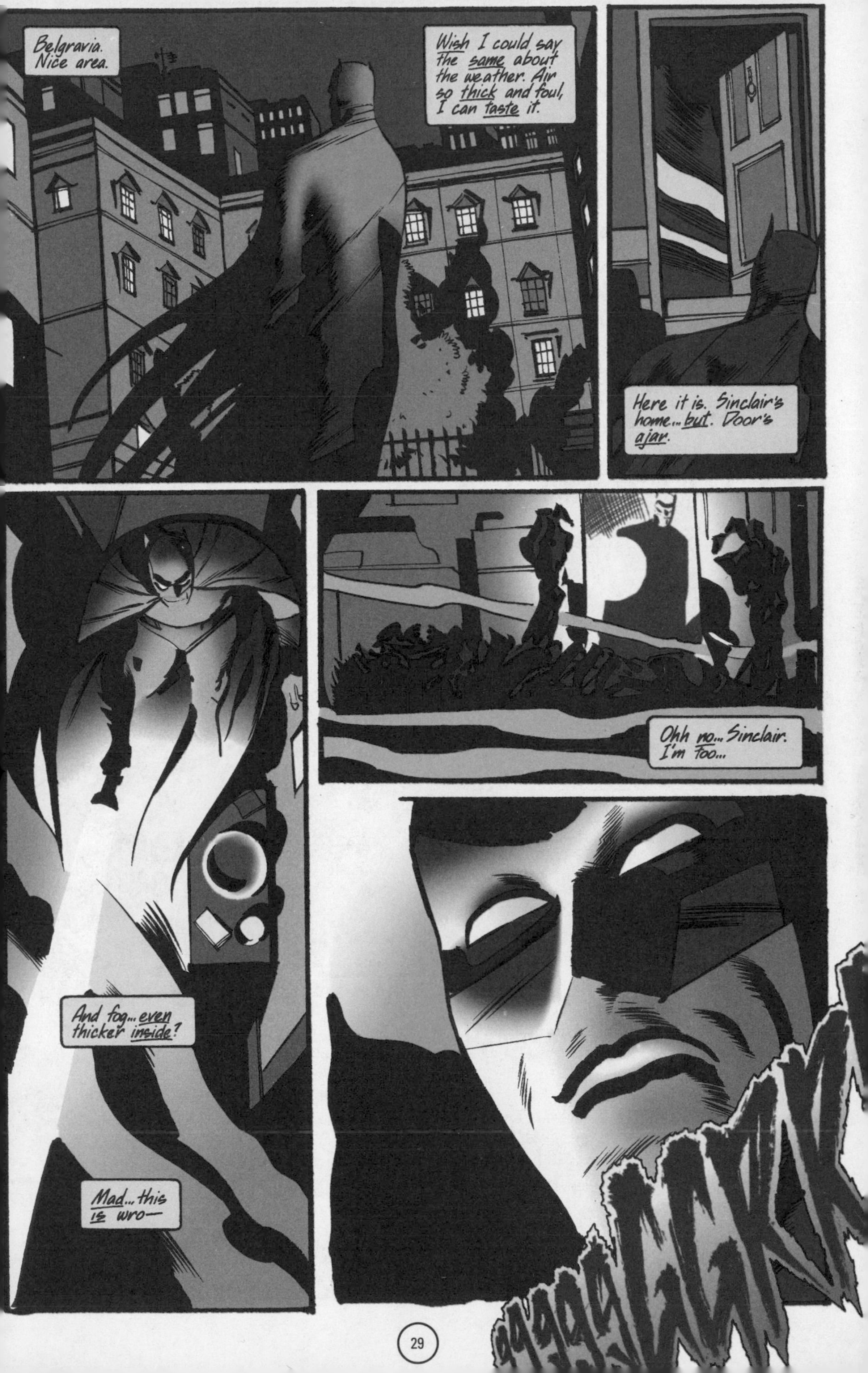
Belgravia. Nice area.
Wish I could say the same about the weather. Air so thick and foul, I can taste it.
Here it is. Sinclair's home... but. Door's ajar.
And fog... even thicker inside?
Mad... this is wro—
Ohh no... Sinclair. I'm too...
aaaaaGGGKKK

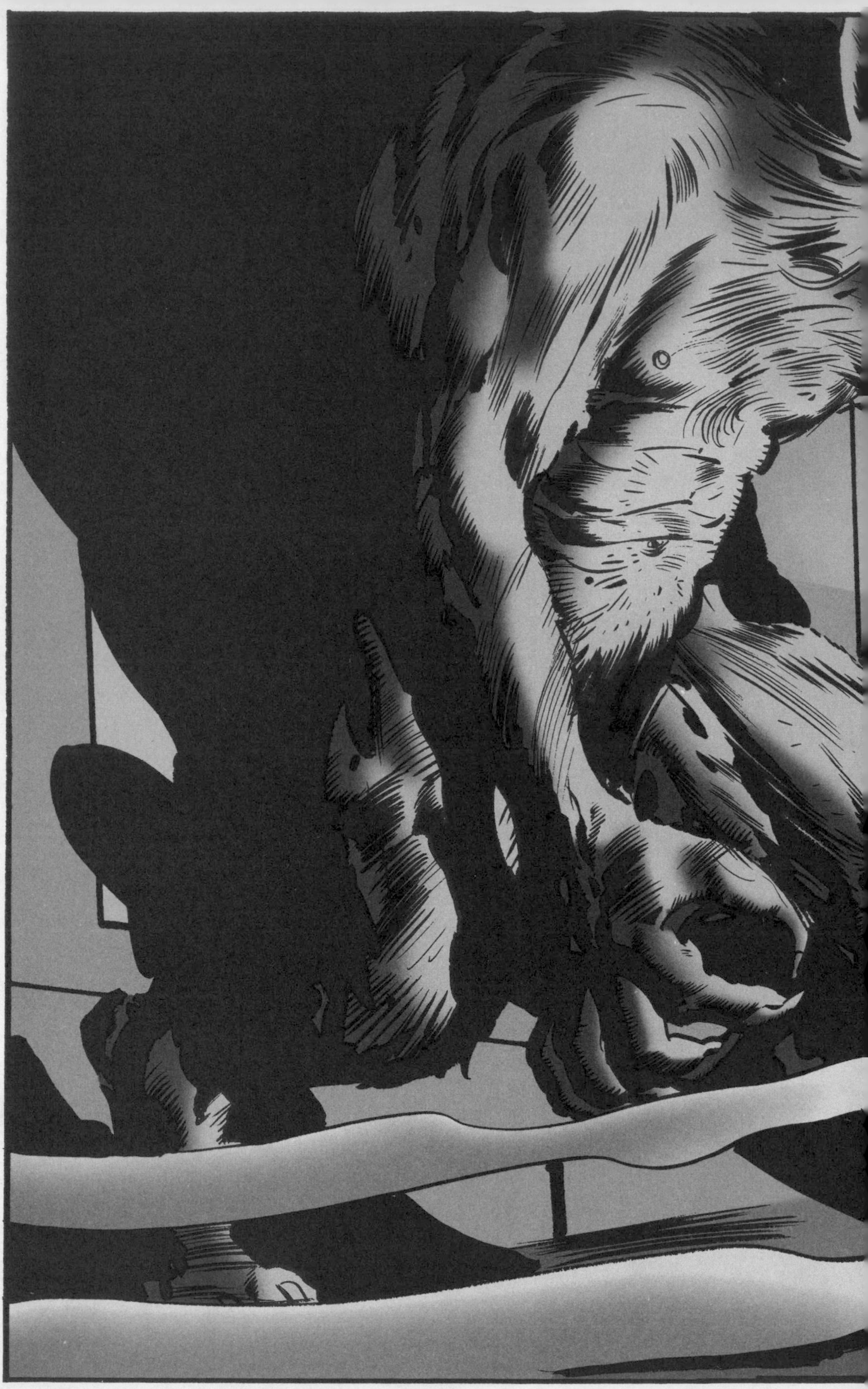

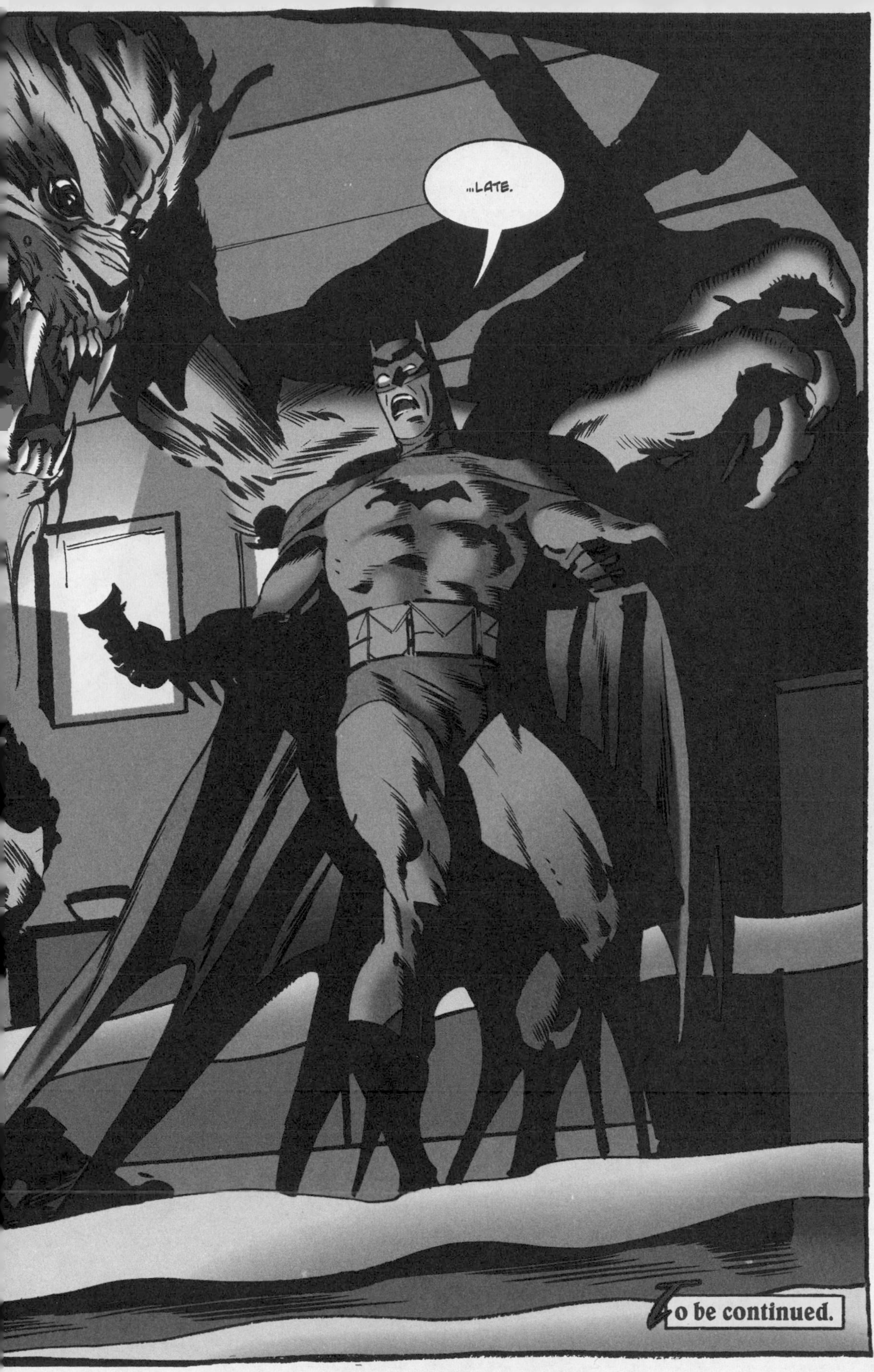
...LATE.
To be continued.

BATMAN
LEGENDS OF THE
DARK KNIGHT
NO 72 JUN 95
WATKISS
WEREWOLF
PART TWO OF THREE
JAMES ROBINSON JOHN WATKISS

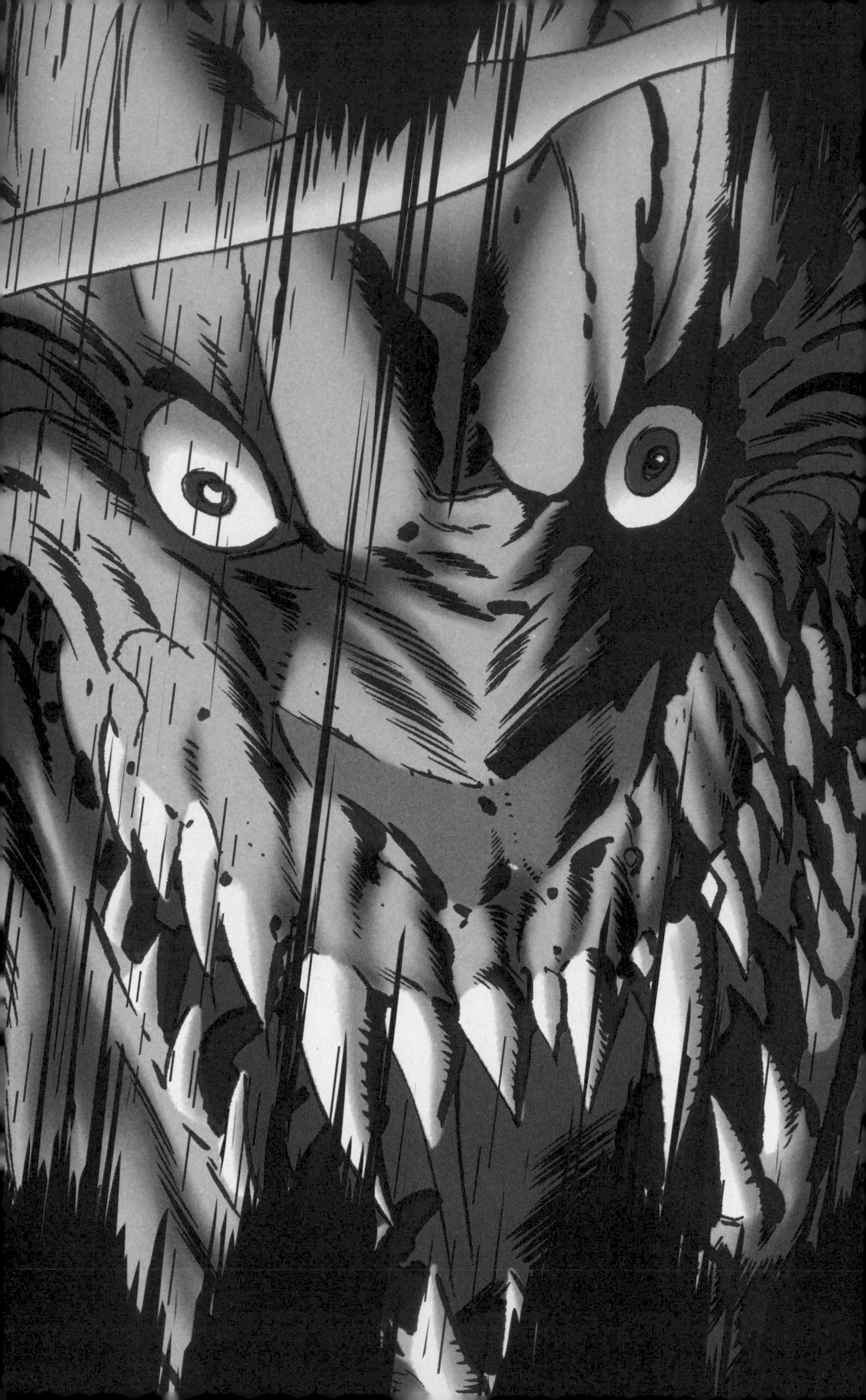

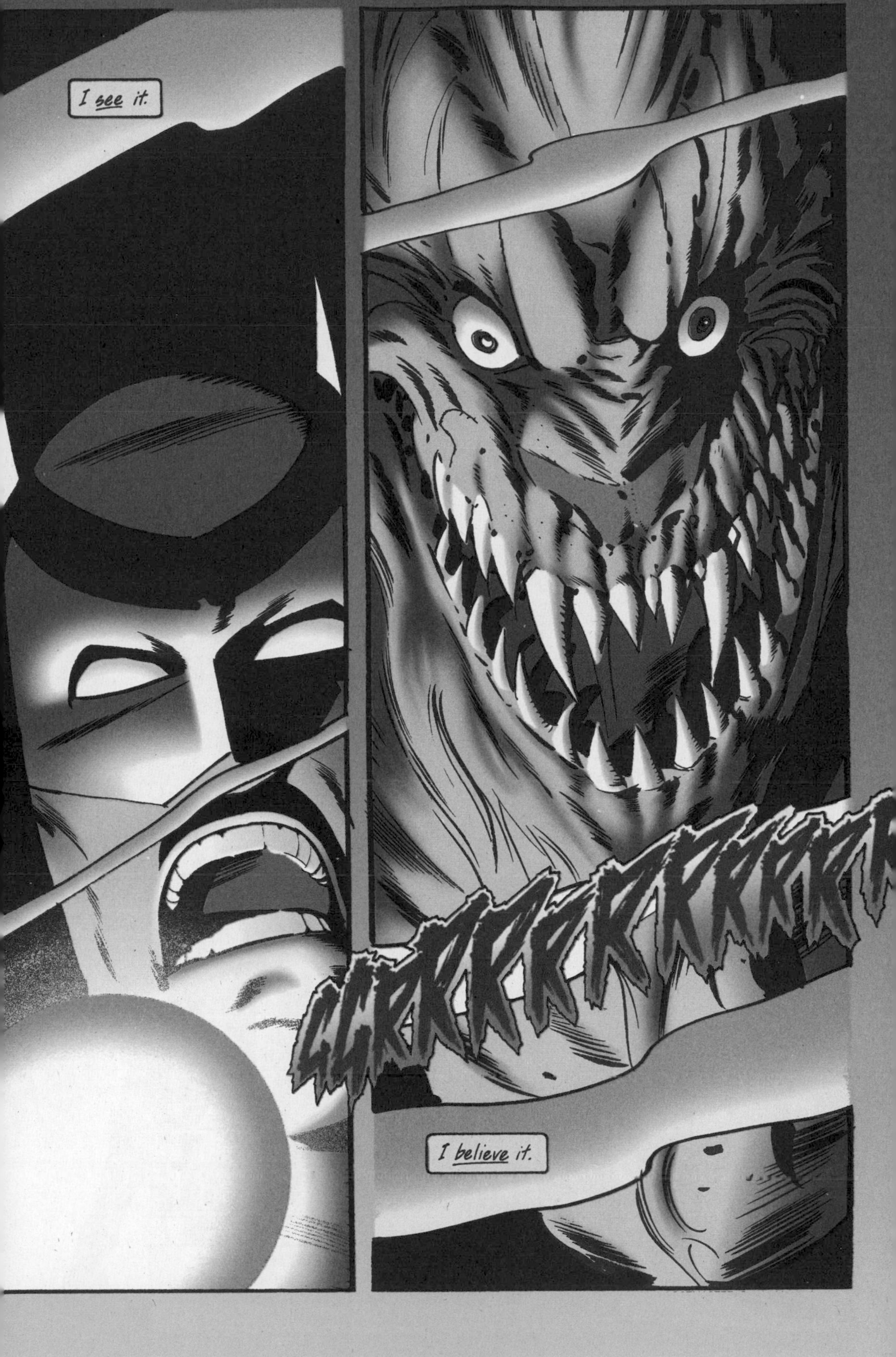
I see it.
GRRRRRRRRRR
I believe it.

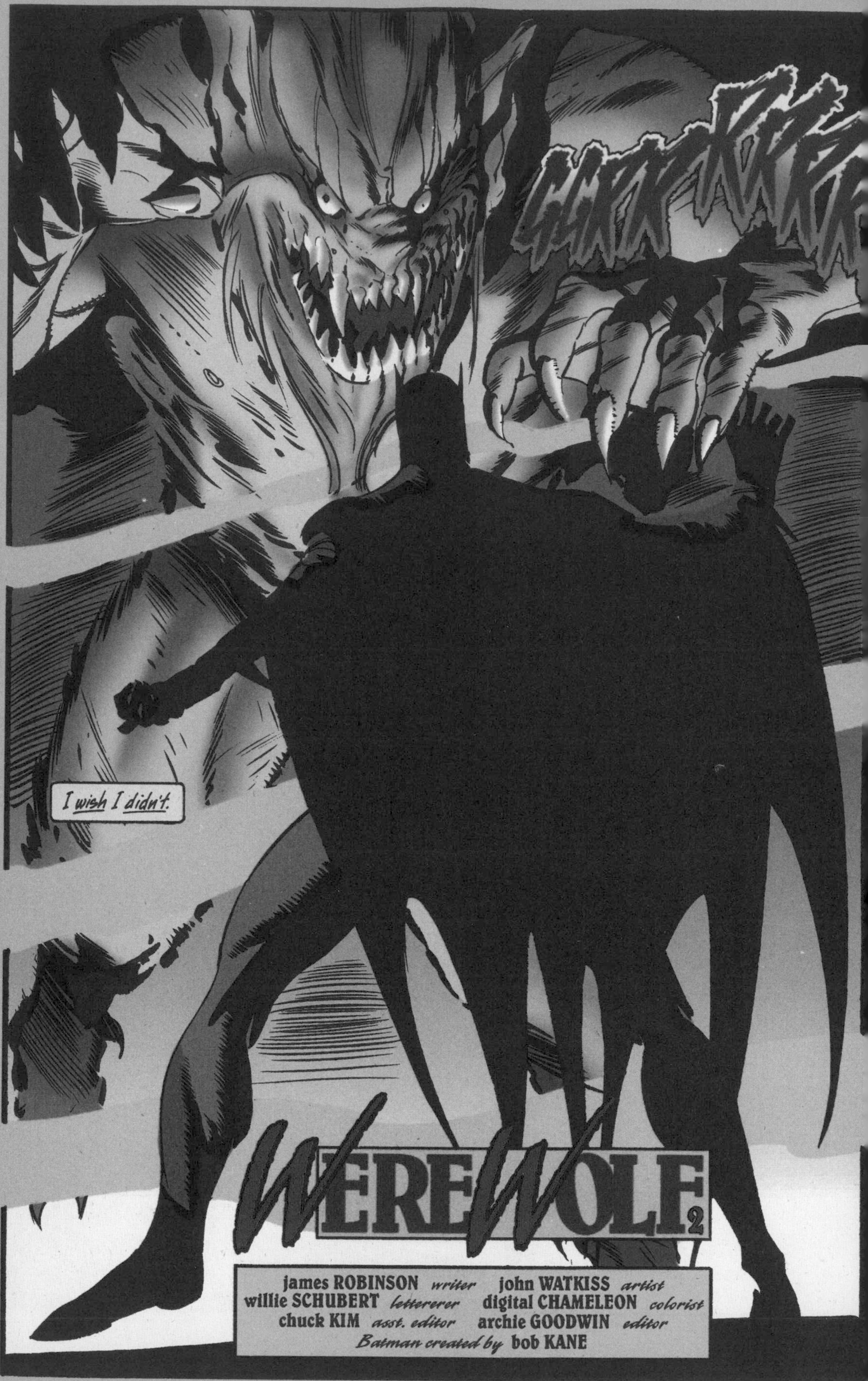
I wish I didn't.
WEREWOLF 2
james ROBINSON writer john WATKISS artist
willie SCHUBERT lettererer digital CHAMELEON colorist
chuck KIM asst. editor archie GOODWIN editor
Batman created by bob KANE

ARKH

SGRAHHH

Too strong.

Use speed.

And gas.

Try.

GRORR

Hopefully that—

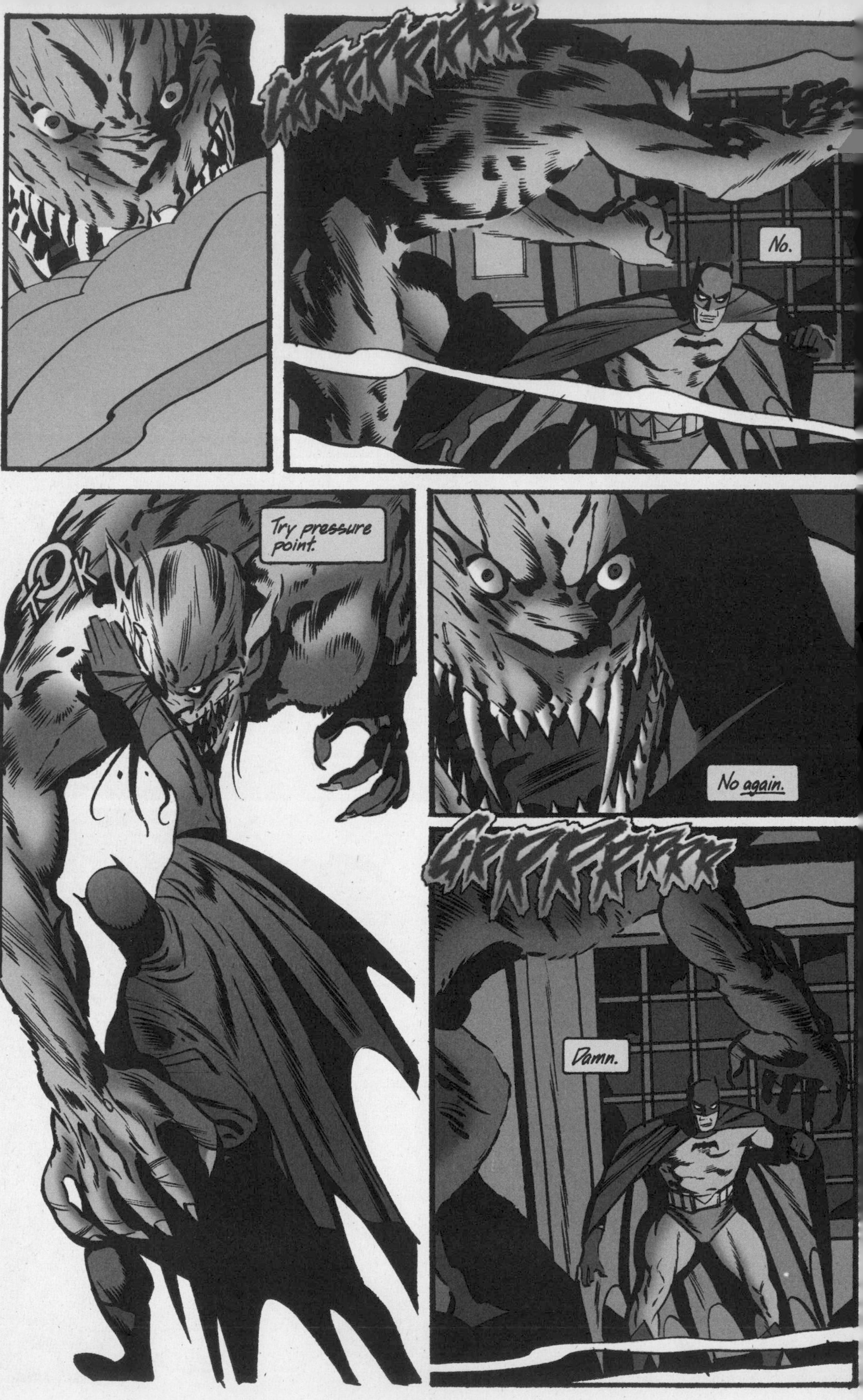

GRRRRRRRRR
No.
Try pressure point.
OK
No again.
GRRRRRRRRR
Damn.

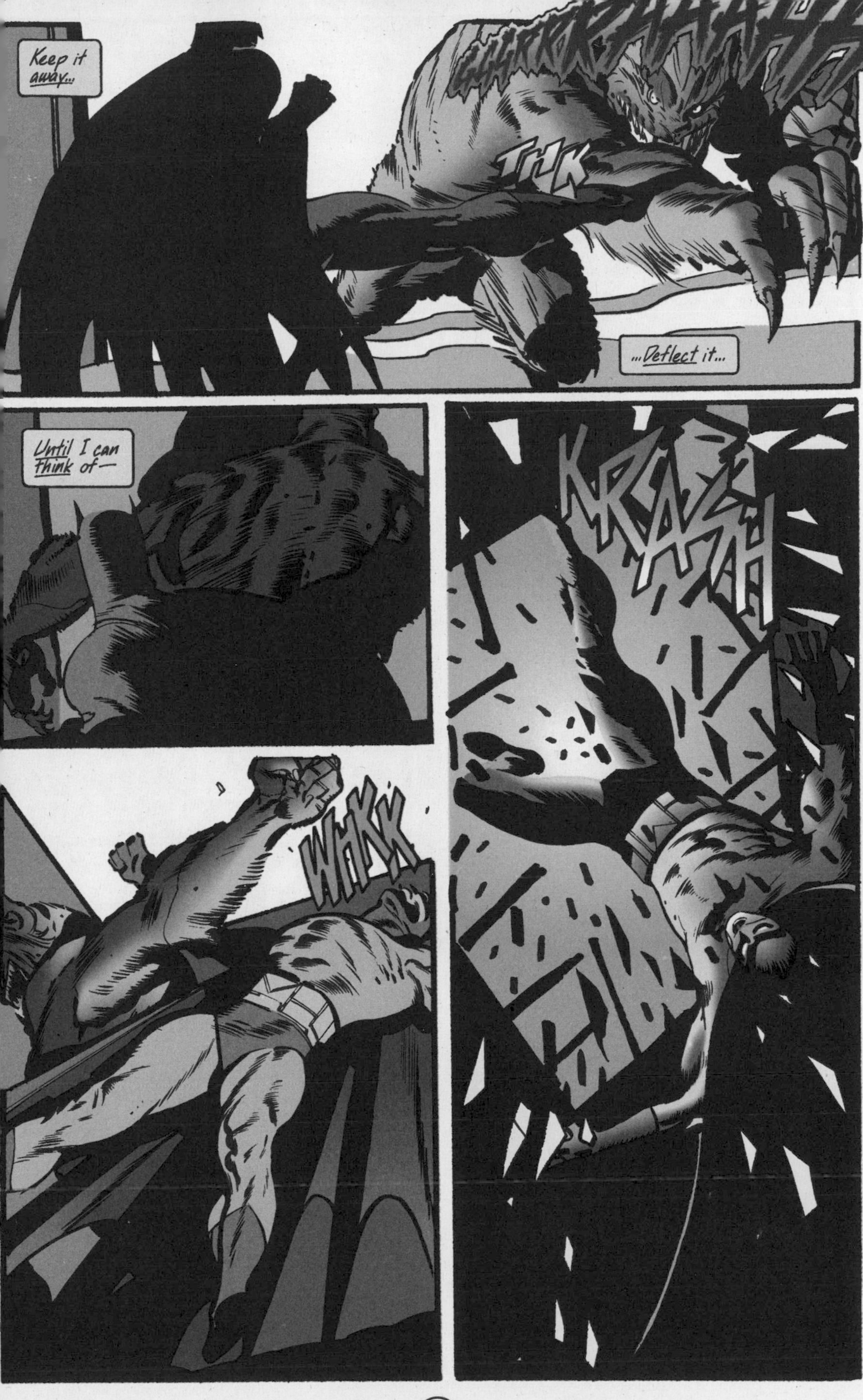
Keep it away...
THK
...Deflect it...
Until I can think of—
WHKK

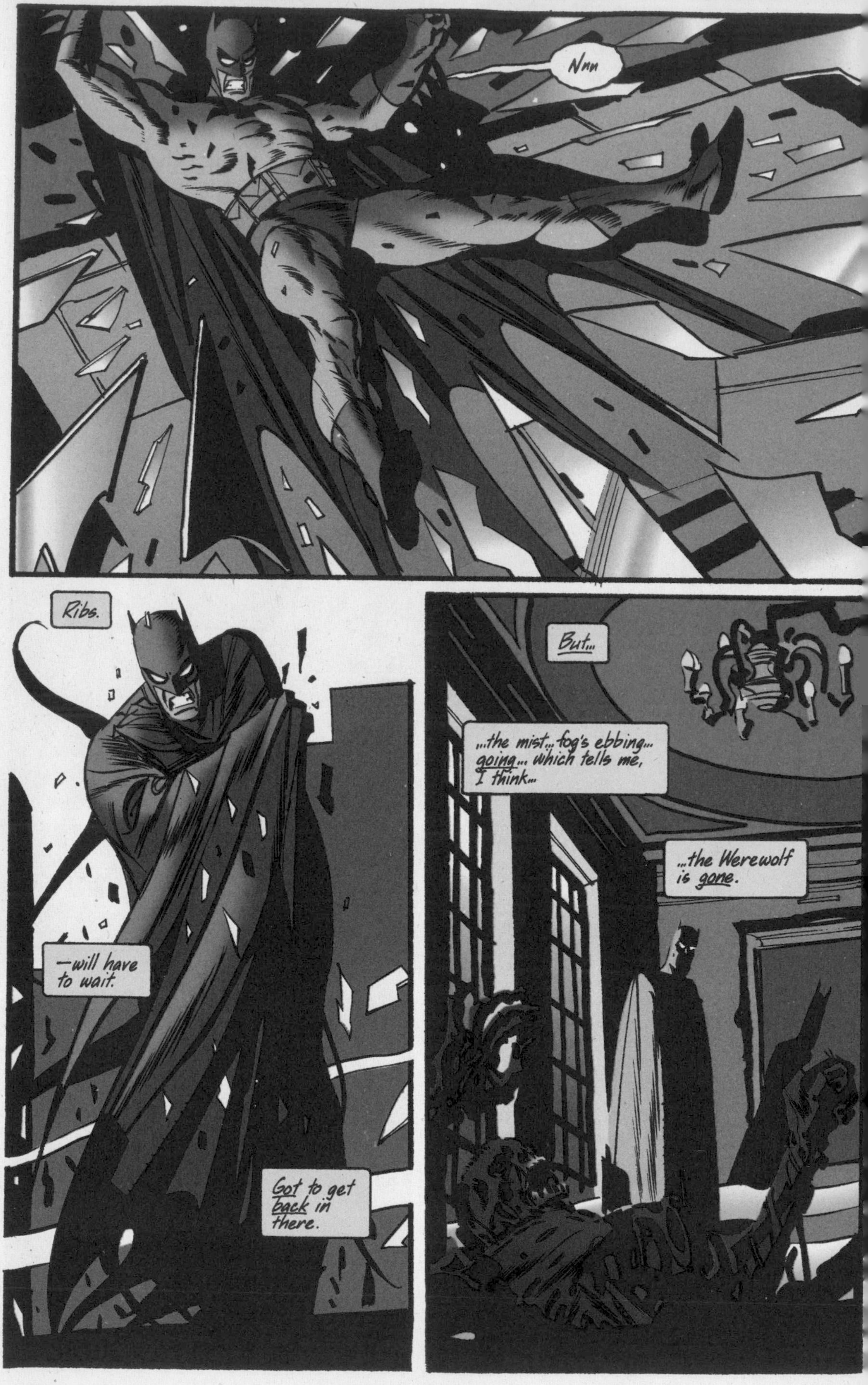
Nnn
Ribs.
—will have to wait.
Got to get back in there.
But...
...the mist... fog's ebbing... going... which tells me, I think...
...the Werewolf is gone.

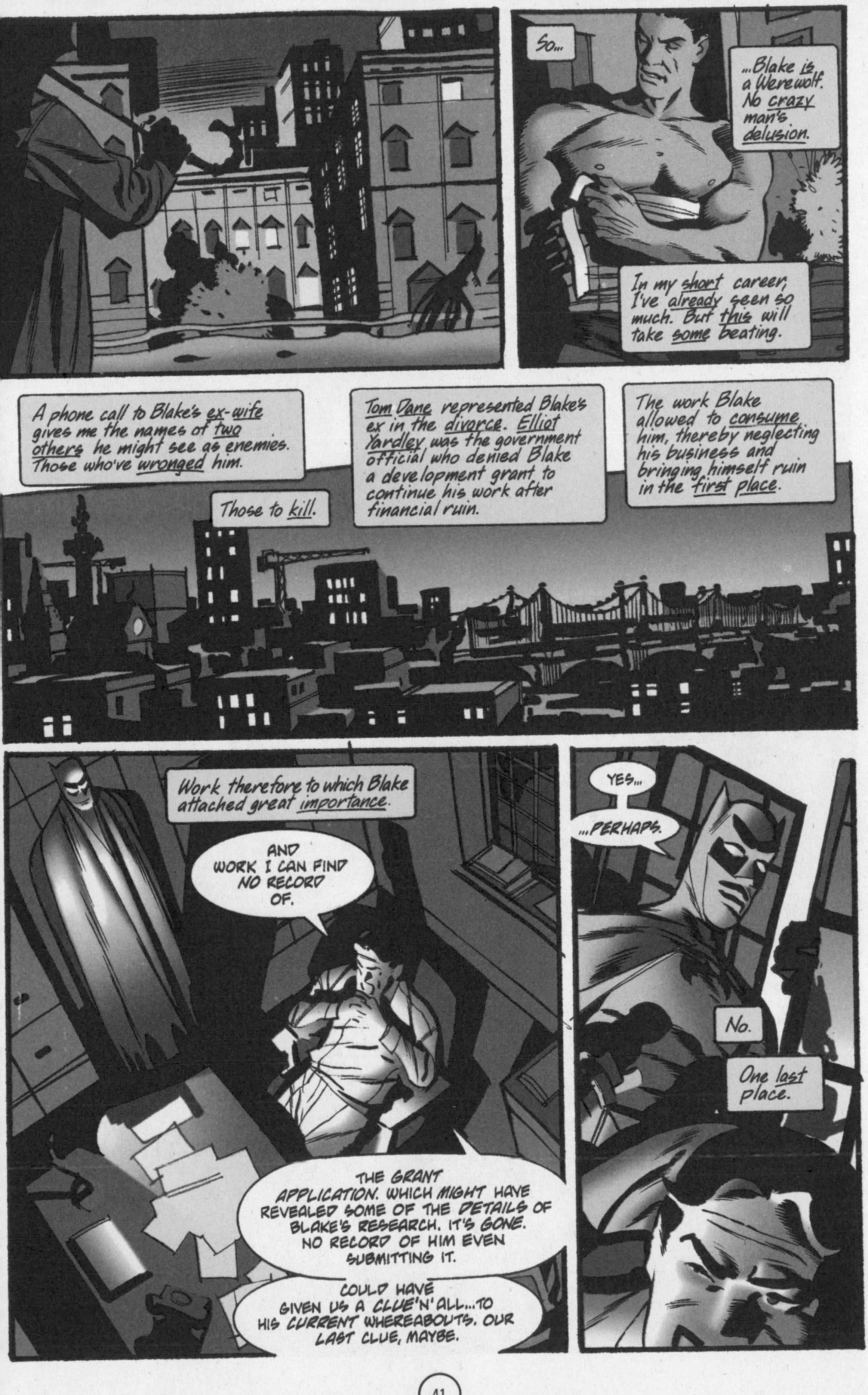

So...
...Blake is a Werewolf. No crazy man's delusion.
In my short career, I've already seen so much. But this will take some beating.
A phone call to Blake's ex-wife gives me the names of two others he might see as enemies. Those who've wronged him.
Those to kill.
Tom Dane represented Blake's ex in the divorce. Elliot Yardley was the government official who denied Blake a development grant to continue his work after financial ruin.
The work Blake allowed to consume him, thereby neglecting his business and bringing himself ruin in the first place.
Work therefore to which Blake attached great importance.
AND WORK I CAN FIND NO RECORD OF.
THE GRANT APPLICATION. WHICH MIGHT HAVE REVEALED SOME OF THE DETAILS OF BLAKE'S RESEARCH. IT'S GONE. NO RECORD OF HIM EVEN SUBMITTING IT.
COULD HAVE GIVEN US A CLUE'N'ALL...TO HIS CURRENT WHEREABOUTS. OUR LAST CLUE, MAYBE.
YES...
...PERHAPS.
No.
One last place.

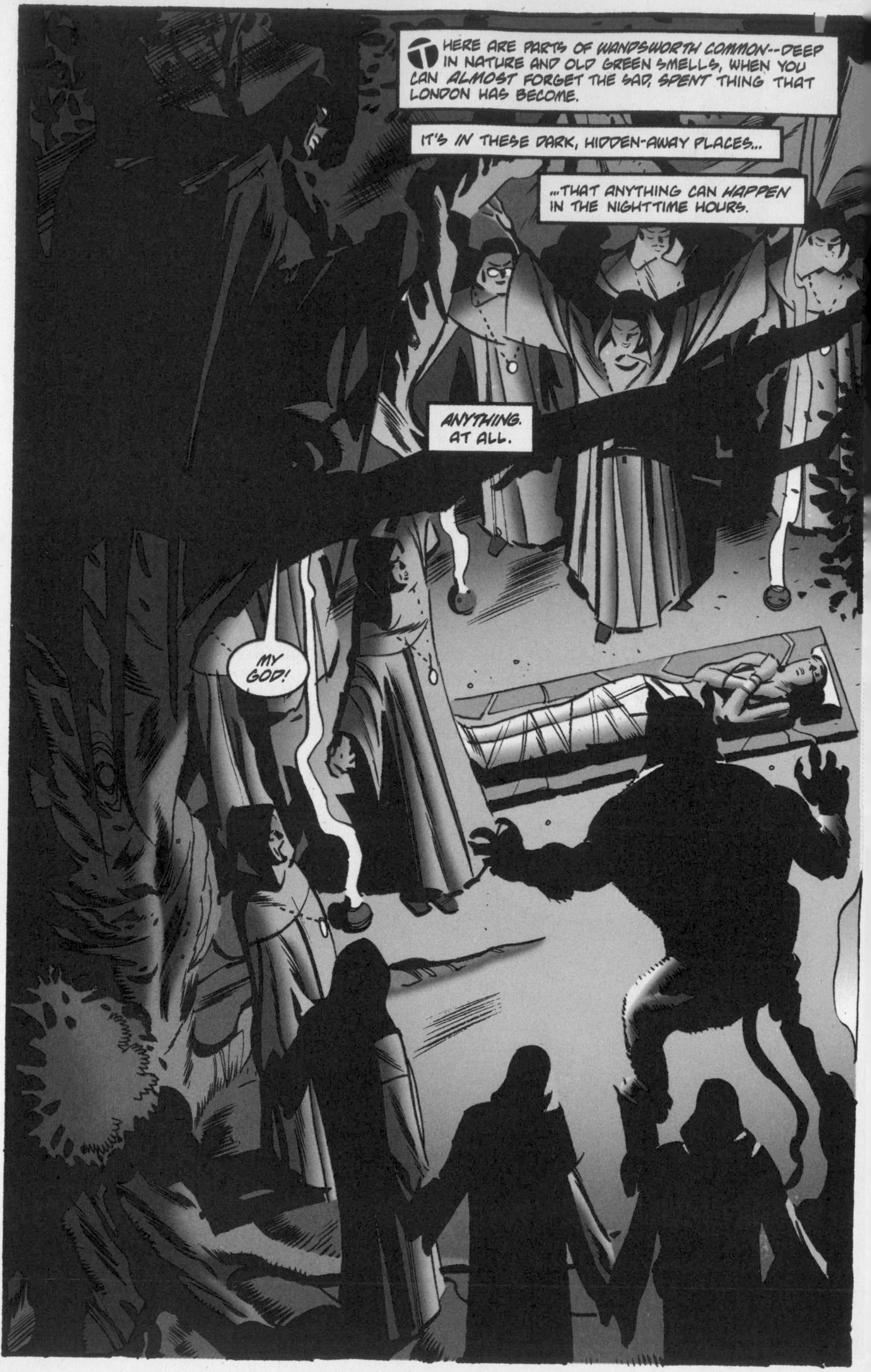
THERE ARE PARTS OF WANDSWORTH COMMON--DEEP IN NATURE AND OLD GREEN SMELLS, WHEN YOU CAN ALMOST FORGET THE SAD, SPENT THING THAT LONDON HAS BECOME.
IT'S IN THESE DARK, HIDDEN-AWAY PLACES...
...THAT ANYTHING CAN HAPPEN IN THE NIGHTTIME HOURS.
ANYTHING. AT ALL.
MY GOD!

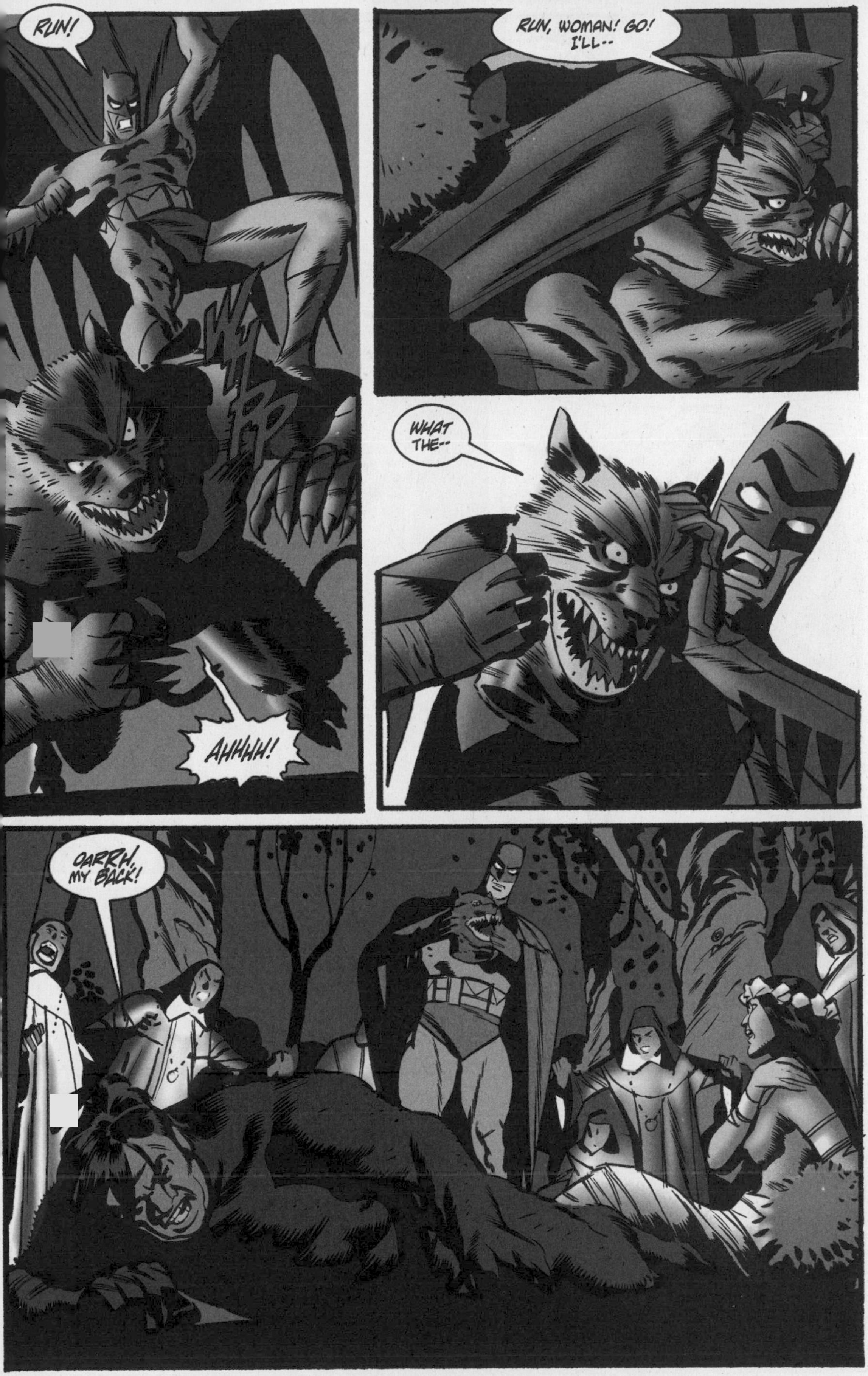
RUN!
RUN, WOMAN! GO! I'LL--
AHHHH!
WHAT THE--
OARRH, MY BACK!

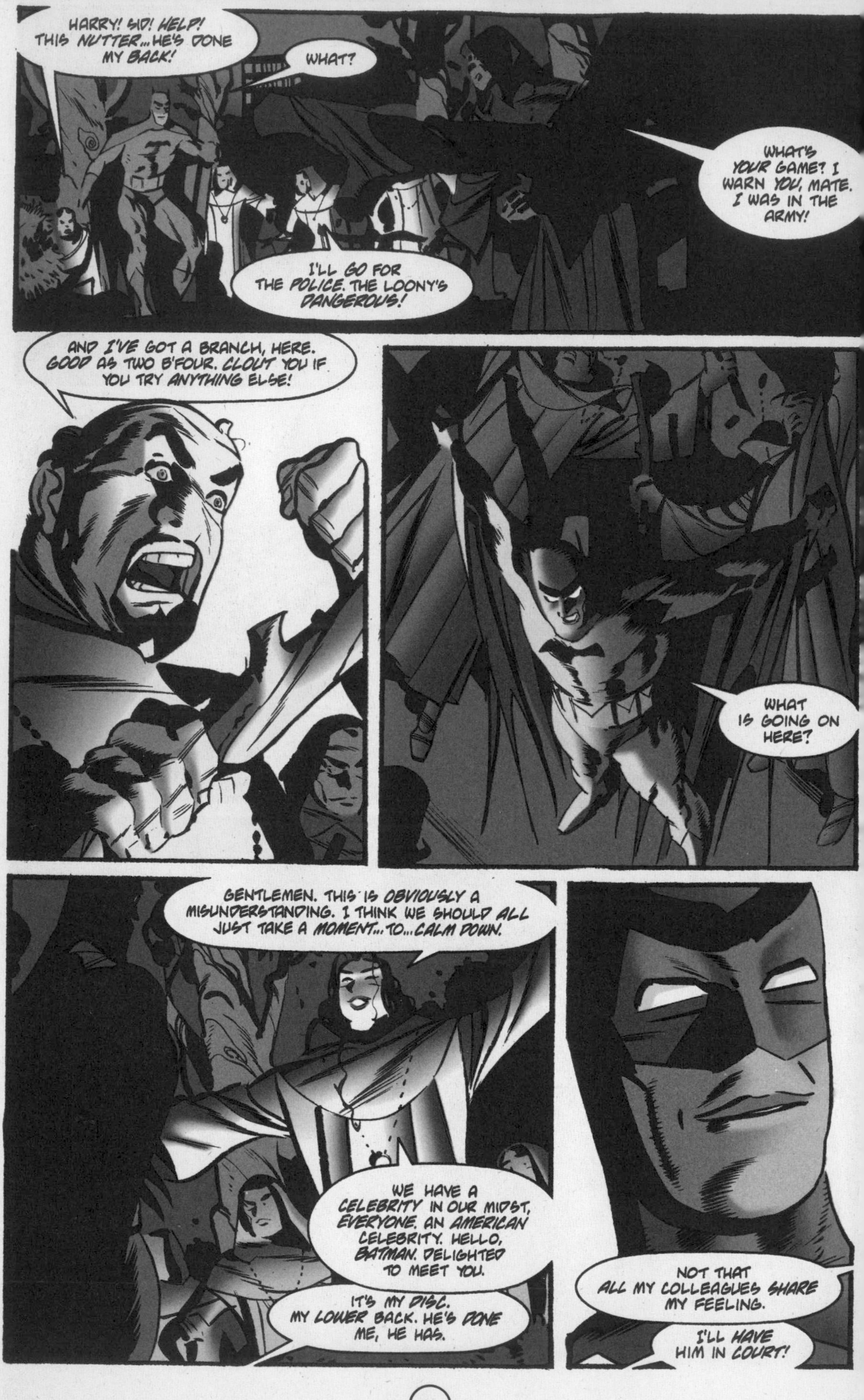
HARRY! SID! HELP! THIS NUTTER... HE'S DONE MY BACK!
WHAT?
WHAT'S YOUR GAME? I WARN YOU, MATE. I WAS IN THE ARMY!
I'LL GO FOR THE POLICE. THE LOONY'S DANGEROUS!
AND I'VE GOT A BRANCH, HERE. GOOD AS TWO B'FOUR. CLOUT YOU IF YOU TRY ANYTHING ELSE!
WHAT IS GOING ON HERE?
GENTLEMEN. THIS IS OBVIOUSLY A MISUNDERSTANDING. I THINK WE SHOULD ALL JUST TAKE A MOMENT... TO... CALM DOWN.
WE HAVE A CELEBRITY IN OUR MIDST, EVERYONE. AN AMERICAN CELEBRITY. HELLO, BATMAN. DELIGHTED TO MEET YOU.
IT'S MY DISC. MY LOWER BACK. HE'S DONE ME, HE HAS.
NOT THAT ALL MY COLLEAGUES SHARE MY FEELING.
I'LL HAVE HIM IN COURT!

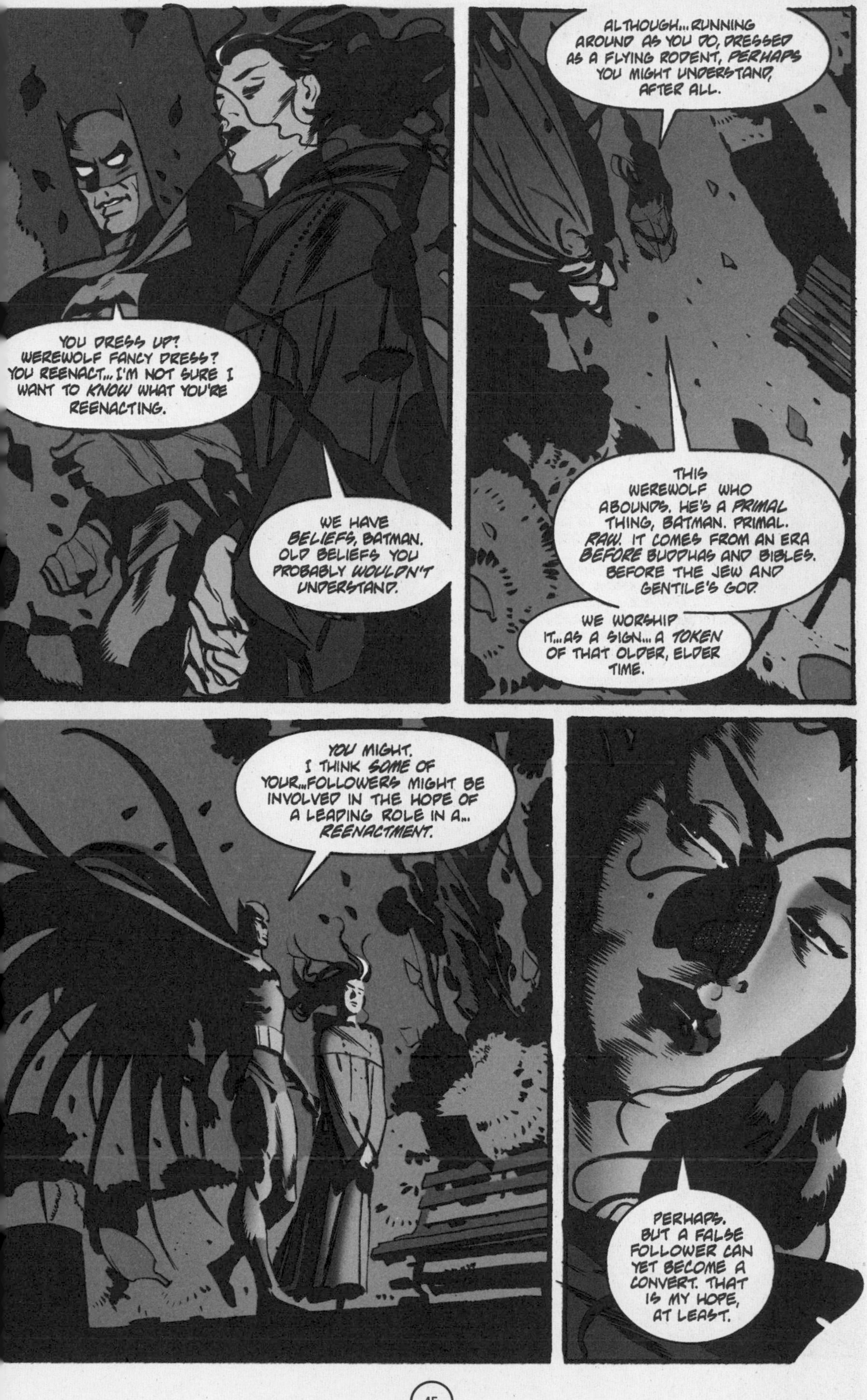
YOU DRESS UP? WEREWOLF FANCY DRESS? YOU REENACT... I'M NOT SURE I WANT TO KNOW WHAT YOU'RE REENACTING.
WE HAVE BELIEFS, BATMAN. OLD BELIEFS YOU PROBABLY WOULDN'T UNDERSTAND.
ALTHOUGH... RUNNING AROUND AS YOU DO, DRESSED AS A FLYING RODENT, PERHAPS YOU MIGHT UNDERSTAND, AFTER ALL.
THIS WEREWOLF WHO ABOUNDS. HE'S A PRIMAL THING, BATMAN. PRIMAL. RAW. IT COMES FROM AN ERA BEFORE BUDDHAS AND BIBLES. BEFORE THE JEW AND GENTILE'S GOD.
WE WORSHIP IT... AS A SIGN... A TOKEN OF THAT OLDER, ELDER TIME.
YOU MIGHT. I THINK SOME OF YOUR... FOLLOWERS MIGHT BE INVOLVED IN THE HOPE OF A LEADING ROLE IN A... REENACTMENT.
PERHAPS. BUT A FALSE FOLLOWER CAN YET BECOME A CONVERT. THAT IS MY HOPE, AT LEAST.

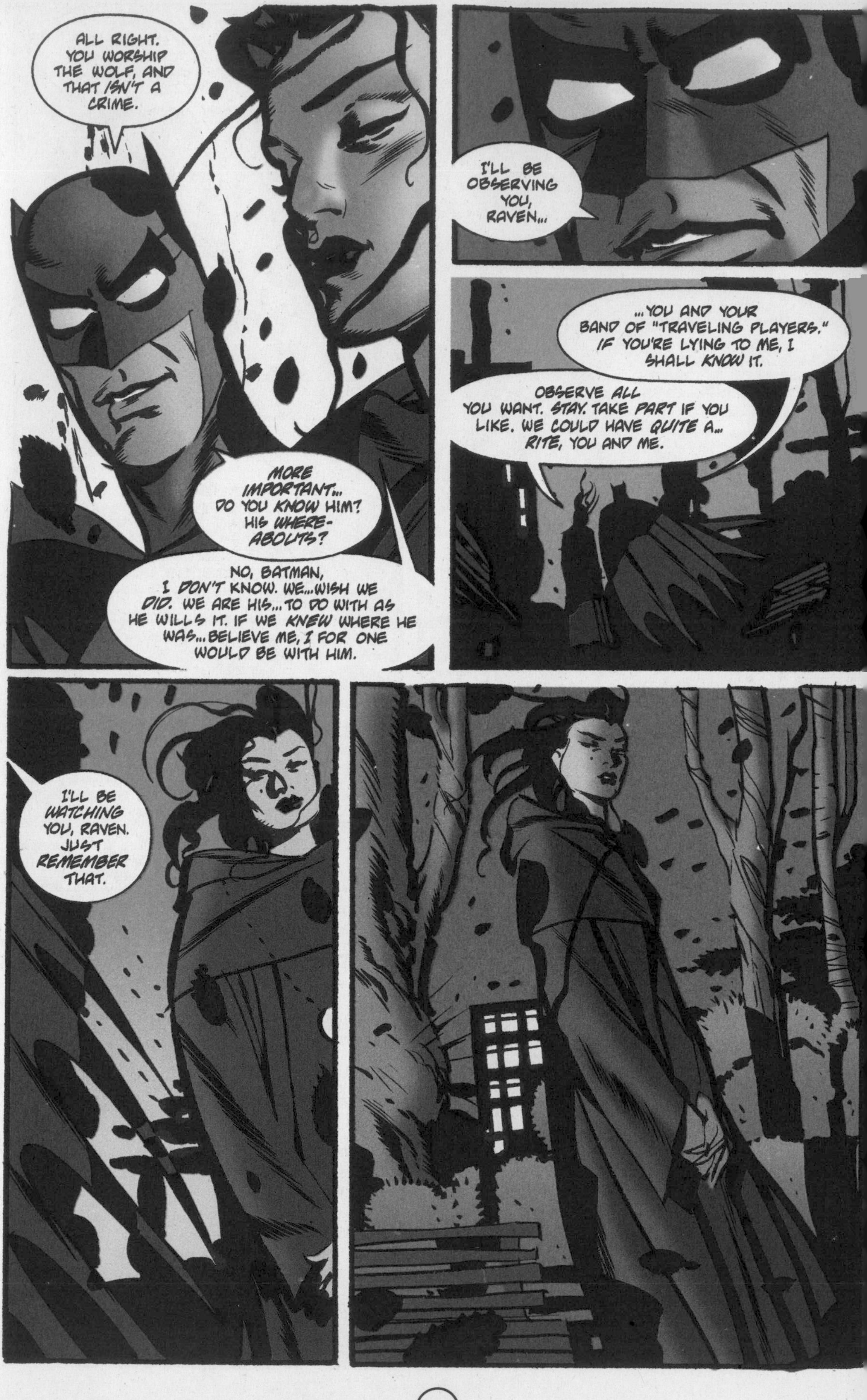

ALL RIGHT. YOU WORSHIP THE WOLF, AND THAT ISN'T A CRIME.
MORE IMPORTANT... DO YOU KNOW HIM? HIS WHERE-ABOUTS?
NO, BATMAN, I DON'T KNOW. WE...WISH WE DID. WE ARE HIS... TO DO WITH AS HE WILLS IT. IF WE KNEW WHERE HE WAS...BELIEVE ME, I FOR ONE WOULD BE WITH HIM.
I'LL BE OBSERVING YOU, RAVEN...
...YOU AND YOUR BAND OF "TRAVELING PLAYERS." IF YOU'RE LYING TO ME, I SHALL KNOW IT.
OBSERVE ALL YOU WANT. STAY. TAKE PART IF YOU LIKE. WE COULD HAVE QUITE A... RITE, YOU AND ME.
I'LL BE WATCHING YOU, RAVEN. JUST REMEMBER THAT.

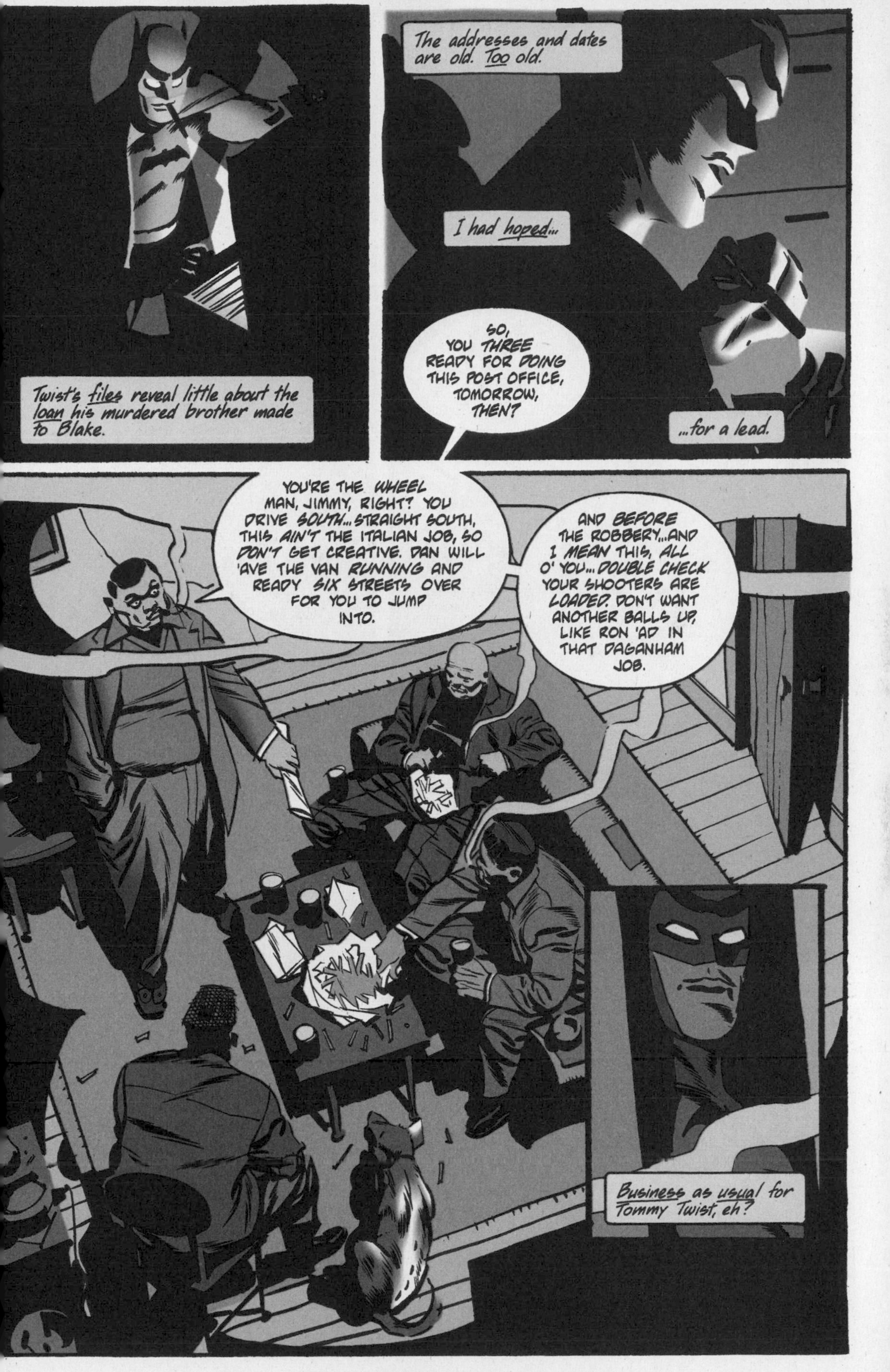

Twist's files reveal little about the loan his murdered brother made to Blake.
The addresses and dates are old. Too old.
I had hoped...
...for a lead.
SO, YOU THREE READY FOR DOING THIS POST OFFICE, TOMORROW, THEN?
YOU'RE THE WHEEL MAN, JIMMY, RIGHT? YOU DRIVE SOUTH... STRAIGHT SOUTH, THIS AIN'T THE ITALIAN JOB, SO DON'T GET CREATIVE. DAN WILL 'AVE THE VAN RUNNING AND READY SIX STREETS OVER FOR YOU TO JUMP INTO.
AND BEFORE THE ROBBERY... AND I MEAN THIS, ALL O' YOU... DOUBLE CHECK YOUR SHOOTERS ARE LOADED. DON'T WANT ANOTHER BALLS UP, LIKE RON 'AD IN THAT DAGANHAM JOB.
Business as usual for Tommy Twist, eh?

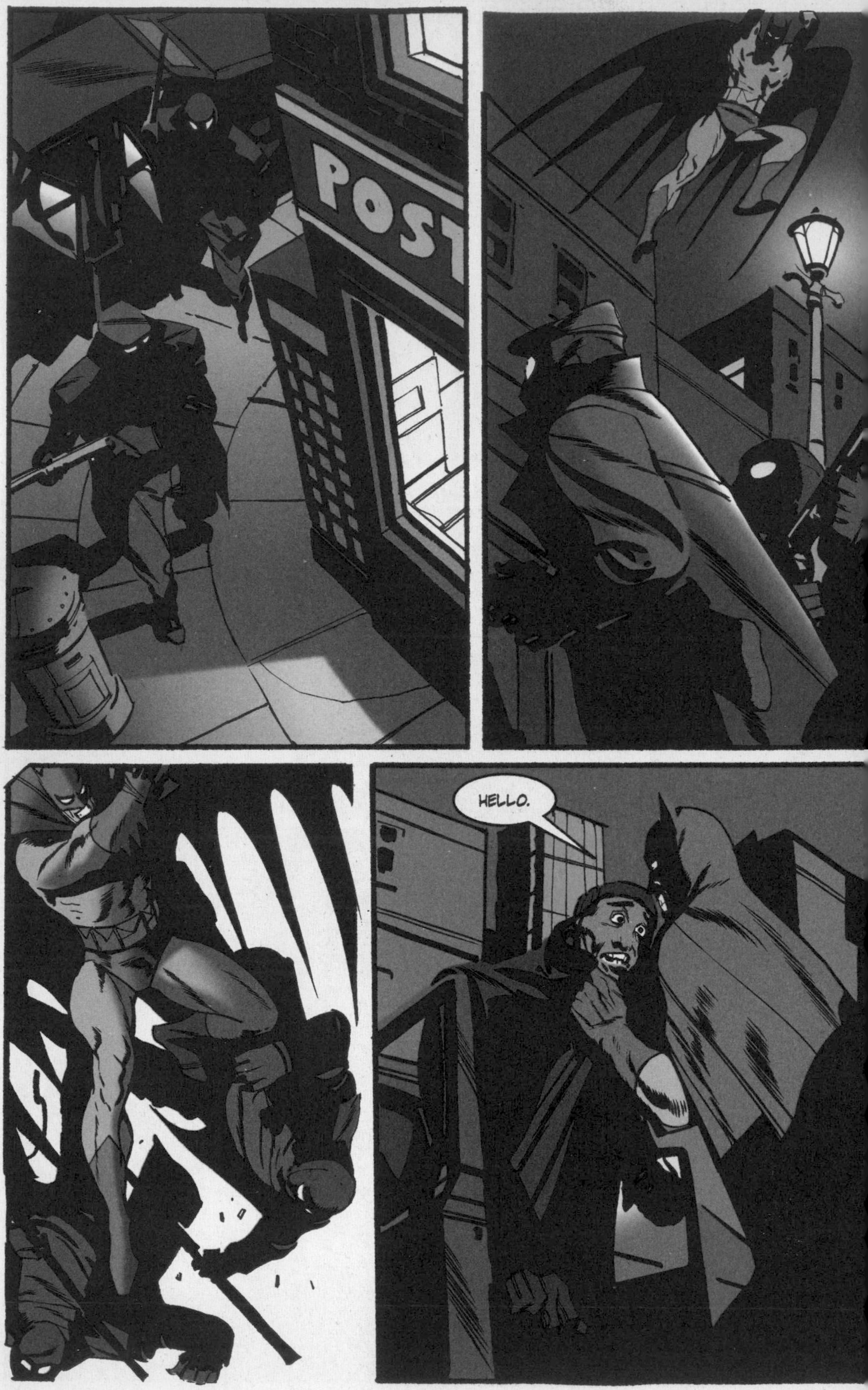
POST
HELLO.

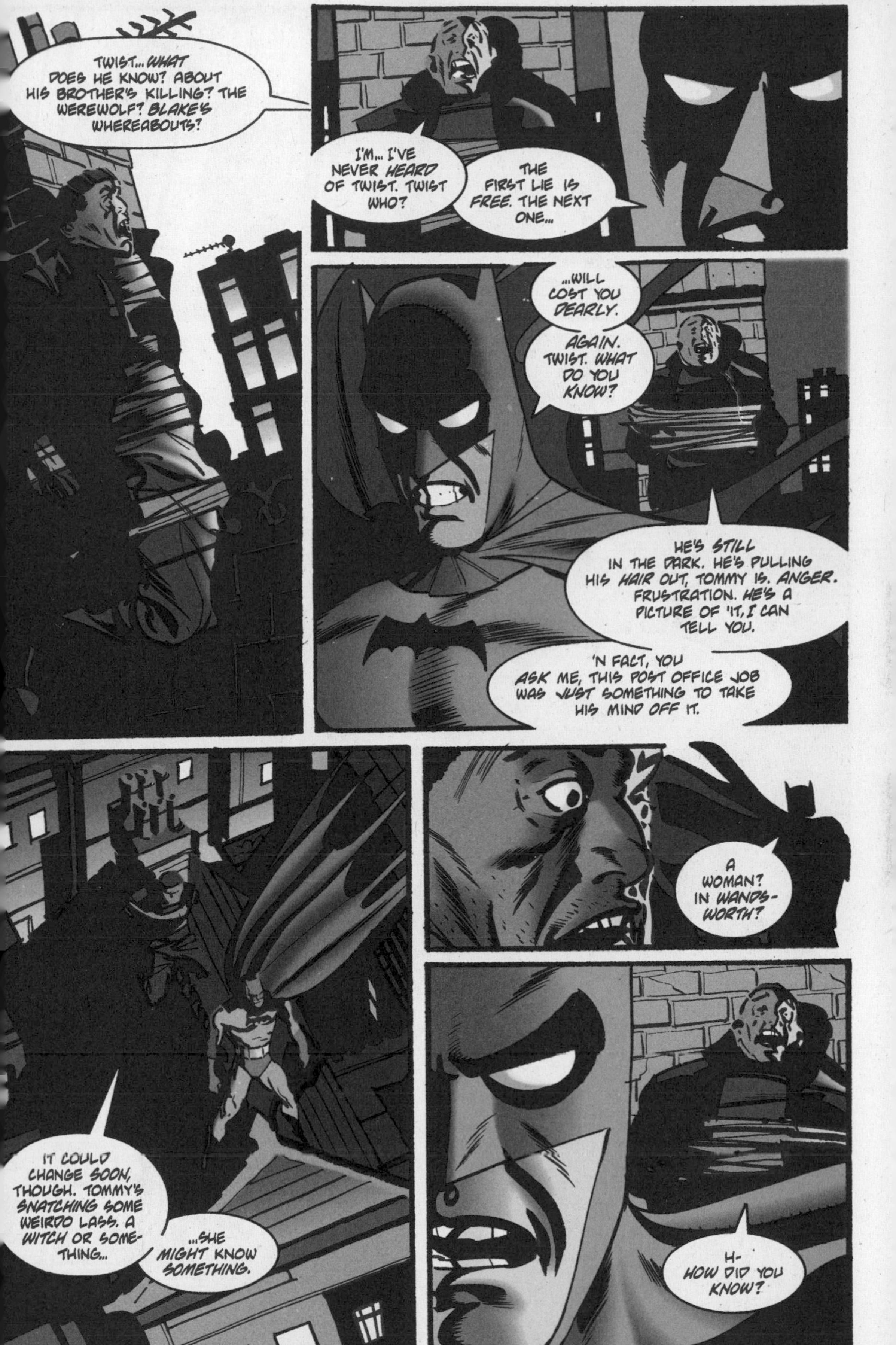
TWIST... WHAT DOES HE KNOW? ABOUT HIS BROTHER'S KILLING? THE WEREWOLF? BLAKE'S WHEREABOUTS?
I'M... I'VE NEVER HEARD OF TWIST. TWIST WHO?
THE FIRST LIE IS FREE. THE NEXT ONE...
...WILL COST YOU DEARLY.
AGAIN. TWIST. WHAT DO YOU KNOW?
HE'S STILL IN THE DARK. HE'S PULLING HIS HAIR OUT, TOMMY IS. ANGER. FRUSTRATION. HE'S A PICTURE OF 'IT, I CAN TELL YOU.
'N FACT, YOU ASK ME, THIS POST OFFICE JOB WAS JUST SOMETHING TO TAKE HIS MIND OFF IT.
IT COULD CHANGE SOON, THOUGH. TOMMY'S SNATCHING SOME WEIRDO LASS. A WITCH OR SOME-THING...
...SHE MIGHT KNOW SOMETHING.
A WOMAN? IN WANDS-WORTH?
H- HOW DID YOU KNOW?

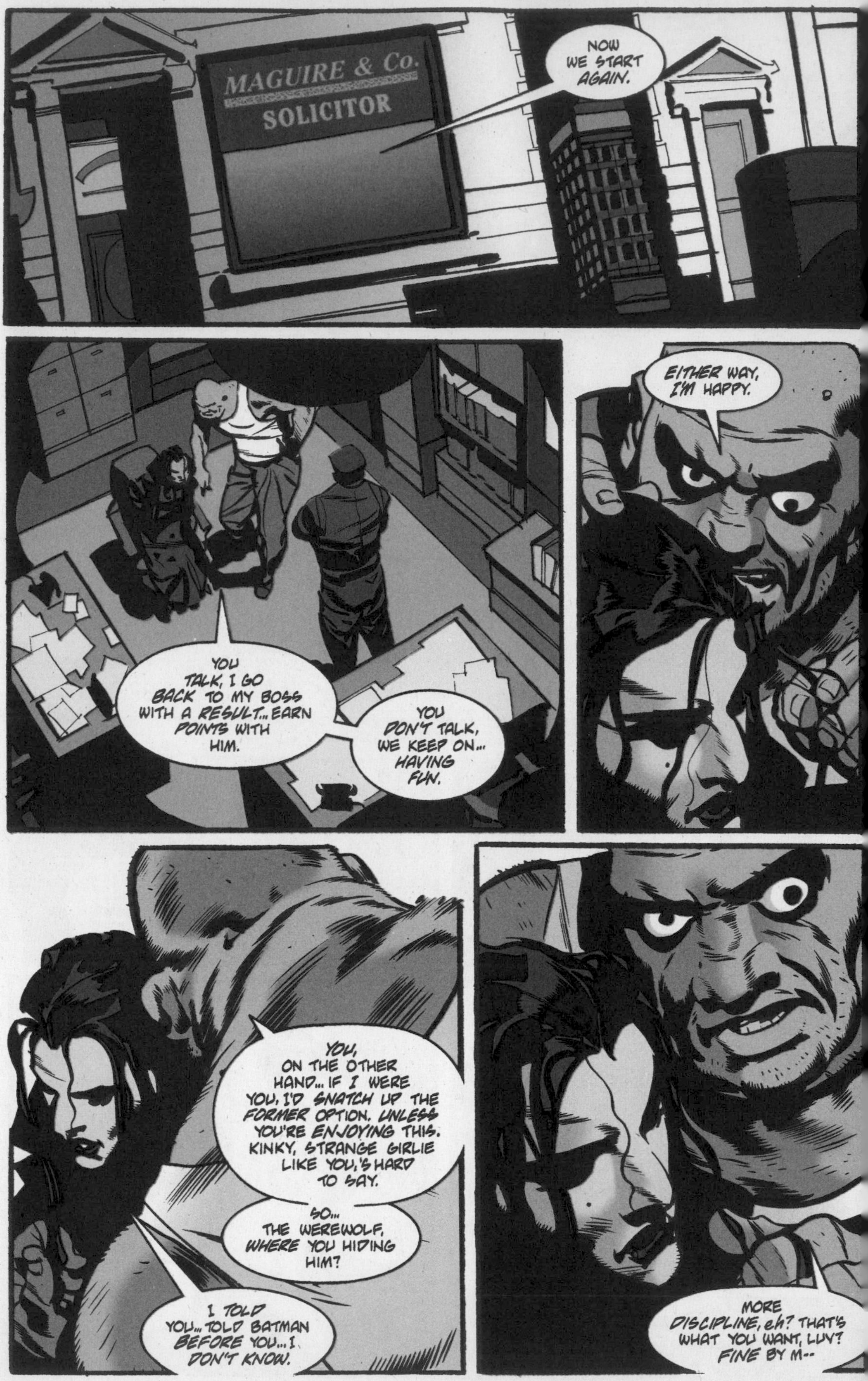
MAGUIRE & Co.
SOLICITOR
NOW WE START AGAIN.
YOU TALK, I GO BACK TO MY BOSS WITH A RESULT... EARN POINTS WITH HIM.
YOU DON'T TALK, WE KEEP ON... HAVING FUN.
EITHER WAY, I'M HAPPY.
YOU, ON THE OTHER HAND... IF I WERE YOU, I'D SNATCH UP THE FORMER OPTION. UNLESS YOU'RE ENJOYING THIS. KINKY, STRANGE GIRLIE LIKE YOU,'S HARD TO SAY.
SO... THE WEREWOLF, WHERE YOU HIDING HIM?
I TOLD YOU... TOLD BATMAN BEFORE YOU... I DON'T KNOW.
MORE DISCIPLINE, eh? THAT'S WHAT YOU WANT, LUV? FINE BY M--

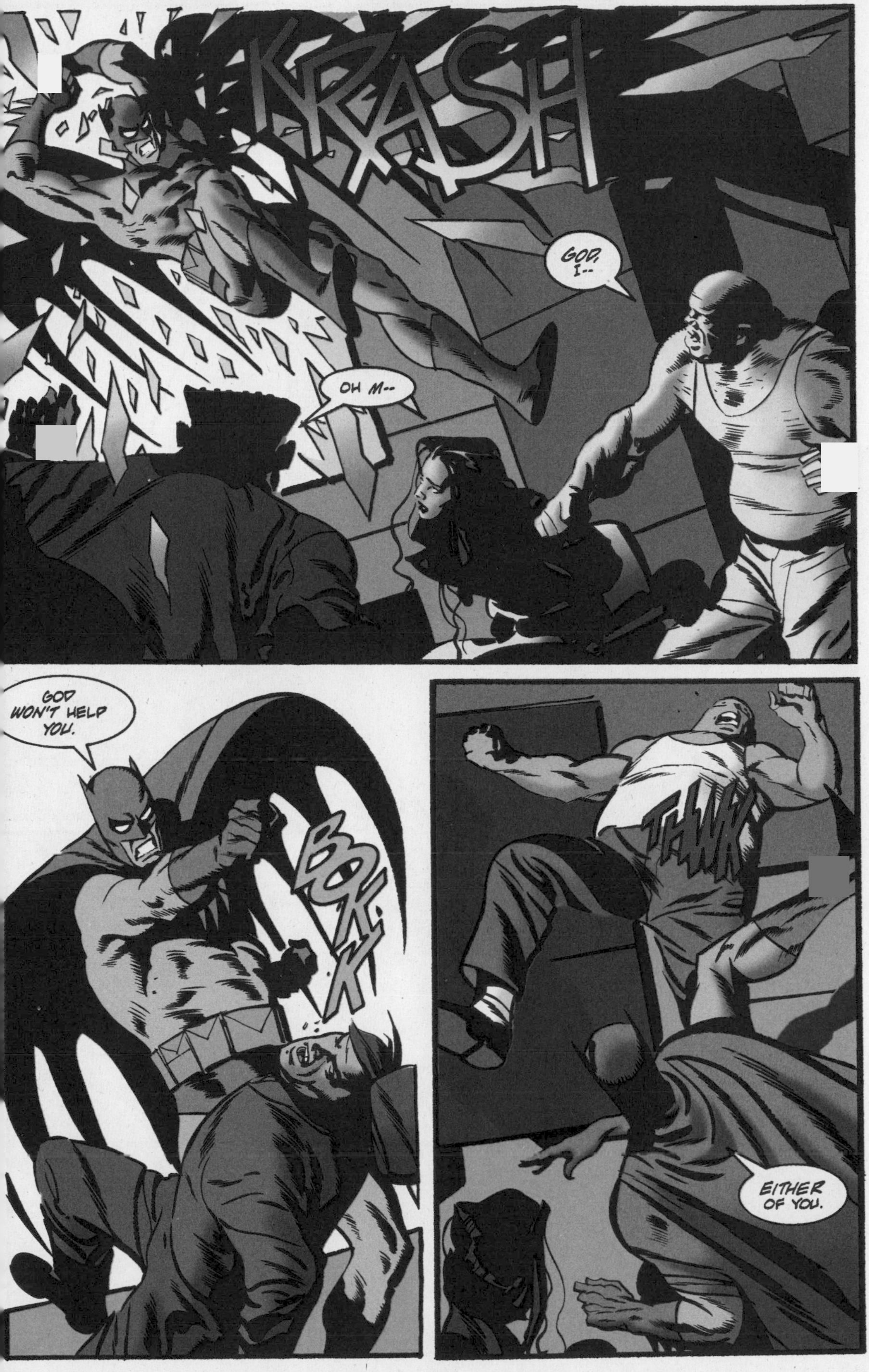
KRASH
GOD, I--
OH M--
GOD WON'T HELP YOU.
BOK
THWK
EITHER OF YOU.

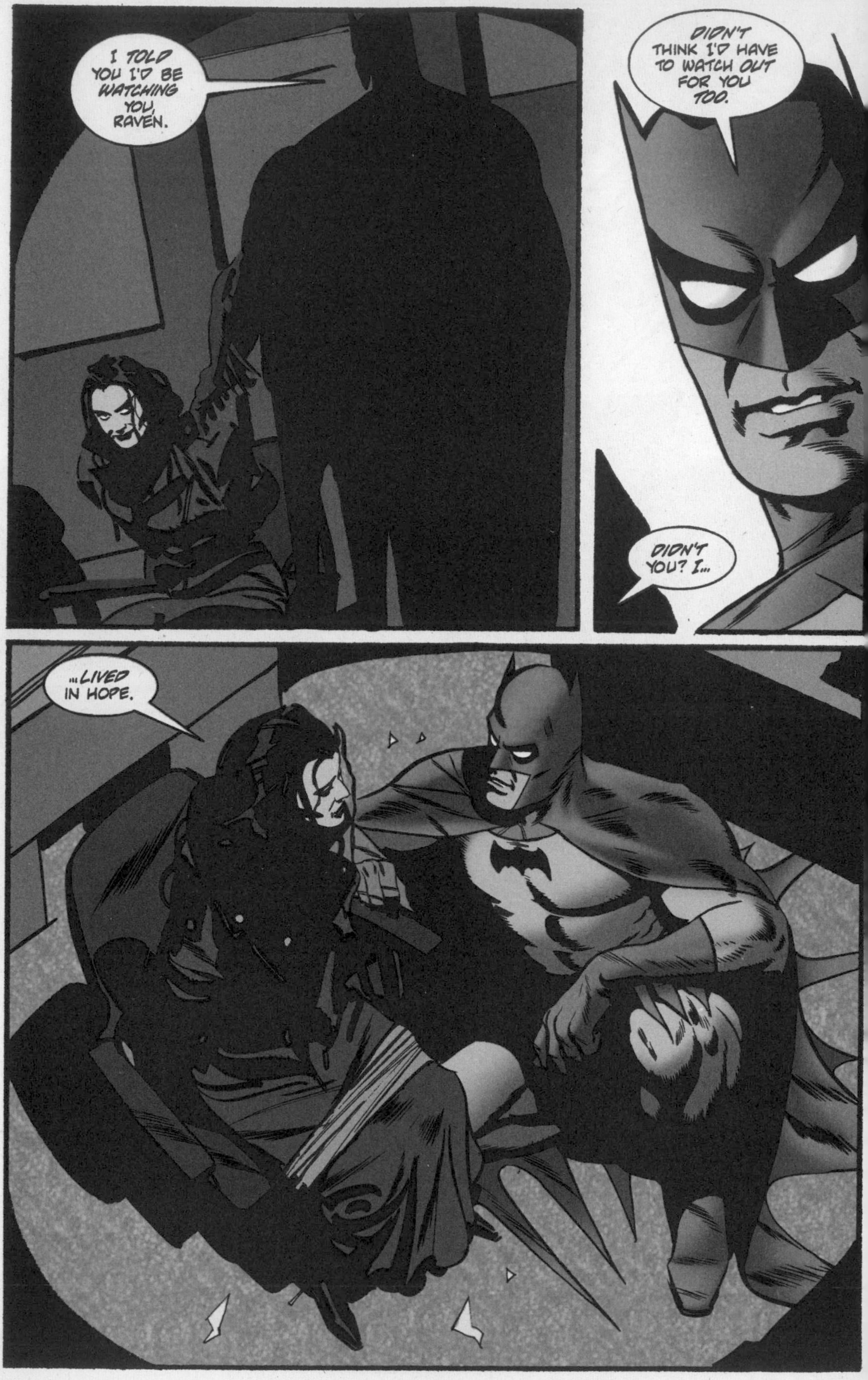
I TOLD YOU I'D BE WATCHING YOU, RAVEN.
DIDN'T THINK I'D HAVE TO WATCH OUT FOR YOU TOO.
DIDN'T YOU? I...
...LIVED IN HOPE.

BATMAN, IT'S NASH.

I'M AFRAID THE NEWS ISN'T GOOD.

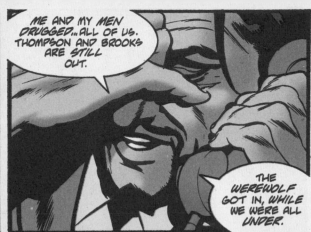

ME AND MY MEN DRUGGED...ALL OF US. THOMPSON AND BROOKS ARE STILL OUT.

THE WEREWOLF GOT IN, WHILE WE WERE ALL UNDER.

YARDLEY'S DEAD.

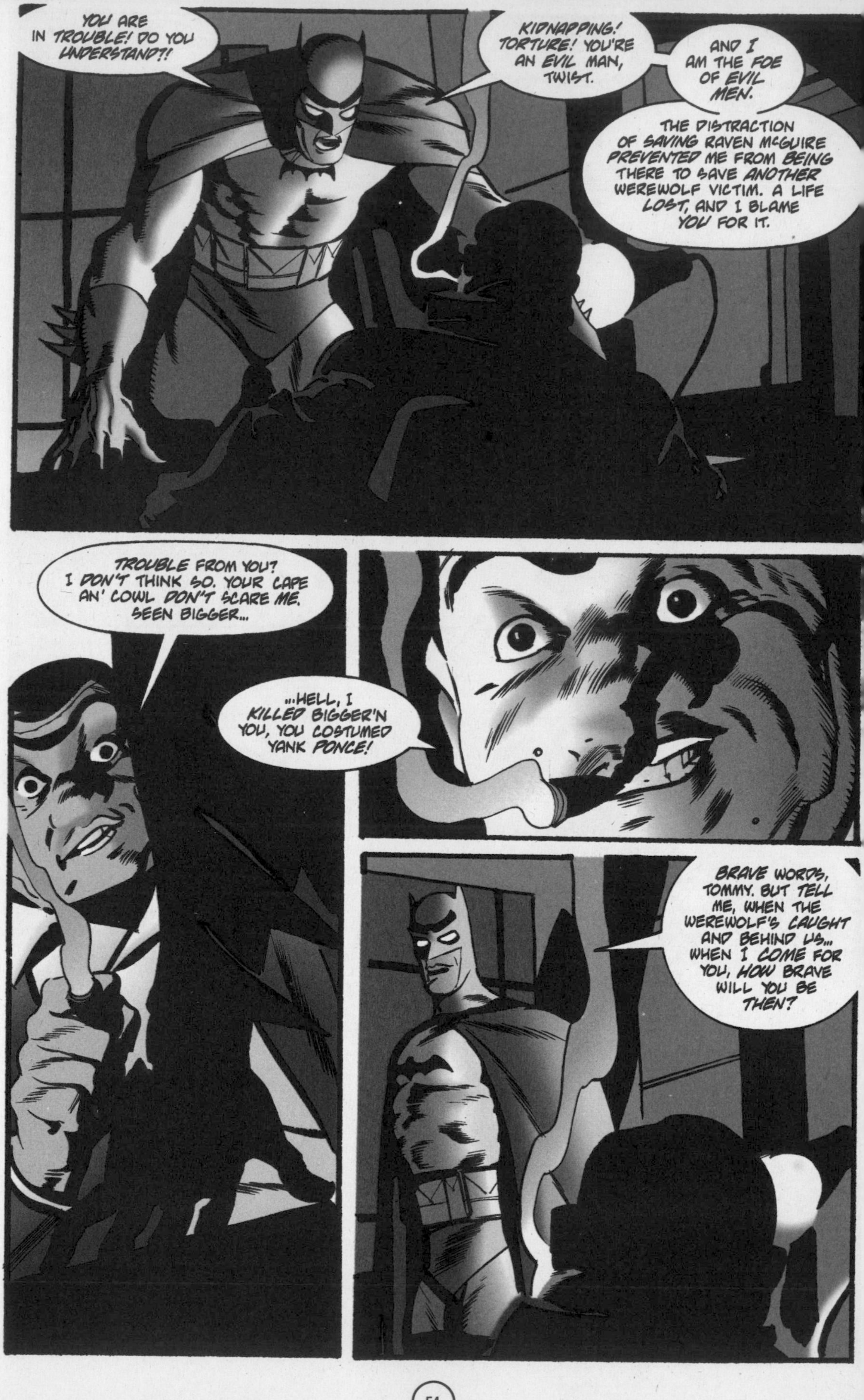
YOU ARE IN TROUBLE! DO YOU UNDERSTAND?!
KIDNAPPING! TORTURE! YOU'RE AN EVIL MAN, TWIST.
AND I AM THE FOE OF EVIL MEN.
THE DISTRACTION OF SAVING RAVEN McGUIRE PREVENTED ME FROM BEING THERE TO SAVE ANOTHER WEREWOLF VICTIM. A LIFE LOST, AND I BLAME YOU FOR IT.
TROUBLE FROM YOU? I DON'T THINK SO. YOUR CAPE AN' COWL DON'T SCARE ME. SEEN BIGGER...
...HELL, I KILLED BIGGER'N YOU, YOU COSTUMED YANK PONCE!
BRAVE WORDS, TOMMY. BUT TELL ME, WHEN THE WEREWOLF'S CAUGHT AND BEHIND US... WHEN I COME FOR YOU, HOW BRAVE WILL YOU BE THEN?

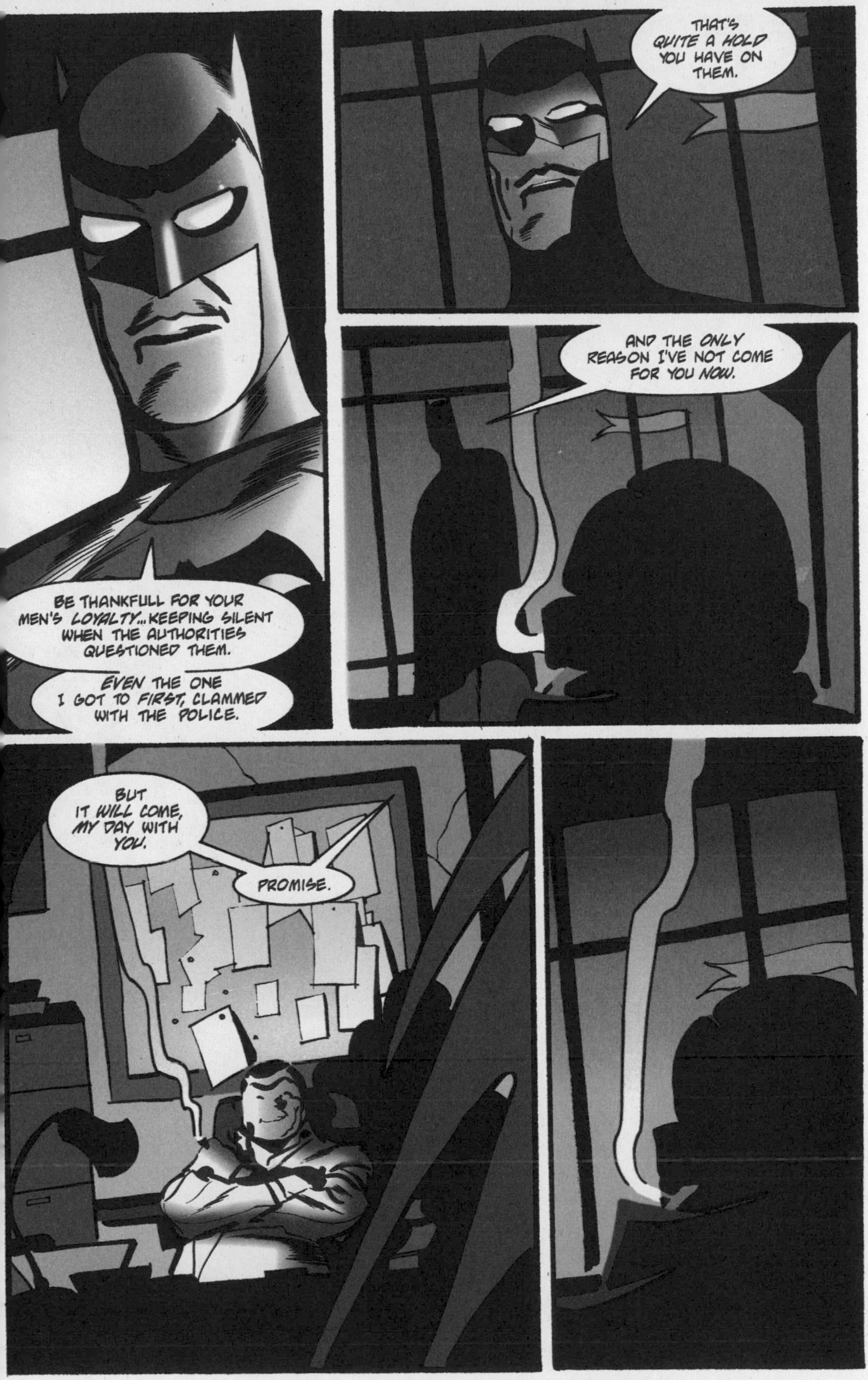
THAT'S QUITE A HOLD YOU HAVE ON THEM.
AND THE ONLY REASON I'VE NOT COME FOR YOU NOW.
BE THANKFULL FOR YOUR MEN'S LOYALTY... KEEPING SILENT WHEN THE AUTHORITIES QUESTIONED THEM.
EVEN THE ONE I GOT TO FIRST, CLAMMED WITH THE POLICE.
BUT IT WILL COME, MY DAY WITH YOU.
PROMISE.

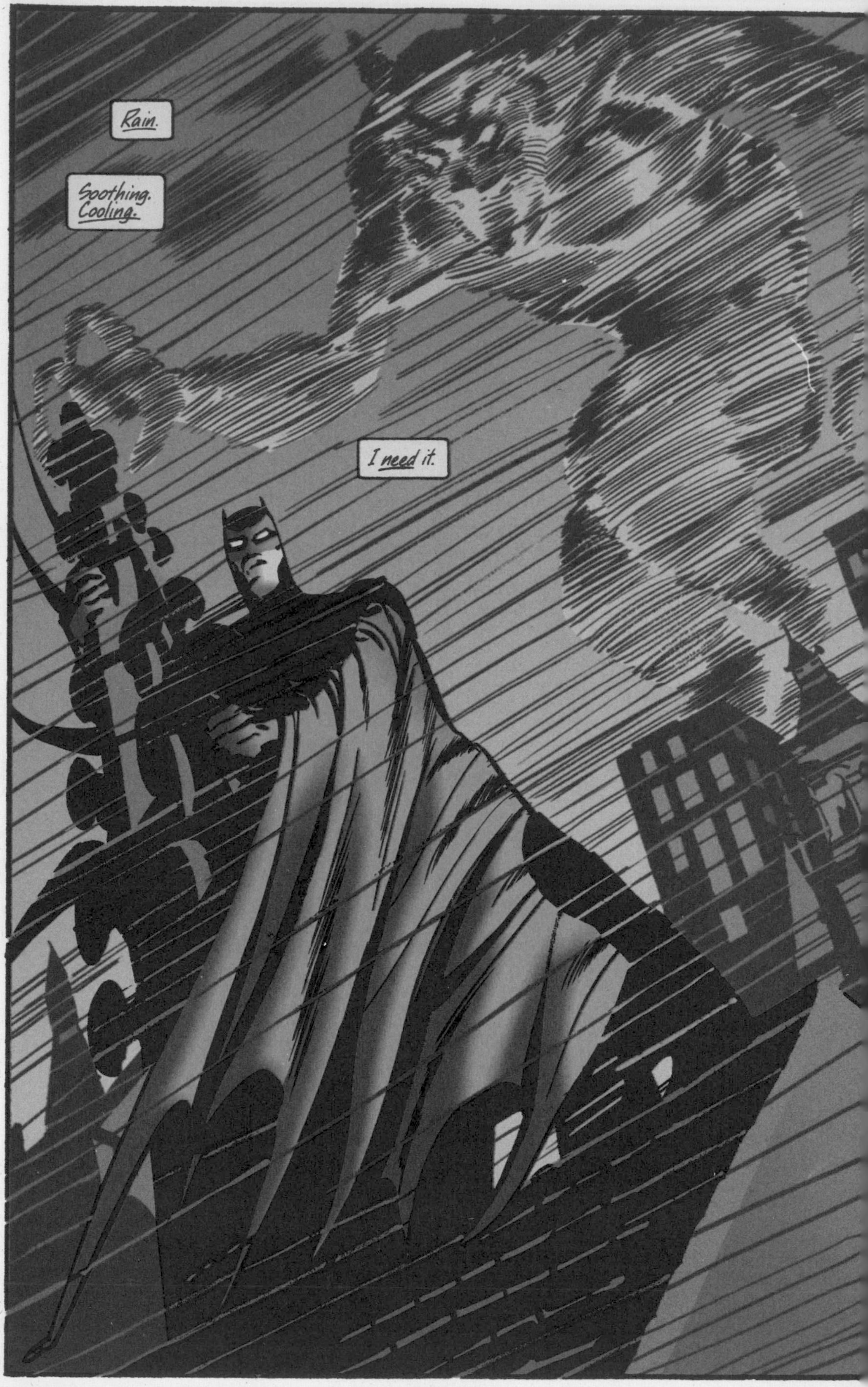
Rain.
Soothing. Cooling.
I need it.

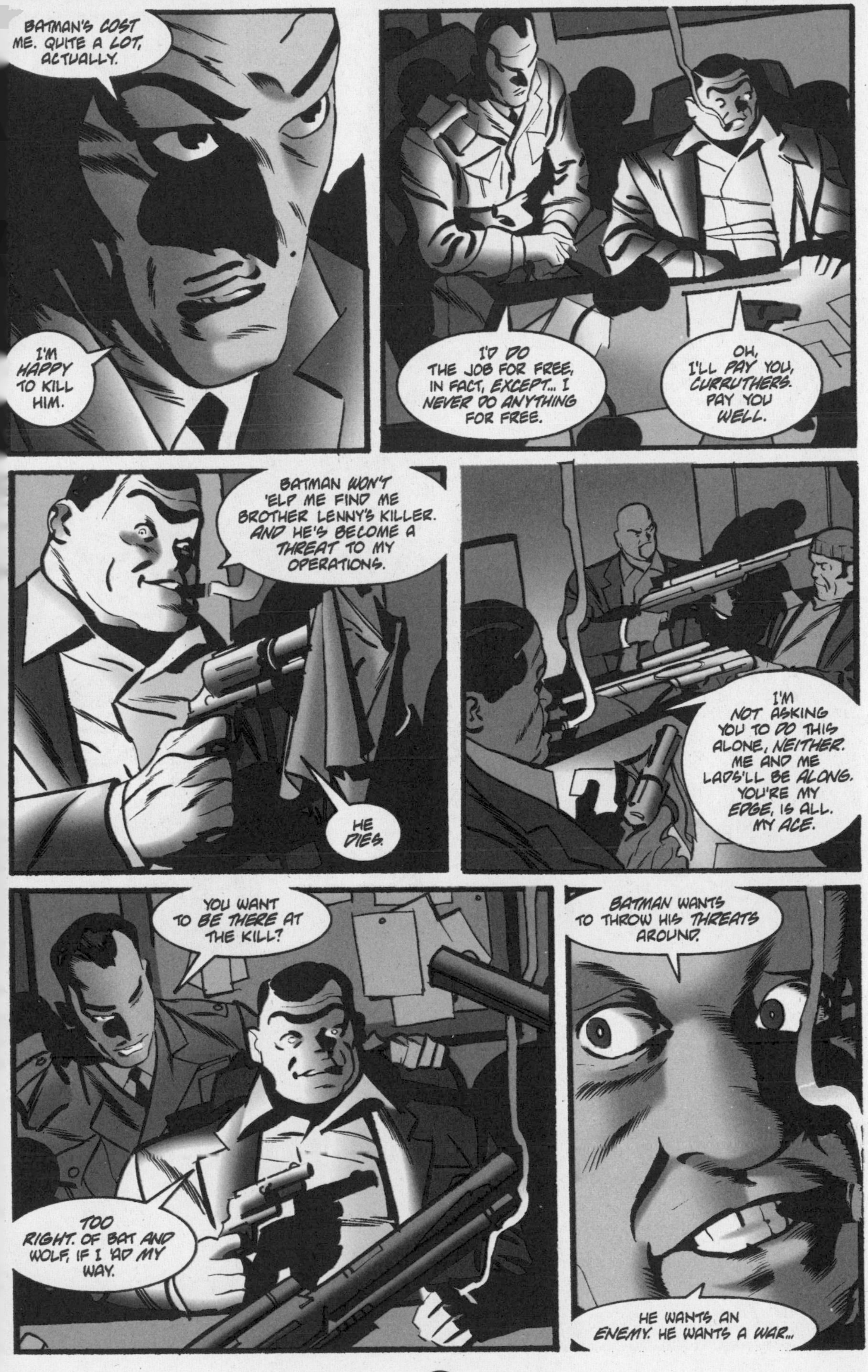
BATMAN'S COST ME. QUITE A LOT, ACTUALLY.
I'M HAPPY TO KILL HIM.
I'D DO THE JOB FOR FREE, IN FACT, EXCEPT... I NEVER DO ANYTHING FOR FREE.
OH, I'LL PAY YOU, CURRUTHERS. PAY YOU WELL.
BATMAN WON'T 'ELP ME FIND ME BROTHER LENNY'S KILLER. AND HE'S BECOME A THREAT TO MY OPERATIONS.
HE DIES.
I'M NOT ASKING YOU TO DO THIS ALONE, NEITHER. ME AND ME LADS'LL BE ALONG. YOU'RE MY EDGE, IS ALL. MY ACE.
YOU WANT TO BE THERE AT THE KILL?
TOO RIGHT. OF BAT AND WOLF, IF I 'AD MY WAY.
BATMAN WANTS TO THROW HIS THREATS AROUND.
HE WANTS AN ENEMY. HE WANTS A WAR...

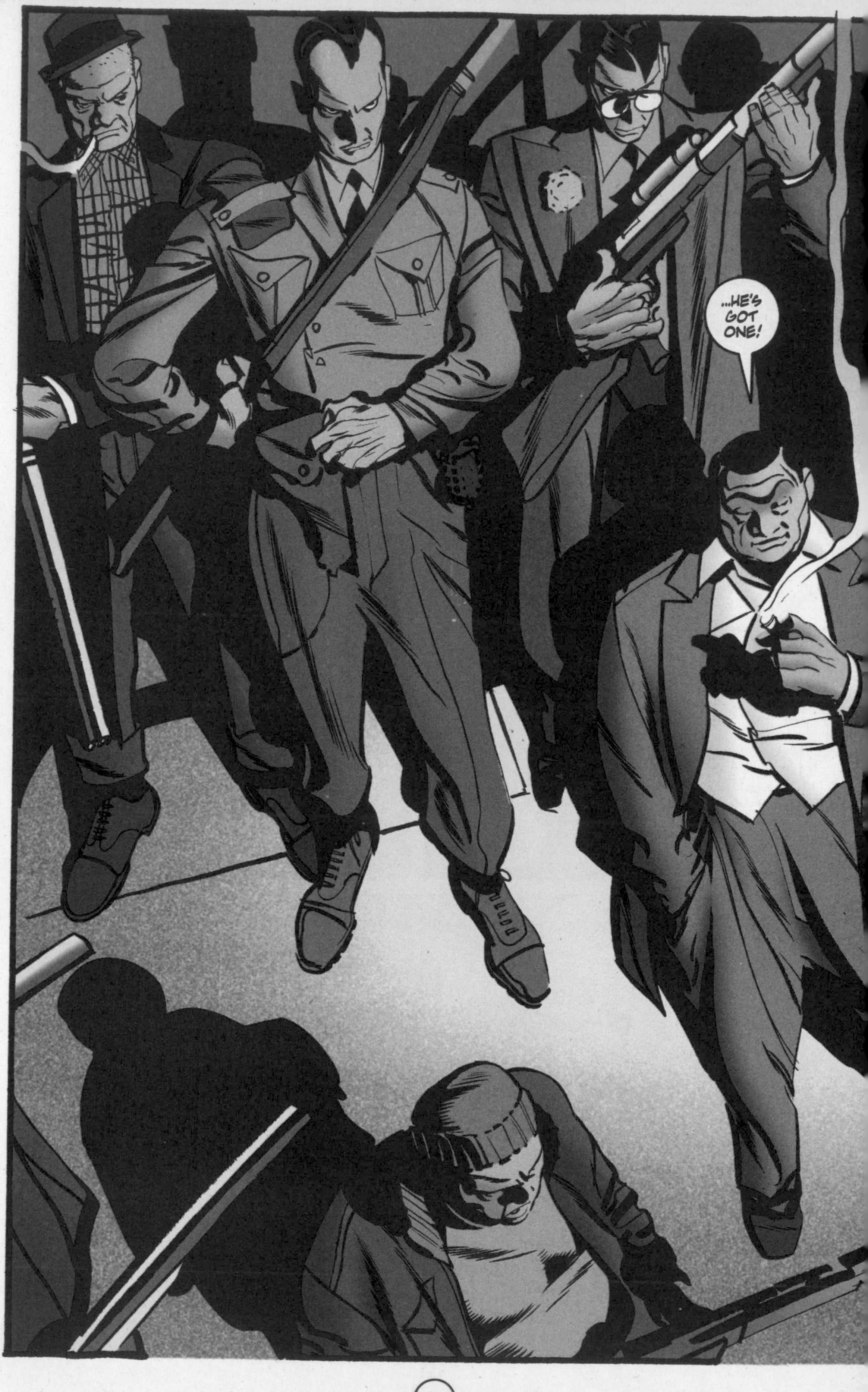
...HE'S GOT ONE!

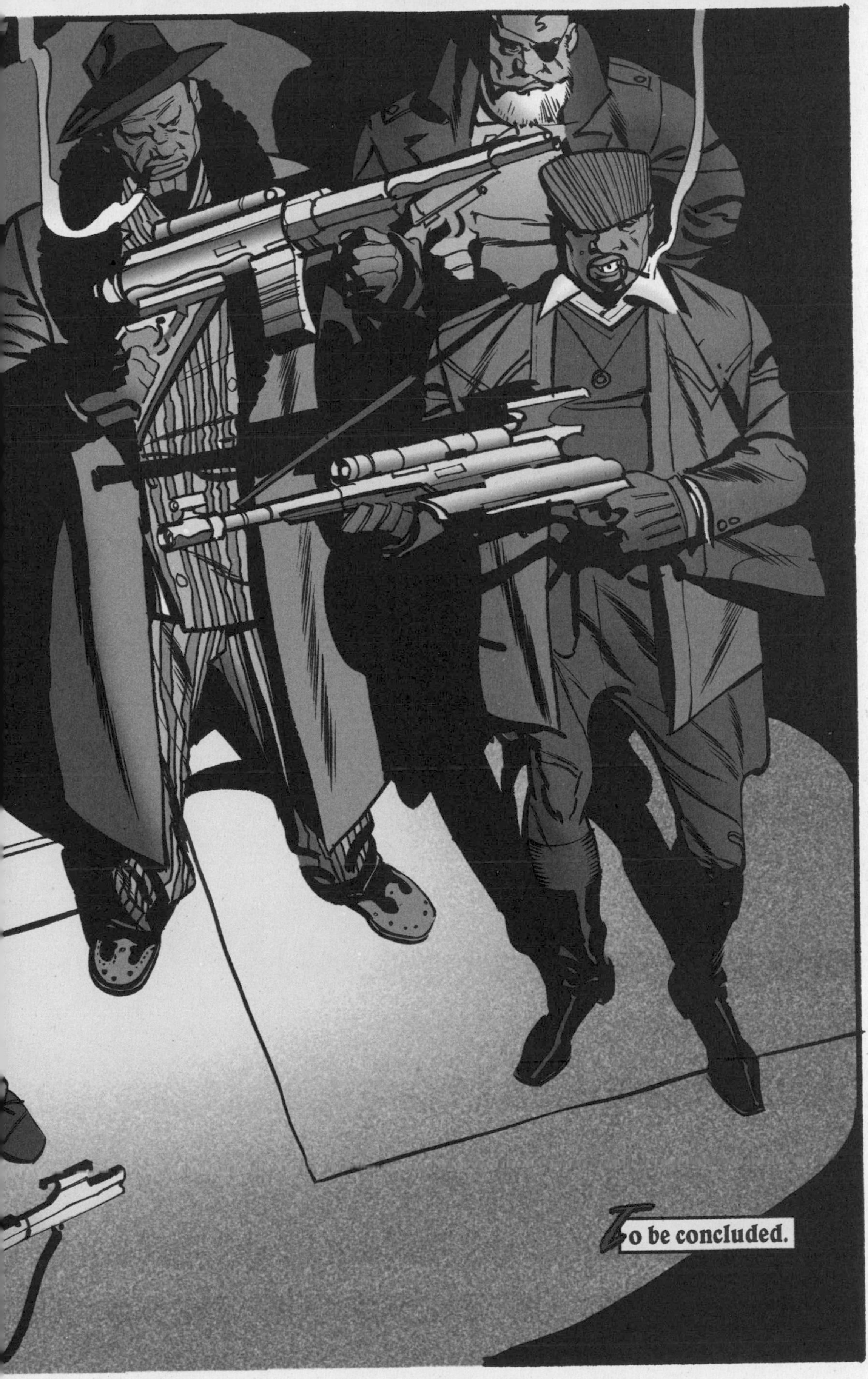
To be concluded.

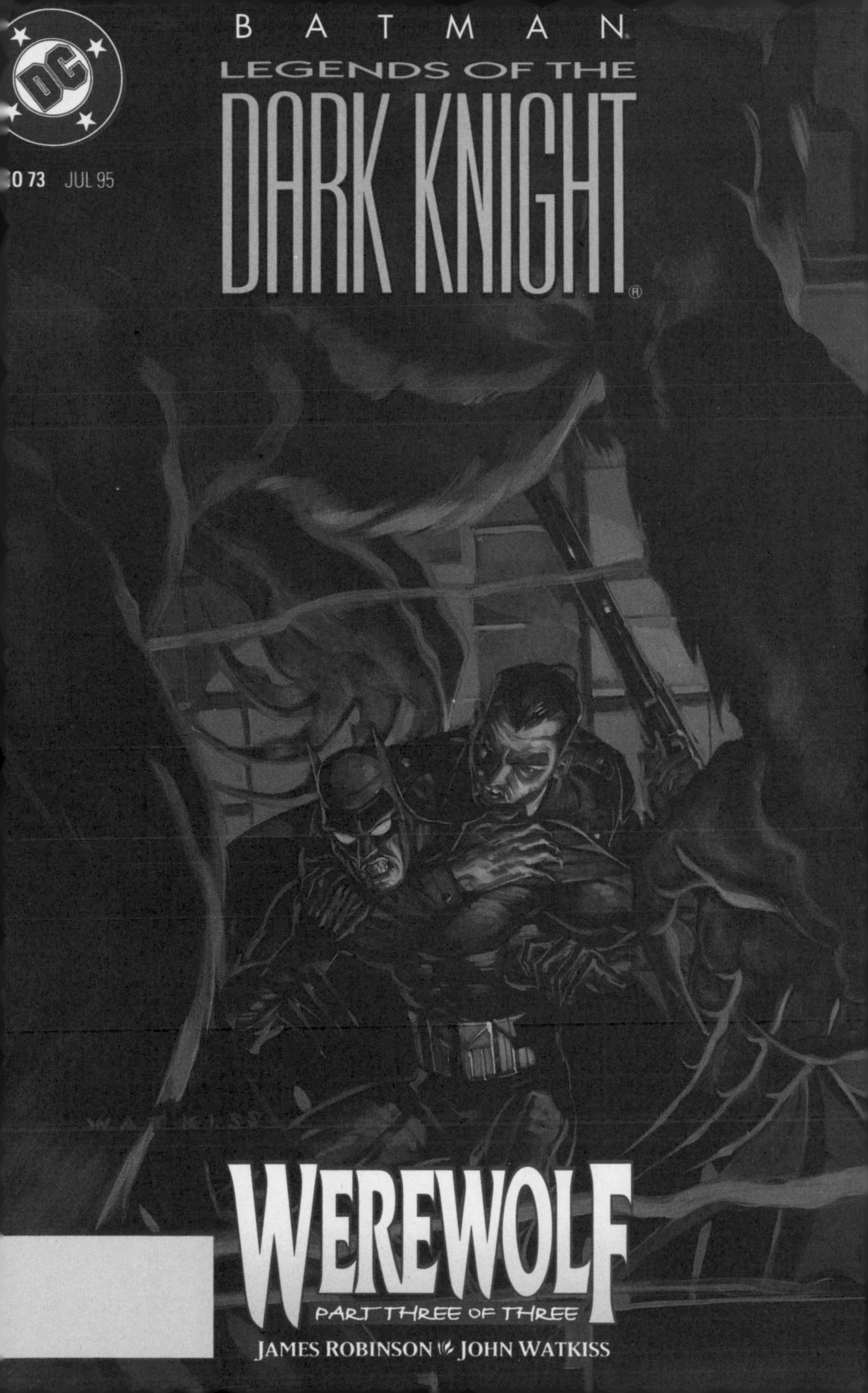
BATMAN
LEGENDS OF THE
DARK KNIGHT
73 JUL 95
WEREWOLF
PART THREE OF THREE
JAMES ROBINSON JOHN WATKISS

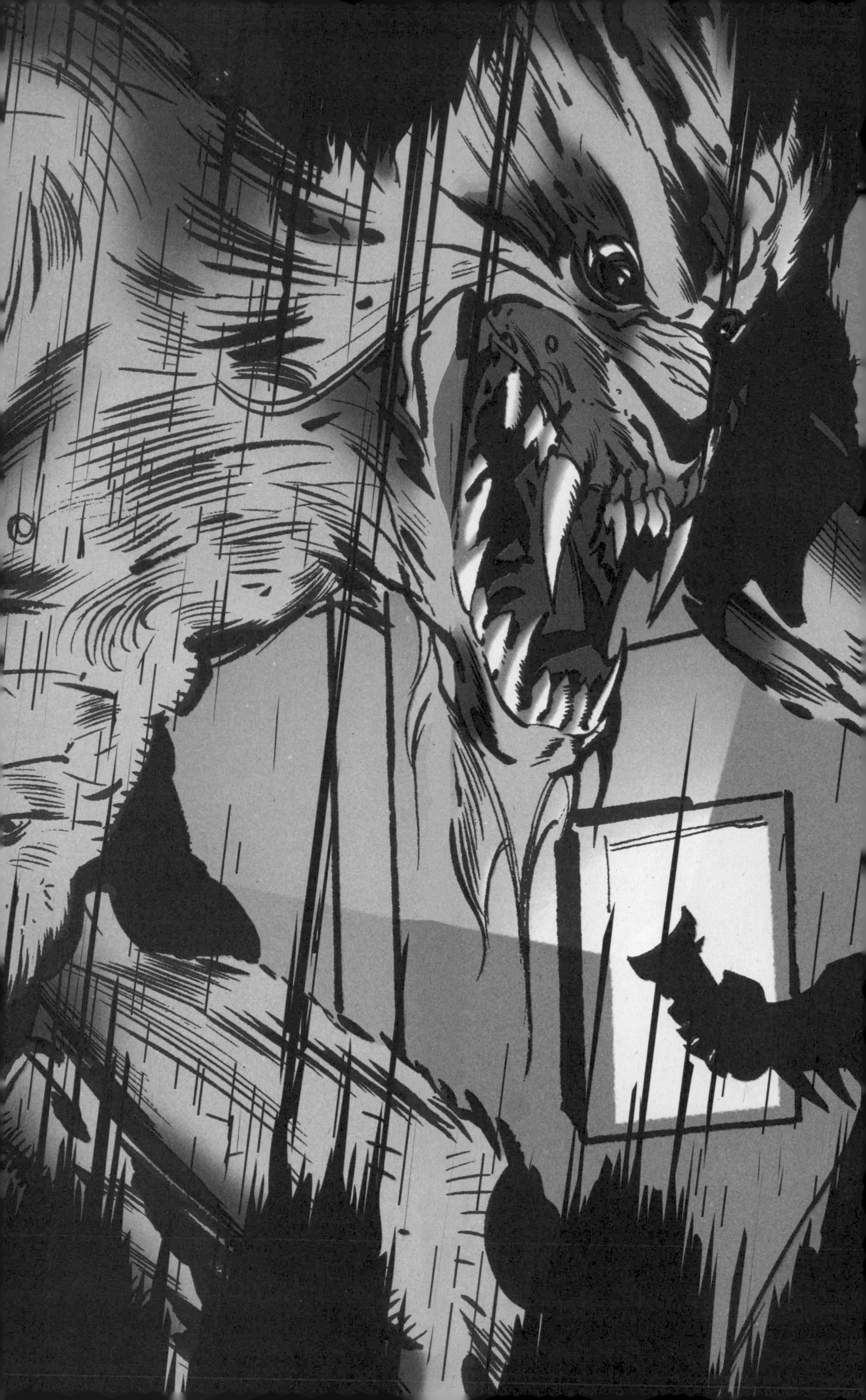

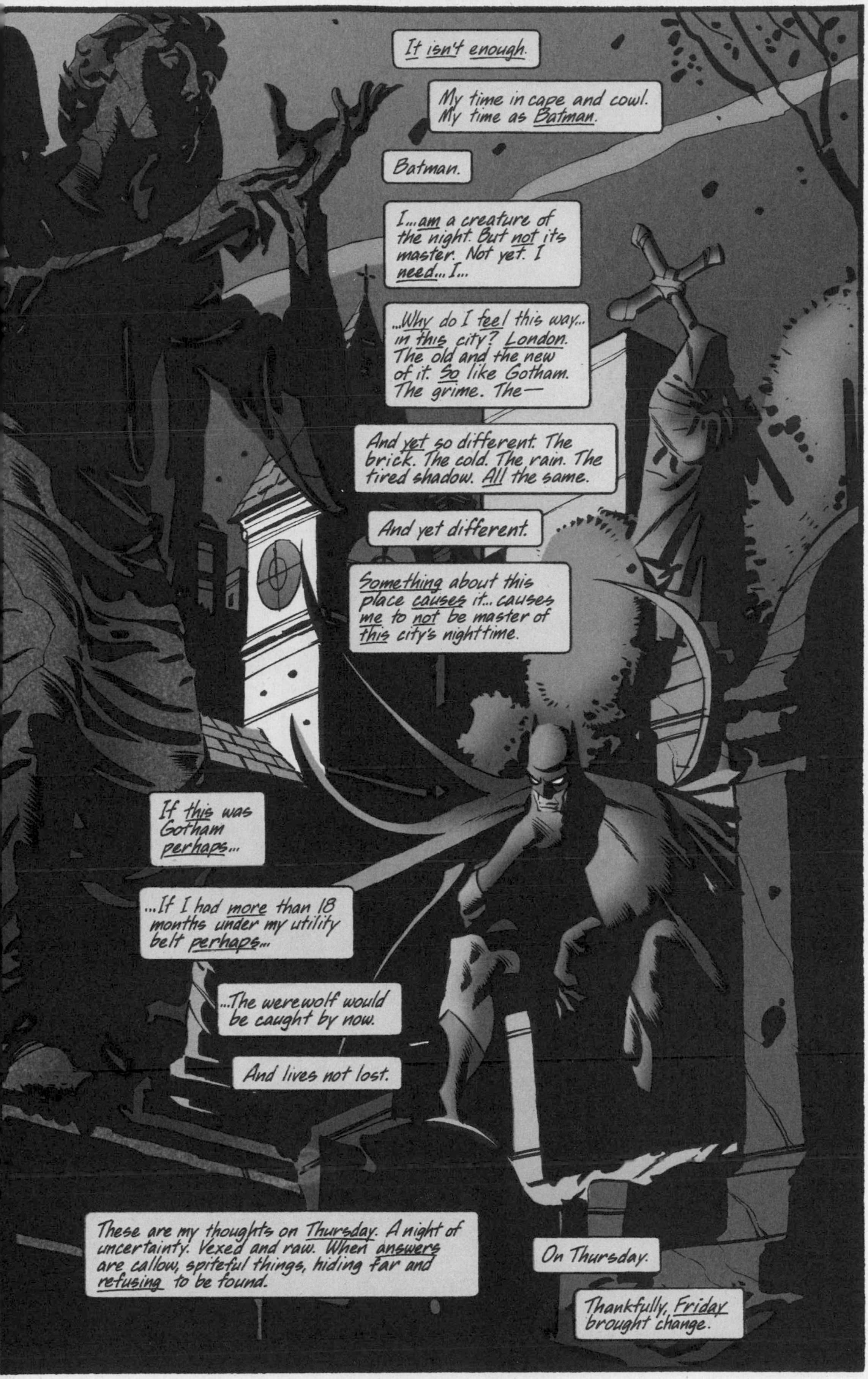
It isn't enough.
My time in cape and cowl. My time as Batman.
Batman.
I...am a creature of the night. But not its master. Not yet. I need... I...
...Why do I feel this way... in this city? London. The old and the new of it. So like Gotham. The grime. The—
And yet so different. The brick. The cold. The rain. The tired shadow. All the same.
And yet different.
Something about this place causes it... causes me to not be master of this city's nighttime.
If this was Gotham perhaps...
...If I had more than 18 months under my utility belt perhaps...
...The werewolf would be caught by now.
And lives not lost.
These are my thoughts on Thursday. A night of uncertainty. Vexed and raw. When answers are callow, spiteful things, hiding far and refusing to be found.
On Thursday.
Thankfully, Friday brought change.

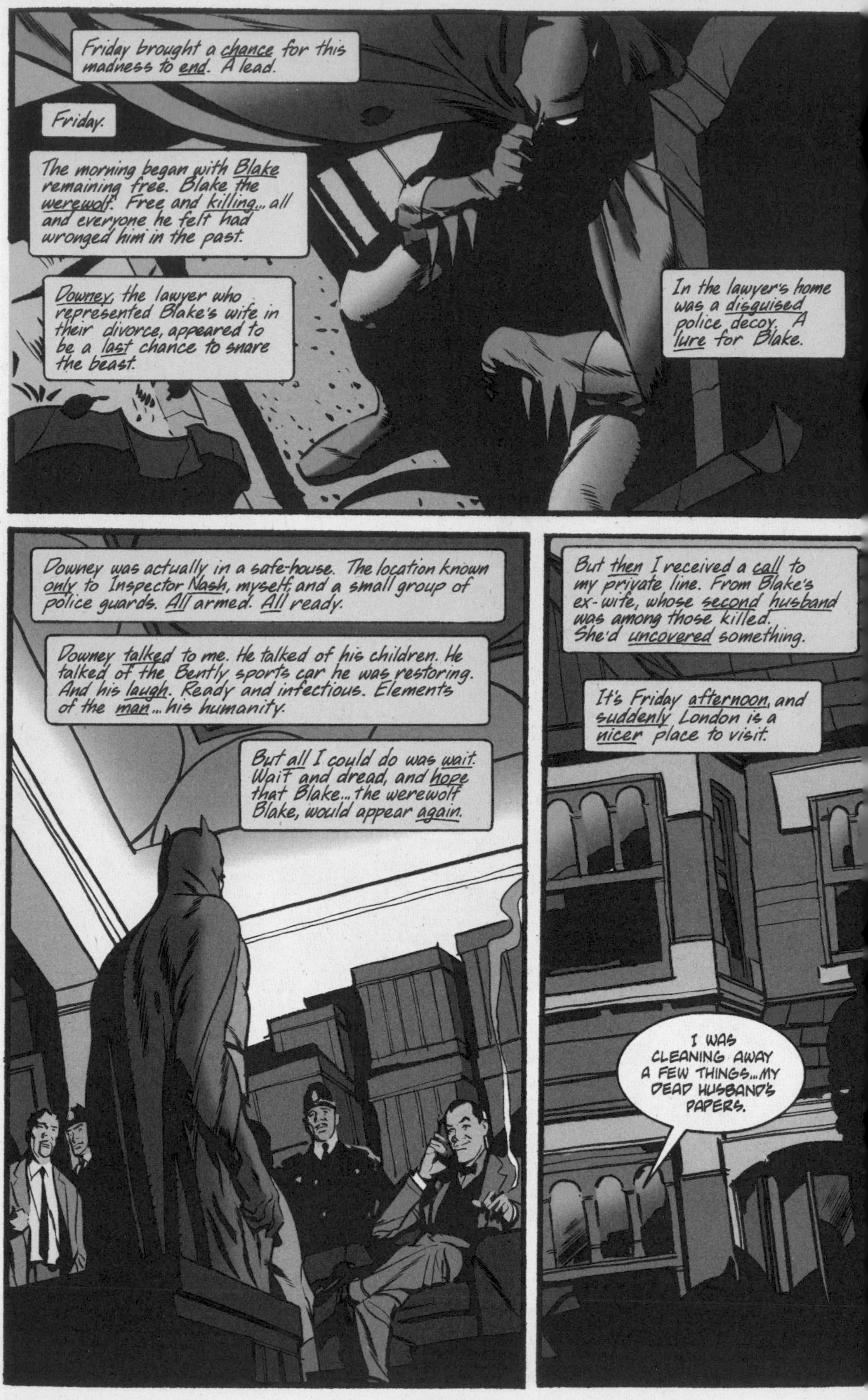
Friday brought a chance for this madness to end. A lead.
Friday.
The morning began with Blake remaining free. Blake the werewolf. Free and killing... all and everyone he felt had wronged him in the past.
Downey, the lawyer who represented Blake's wife in their divorce, appeared to be a last chance to snare the beast.
In the lawyer's home was a disguised police decoy. A lure for Blake.
Downey was actually in a safe-house. The location known only to Inspector Nash, myself, and a small group of police guards. All armed. All ready.
Downey talked to me. He talked of his children. He talked of the Bently sports car he was restoring. And his laugh. Ready and infectious. Elements of the man... his humanity.
But all I could do was wait. Wait and dread, and hope that Blake... the werewolf Blake, would appear again.
But then I received a call to my private line. From Blake's ex-wife, whose second husband was among those killed. She'd uncovered something.
It's Friday afternoon, and suddenly London is a nicer place to visit.
I WAS CLEANING AWAY A FEW THINGS... MY DEAD HUSBAND'S PAPERS.

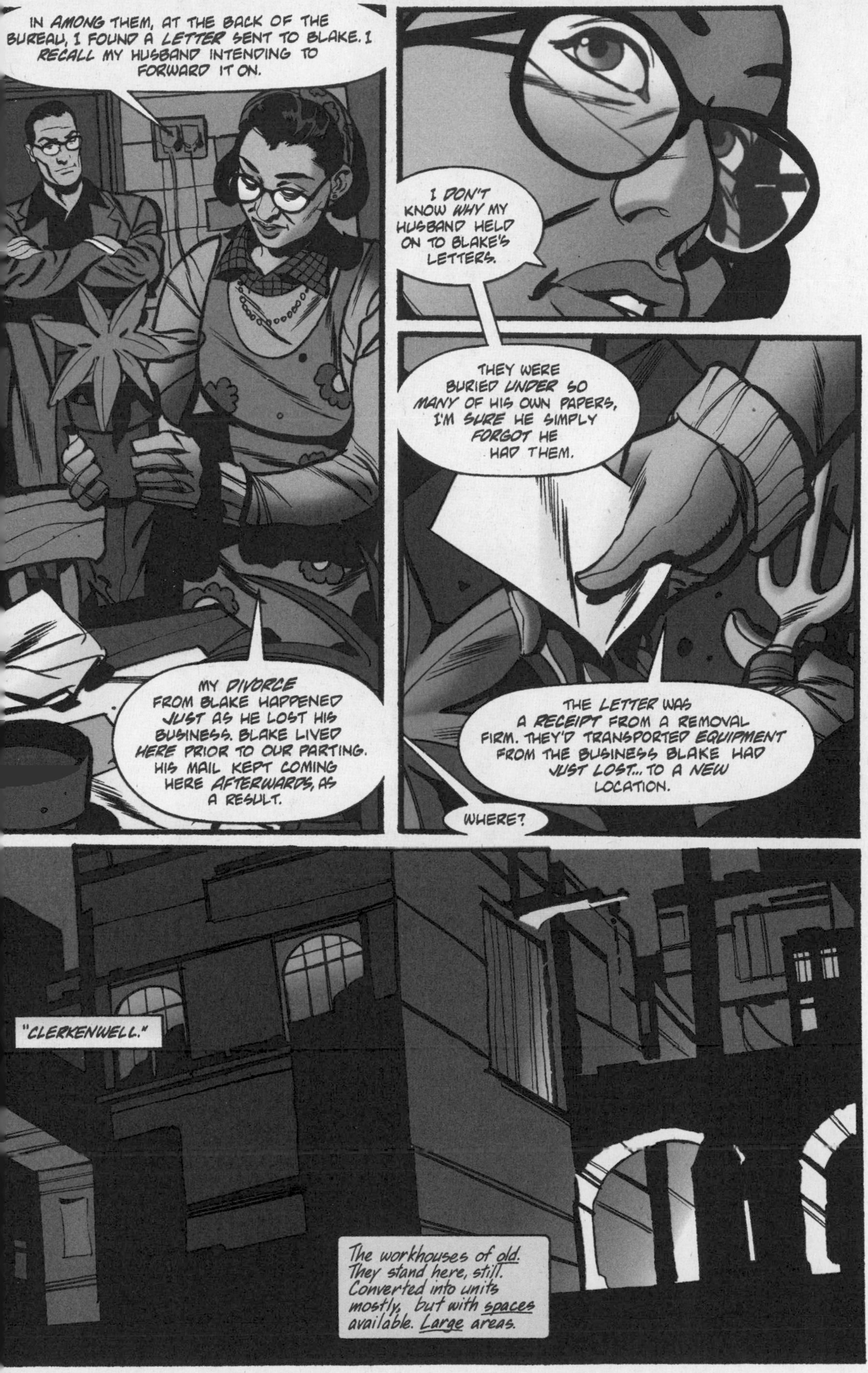
IN AMONG THEM, AT THE BACK OF THE BUREAU, I FOUND A LETTER SENT TO BLAKE. I RECALL MY HUSBAND INTENDING TO FORWARD IT ON.
MY DIVORCE FROM BLAKE HAPPENED JUST AS HE LOST HIS BUSINESS. BLAKE LIVED HERE PRIOR TO OUR PARTING. HIS MAIL KEPT COMING HERE AFTERWARDS, AS A RESULT.
I DON'T KNOW WHY MY HUSBAND HELD ON TO BLAKE'S LETTERS.
THEY WERE BURIED UNDER SO MANY OF HIS OWN PAPERS, I'M SURE HE SIMPLY FORGOT HE HAD THEM.
THE LETTER WAS A RECEIPT FROM A REMOVAL FIRM. THEY'D TRANSPORTED EQUIPMENT FROM THE BUSINESS BLAKE HAD JUST LOST... TO A NEW LOCATION.
WHERE?
"CLERKENWELL."
The workhouses of old. They stand here, still. Converted into units mostly, but with spaces available. Large areas.

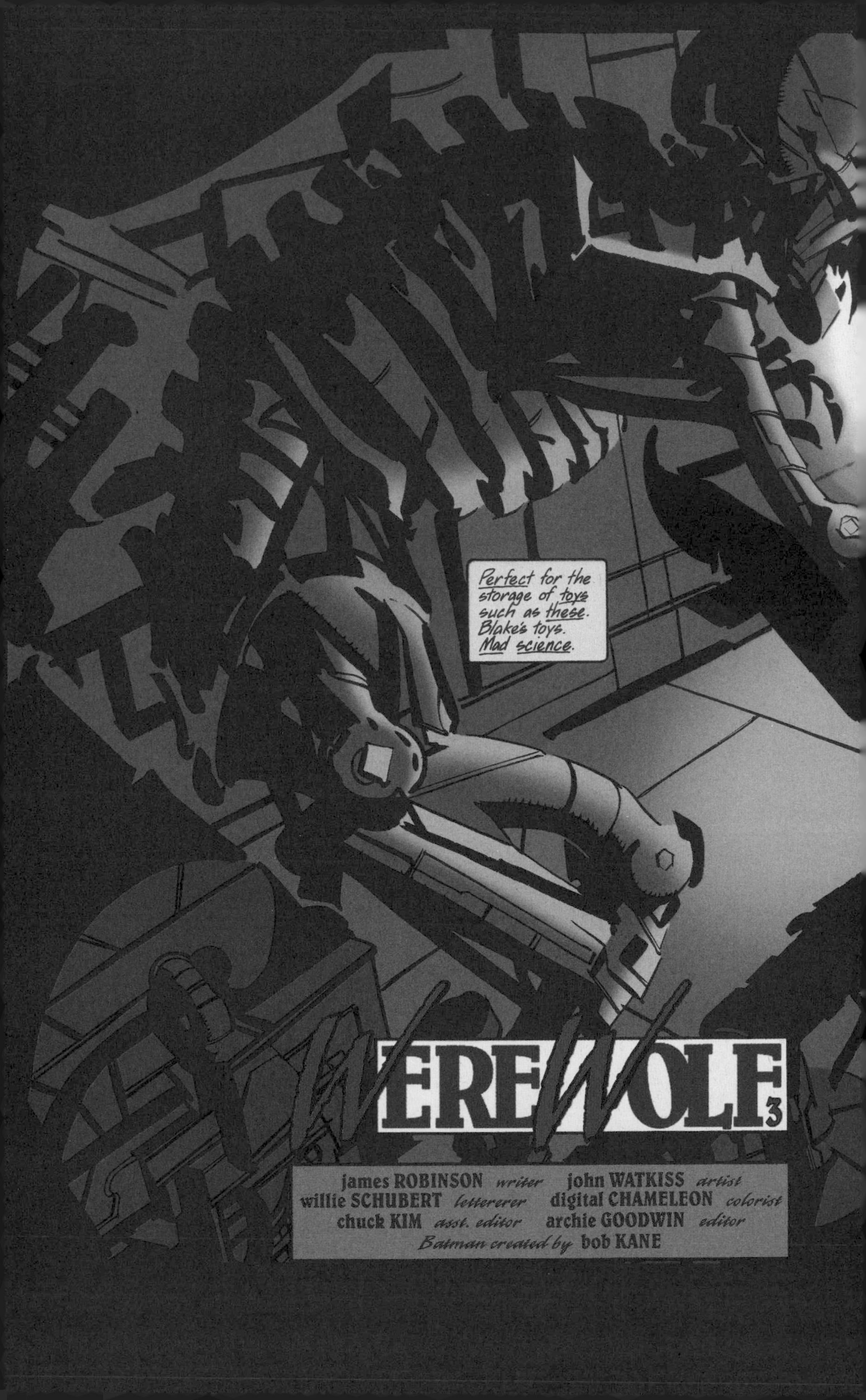
Perfect for the storage of toys such as these. Blake's toys. Mad science.
WEREWOLF 3
james ROBINSON writer john WATKISS artist
willie SCHUBERT lettererer digital CHAMELEON colorist
chuck KIM asst. editor archie GOODWIN editor
Batman created by bob KANE

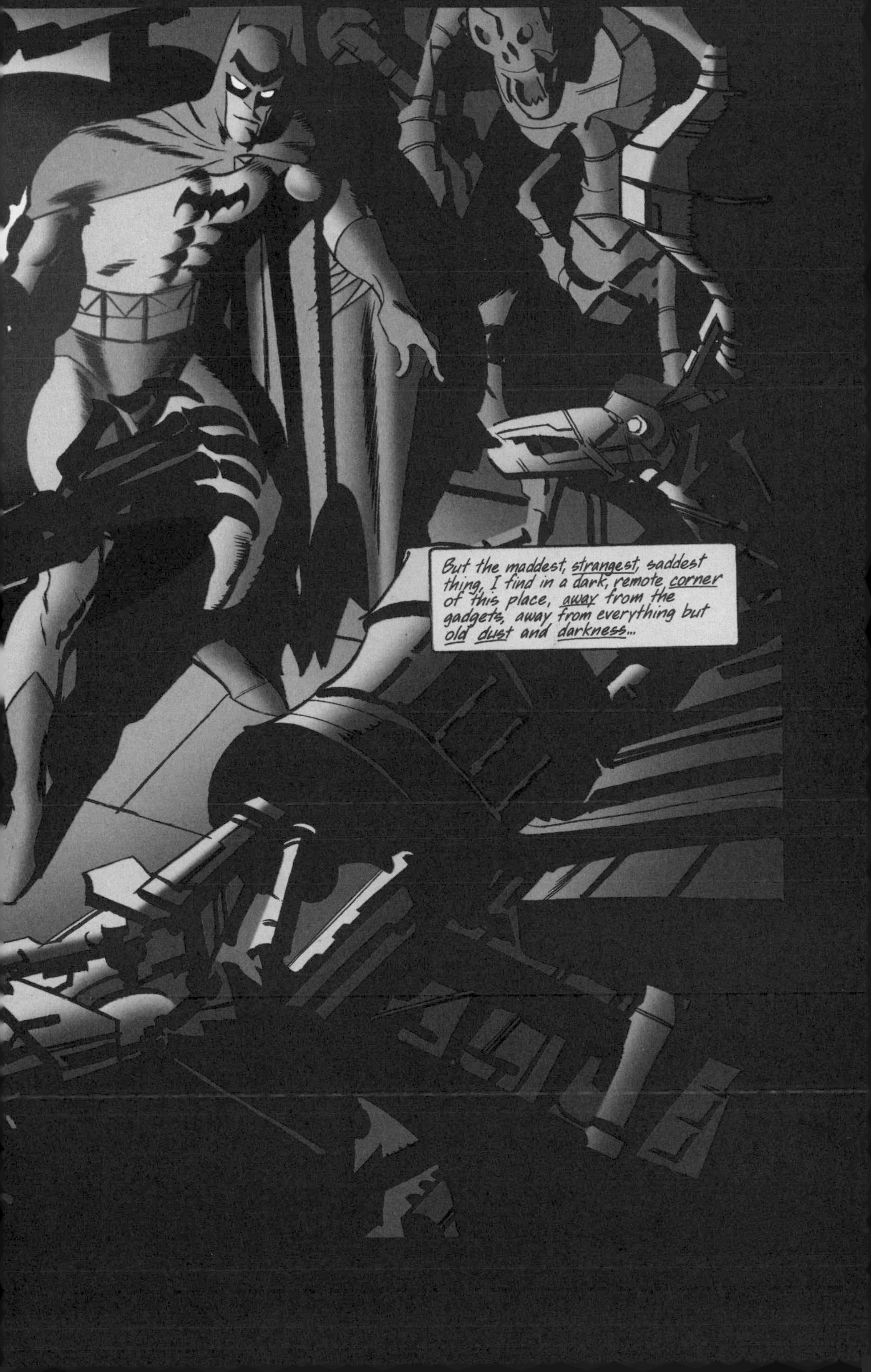
But the maddest, strangest, saddest thing, I find in a dark, remote corner of this place, away from the gadgets, away from everything but old dust and darkness...

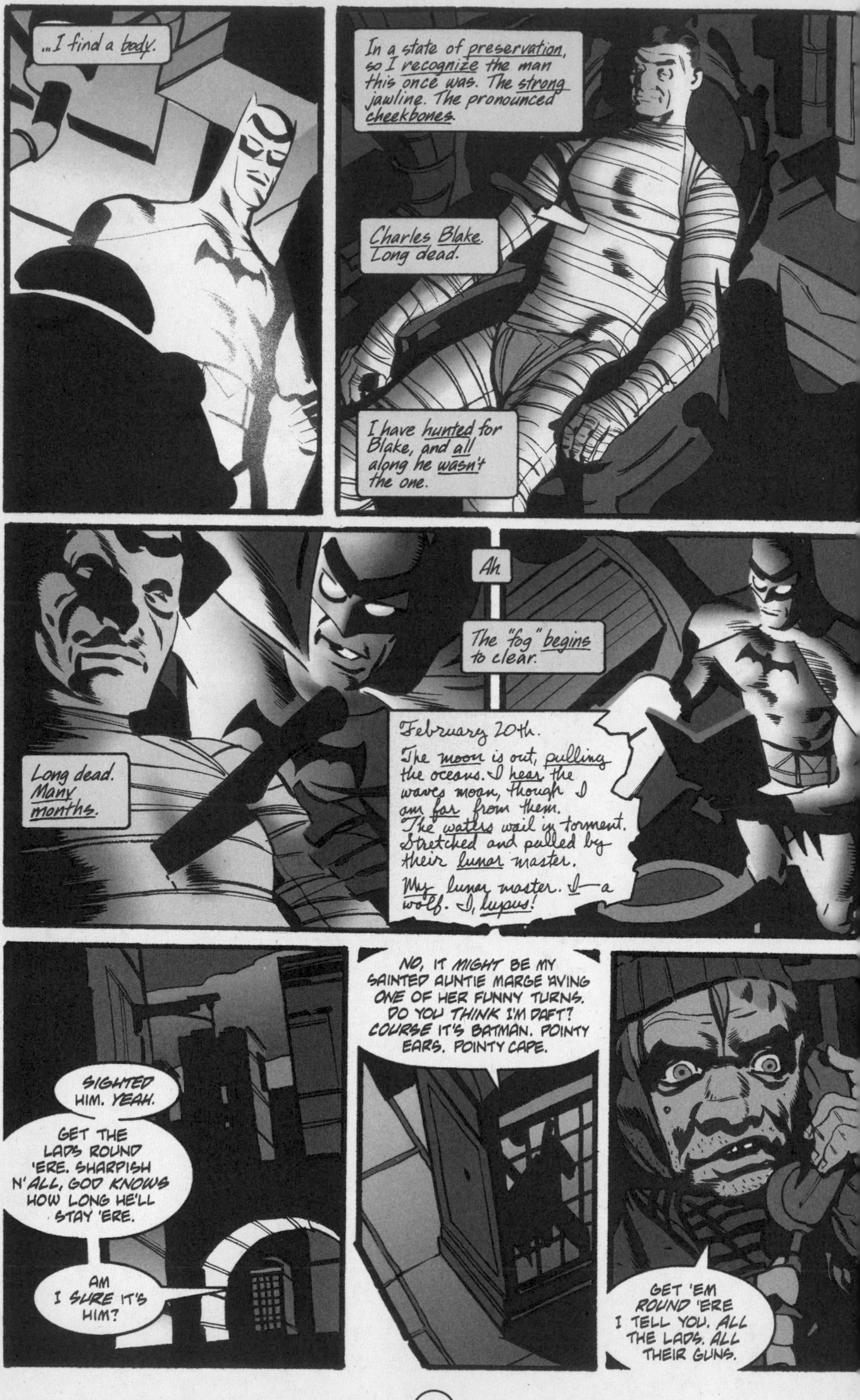
...I find a body.
In a state of preservation, so I recognize the man this once was. The strong jawline. The pronounced cheekbones.
Charles Blake. Long dead.
I have hunted for Blake, and all along he wasn't the one.
Long dead. Many months.
Ah.
The "fog" begins to clear.
February 20th.
The moon is out, pulling the oceans. I hear the waves moan, though I am far from them. The waters wail in torment. Stretched and pulled by their lunar master.
My lunar master. I—a wolf. I, lupus!
SIGHTED HIM. YEAH.
GET THE LADS ROUND 'ERE. SHARPISH N' ALL, GOD KNOWS HOW LONG HE'LL STAY 'ERE.
AM I SURE IT'S HIM?
NO, IT MIGHT BE MY SAINTED AUNTIE MARGE 'AVING ONE OF HER FUNNY TURNS. DO YOU THINK I'M DAFT? COURSE IT'S BATMAN. POINTY EARS. POINTY CAPE.
GET 'EM ROUND 'ERE I TELL YOU. ALL THE LADS. ALL THEIR GUNS.

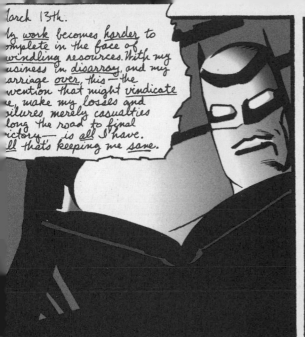

March 13th.

My work becomes harder to complete in the face of dwindling resources. With my business in disarray, and my marriage over, this — the invention that might vindicate me, make my losses and failures merely casualties along the road to final victory — is all I have. All that's keeping me sane.

March 21st.

I — am — I know I am a — werewolf. I feel the moon calling. I will transform if I do not con—centrate. I must remain a man — a thinker. I must finish what I've started — my creation.

In the face of divorce. In the face of ruin. I will persevere. And I will bring those who've wronged me to their knees.

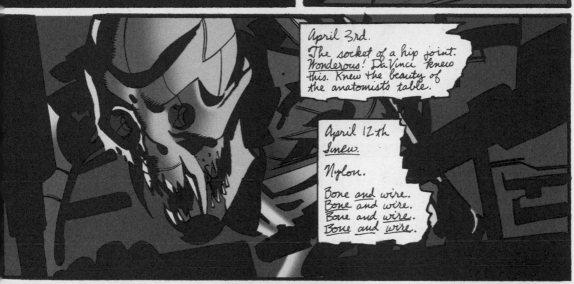

April 3rd.
The socket of a hip joint. Wonderous! DaVinci knew this. Knew the beauty of the anatomist's table.

April 12th.
Sinew.

Nylon.

Bone and wire.
Bone and wire.
Bone and wire.
Bone and wire.

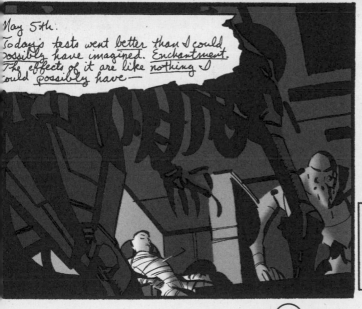

May 5th.
Today's tests went better than I could possibly have imagined. Enchantment. The effects of it are like nothing I could possibly have —

Outside of how it will aid my creation, the possibilities of application for this are —
This patent alone will make me a millionaire. Perhaps then my wife will —

These are the words of someone under _great_ strain, _but_... there's a _lack_ of malice here. The _man_ who wrote this _isn't_ even _close_ to _killing_ anyone.

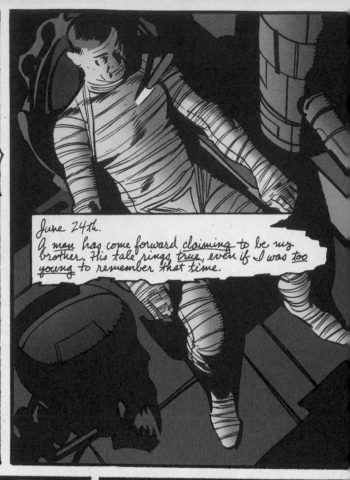

June 23rd.
My loneliness _may_ be over. Alone. _Too much._ It's—without my wife—the feelings of _despair_ have been—

In my childhood—the orphanage. Perhaps _there_ lies the root of my sorrow. A constant subconscious _fear_ of—

But _now_...that isolation may be at an _end_.

June 24th.
A man has come forward _claiming_ to be my brother. His tale rings _true_, even if I was _too young_ to remember that time.

We were both young in fact. He was _adopted_. I was _not_. Neither of us remembered the _other_ as we grew up and into our _separate_ lives. My brother uncovered our pasts recently. He contacted me. Blood tests _prove_ we _are_ brothers...and the thought that my _loneliness_ might be at an _end_ is—

September 3rd.
Two months. Things have _happened_, good _and_ bad.

My device is complete. Working. _Wonderful._ I am proud. Like a _father_ I'm proud. Now _all_ I have to do is contact the _organization_ in _France._ I'm confident they'll buy it. Confident I'll be _wealthy._

The _bad_...my concern is that—well—it _began_ when my brother, inspired by the success in finding _me_, began to investigate our parents—who they were. He used his _job._ He found records.

What he found _wasn't_ good. Our father was a _maniac._ He killed our mother. He _then_ took his _own_ life.

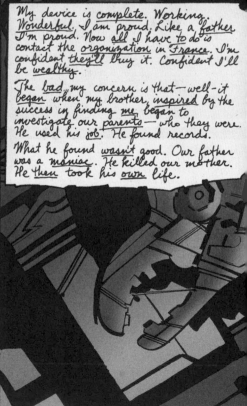

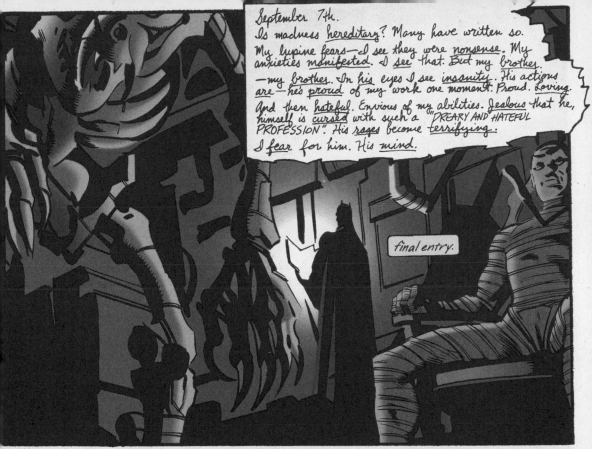

September 7th.
Is madness _hereditary_? Many have written so. My lupine fears—I see they were _nonsense_. My anxieties _manifested_. I _see_ that. But my _brother._ —my _brother._ In his eyes I see _insanity._ His actions _are_—he's proud of my work one moment. Proud. _Loving._ And then _hateful._ Envious of my abilities. Jealous that he, himself is _cursed_ with such a "_DREARY AND HATEFUL PROFESSION_". His _rages_ become _terrifying._ I _fear_ for him. His _mind._

final entry.

plus loose notes.

Some _calculus_ from the _look_ of things. And a _phot..._

...Oh.

WH—

KPOW

KPOW

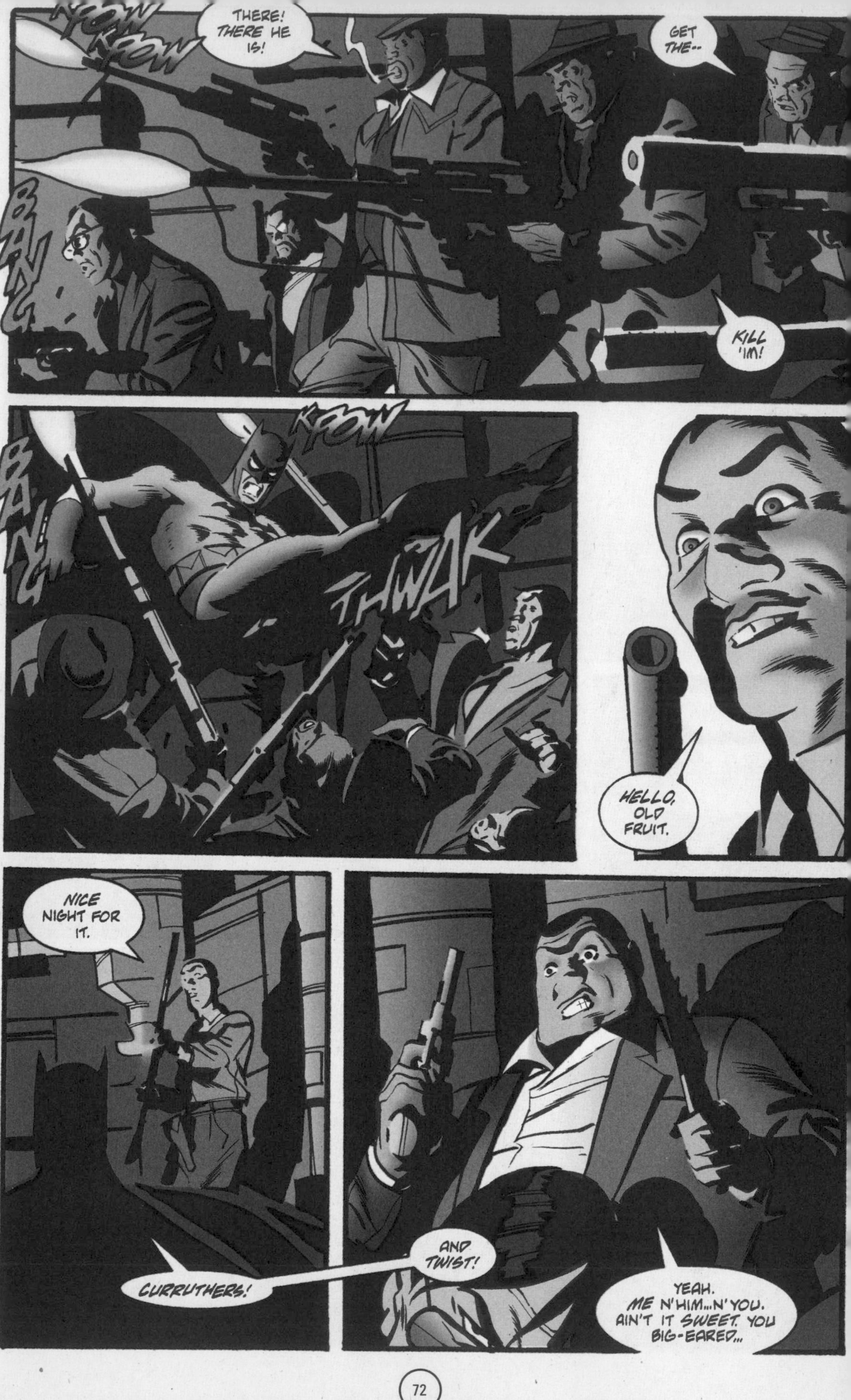
KPOW
THERE! THERE HE IS!
GET THE..
BANG
KILL 'IM!
BANG
KPOW
THWAK
HELLO, OLD FRUIT.
NICE NIGHT FOR IT.
CURRUTHERS!
AND TWIST!
YEAH. ME N'HIM...N'YOU. AIN'T IT SWEET. YOU BIG-EARED...

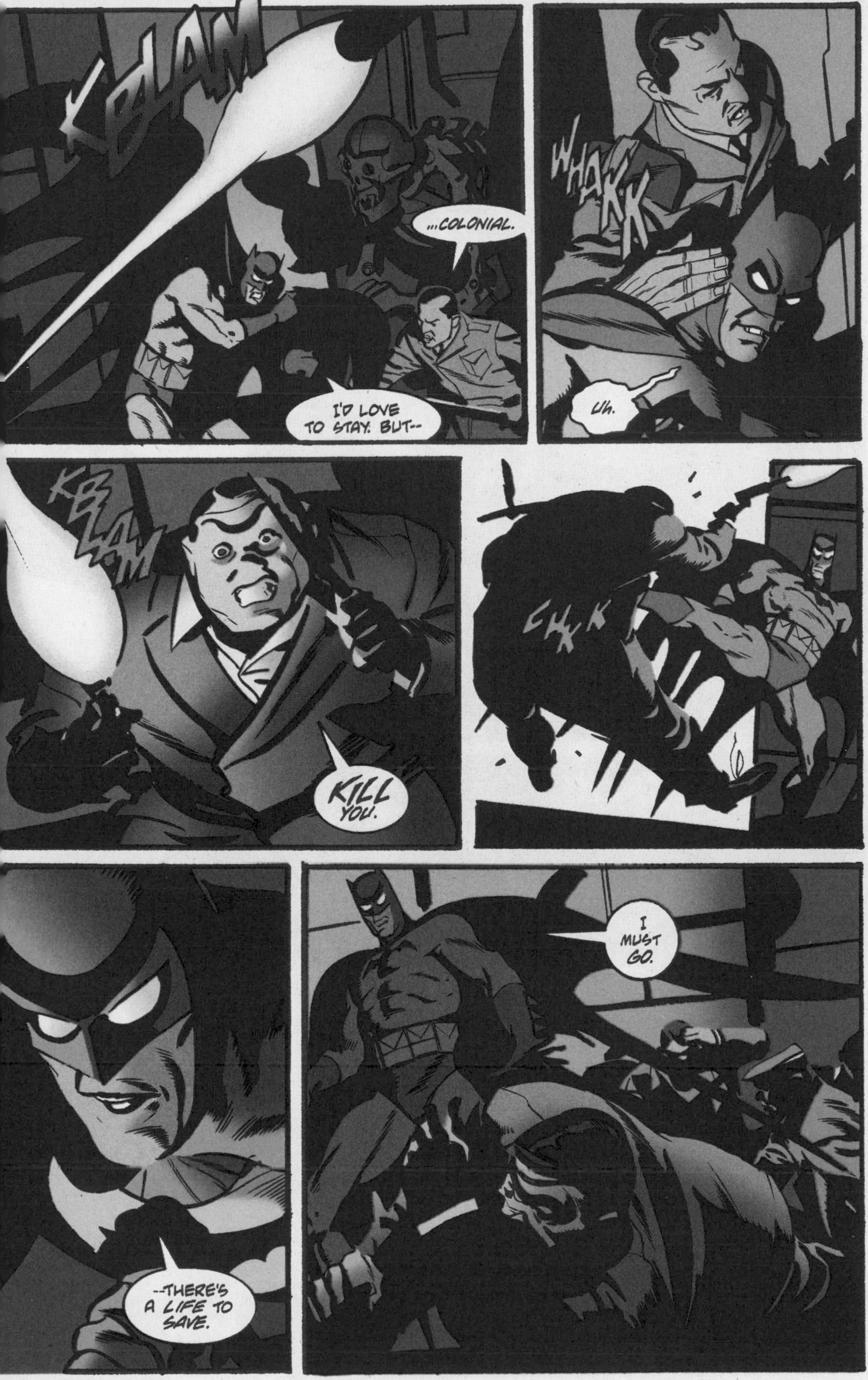
KBLAM
...COLONIAL.
I'D LOVE TO STAY. BUT--
WHAKK
Uh.
KBLAM
KILL YOU.
CHKK
--THERE'S A LIFE TO SAVE.
I MUST GO.

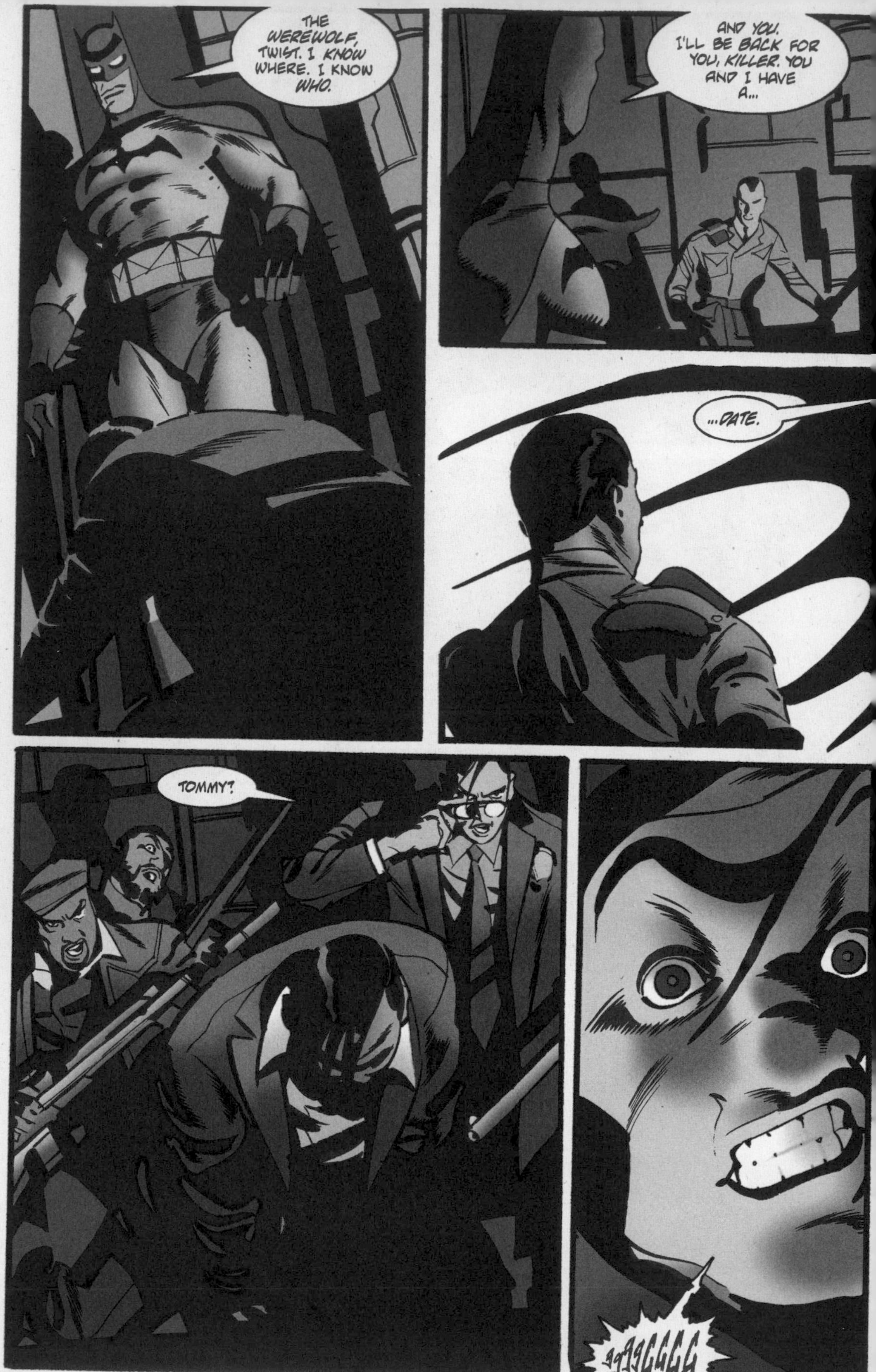
THE WEREWOLF, TWIST. I KNOW WHERE. I KNOW WHO.
AND YOU. I'LL BE BACK FOR YOU, KILLER. YOU AND I HAVE A...
...DATE.
TOMMY?
ggggGGGG

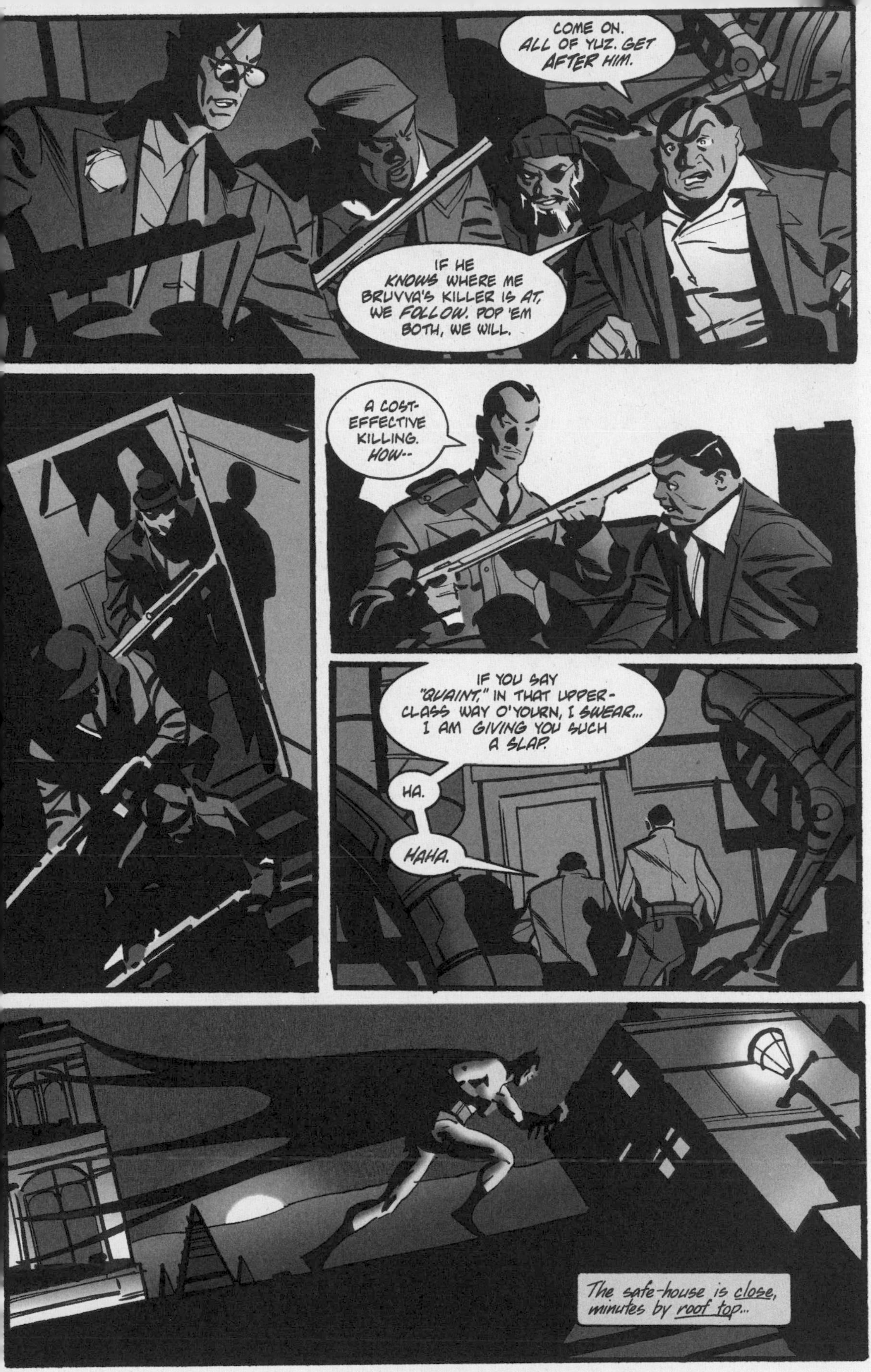
COME ON. ALL OF YUZ. GET AFTER HIM.
IF HE KNOWS WHERE ME BRUVVA'S KILLER IS AT, WE FOLLOW. POP 'EM BOTH, WE WILL.
A COST-EFFECTIVE KILLING. HOW--
IF YOU SAY "QUAINT," IN THAT UPPER-CLASS WAY O'YOURN, I SWEAR... I AM GIVING YOU SUCH A SLAP.
HA.
HAHA.
The safe-house is close, minutes by roof top...

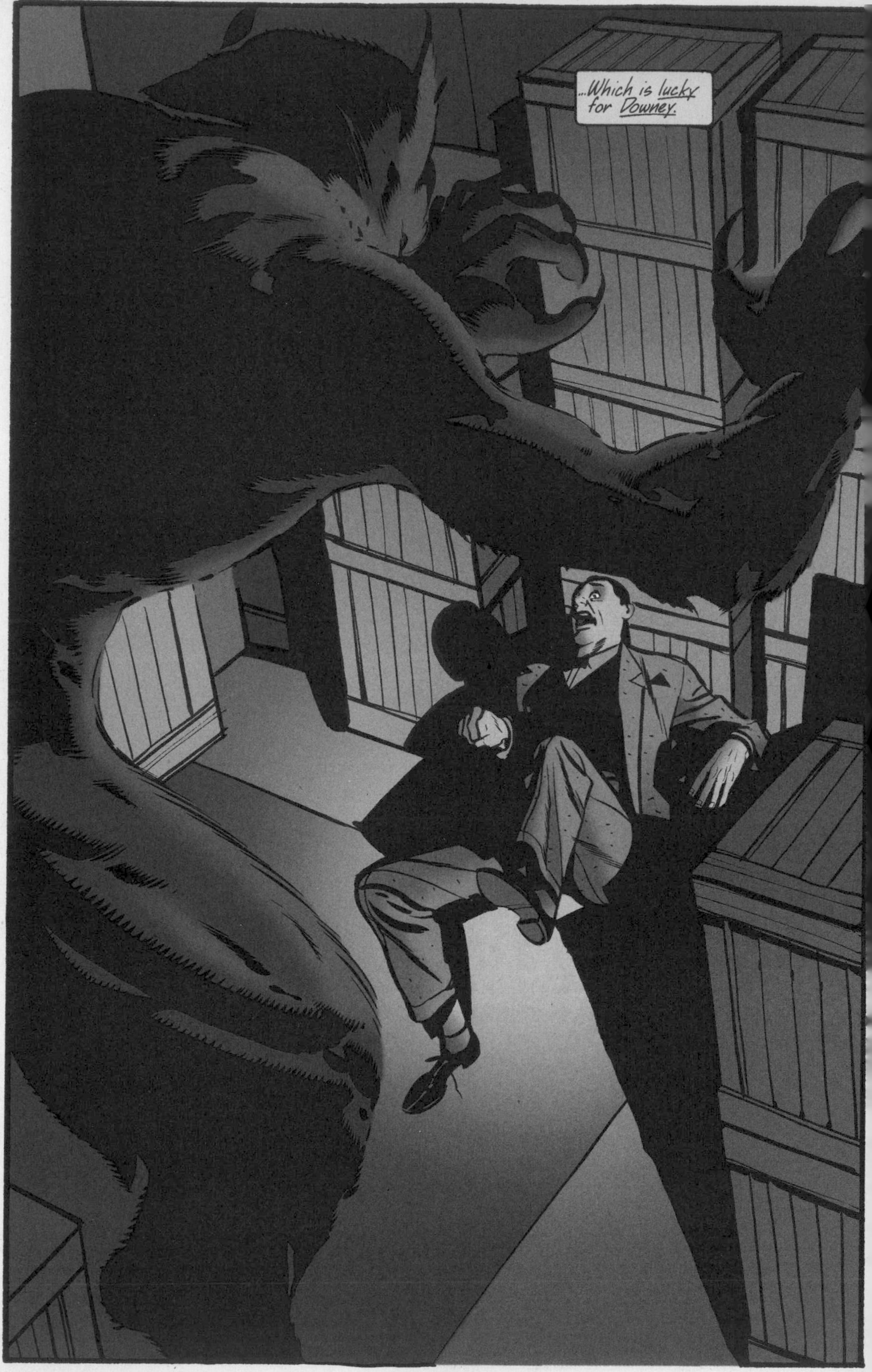
...Which is lucky for Downey.

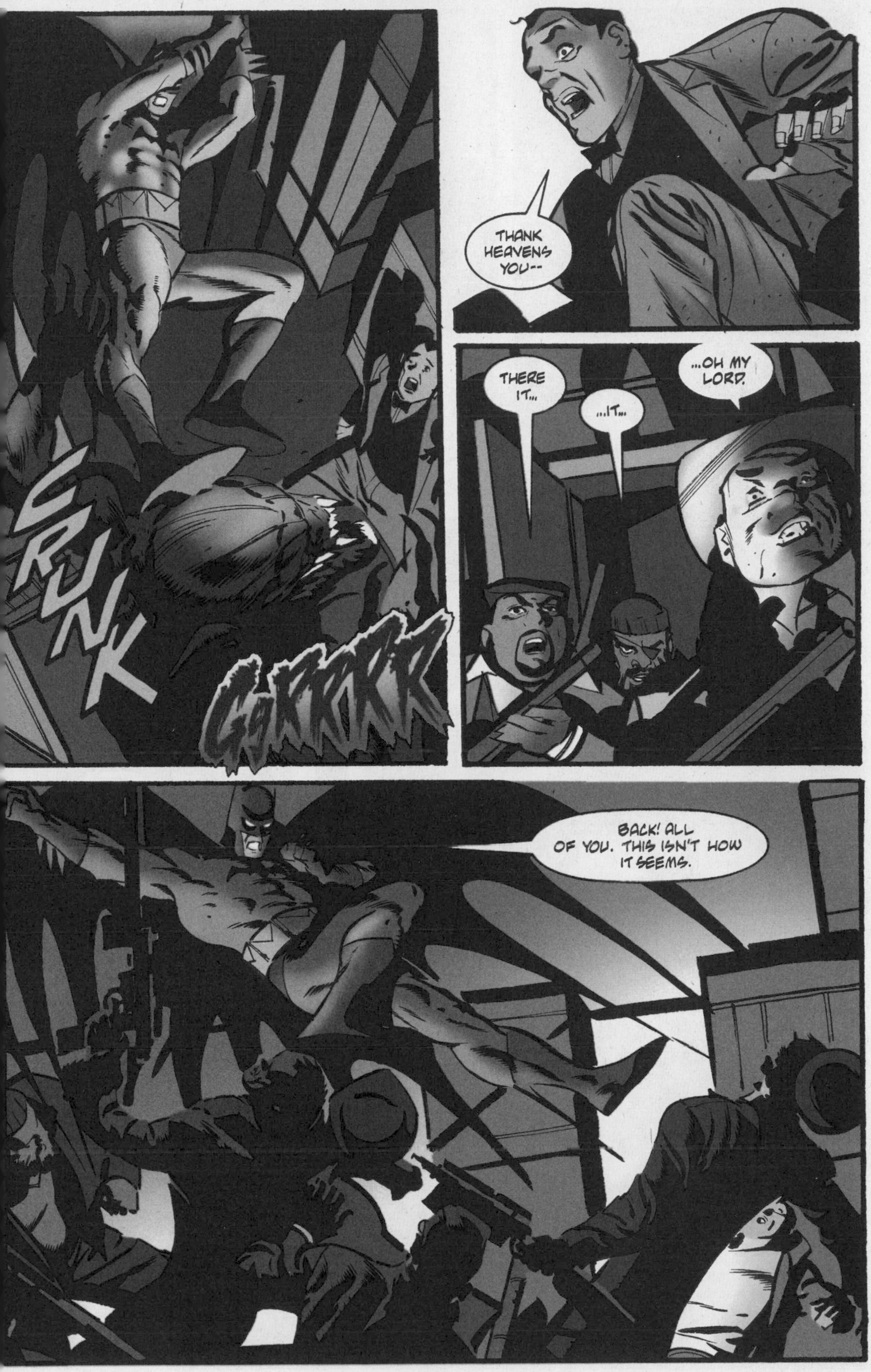
THANK HEAVENS YOU--
THERE IT...
...IT...
...OH MY LORD.
SHRUNK
GRRRRR
BACK! ALL OF YOU. THIS ISN'T HOW IT SEEMS.

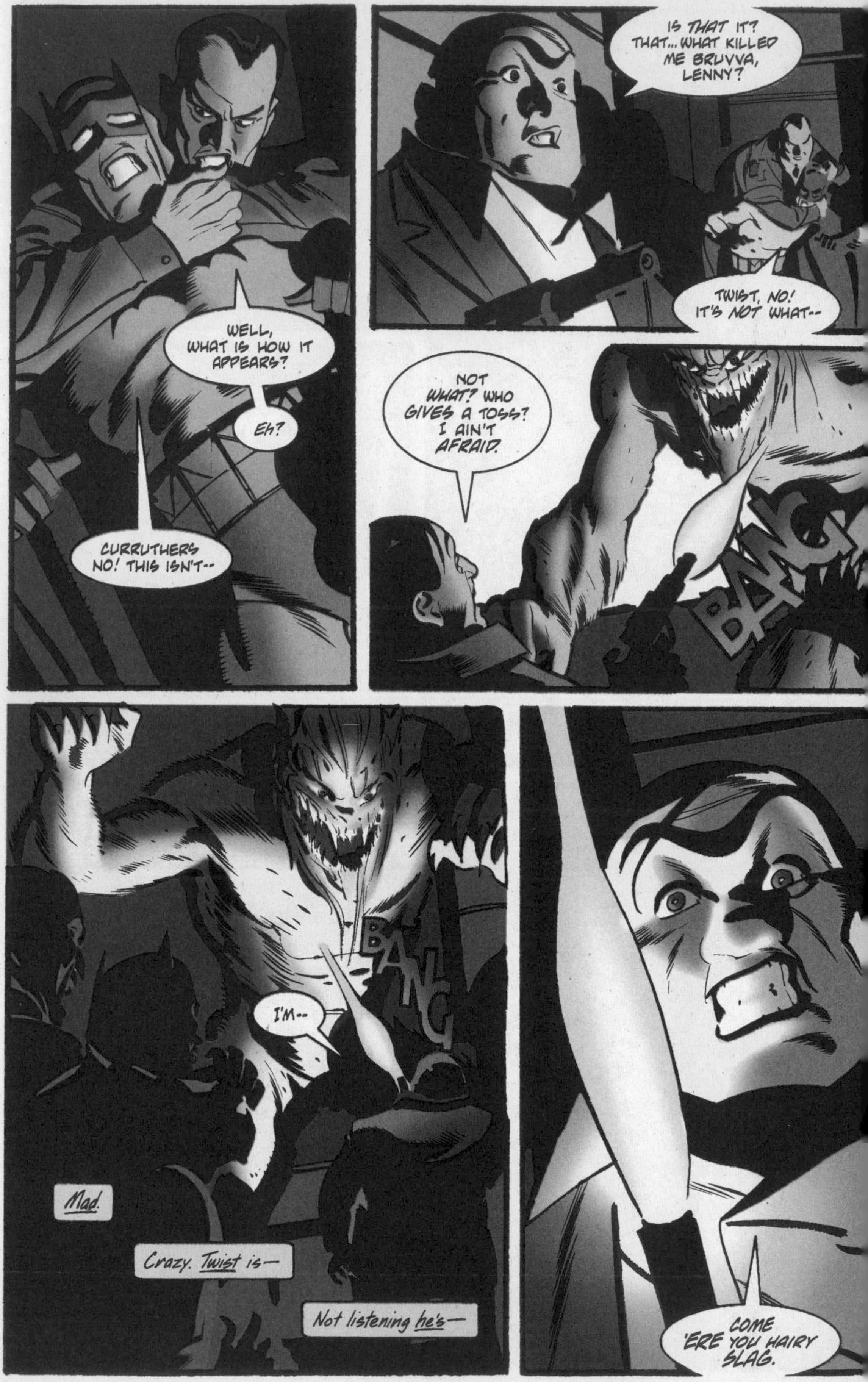
WELL, WHAT IS HOW IT APPEARS?
Eh?
CURRUTHERS NO! THIS ISN'T--
IS THAT IT? THAT... WHAT KILLED ME BRUVVA, LENNY?
TWIST, NO! IT'S NOT WHAT--
NOT WHAT? WHO GIVES A TOSS? I AIN'T AFRAID.
BANG
BANG
I'M--
Mad.
Crazy. Twist is—
Not listening he's—
COME 'ERE YOU HAIRY SLAG.

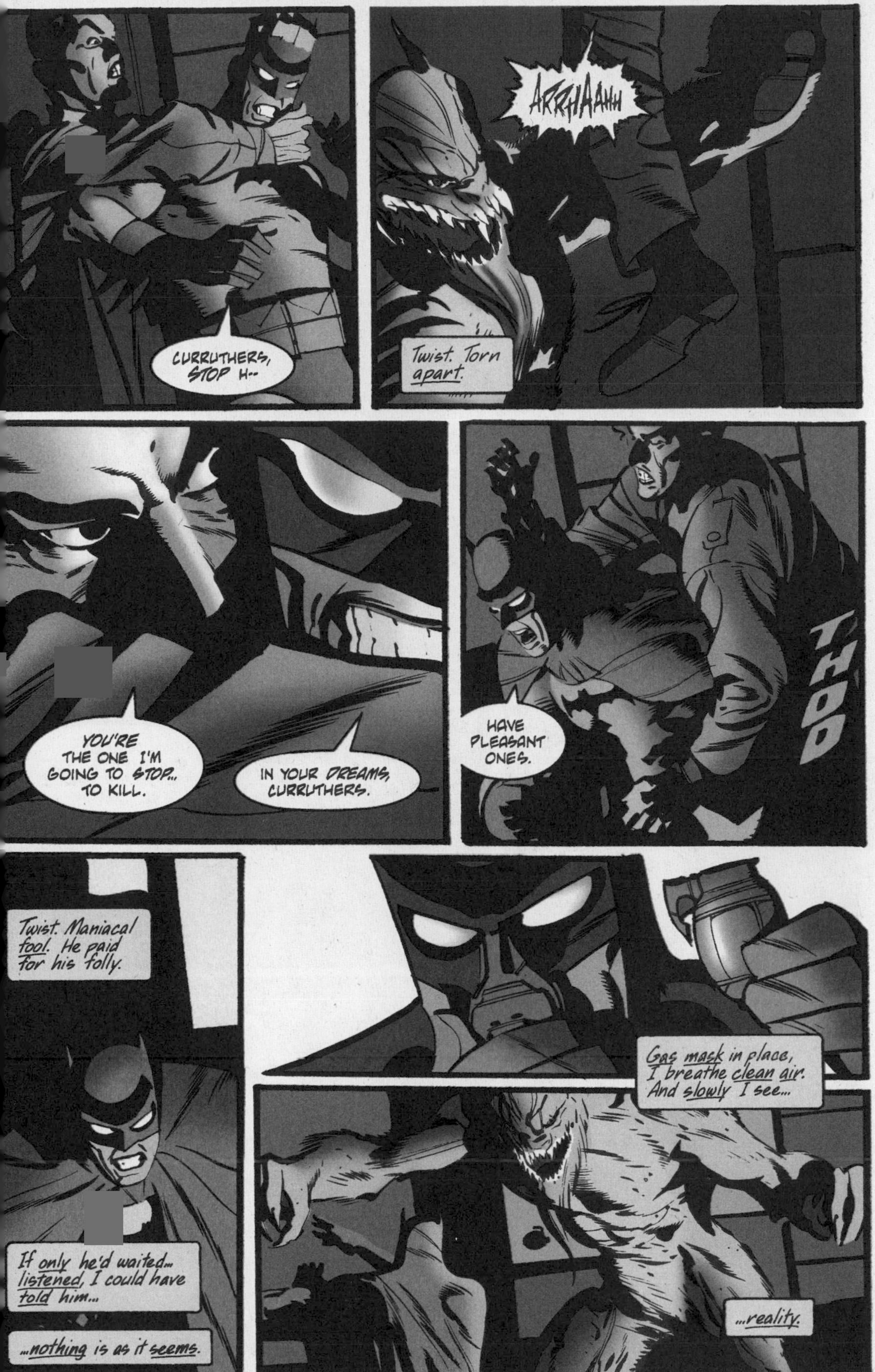
CURRUTHERS, STOP H--
ARRHAAHH
Twist. Torn apart.
YOU'RE THE ONE I'M GOING TO STOP... TO KILL.
IN YOUR DREAMS, CURRUTHERS.
HAVE PLEASANT ONES.
THOD
Twist. Maniacal fool. He paid for his folly.
If only he'd waited... listened, I could have told him...
...nothing is as it seems.
Gas mask in place, I breathe clean air. And slowly I see...
...reality.

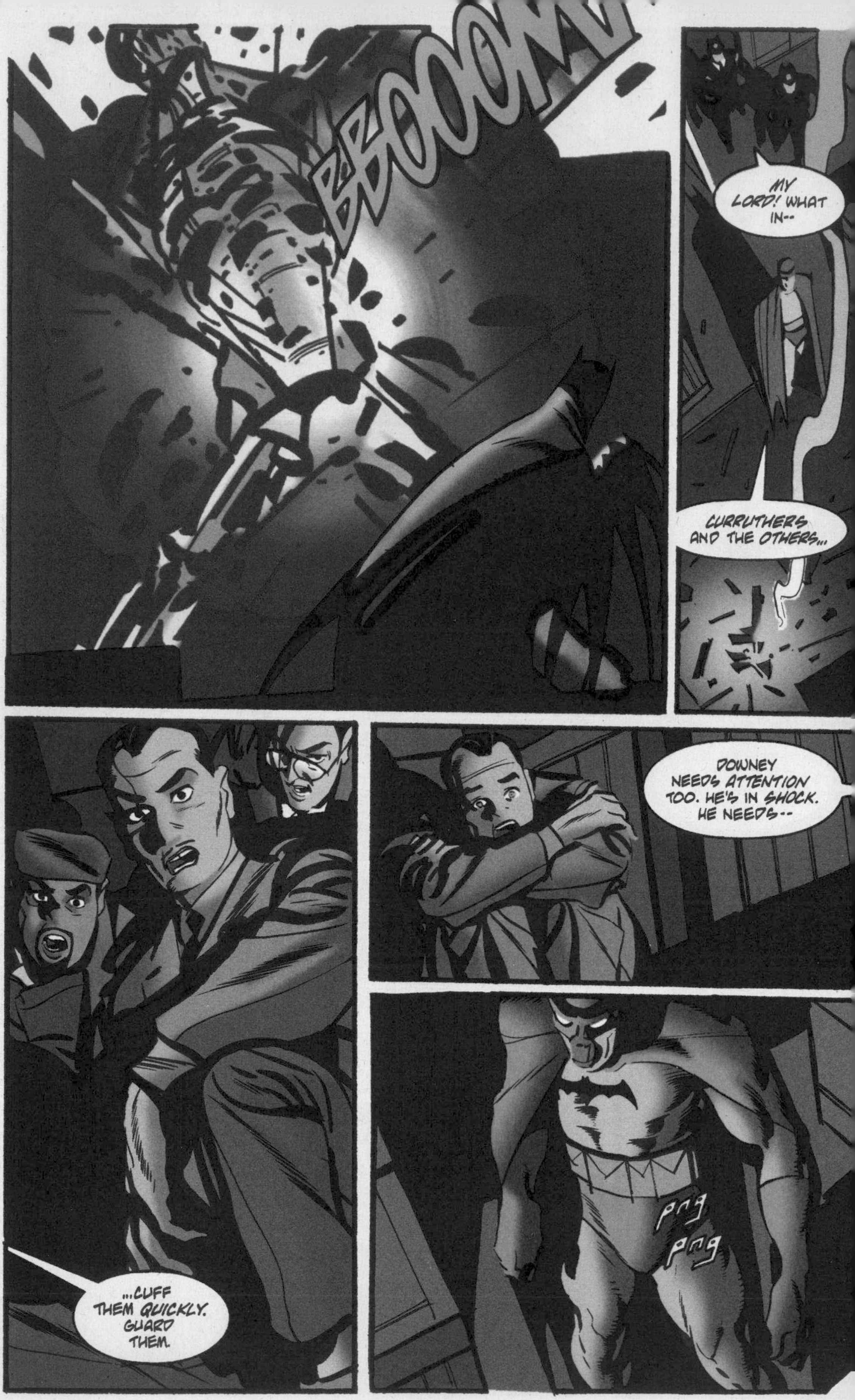
BOOOM
MY LORD! WHAT IN--
CURRUTHERS AND THE OTHERS...
...CUFF THEM QUICKLY. GUARD THEM.
DOWNEY NEEDS ATTENTION TOO. HE'S IN SHOCK. HE NEEDS--
PNG
PNG

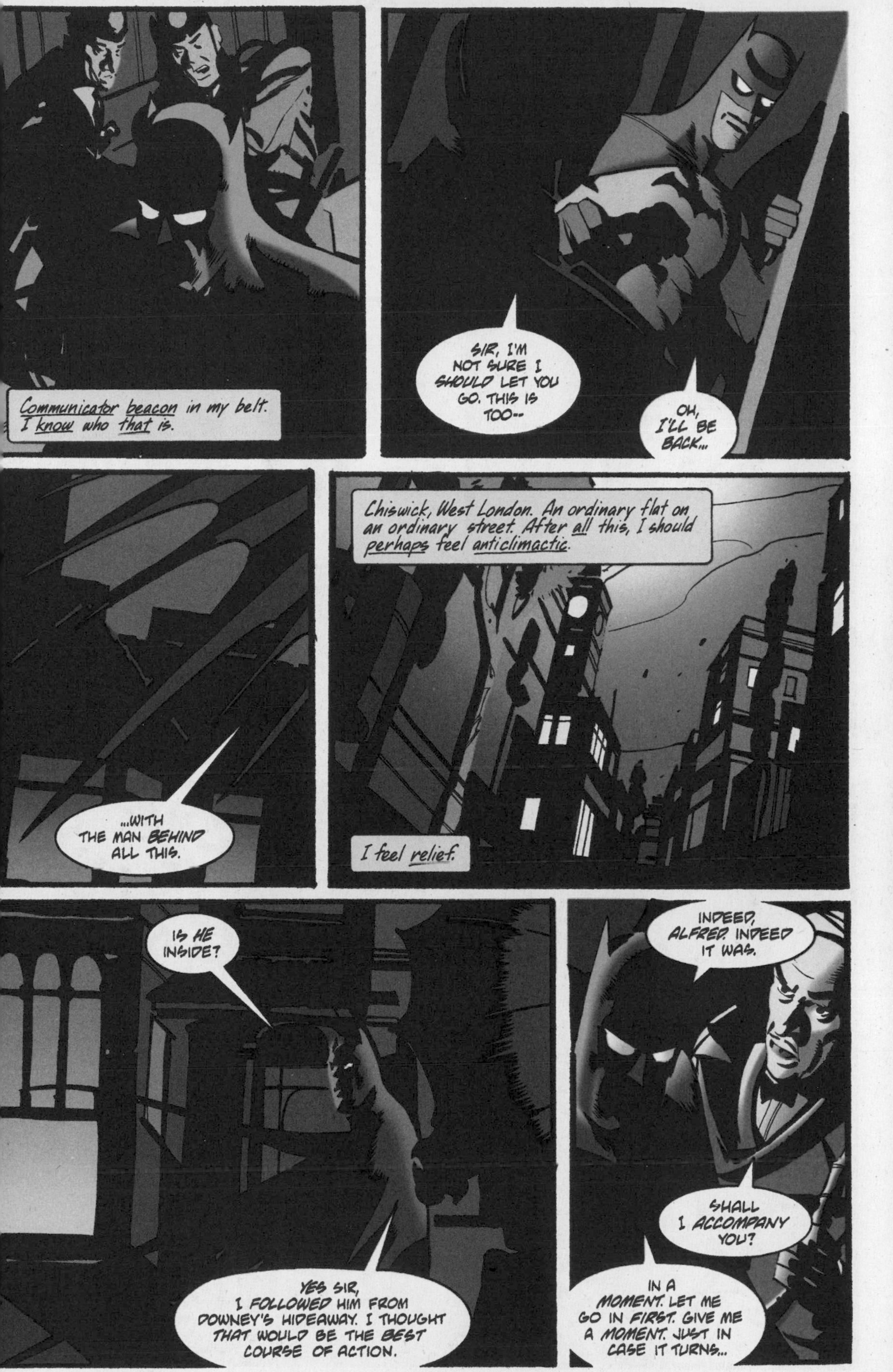
Communicator beacon in my belt. I know who that is.
SIR, I'M NOT SURE I SHOULD LET YOU GO. THIS IS TOO--
OH, I'LL BE BACK...
...WITH THE MAN BEHIND ALL THIS.
Chiswick, West London. An ordinary flat on an ordinary street. After all this, I should perhaps feel anticlimactic.
I feel relief.
IS HE INSIDE?
YES SIR, I FOLLOWED HIM FROM DOWNEY'S HIDEAWAY. I THOUGHT THAT WOULD BE THE BEST COURSE OF ACTION.
INDEED, ALFRED. INDEED IT WAS.
SHALL I ACCOMPANY YOU?
IN A MOMENT. LET ME GO IN FIRST. GIVE ME A MOMENT. JUST IN CASE IT TURNS...

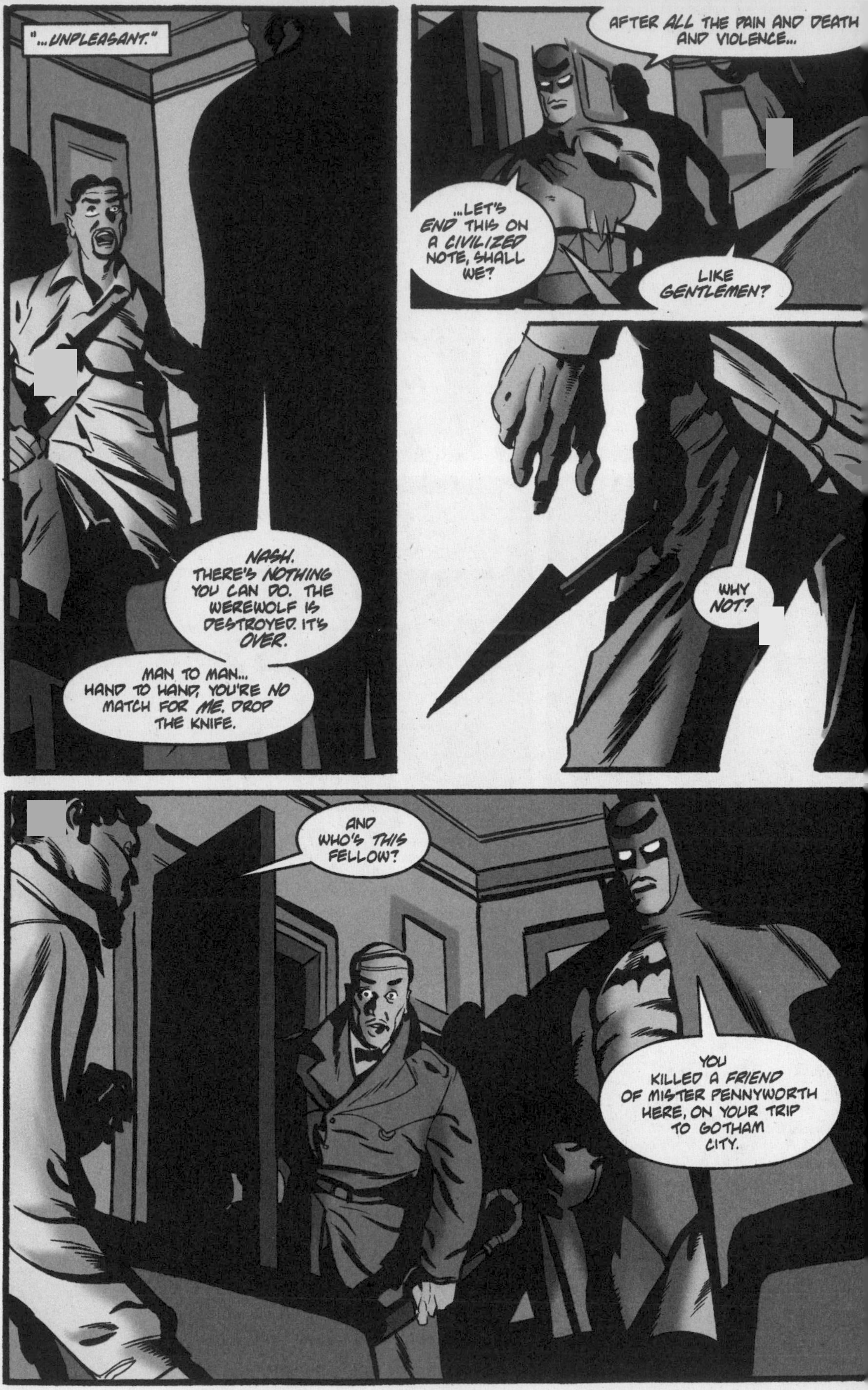
"...UNPLEASANT."
NASH. THERE'S NOTHING YOU CAN DO. THE WEREWOLF IS DESTROYED. IT'S OVER.
MAN TO MAN... HAND TO HAND, YOU'RE NO MATCH FOR ME. DROP THE KNIFE.
AFTER ALL THE PAIN AND DEATH AND VIOLENCE...
...LET'S END THIS ON A CIVILIZED NOTE, SHALL WE?
LIKE GENTLEMEN?
WHY NOT?
AND WHO'S THIS FELLOW?
YOU KILLED A FRIEND OF MISTER PENNYWORTH HERE, ON YOUR TRIP TO GOTHAM CITY.

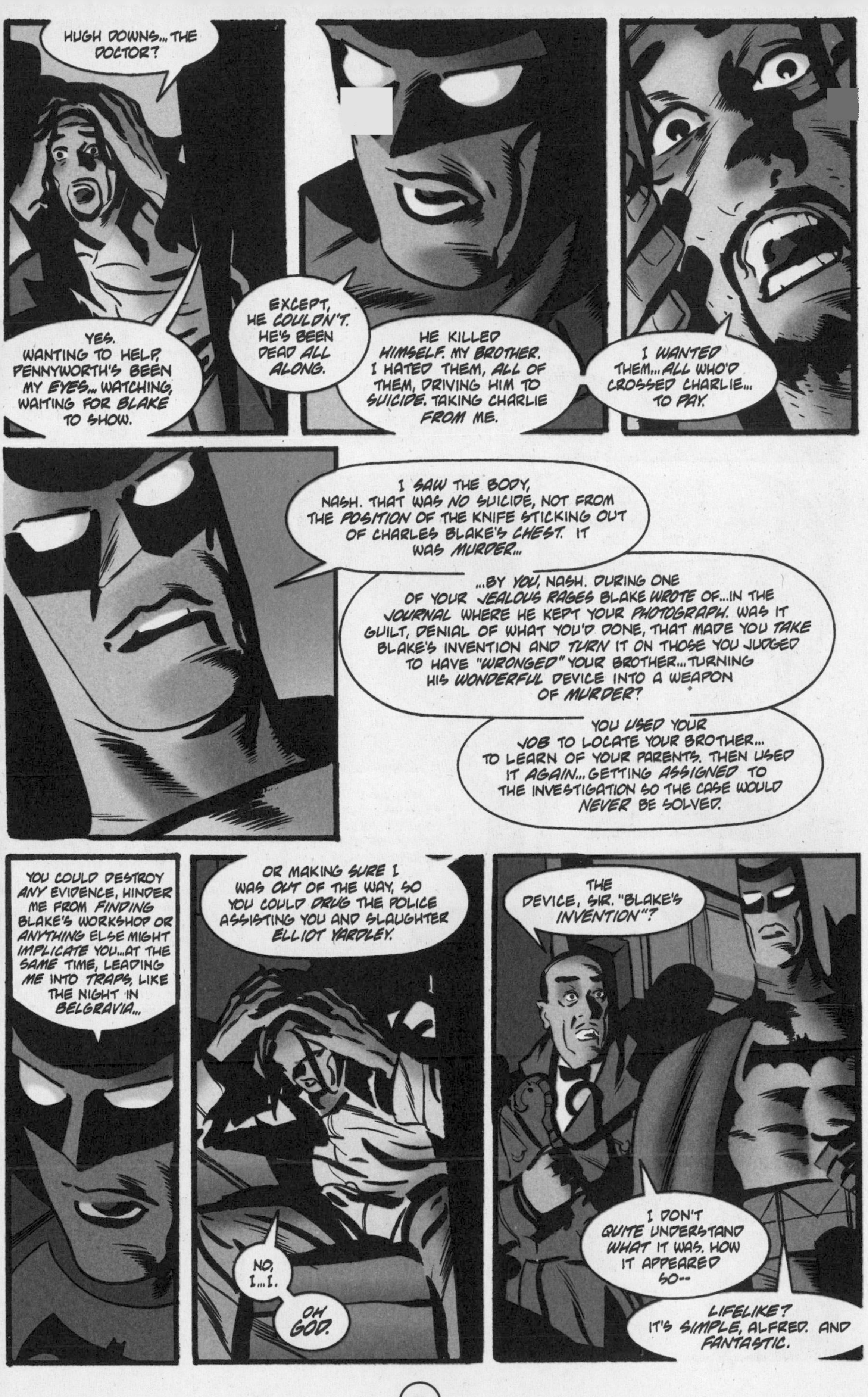
HUGH DOWNS... THE DOCTOR?
YES. WANTING TO HELP, PENNYWORTH'S BEEN MY EYES... WATCHING, WAITING FOR BLAKE TO SHOW.
EXCEPT, HE COULDN'T. HE'S BEEN DEAD ALL ALONG.
HE KILLED HIMSELF. MY BROTHER. I HATED THEM, ALL OF THEM, DRIVING HIM TO SUICIDE. TAKING CHARLIE FROM ME.
I WANTED THEM... ALL WHO'D CROSSED CHARLIE... TO PAY.
I SAW THE BODY, NASH. THAT WAS NO SUICIDE, NOT FROM THE POSITION OF THE KNIFE STICKING OUT OF CHARLES BLAKE'S CHEST. IT WAS MURDER...
...BY YOU, NASH. DURING ONE OF YOUR JEALOUS RAGES BLAKE WROTE OF... IN THE JOURNAL WHERE HE KEPT YOUR PHOTOGRAPH. WAS IT GUILT, DENIAL OF WHAT YOU'D DONE, THAT MADE YOU TAKE BLAKE'S INVENTION AND TURN IT ON THOSE YOU JUDGED TO HAVE "WRONGED" YOUR BROTHER... TURNING HIS WONDERFUL DEVICE INTO A WEAPON OF MURDER?
YOU USED YOUR JOB TO LOCATE YOUR BROTHER... TO LEARN OF YOUR PARENTS. THEN USED IT AGAIN... GETTING ASSIGNED TO THE INVESTIGATION SO THE CASE WOULD NEVER BE SOLVED.
YOU COULD DESTROY ANY EVIDENCE, HINDER ME FROM FINDING BLAKE'S WORKSHOP OR ANYTHING ELSE MIGHT IMPLICATE YOU... AT THE SAME TIME, LEADING ME INTO TRAPS, LIKE THE NIGHT IN BELGRAVIA...
OR MAKING SURE I WAS OUT OF THE WAY, SO YOU COULD DRUG THE POLICE ASSISTING YOU AND SLAUGHTER ELLIOT YARDLEY.
NO, I... I.
OH GOD.
THE DEVICE, SIR. "BLAKE'S INVENTION"?
I DON'T QUITE UNDERSTAND WHAT IT WAS. HOW IT APPEARED SO--
LIFELIKE? IT'S SIMPLE, ALFRED. AND FANTASTIC.

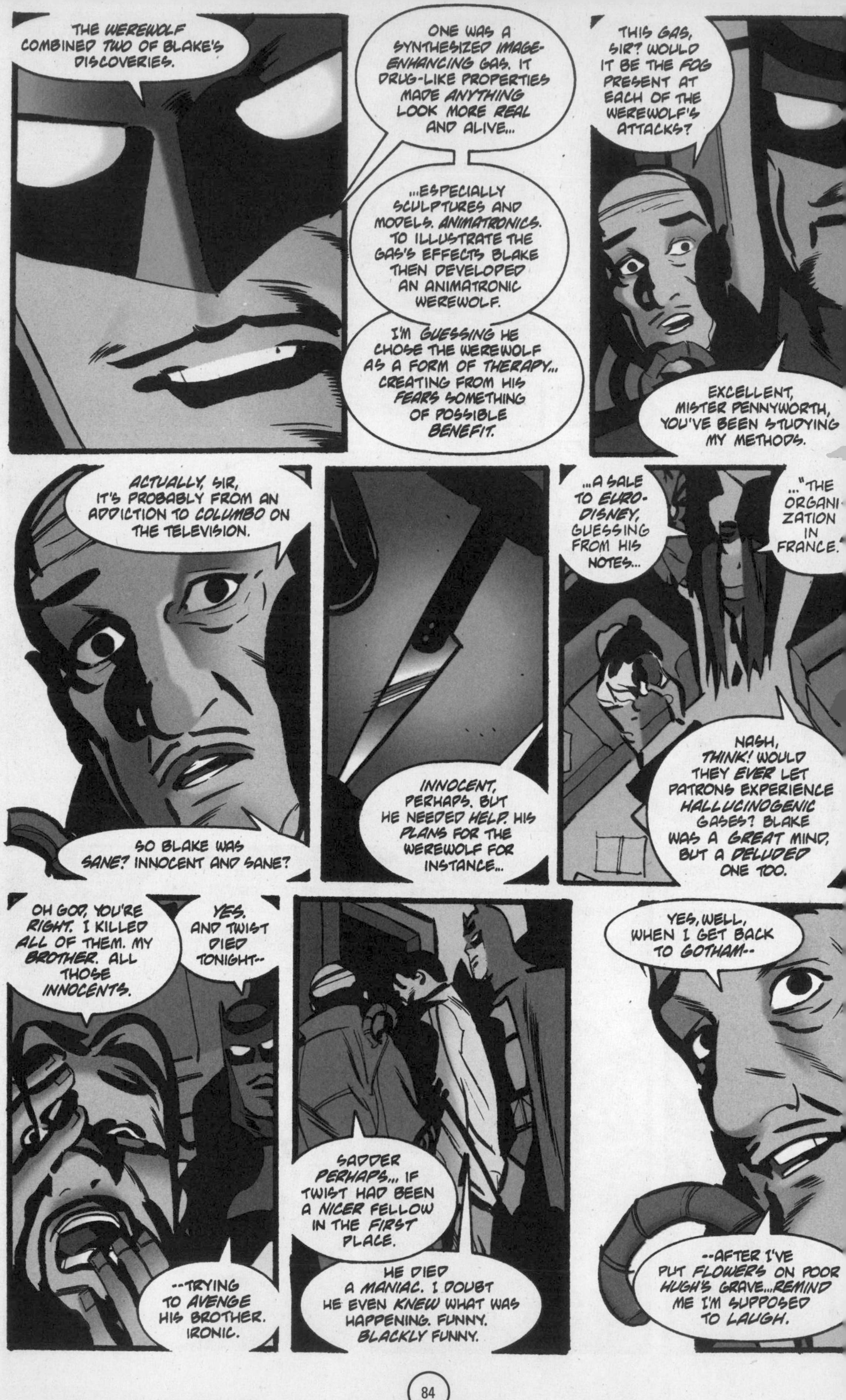
THE WEREWOLF COMBINED TWO OF BLAKE'S DISCOVERIES.
ONE WAS A SYNTHESIZED IMAGE-ENHANCING GAS. IT DRUG-LIKE PROPERTIES MADE ANYTHING LOOK MORE REAL AND ALIVE...
...ESPECIALLY SCULPTURES AND MODELS. ANIMATRONICS. TO ILLUSTRATE THE GAS'S EFFECTS BLAKE THEN DEVELOPED AN ANIMATRONIC WEREWOLF.
I'M GUESSING HE CHOSE THE WEREWOLF AS A FORM OF THERAPY... CREATING FROM HIS FEARS SOMETHING OF POSSIBLE BENEFIT.
THIS GAS, SIR? WOULD IT BE THE FOG PRESENT AT EACH OF THE WEREWOLF'S ATTACKS?
EXCELLENT, MISTER PENNYWORTH, YOU'VE BEEN STUDYING MY METHODS.
ACTUALLY, SIR, IT'S PROBABLY FROM AN ADDICTION TO COLUMBO ON THE TELEVISION.
SO BLAKE WAS SANE? INNOCENT AND SANE?
INNOCENT, PERHAPS. BUT HE NEEDED HELP. HIS PLANS FOR THE WEREWOLF FOR INSTANCE...
...A SALE TO EURO-DISNEY, GUESSING FROM HIS NOTES...
..."THE ORGANIZATION IN FRANCE."
NASH, THINK! WOULD THEY EVER LET PATRONS EXPERIENCE HALLUCINOGENIC GASES? BLAKE WAS A GREAT MIND, BUT A DELUDED ONE TOO.
OH GOD, YOU'RE RIGHT. I KILLED ALL OF THEM. MY BROTHER. ALL THOSE INNOCENTS.
YES. AND TWIST DIED TONIGHT--
--TRYING TO AVENGE HIS BROTHER. IRONIC.
SADDER PERHAPS... IF TWIST HAD BEEN A NICER FELLOW IN THE FIRST PLACE.
HE DIED A MANIAC. I DOUBT HE EVEN KNEW WHAT WAS HAPPENING. FUNNY. BLACKLY FUNNY.
YES, WELL, WHEN I GET BACK TO GOTHAM--
--AFTER I'VE PUT FLOWERS ON POOR HUGH'S GRAVE...REMIND ME I'M SUPPOSED TO LAUGH.

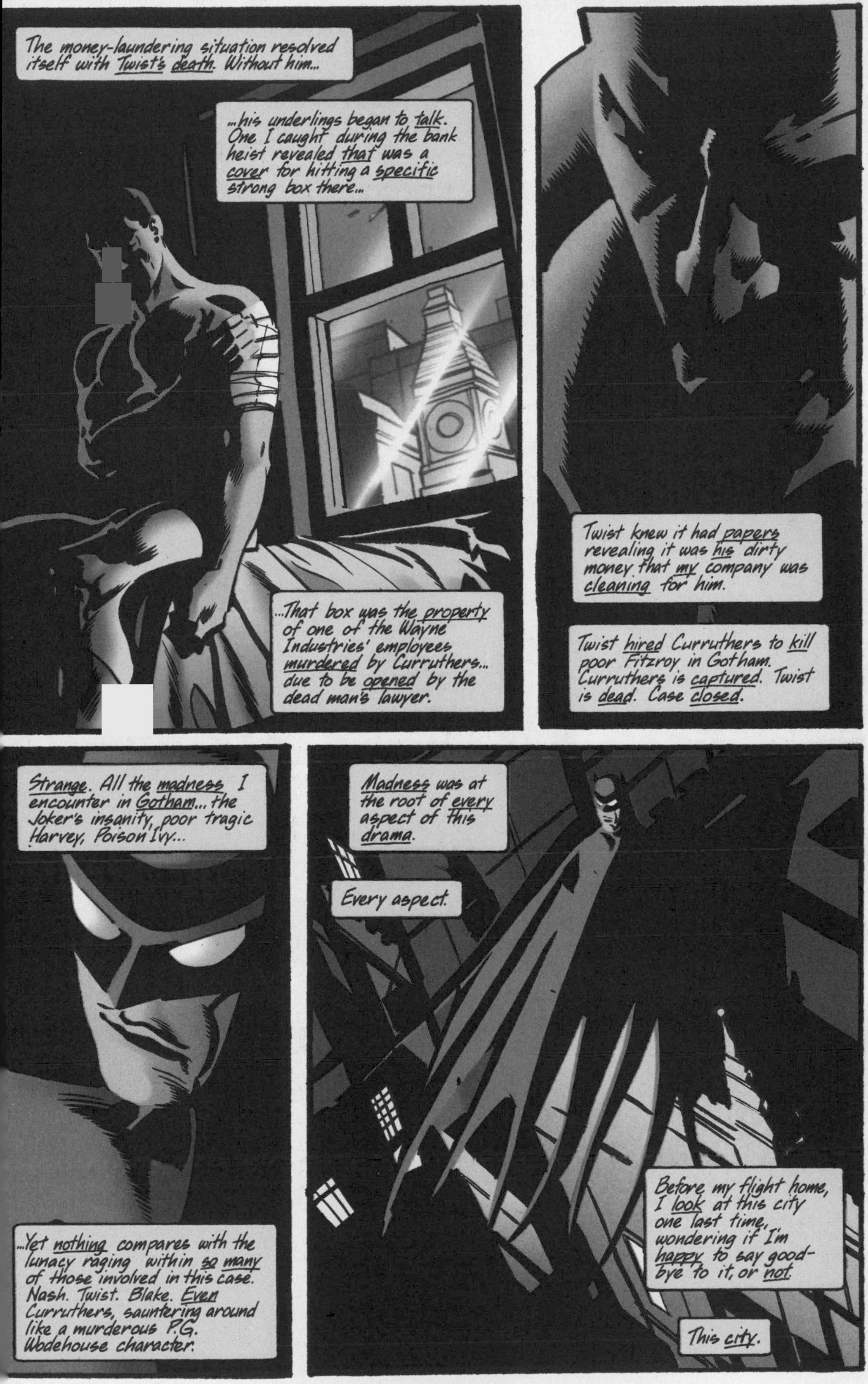
The money-laundering situation resolved itself with Twist's death. Without him...
...his underlings began to talk. One I caught during the bank heist revealed that was a cover for hitting a specific strong box there...
...That box was the property of one of the Wayne Industries' employees murdered by Curruthers... due to be opened by the dead man's lawyer.
Twist knew it had papers revealing it was his dirty money that my company was cleaning for him.
Twist hired Curruthers to kill poor Fitzroy in Gotham. Curruthers is captured. Twist is dead. Case closed.
Strange. All the madness I encounter in Gotham... the Joker's insanity, poor tragic Harvey, Poison Ivy...
...Yet nothing compares with the lunacy raging within so many of those involved in this case. Nash. Twist. Blake. Even Curruthers, sauntering around like a murderous P.G. Wodehouse character.
Madness was at the root of every aspect of this drama.
Every aspect.
Before my flight home, I look at this city one last time, wondering if I'm happy to say good-bye to it, or not.
This city.

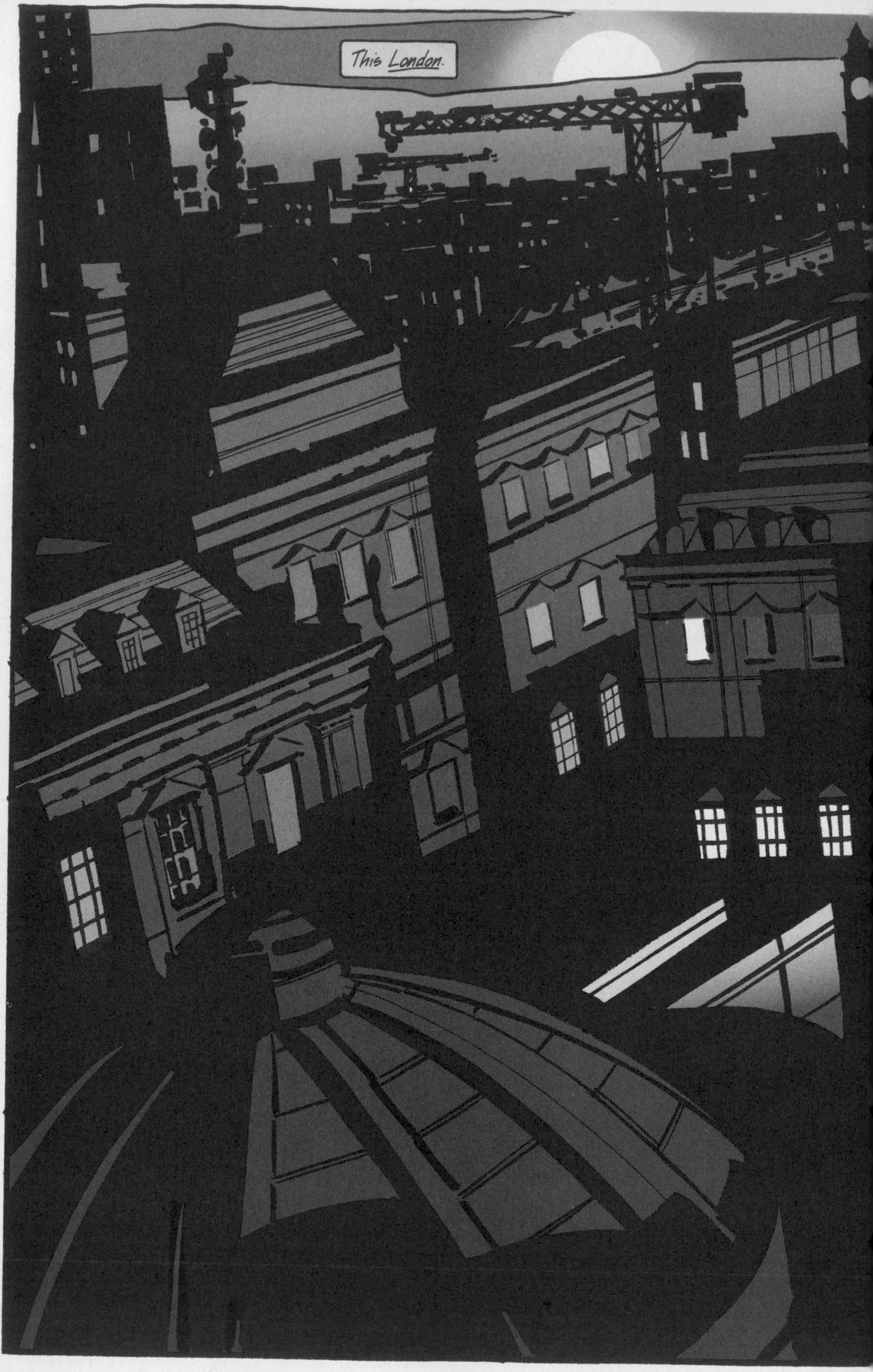
This London.

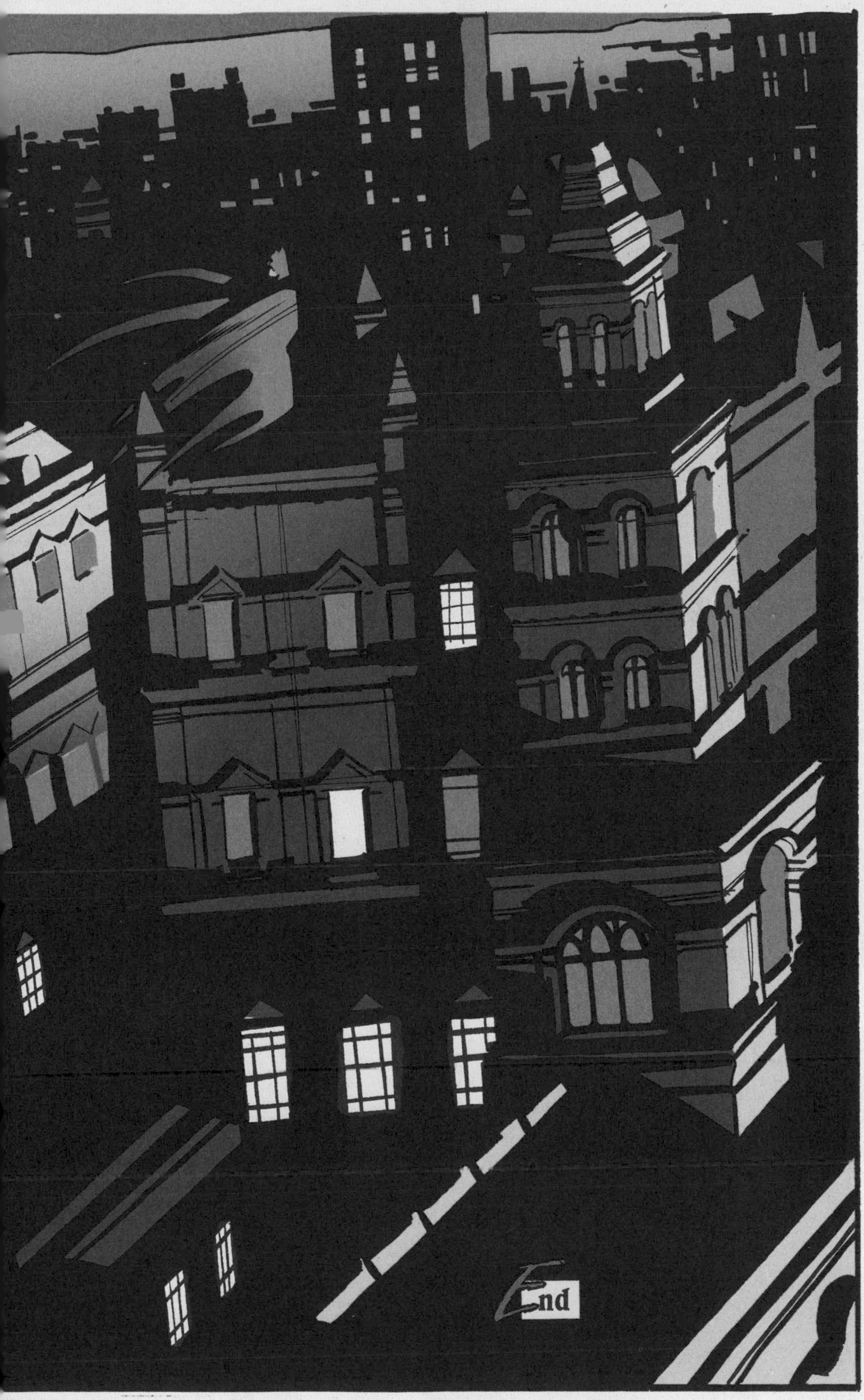
End

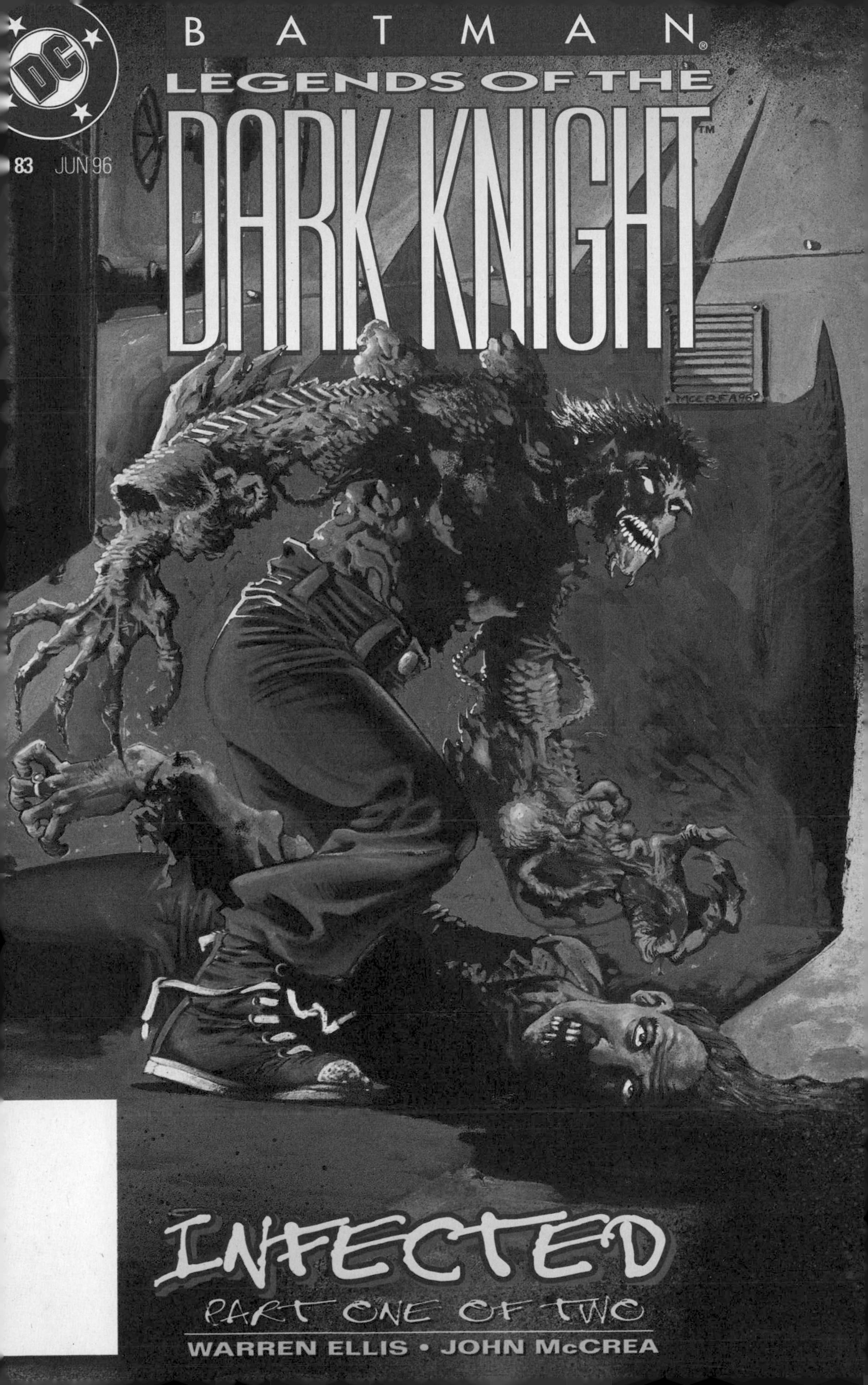
DC
BATMAN®
LEGENDS OF THE
DARK KNIGHT™
83 JUN 96
INFECTED
PART ONE OF TWO
WARREN ELLIS • JOHN McCREA

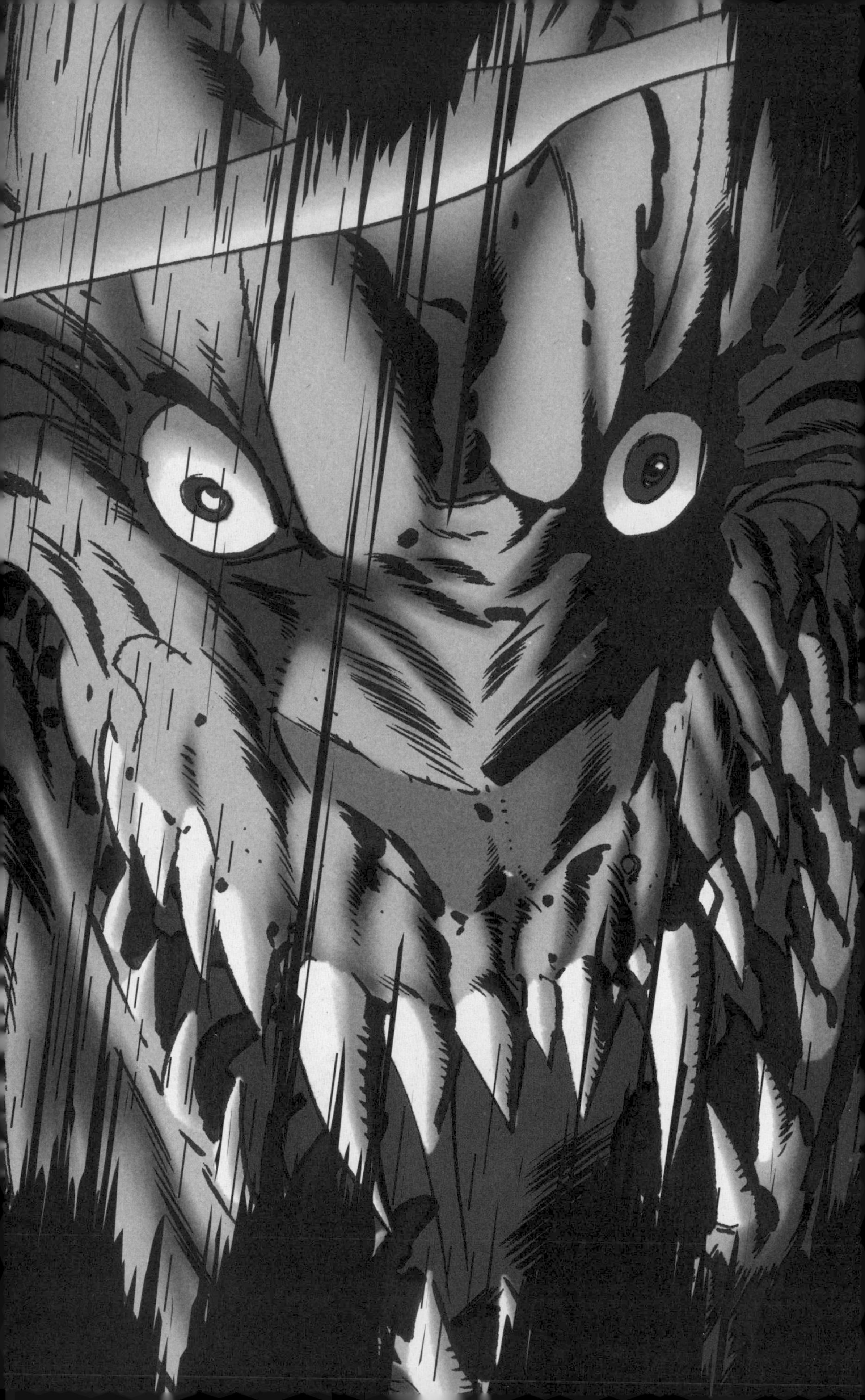

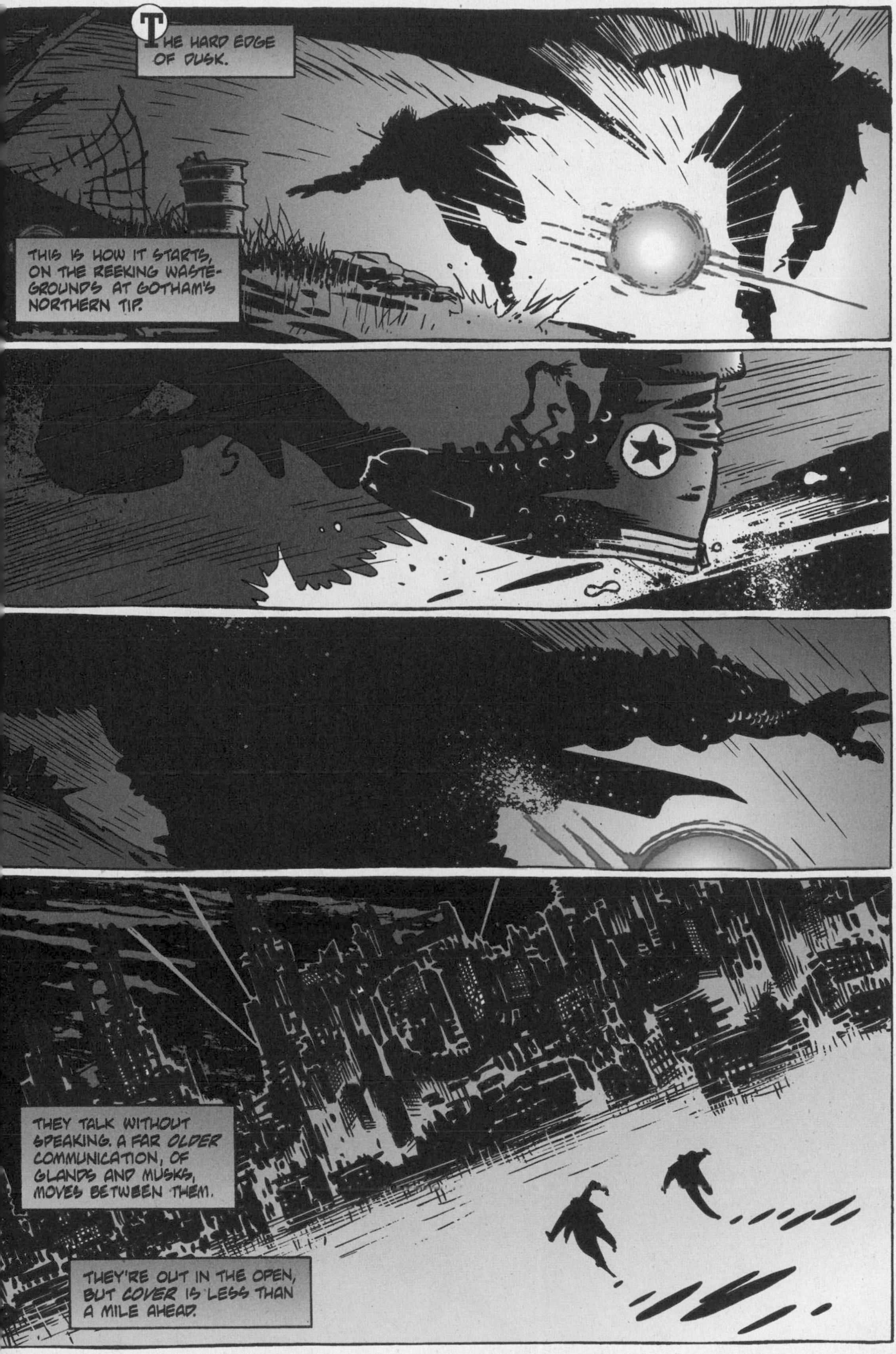
THE HARD EDGE OF DUSK.
THIS IS HOW IT STARTS, ON THE REEKING WASTE-GROUNDS AT GOTHAM'S NORTHERN TIP.
THEY TALK WITHOUT SPEAKING. A FAR OLDER COMMUNICATION, OF GLANDS AND MUSKS, MOVES BETWEEN THEM.
THEY'RE OUT IN THE OPEN, BUT COVER IS LESS THAN A MILE AHEAD.

just keep running.

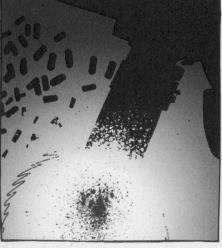

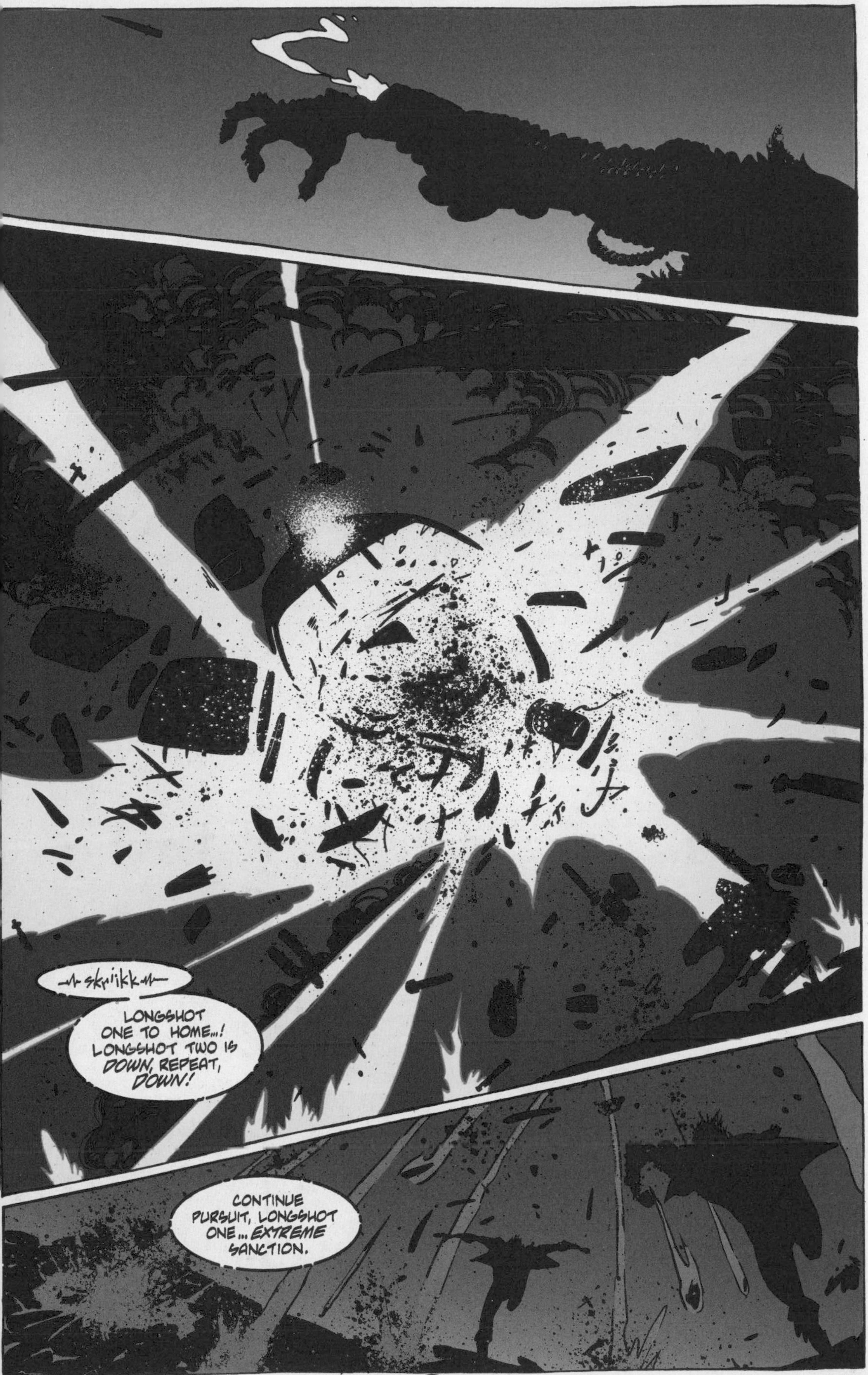
skriikk
LONGSHOT ONE TO HOME...! LONGSHOT TWO IS DOWN, REPEAT, DOWN!
CONTINUE PURSUIT, LONGSHOT ONE... EXTREME SANCTION.

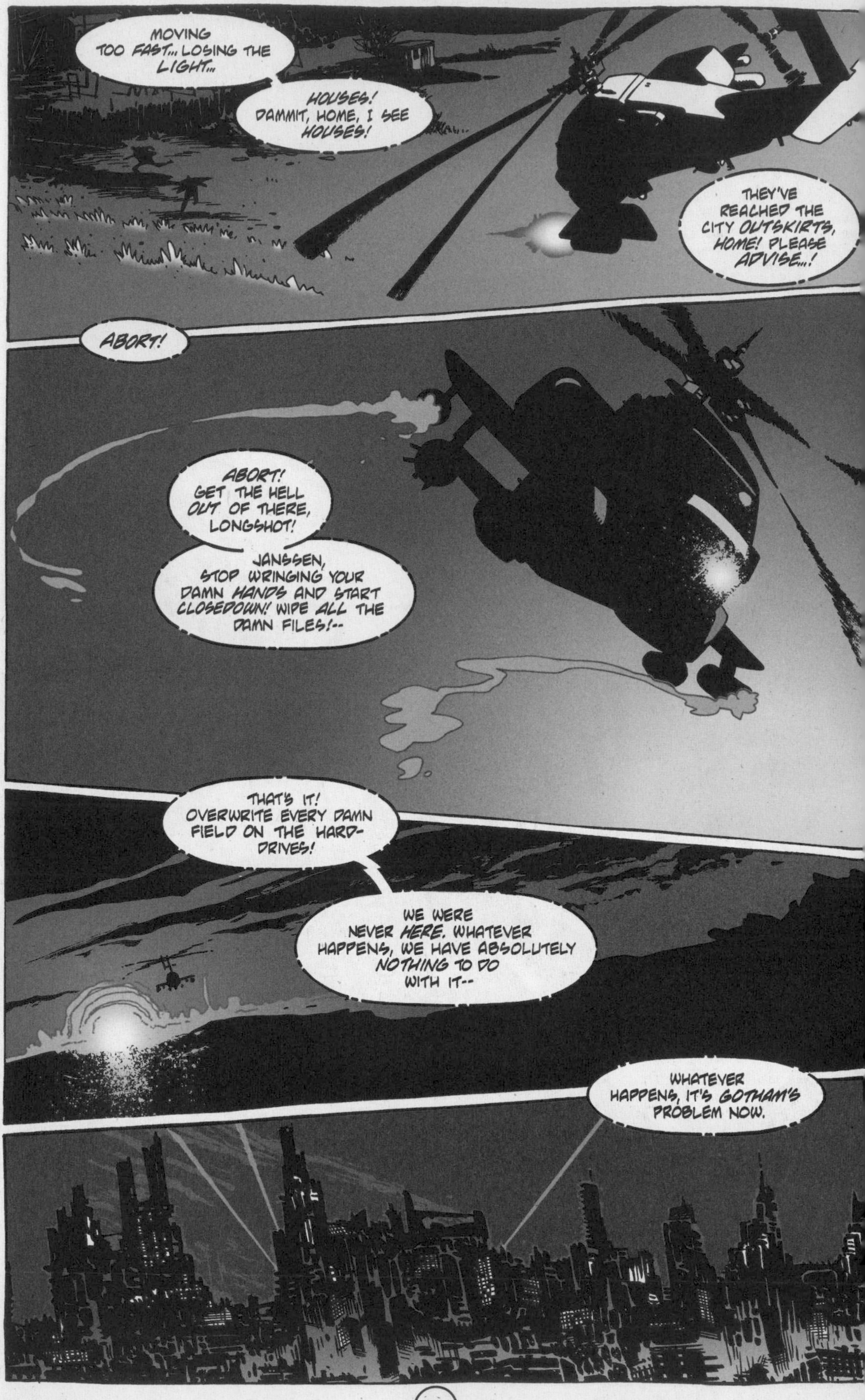
MOVING TOO FAST... LOSING THE LIGHT...
HOUSES! DAMMIT, HOME, I SEE HOUSES!
THEY'VE REACHED THE CITY OUTSKIRTS, HOME! PLEASE ADVISE...!
ABORT!
ABORT! GET THE HELL OUT OF THERE, LONGSHOT!
JANSSEN, STOP WRINGING YOUR DAMN HANDS AND START CLOSEDOWN! WIPE ALL THE DAMN FILES!--
THAT'S IT! OVERWRITE EVERY DAMN FIELD ON THE HARD-DRIVES!
WE WERE NEVER HERE. WHATEVER HAPPENS, WE HAVE ABSOLUTELY NOTHING TO DO WITH IT--
WHATEVER HAPPENS, IT'S GOTHAM'S PROBLEM NOW.

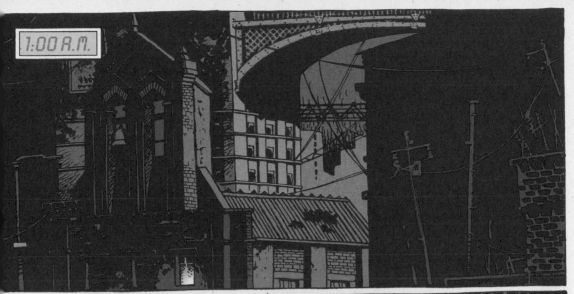

ANY O' THAT GOOD STUFF LEFT, JANIE?

AWW, MURF--IF THAT AIN'T THE EIGHTH TIME YOU ASKED THAT, AN' YOU KNOW I NEED IT MORE'N--

HEYYY! WE GOT SOME COMPANY HERE, GUYS!

SPIDER, MAN, I AIN'T GIVIN' 'EM MY GOOD STUFF--

SHUTCHA HOLE, MURF, YOU AIN'T GOT NO "STUFF."

'SIDES, THEY JUST WANT A PIECE OF OUR FIRE HERE.

HEY, YOU GUYS LOOK LIKE GOOD ARMY BOYS IN THEM DRABS. COLD TO BE WALKIN' AROUND WITHOUT SLEEVES--HELL!

YOUR ARMS LOOK...YOUR ARMS...

EEEEEE

KLUNG

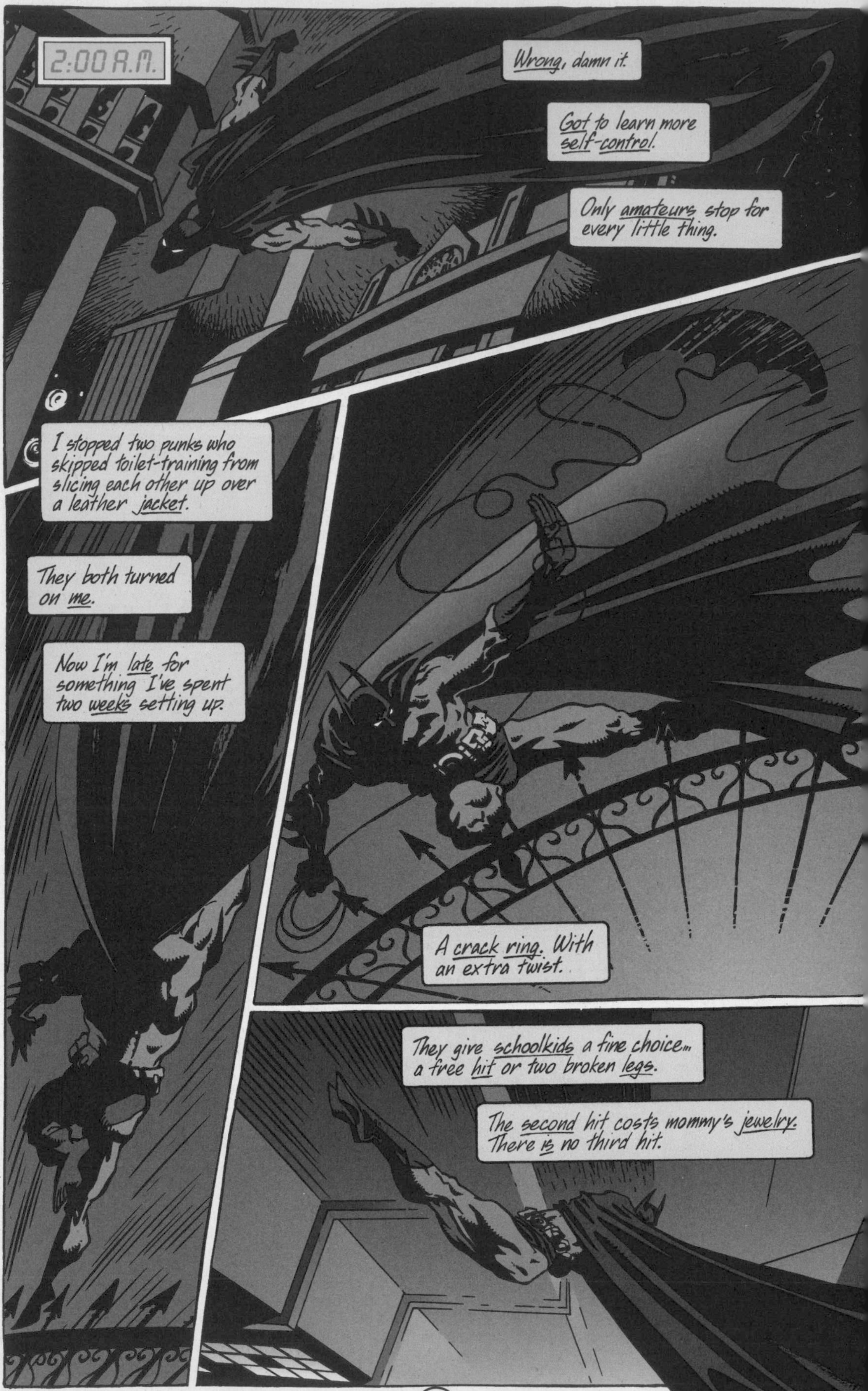
2:00 A.M.
Wrong, damn it.
Got to learn more self-control.
Only amateurs stop for every little thing.
I stopped two punks who skipped toilet-training from slicing each other up over a leather jacket.
They both turned on me.
Now I'm late for something I've spent two weeks setting up.
A crack ring. With an extra twist.
They give schoolkids a fine choice... a free hit or two broken legs.
The second hit costs mommy's jewelry. There is no third hit.

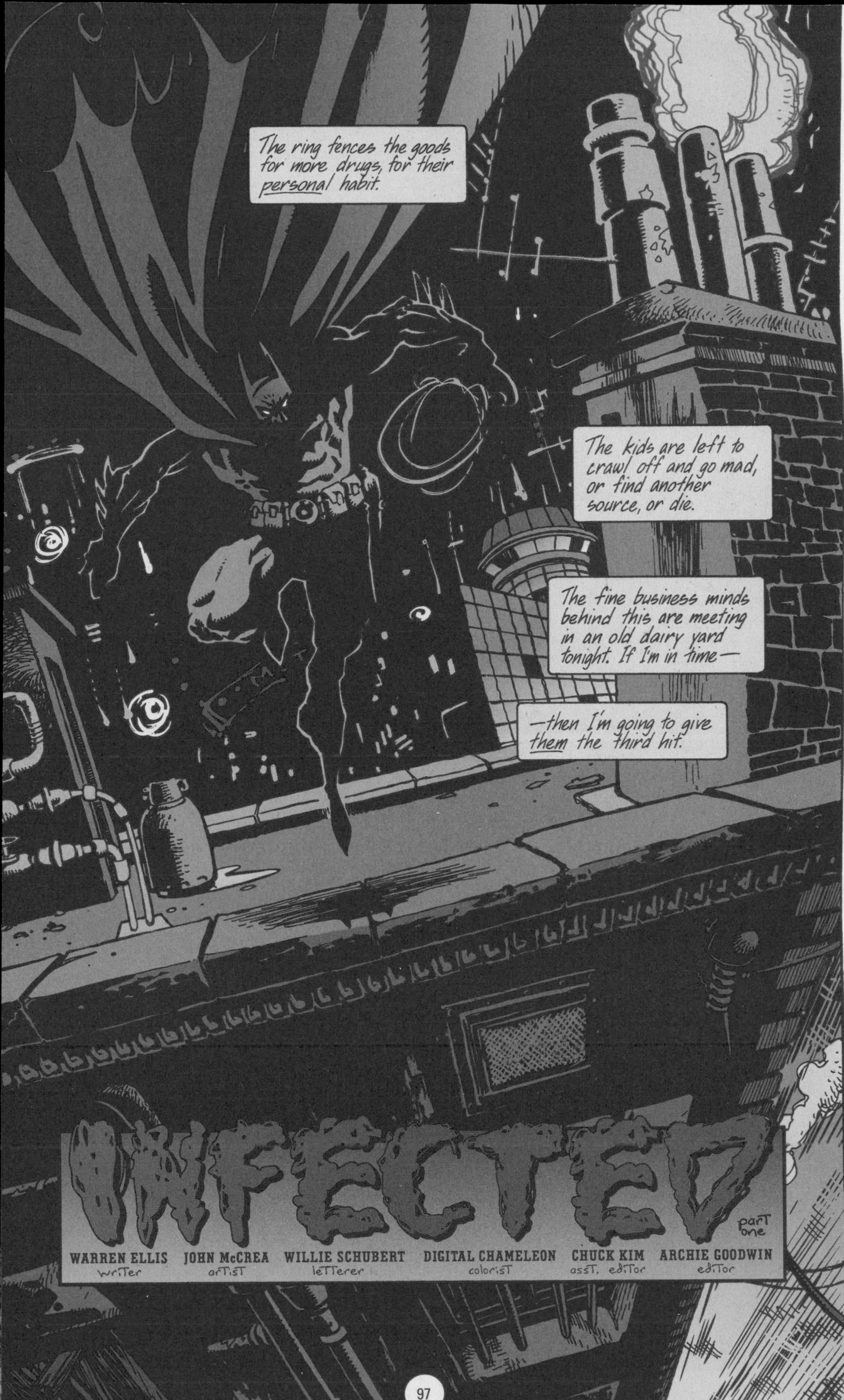

The ring fences the goods for more drugs, for their personal habit.
The kids are left to crawl off and go mad, or find another source, or die.
The fine business minds behind this are meeting in an old dairy yard tonight. If I'm in time—
—then I'm going to give them the third hit.
INFECTED
PART ONE
WARREN ELLIS writer
JOHN McCREA artist
WILLIE SCHUBERT letterer
DIGITAL CHAMELEON colorist
CHUCK KIM asst. editor
ARCHIE GOODWIN editor

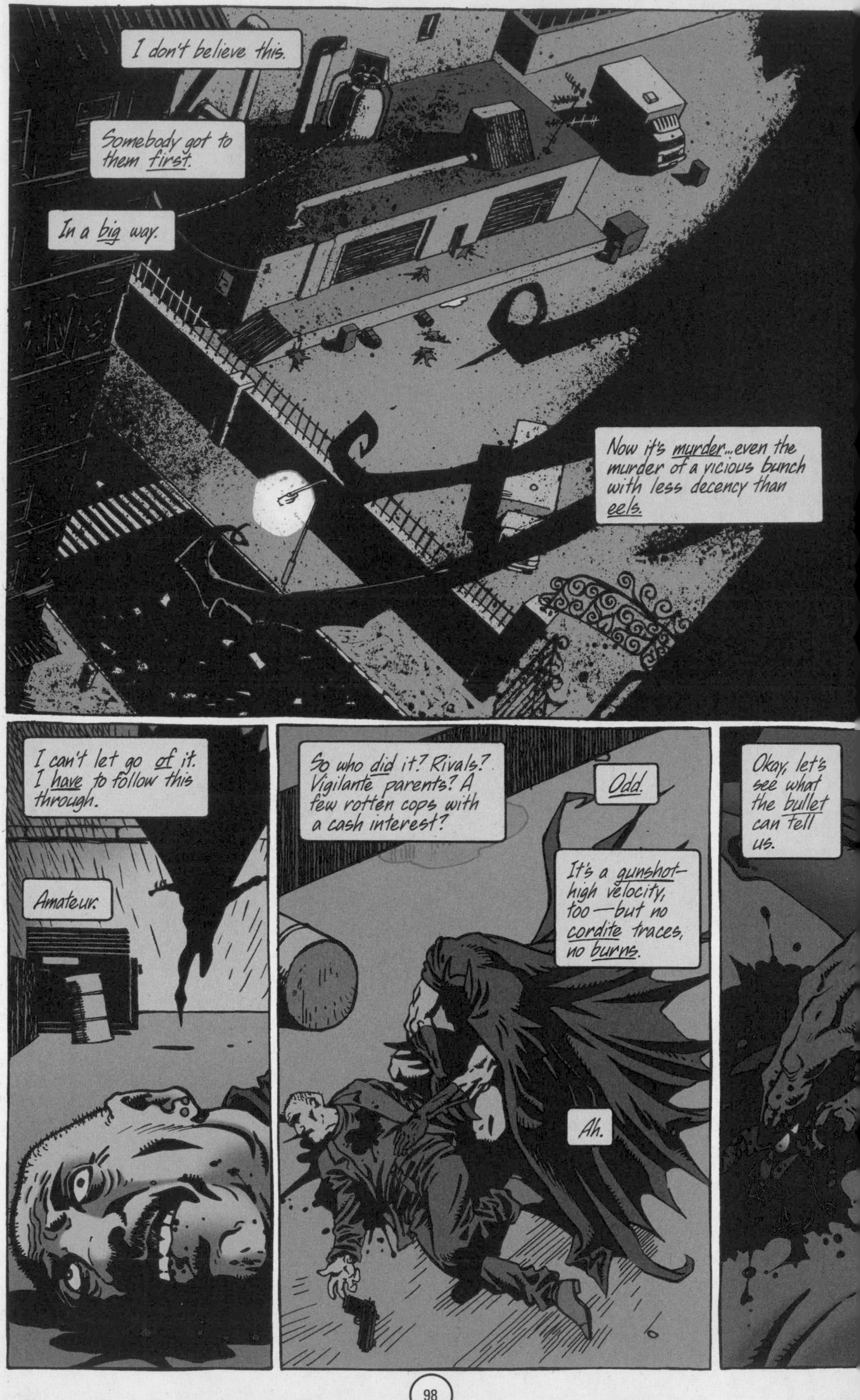
I don't believe this.
Somebody got to them first.
In a big way.
Now it's murder...even the murder of a vicious bunch with less decency than eels.
I can't let go of it. I have to follow this through.
Amateur.
So who did it? Rivals? Vigilante parents? A few rotten cops with a cash interest?
Odd.
It's a gunshot—high velocity, too—but no cordite traces, no burns.
Ah.
Okay, let's see what the bullet can tell us.

Never seen a bullet *like* it.

More like *bone*.

Can't fire *bone* from a *gun*. It'd be pulverized.

Sirens.

Tonight's fast becoming an unmitigated disaster.

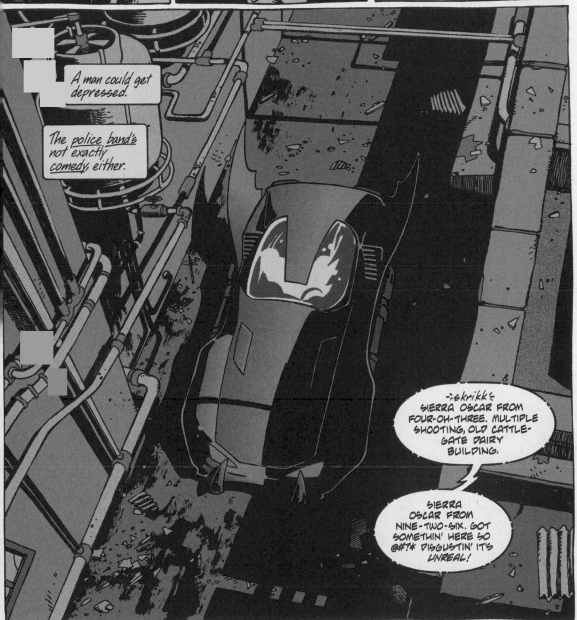

A man could get depressed.

The *police band's* not exactly *comedy,* either.

≈skrikk≈ SIERRA OSCAR FROM FOUR-OH-THREE. MULTIPLE SHOOTING, OLD CATTLE-GATE DAIRY BUILDING.

SIERRA OSCAR FROM NINE-TWO-SIX. GOT SOMETHIN' HERE SO @#?# DISGUSTIN' IT'S UNREAL!

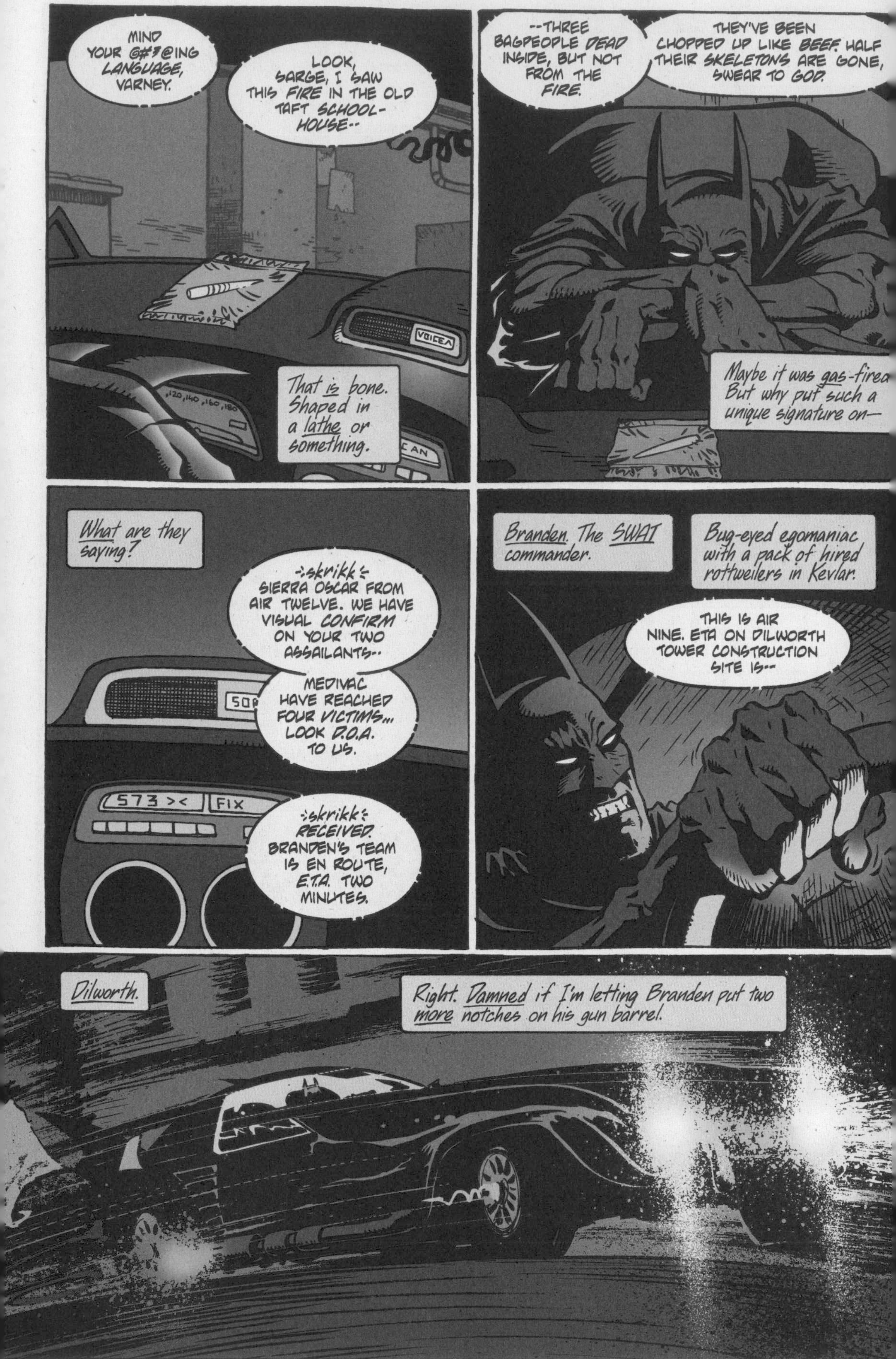

MIND YOUR @#$@ING LANGUAGE, VARNEY.
LOOK, SARGE, I SAW THIS FIRE IN THE OLD TAFT SCHOOL-HOUSE--
That is bone. Shaped in a lathe or something.
--THREE BAGPEOPLE DEAD INSIDE, BUT NOT FROM THE FIRE.
THEY'VE BEEN CHOPPED UP LIKE BEEF. HALF THEIR SKELETONS ARE GONE, SWEAR TO GOD.
Maybe it was gas-fired. But why put such a unique signature on—
What are they saying?
-skrikk- SIERRA OSCAR FROM AIR TWELVE. WE HAVE VISUAL CONFIRM ON YOUR TWO ASSAILANTS--
MEDIVAC HAVE REACHED FOUR VICTIMS... LOOK D.O.A. TO US.
-skrikk- RECEIVED. BRANDEN'S TEAM IS EN ROUTE, E.T.A. TWO MINUTES.
Branden. The SWAT commander.
Bug-eyed egomaniac with a pack of hired rottweilers in Kevlar.
THIS IS AIR NINE. ETA ON DILWORTH TOWER CONSTRUCTION SITE IS--
Dilworth.
Right. Damned if I'm letting Branden put two more notches on his gun barrel.

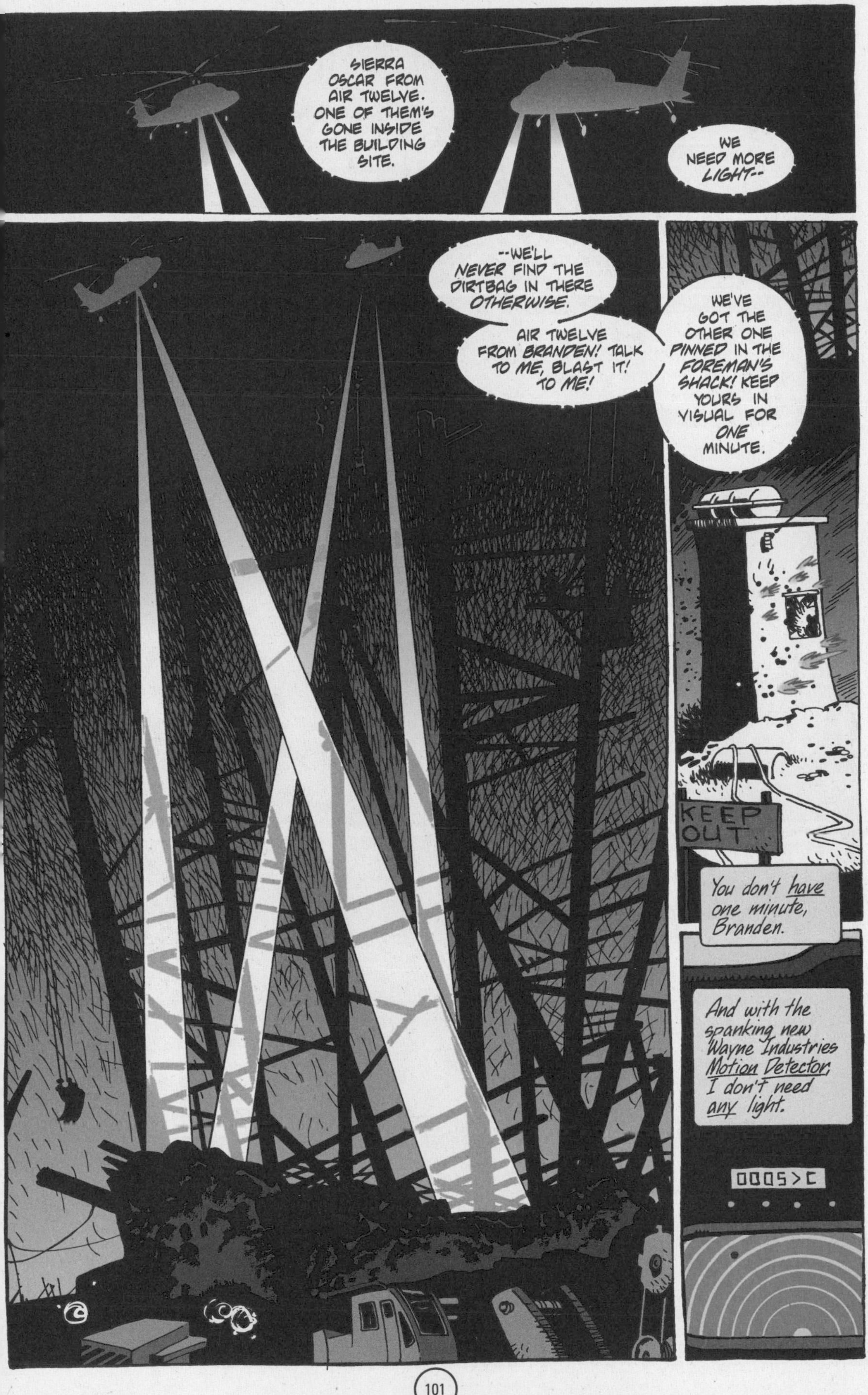
SIERRA OSCAR FROM AIR TWELVE. ONE OF THEM'S GONE INSIDE THE BUILDING SITE.
WE NEED MORE LIGHT--
--WE'LL NEVER FIND THE DIRTBAG IN THERE OTHERWISE.
AIR TWELVE FROM BRANDEN! TALK TO ME, BLAST IT! TO ME!
WE'VE GOT THE OTHER ONE PINNED IN THE FOREMAN'S SHACK! KEEP YOURS IN VISUAL FOR ONE MINUTE.
KEEP OUT
You don't have one minute, Branden.
And with the spanking new Wayne Industries Motion Detector, I don't need any light.
0005>C

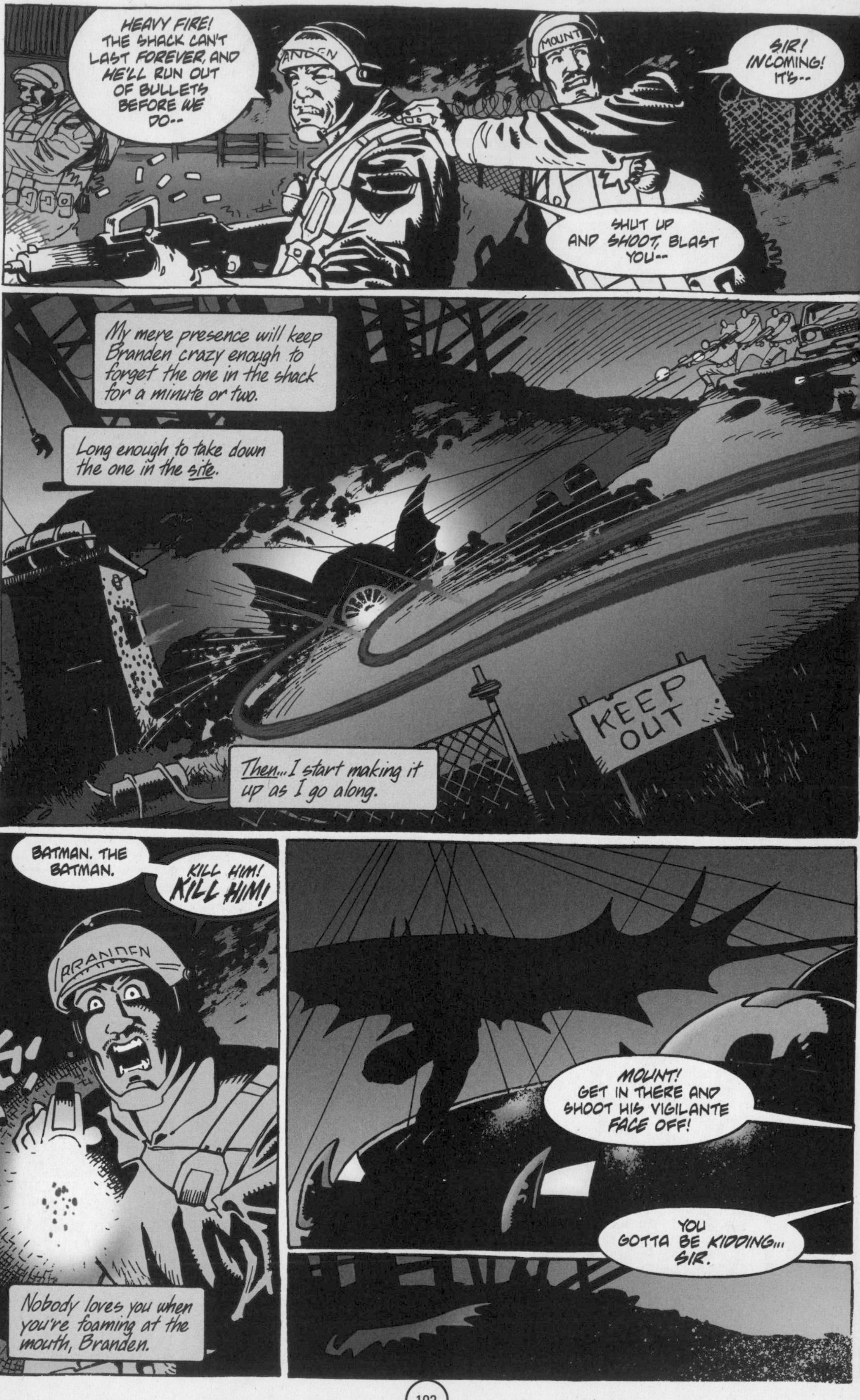

HEAVY FIRE! THE SHACK CAN'T LAST FOREVER, AND HE'LL RUN OUT OF BULLETS BEFORE WE DO--
BRANDEN
MOUNT
SIR! INCOMING! IT'S--
SHUT UP AND SHOOT, BLAST YOU--
My mere presence will keep Branden crazy enough to forget the one in the shack for a minute or two.
Long enough to take down the one in the site.
KEEP OUT
Then...I start making it up as I go along.
BATMAN. THE BATMAN.
KILL HIM! KILL HIM!
BRANDEN
Nobody loves you when you're foaming at the mouth, Branden.
MOUNT! GET IN THERE AND SHOOT HIS VIGILANTE FACE OFF!
YOU GOTTA BE KIDDING... SIR.

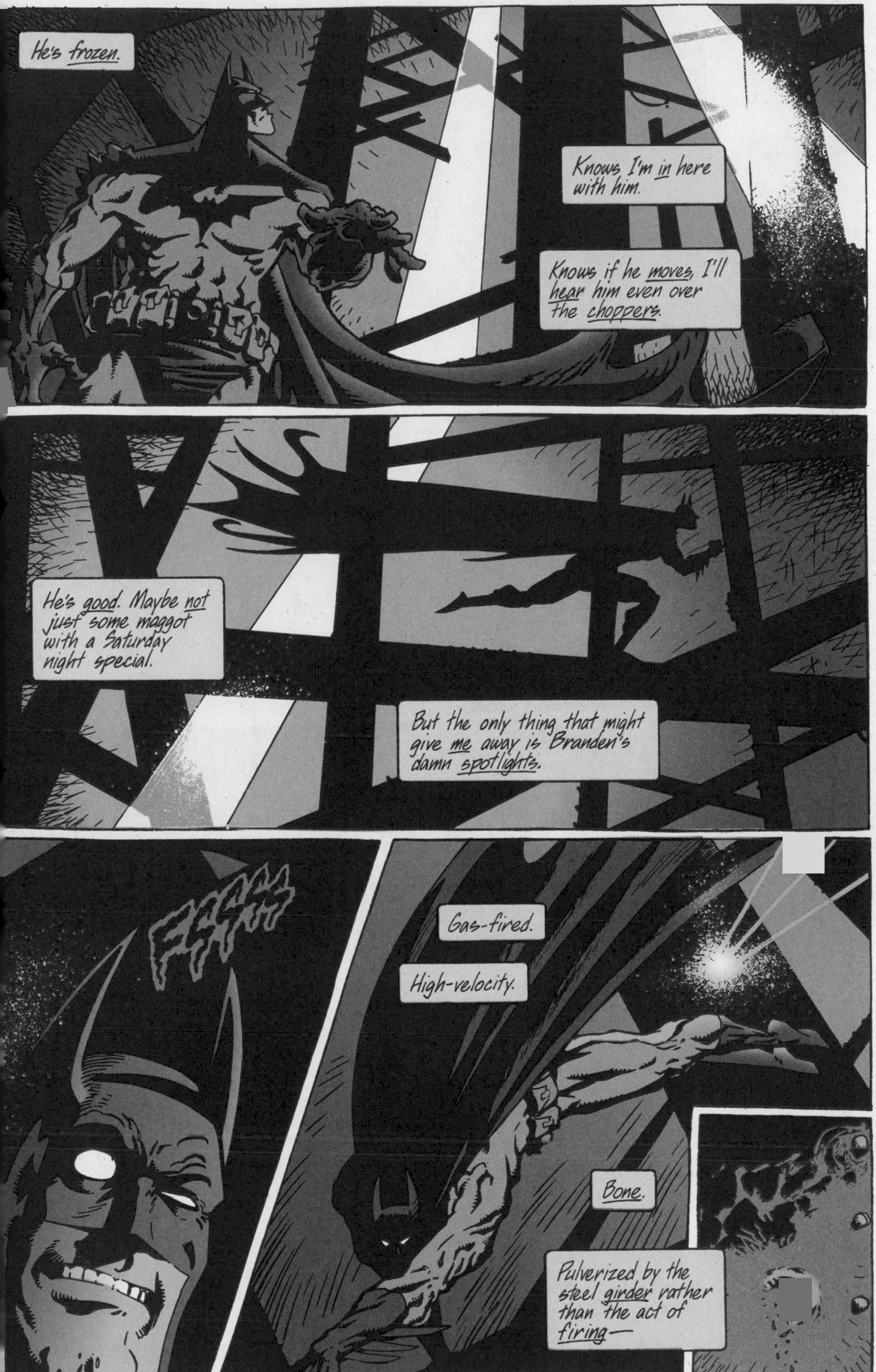

He's frozen.
Knows I'm in here with him.
Knows if he moves, I'll hear him even over the choppers.
He's good. Maybe not just some maggot with a Saturday night special.
But the only thing that might give me away is Branden's damn spotlights.
FSSSH
Gas-fired.
High-velocity.
Bone.
Pulverized by the steel girder rather than the act of firing—

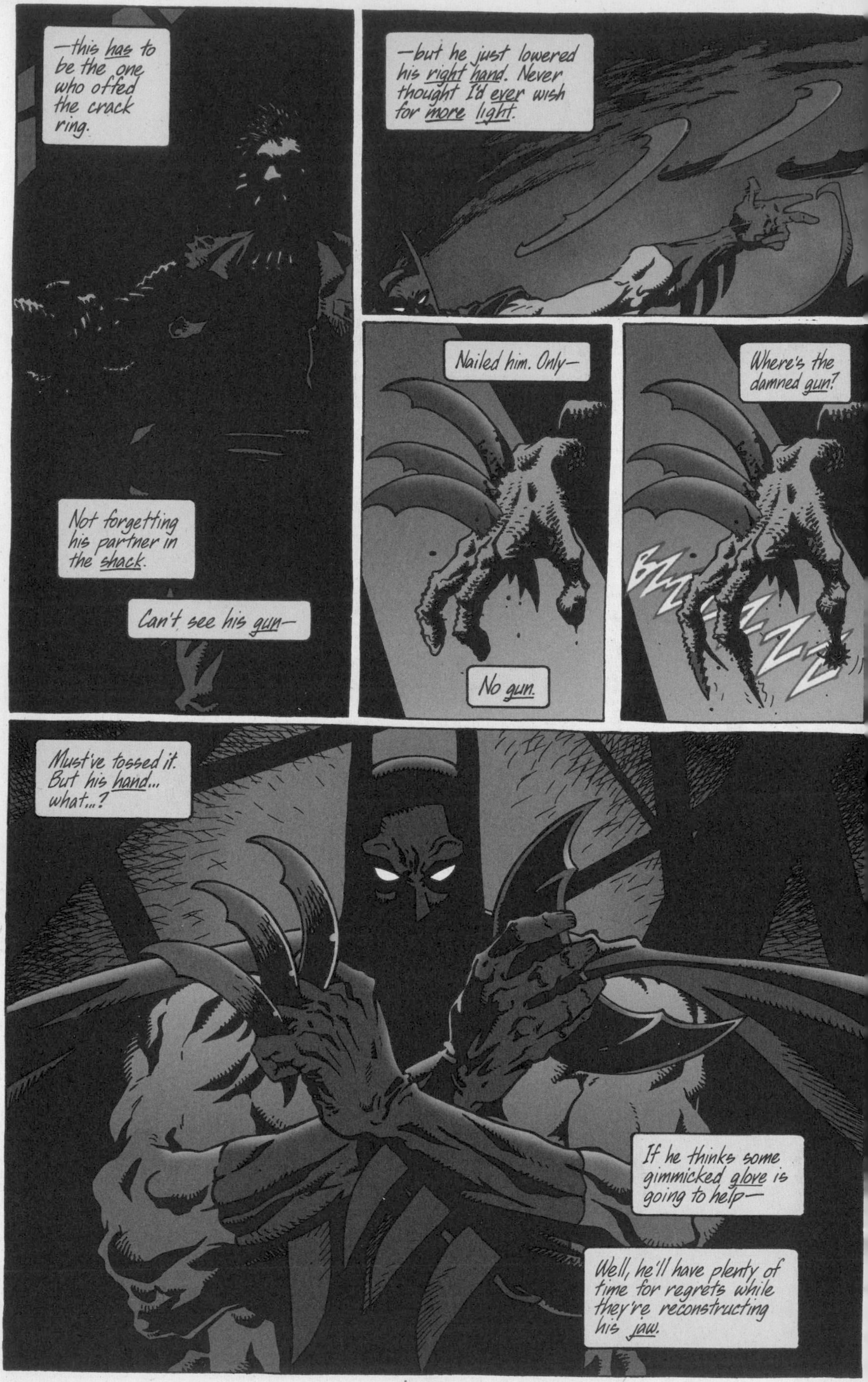
—this has to be the one who offed the crack ring.
Not forgetting his partner in the shack.
Can't see his gun—
—but he just lowered his right hand. Never thought I'd ever wish for more light.
Nailed him. Only—
No gun.
Where's the damned gun?
BZZZZZZ
Must've tossed it. But his hand... what...?
If he thinks some gimmicked glove is going to help—
Well, he'll have plenty of time for regrets while they're reconstructing his jaw.

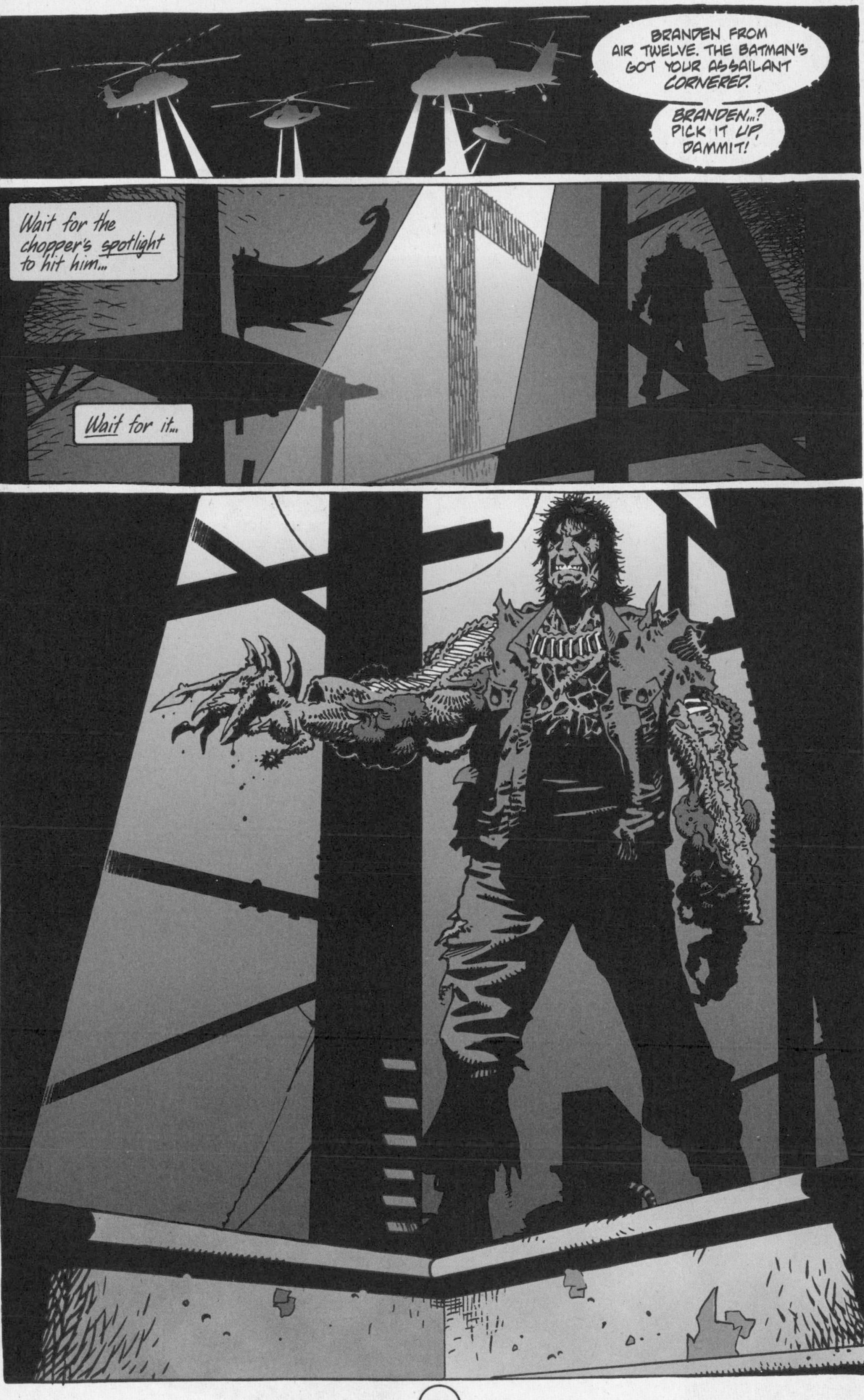
BRANDEN FROM AIR TWELVE. THE BATMAN'S GOT YOUR ASSAILANT CORNERED.
BRANDEN...? PICK IT UP, DAMMIT!
Wait for the chopper's spotlight to hit him...
Wait for it...

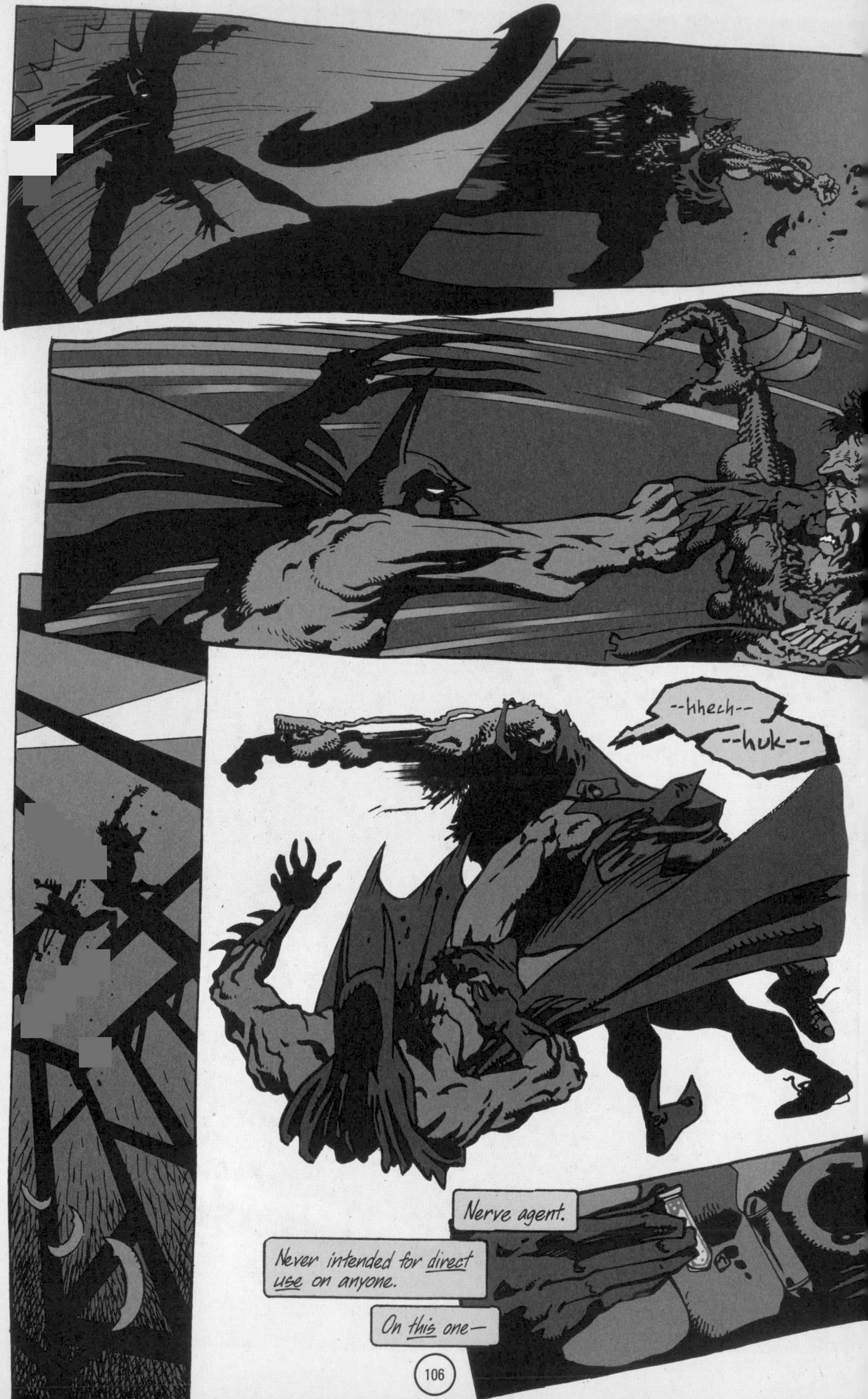
--hhech--
--huk--
Nerve agent.
Never intended for direct use on anyone.
On this one—

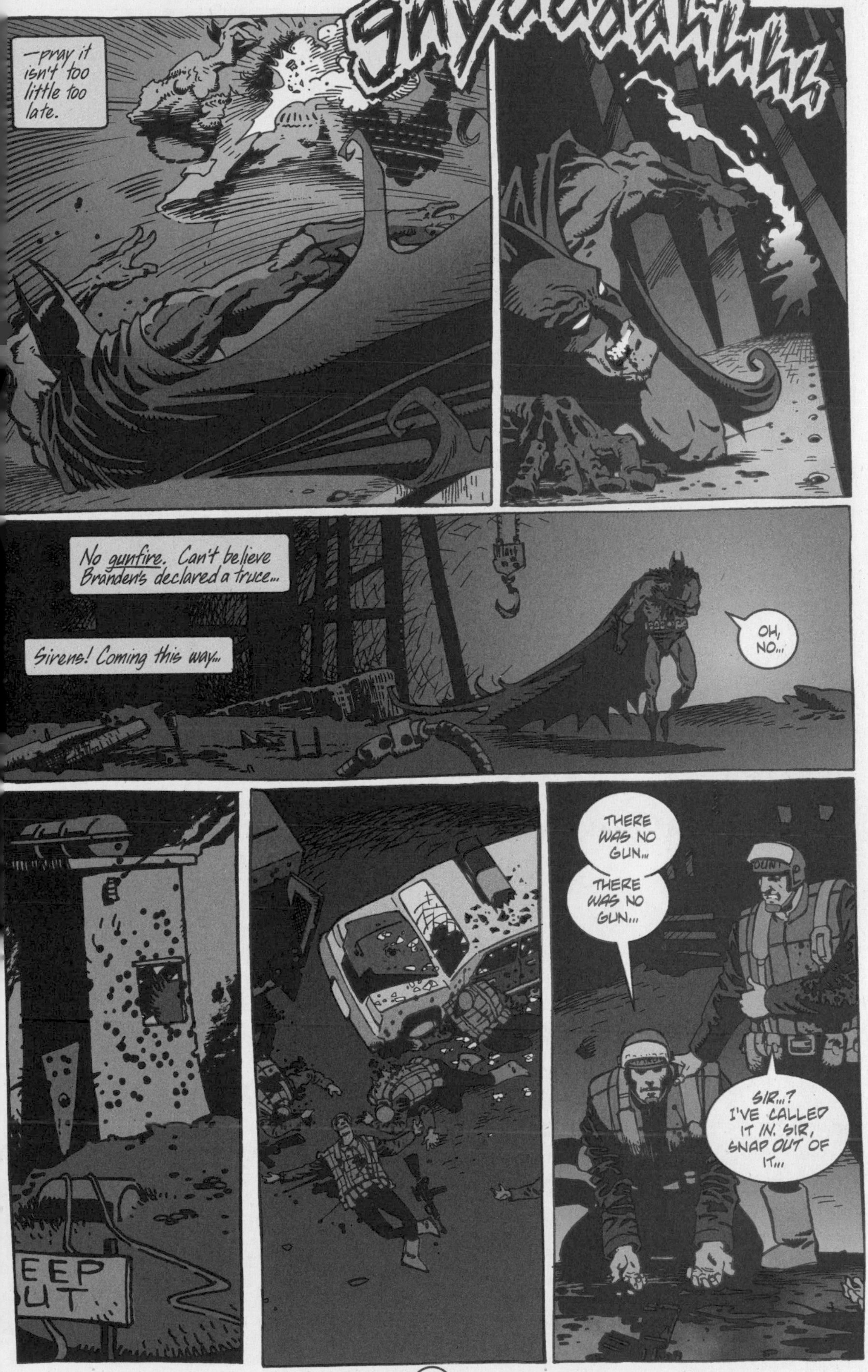
—pray it isn't too little too late.
SNYAAAAHHHHH
No gunfire. Can't believe Branden's declared a truce...
Sirens! Coming this way...
OH, NO...
EEP
UT
THERE WAS NO GUN...
THERE WAS NO GUN...
SIR...? I'VE CALLED IT IN, SIR, SNAP OUT OF IT...

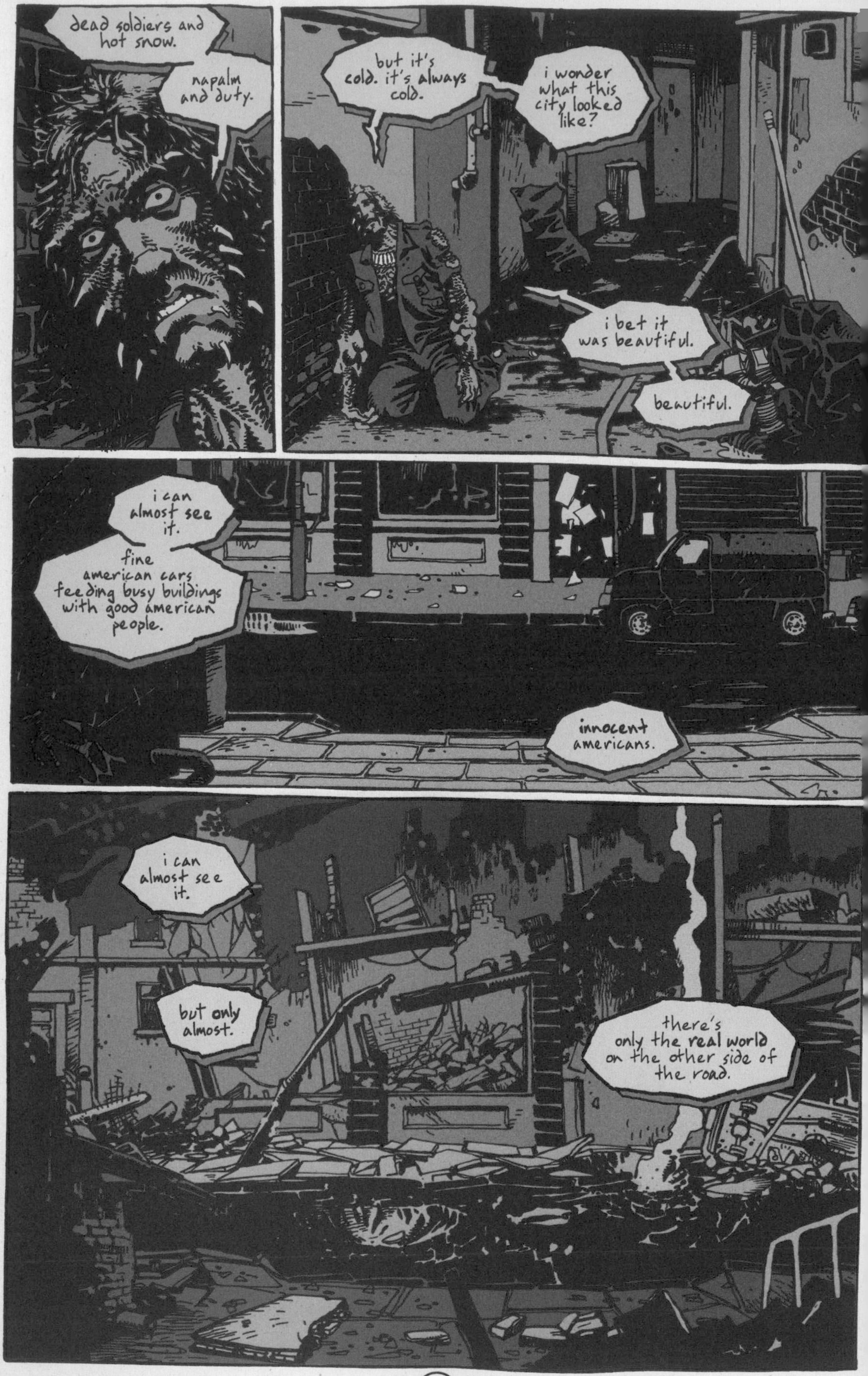
dead soldiers and hot snow.
napalm and duty.
but it's cold. it's always cold.
i wonder what this city looked like?
i bet it was beautiful.
beautiful.
i can almost see it.
fine american cars feeding busy buildings with good american people.
innocent americans.
i can almost see it.
but only almost.
there's only the real world on the other side of the road.

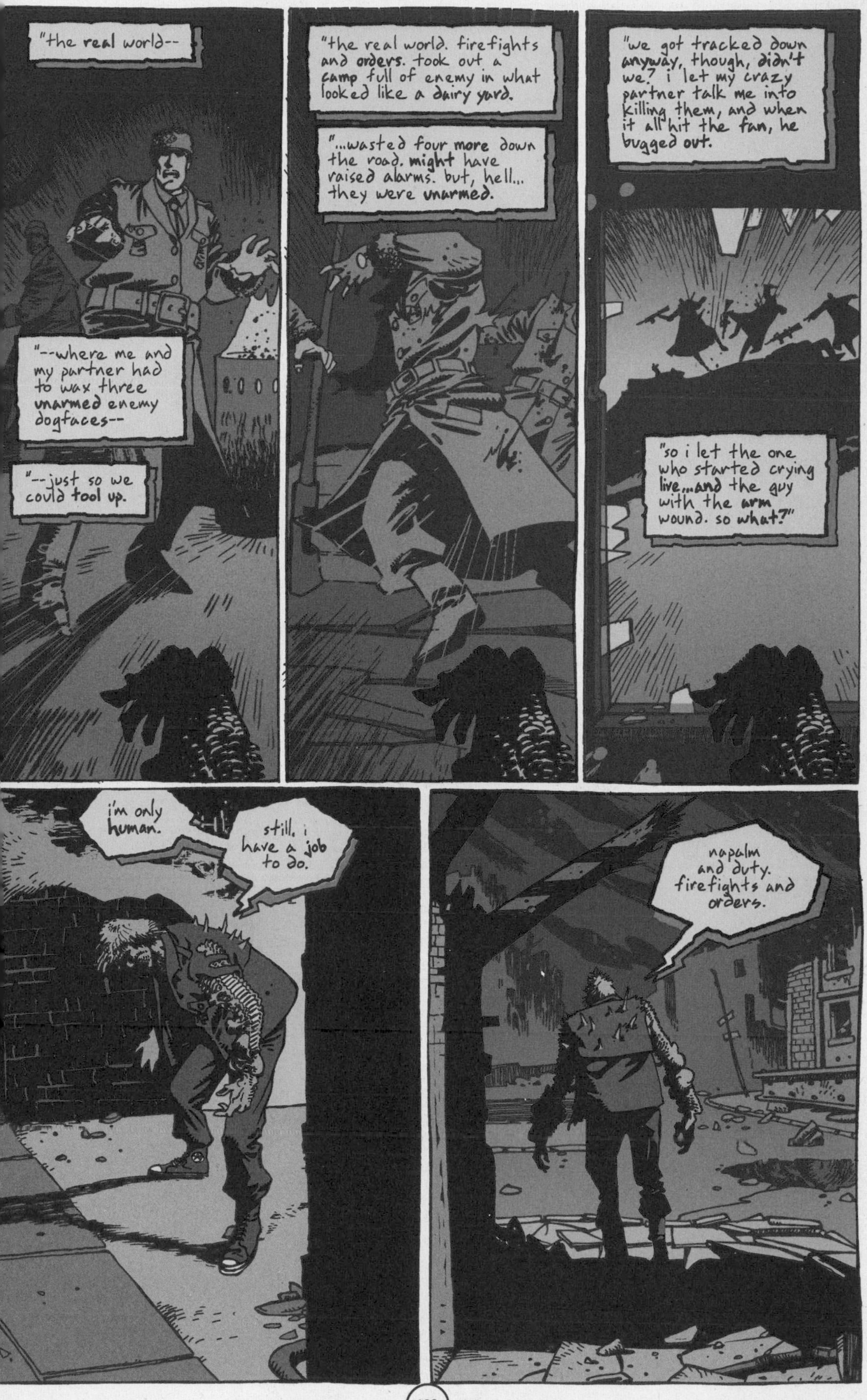
"the real world--
"--where me and my partner had to wax three unarmed enemy dogfaces--
"--just so we could tool up.
"the real world. firefights and orders. took out a camp full of enemy in what looked like a dairy yard.
"...wasted four more down the road. might have raised alarms. but, hell... they were unarmed.
"we got tracked down anyway, though, didn't we? i let my crazy partner talk me into killing them, and when it all hit the fan, he bugged out.
"so i let the one who started crying live...and the guy with the arm wound. so what?"
i'm only human.
still, i have a job to do.
napalm and duty. firefights and orders.

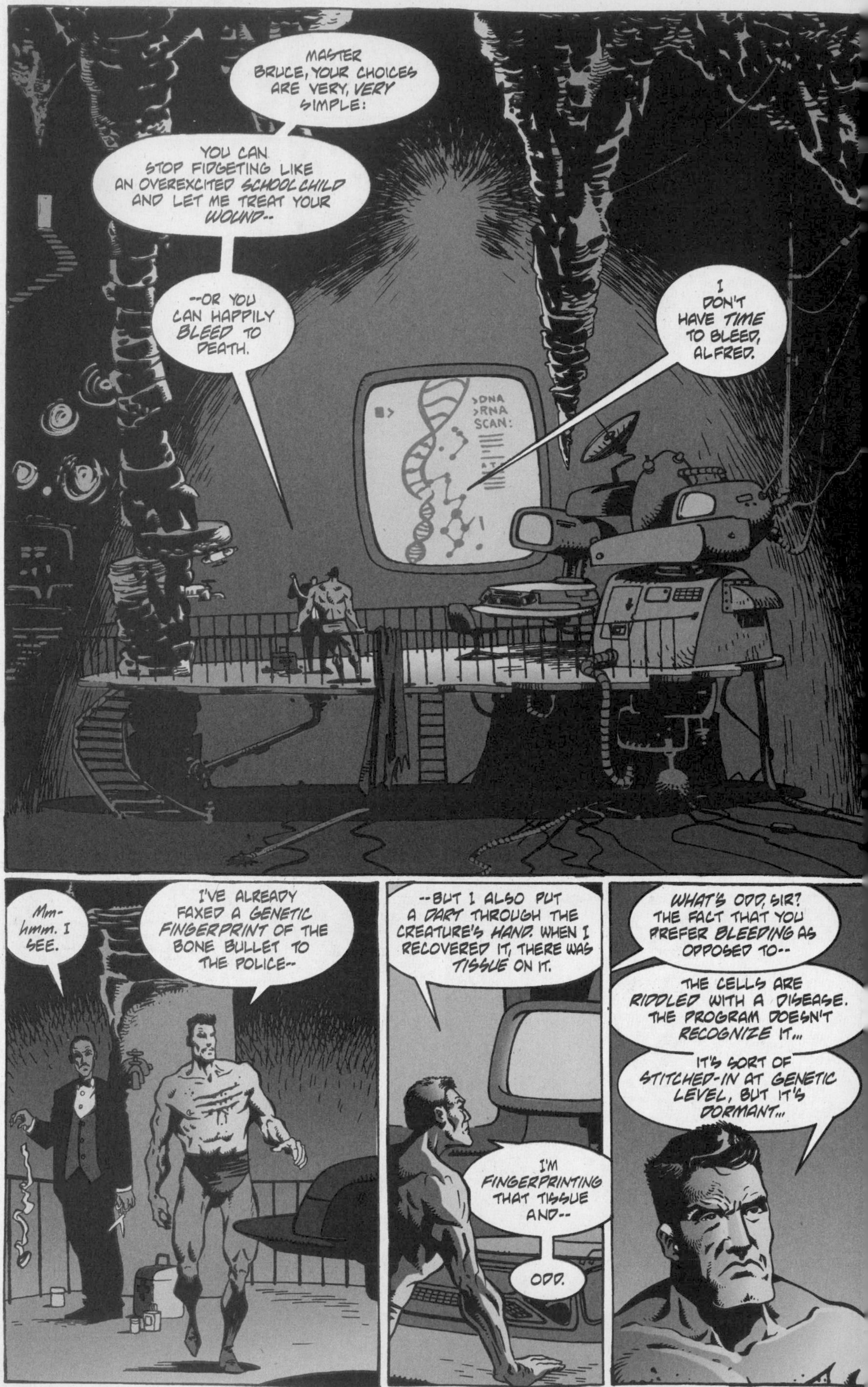
MASTER BRUCE, YOUR CHOICES ARE VERY, VERY SIMPLE:
YOU CAN STOP FIDGETING LIKE AN OVEREXCITED SCHOOLCHILD AND LET ME TREAT YOUR WOUND--
--OR YOU CAN HAPPILY BLEED TO DEATH.
I DON'T HAVE TIME TO BLEED, ALFRED.
>DNA
>RNA
SCAN:
I'VE ALREADY FAXED A GENETIC FINGERPRINT OF THE BONE BULLET TO THE POLICE--
Mm-hmm. I SEE.
--BUT I ALSO PUT A DART THROUGH THE CREATURE'S HAND. WHEN I RECOVERED IT, THERE WAS TISSUE ON IT.
I'M FINGERPRINTING THAT TISSUE AND--
ODD.
WHAT'S ODD, SIR? THE FACT THAT YOU PREFER BLEEDING AS OPPOSED TO--
THE CELLS ARE RIDDLED WITH A DISEASE. THE PROGRAM DOESN'T RECOGNIZE IT...
IT'S SORT OF STITCHED-IN AT GENETIC LEVEL, BUT IT'S DORMANT...

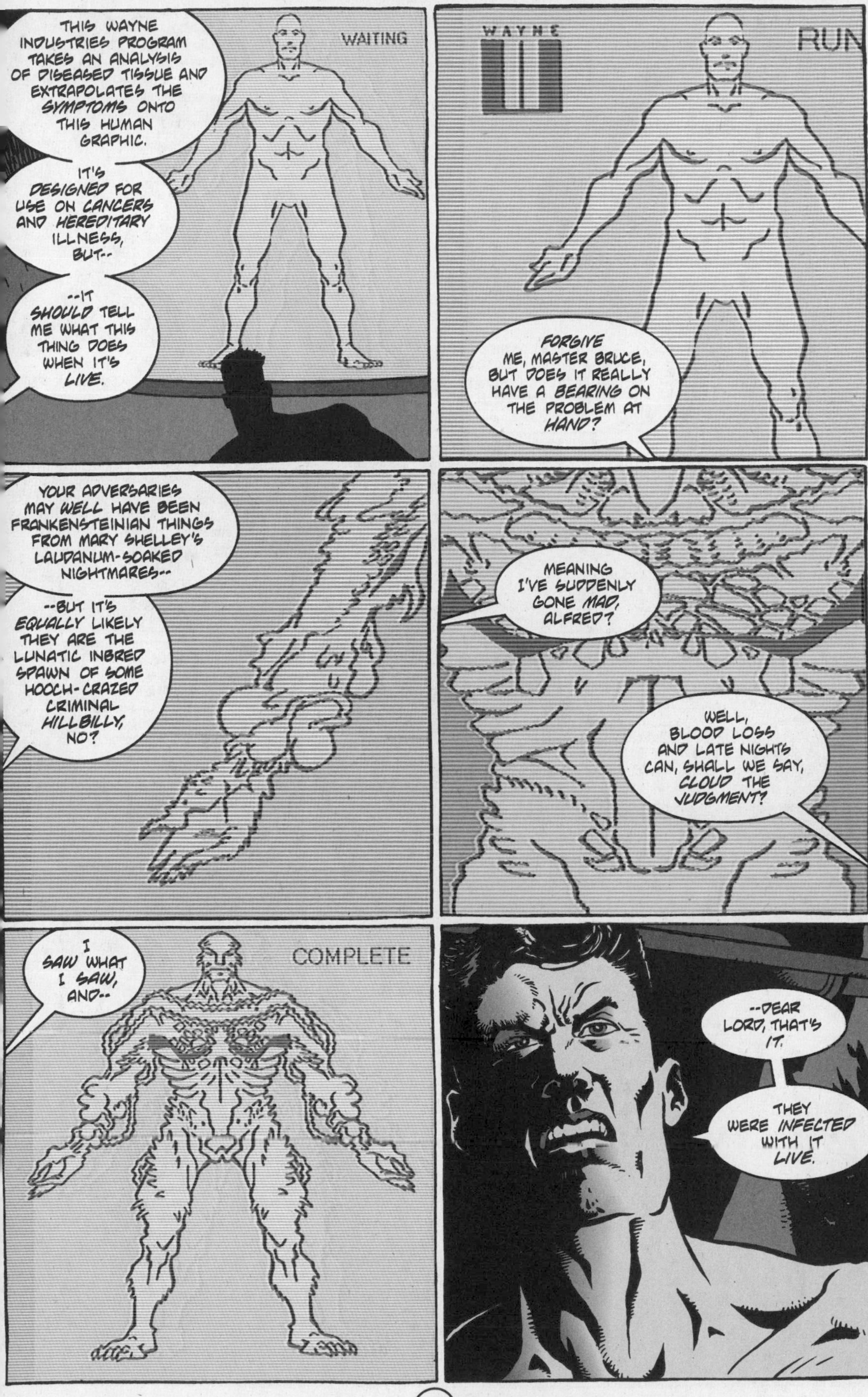
THIS WAYNE INDUSTRIES PROGRAM TAKES AN ANALYSIS OF DISEASED TISSUE AND EXTRAPOLATES THE SYMPTOMS ONTO THIS HUMAN GRAPHIC.
WAITING
IT'S DESIGNED FOR USE ON CANCERS AND HEREDITARY ILLNESS, BUT--
--IT SHOULD TELL ME WHAT THIS THING DOES WHEN IT'S LIVE.
WAYNE
RUN
FORGIVE ME, MASTER BRUCE, BUT DOES IT REALLY HAVE A BEARING ON THE PROBLEM AT HAND?
YOUR ADVERSARIES MAY WELL HAVE BEEN FRANKENSTEINIAN THINGS FROM MARY SHELLEY'S LAUDANUM-SOAKED NIGHTMARES--
--BUT IT'S EQUALLY LIKELY THEY ARE THE LUNATIC INBRED SPAWN OF SOME HOOCH-CRAZED CRIMINAL HILLBILLY, NO?
MEANING I'VE SUDDENLY GONE MAD, ALFRED?
WELL, BLOOD LOSS AND LATE NIGHTS CAN, SHALL WE SAY, CLOUD THE JUDGMENT?
I SAW WHAT I SAW, AND--
COMPLETE
--DEAR LORD, THAT'S IT.
THEY WERE INFECTED WITH IT LIVE.

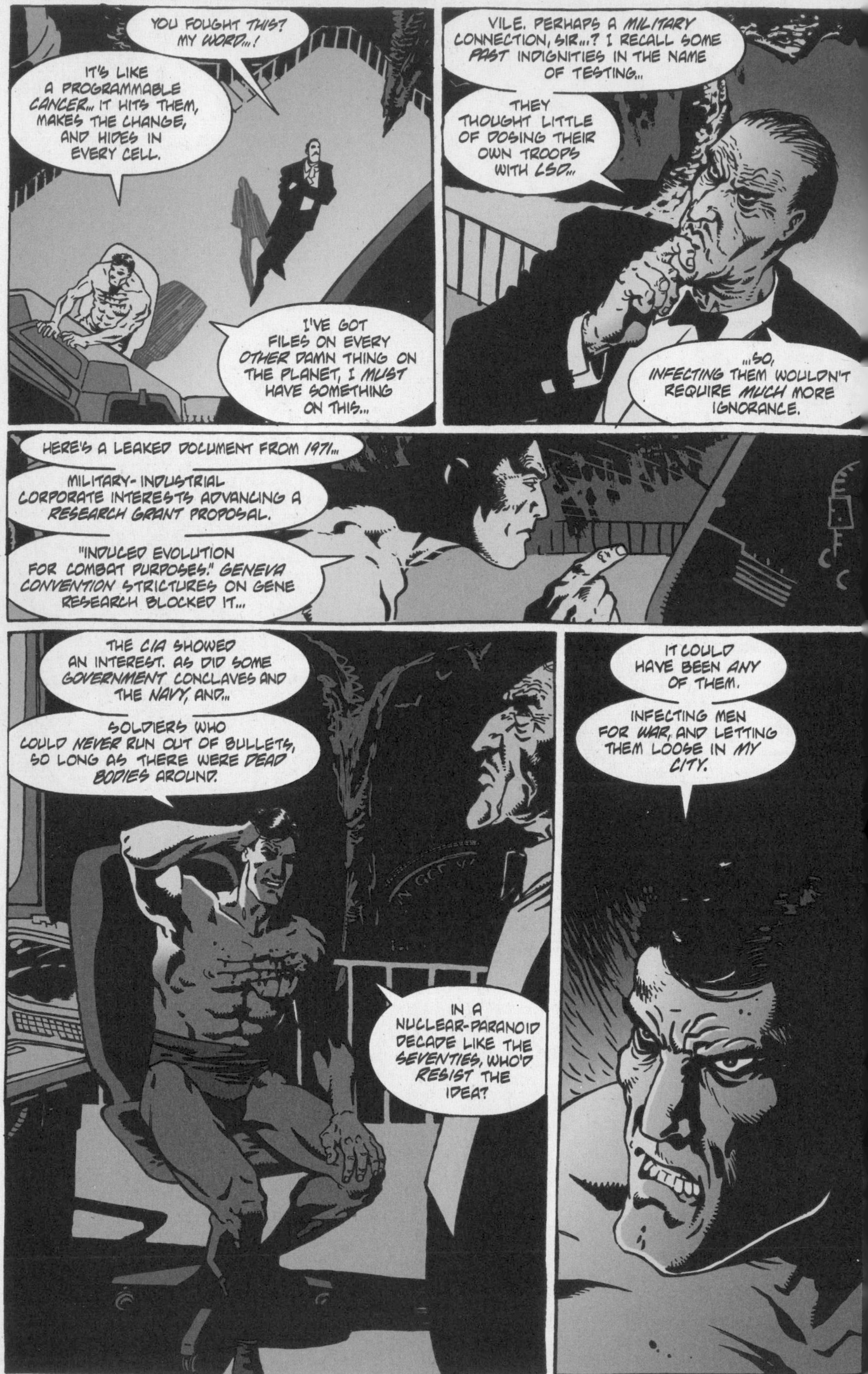
IT'S LIKE A PROGRAMMABLE CANCER... IT HITS THEM, MAKES THE CHANGE, AND HIDES IN EVERY CELL.
YOU FOUGHT THIS? MY WORD...!
I'VE GOT FILES ON EVERY OTHER DAMN THING ON THE PLANET, I MUST HAVE SOMETHING ON THIS...
VILE. PERHAPS A MILITARY CONNECTION, SIR...? I RECALL SOME PAST INDIGNITIES IN THE NAME OF TESTING...
THEY THOUGHT LITTLE OF DOSING THEIR OWN TROOPS WITH LSD...
...SO, INFECTING THEM WOULDN'T REQUIRE MUCH MORE IGNORANCE.
HERE'S A LEAKED DOCUMENT FROM 1971...
MILITARY- INDUSTRIAL CORPORATE INTERESTS ADVANCING A RESEARCH GRANT PROPOSAL.
"INDUCED EVOLUTION FOR COMBAT PURPOSES." GENEVA CONVENTION STRICTURES ON GENE RESEARCH BLOCKED IT...
THE CIA SHOWED AN INTEREST. AS DID SOME GOVERNMENT CONCLAVES AND THE NAVY, AND...
SOLDIERS WHO COULD NEVER RUN OUT OF BULLETS, SO LONG AS THERE WERE DEAD BODIES AROUND.
IN A NUCLEAR-PARANOID DECADE LIKE THE SEVENTIES, WHO'D RESIST THE IDEA?
IT COULD HAVE BEEN ANY OF THEM.
INFECTING MEN FOR WAR, AND LETTING THEM LOOSE IN MY CITY.

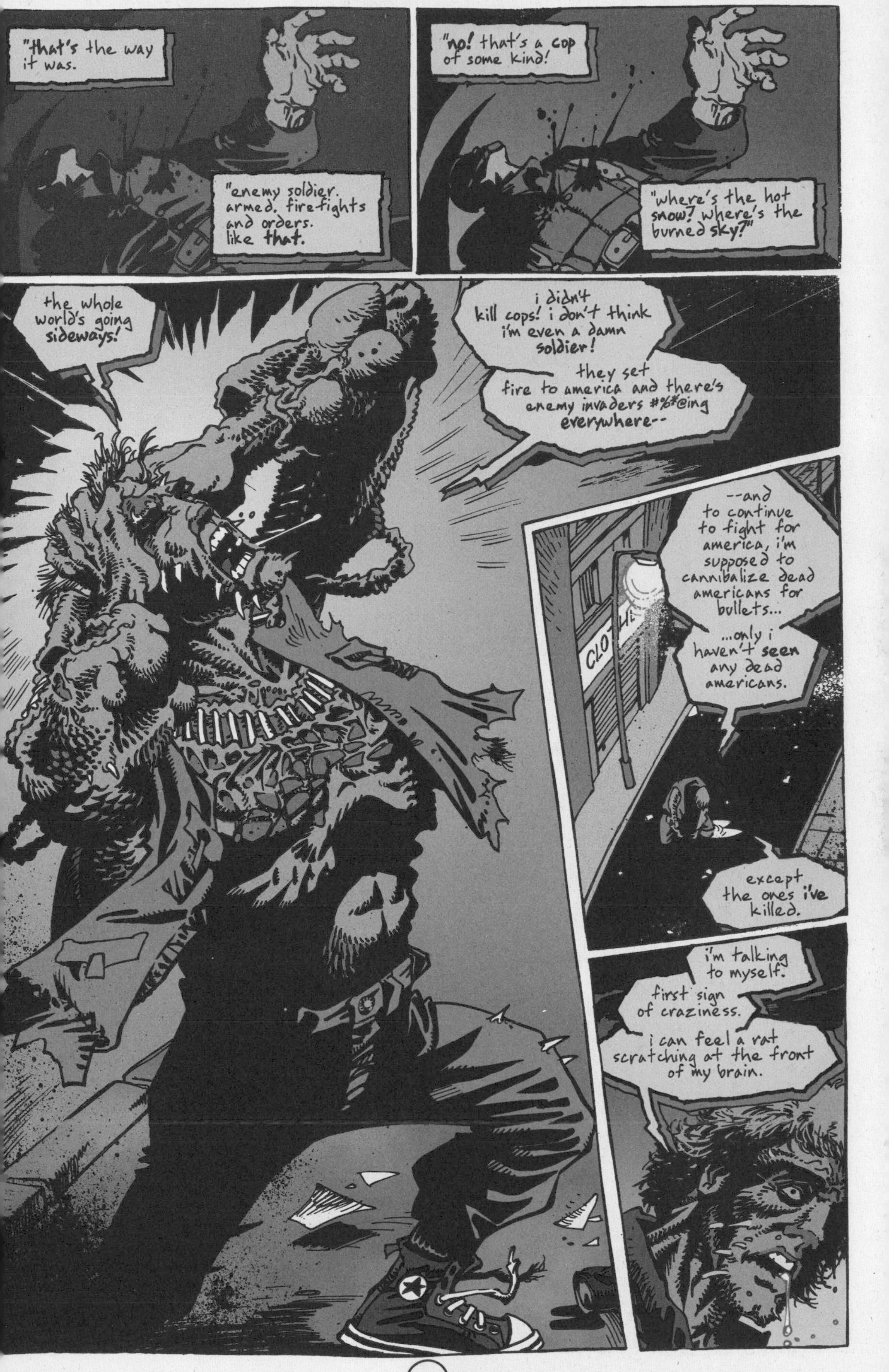
"that's the way it was.
"enemy soldier. armed. firefights and orders. like that.
"no! that's a cop of some kind!
"where's the hot snow? where's the burned sky?"
the whole world's going sideways!
i didn't kill cops! i don't think i'm even a damn soldier!
they set fire to america and there's enemy invaders #%#@ing everywhere--
--and to continue to fight for america, i'm supposed to cannibalize dead americans for bullets...
...only i haven't seen any dead americans.
except the ones i've killed.
i'm talking to myself.
first sign of craziness.
i can feel a rat scratching at the front of my brain.

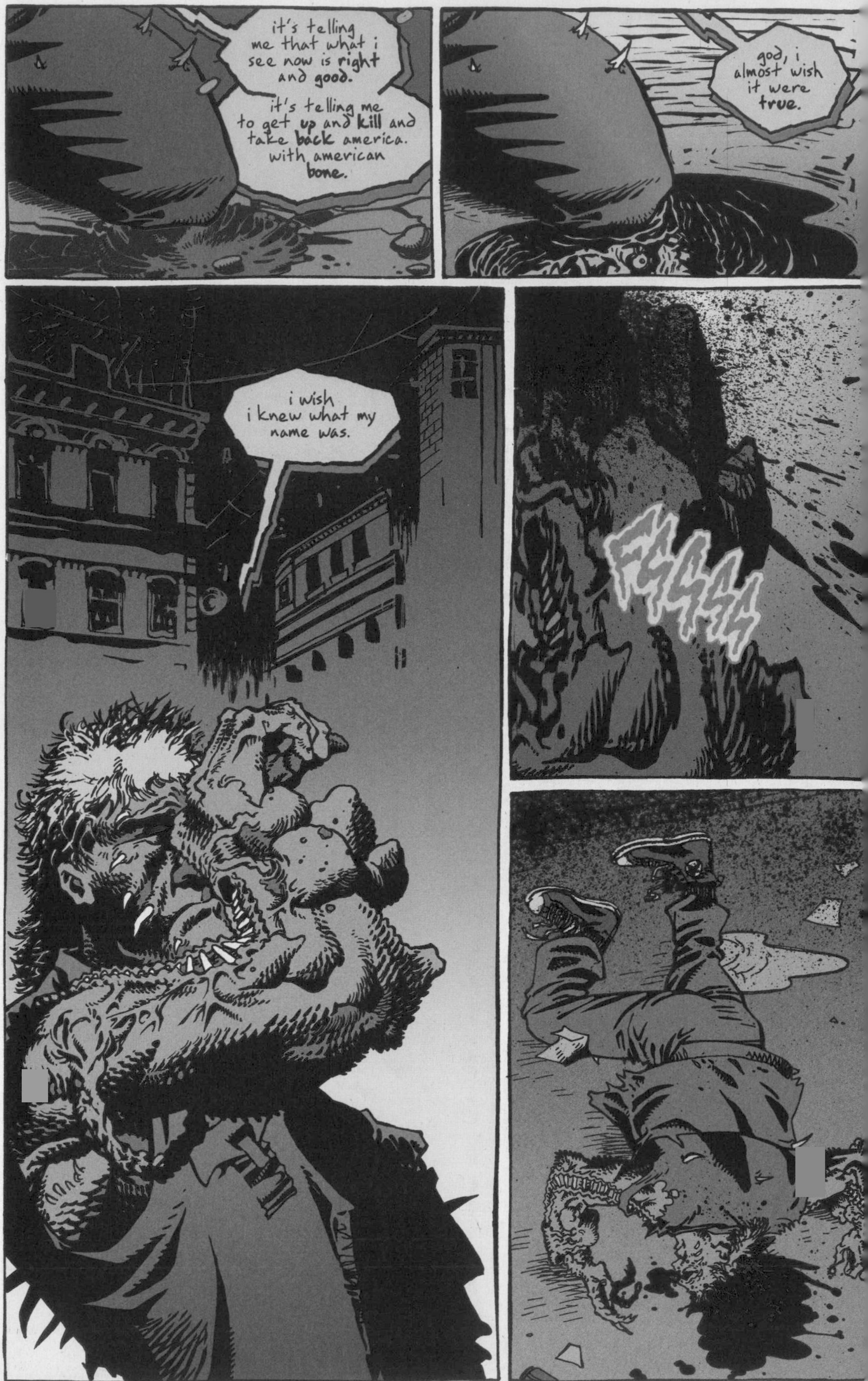
it's telling me that what i see now is right and good.
it's telling me to get up and kill and take back america. with american bone.
god, i almost wish it were true.
i wish i knew what my name was.
FSSSS

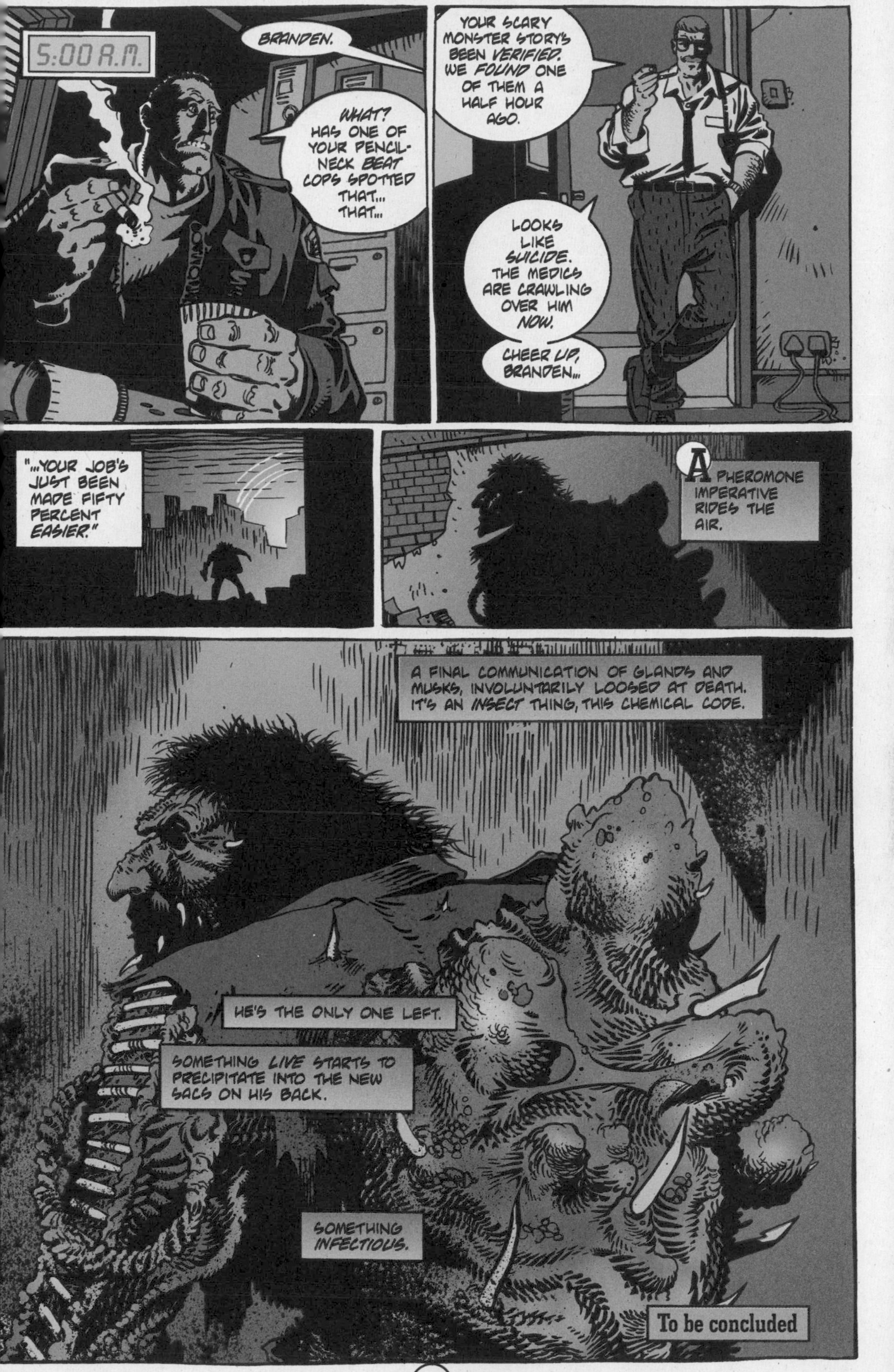
5:00 A.M.
BRANDEN.
WHAT? HAS ONE OF YOUR PENCIL-NECK BEAT COPS SPOTTED THAT... THAT...
YOUR SCARY MONSTER STORY'S BEEN VERIFIED. WE FOUND ONE OF THEM A HALF HOUR AGO.
LOOKS LIKE SUICIDE. THE MEDICS ARE CRAWLING OVER HIM NOW.
CHEER UP, BRANDEN...
"...YOUR JOB'S JUST BEEN MADE FIFTY PERCENT EASIER."
A PHEROMONE IMPERATIVE RIDES THE AIR.
A FINAL COMMUNICATION OF GLANDS AND MUSKS, INVOLUNTARILY LOOSED AT DEATH. IT'S AN INSECT THING, THIS CHEMICAL CODE.
HE'S THE ONLY ONE LEFT.
SOMETHING LIVE STARTS TO PRECIPITATE INTO THE NEW SACS ON HIS BACK.
SOMETHING INFECTIOUS.
To be concluded

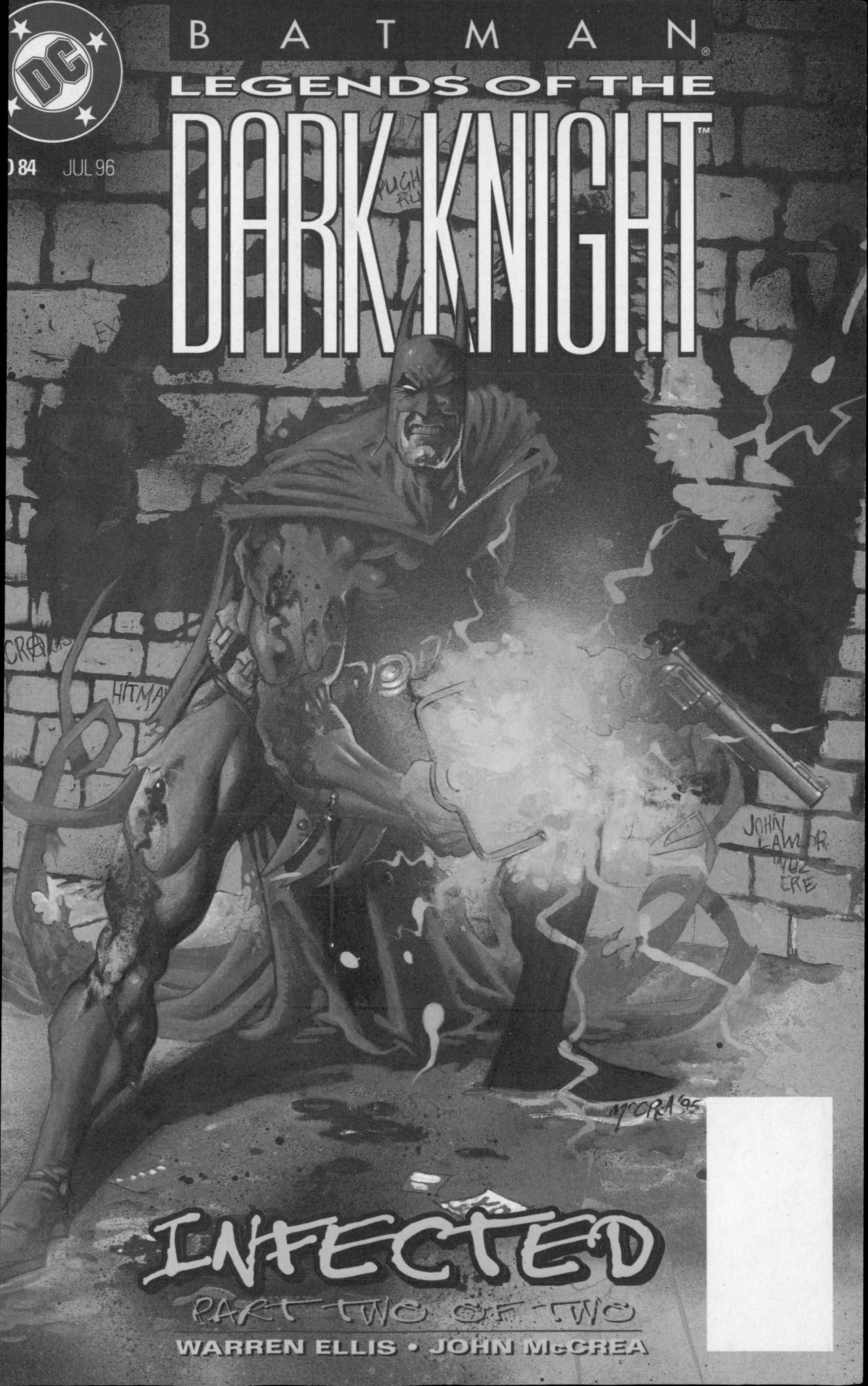
BATMAN
LEGENDS OF THE
DARK KNIGHT
84 JUL 96
INFECTED
PART TWO OF TWO
WARREN ELLIS • JOHN McCREA

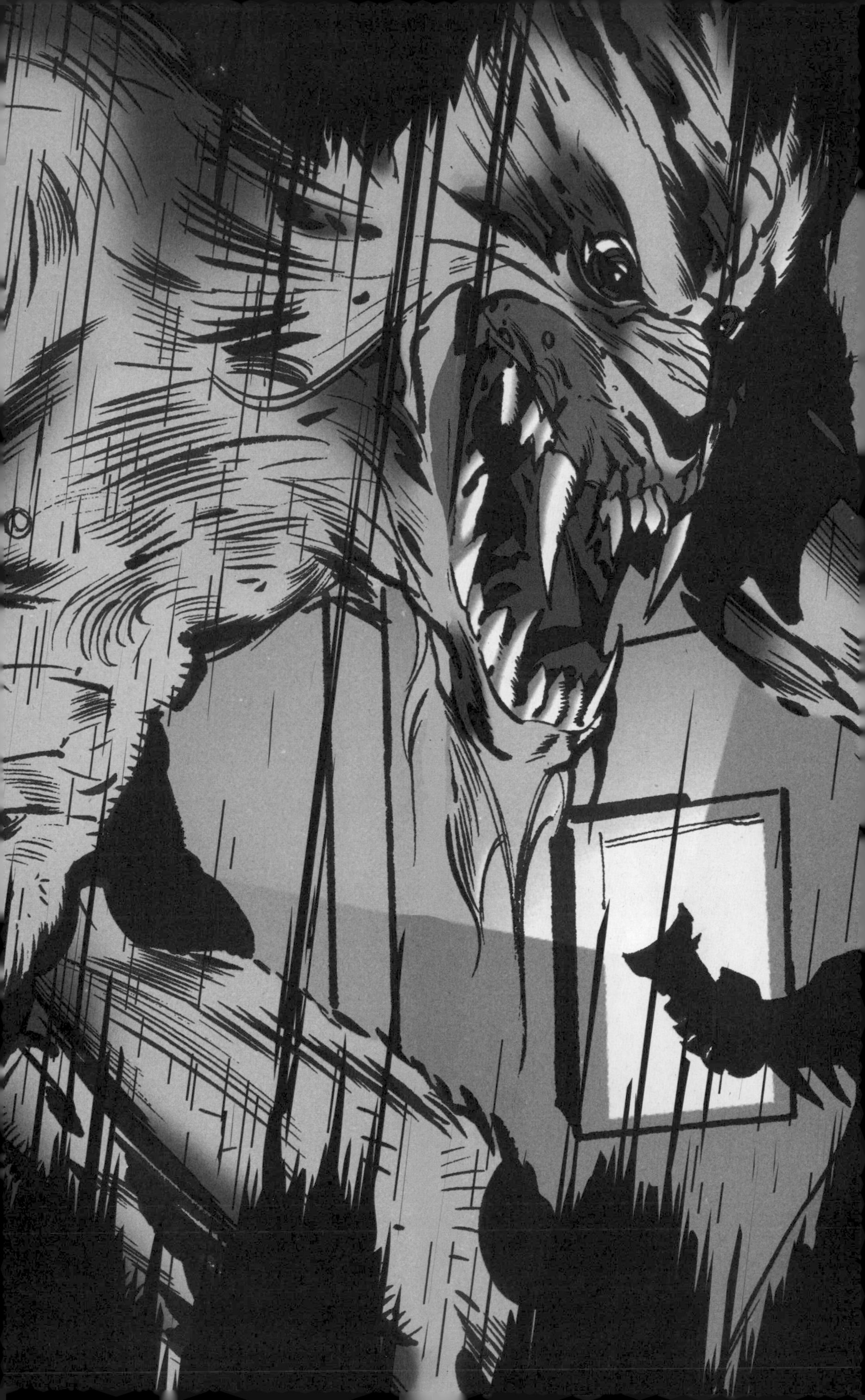

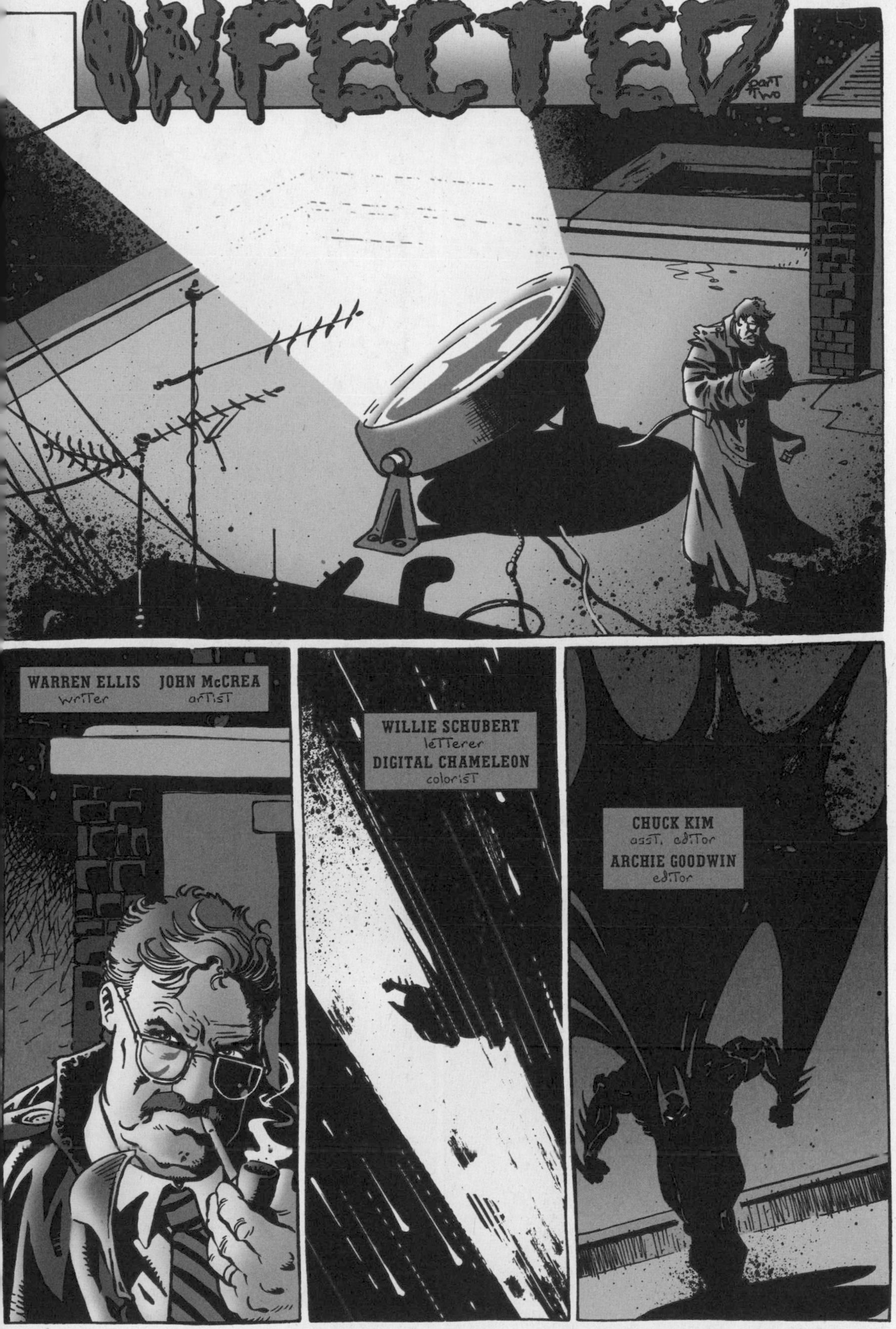
INFECTED
part two
WARREN ELLIS writer
JOHN McCREA artist
WILLIE SCHUBERT letterer
DIGITAL CHAMELEON colorist
CHUCK KIM asst. editor
ARCHIE GOODWIN editor

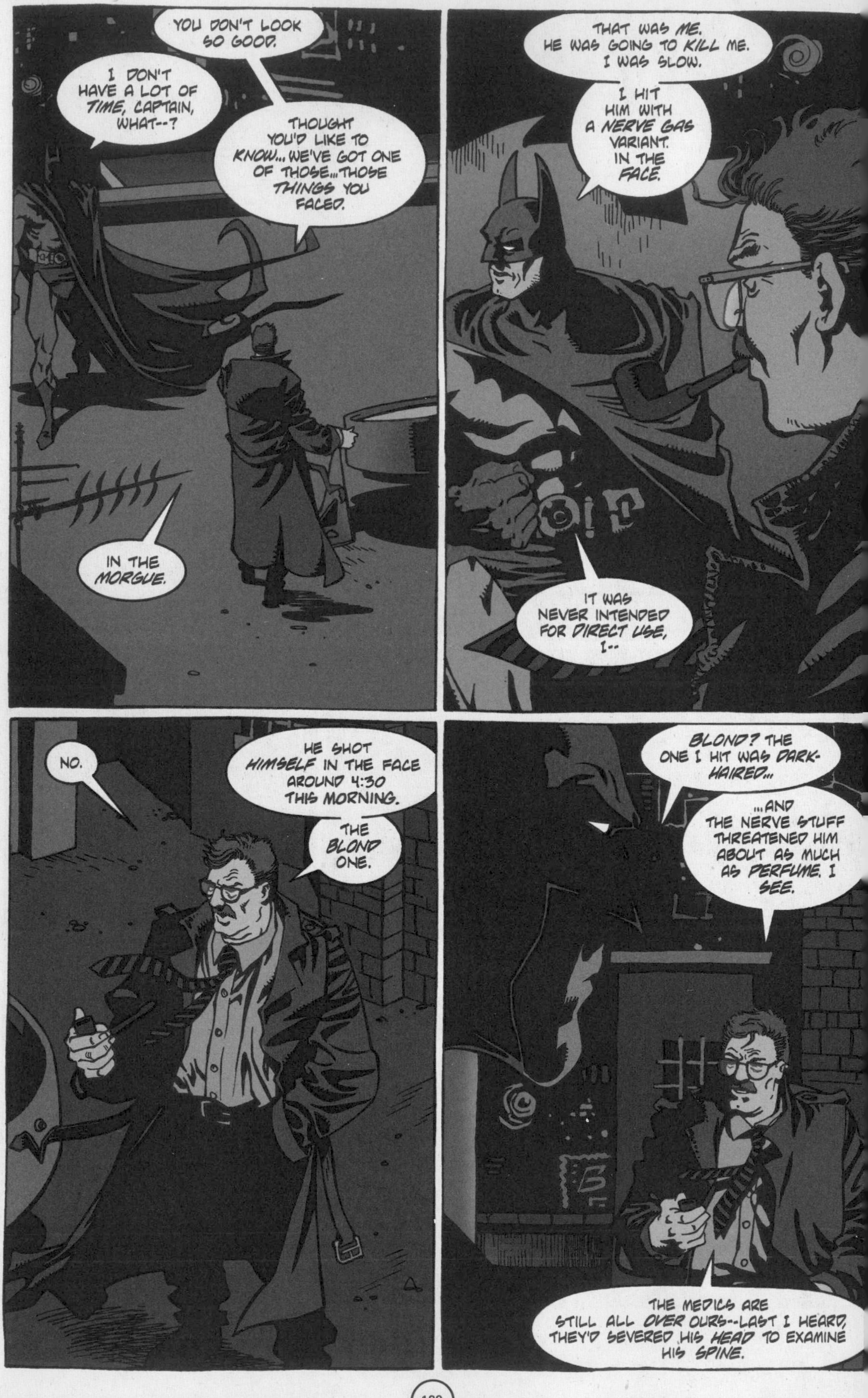
YOU DON'T LOOK SO GOOD.
I DON'T HAVE A LOT OF TIME, CAPTAIN, WHAT--?
THOUGHT YOU'D LIKE TO KNOW... WE'VE GOT ONE OF THOSE... THOSE THINGS YOU FACED.
IN THE MORGUE.
THAT WAS ME. HE WAS GOING TO KILL ME. I WAS SLOW.
I HIT HIM WITH A NERVE GAS VARIANT. IN THE FACE.
IT WAS NEVER INTENDED FOR DIRECT USE, I--
NO.
HE SHOT HIMSELF IN THE FACE AROUND 4:30 THIS MORNING.
THE BLOND ONE.
BLOND? THE ONE I HIT WAS DARK-HAIRED...
...AND THE NERVE STUFF THREATENED HIM ABOUT AS MUCH AS PERFUME. I SEE.
THE MEDICS ARE STILL ALL OVER OURS--LAST I HEARD, THEY'D SEVERED HIS HEAD TO EXAMINE HIS SPINE.

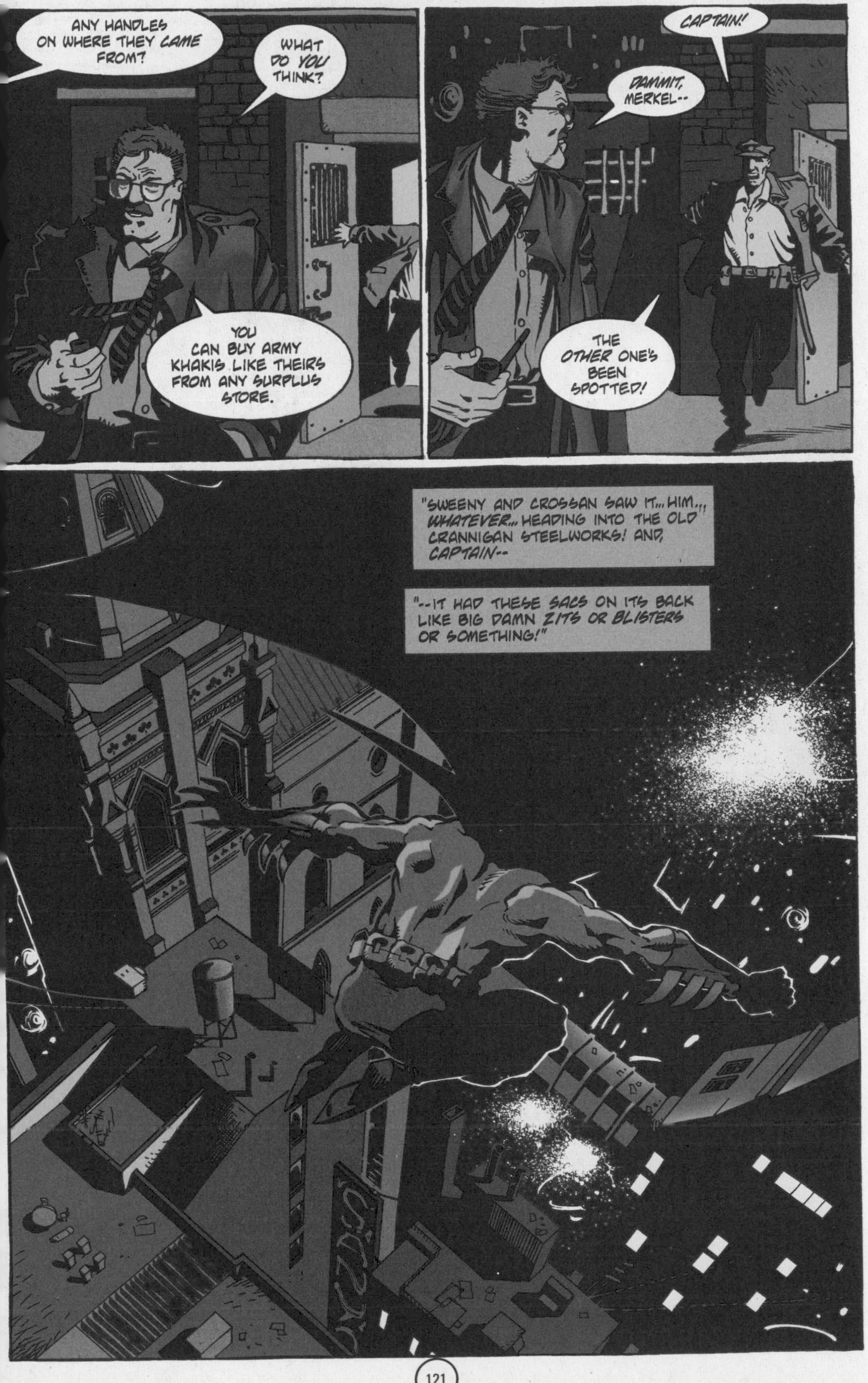
ANY HANDLES ON WHERE THEY CAME FROM?
WHAT DO YOU THINK?
YOU CAN BUY ARMY KHAKIS LIKE THEIRS FROM ANY SURPLUS STORE.
CAPTAIN!
DAMMIT, MERKEL--
THE OTHER ONE'S BEEN SPOTTED!
"SWEENY AND CROSSAN SAW IT... HIM... WHATEVER... HEADING INTO THE OLD CRANNIGAN STEELWORKS! AND, CAPTAIN--
"--IT HAD THESE SACS ON ITS BACK LIKE BIG DAMN ZITS OR BLISTERS OR SOMETHING!"

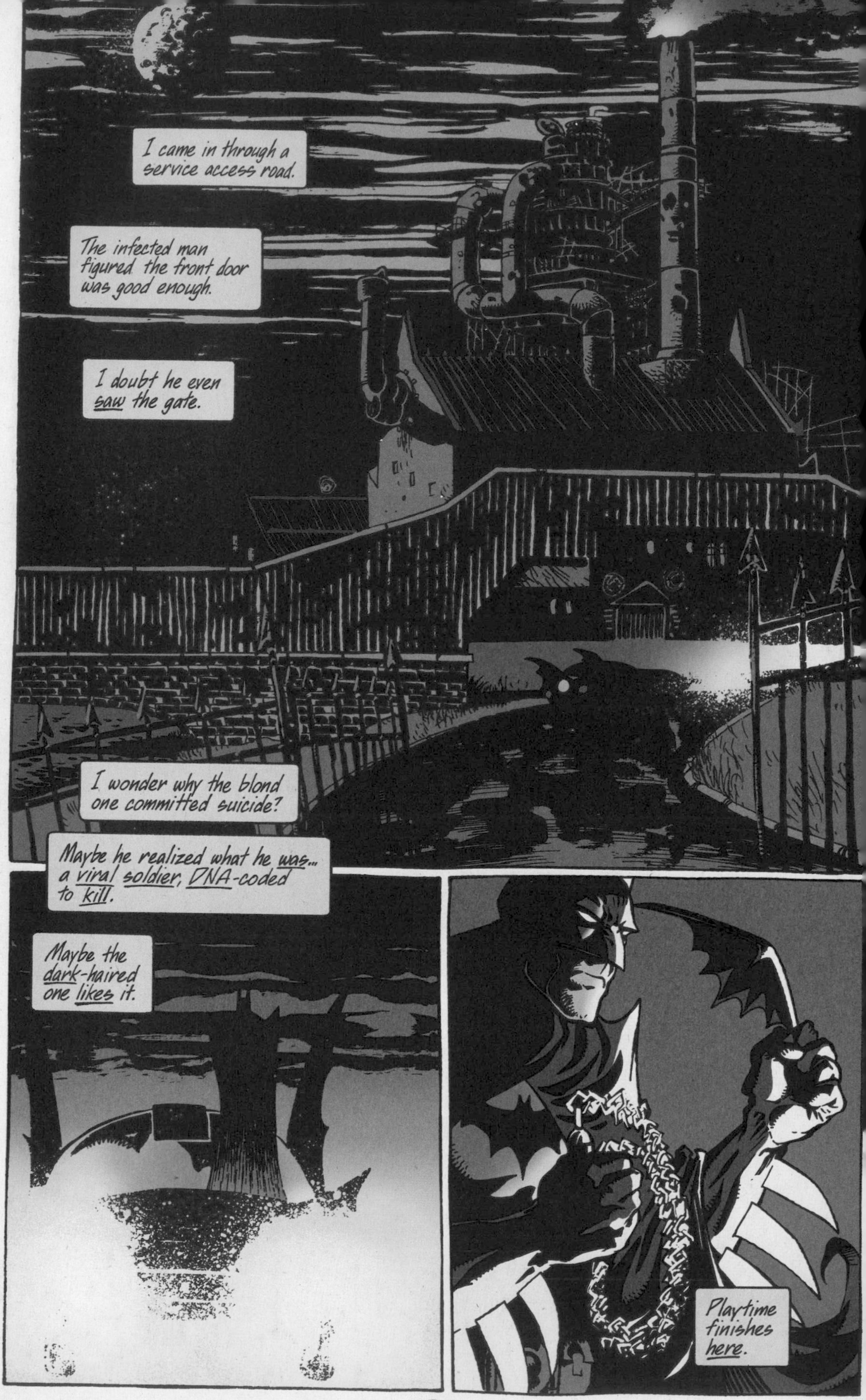
I came in through a service access road.
The infected man figured the front door was good enough.
I doubt he even saw the gate.
I wonder why the blond one committed suicide?
Maybe he realized what he was... a viral soldier, DNA-coded to kill.
Maybe the dark-haired one likes it.
Playtime finishes here.

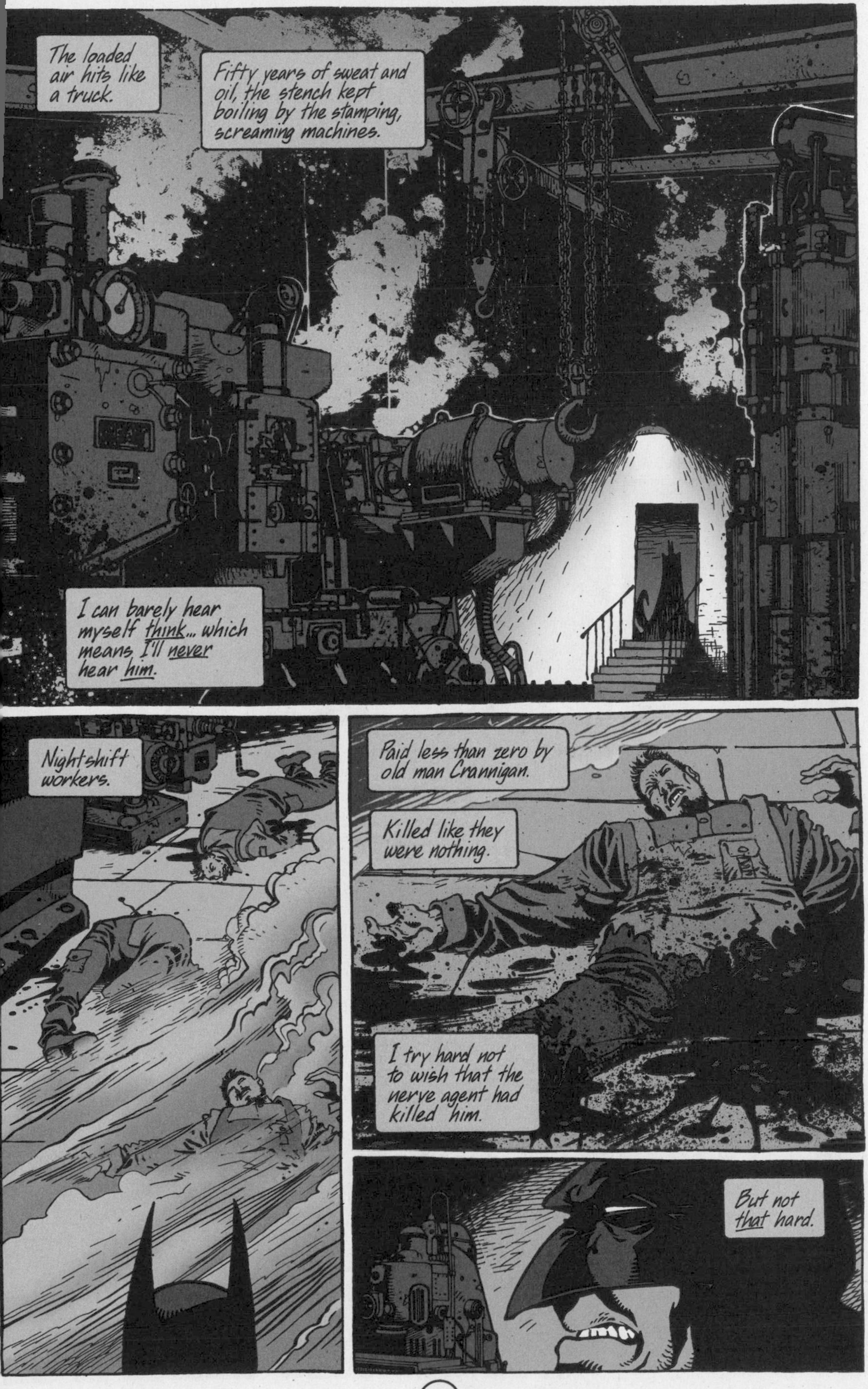
The loaded air hits like a truck.
Fifty years of sweat and oil, the stench kept boiling by the stamping, screaming machines.
I can barely hear myself think... which means I'll never hear him.
Nightshift workers.
Paid less than zero by old man Crannigan.
Killed like they were nothing.
I try hard not to wish that the nerve agent had killed him.
But not that hard.

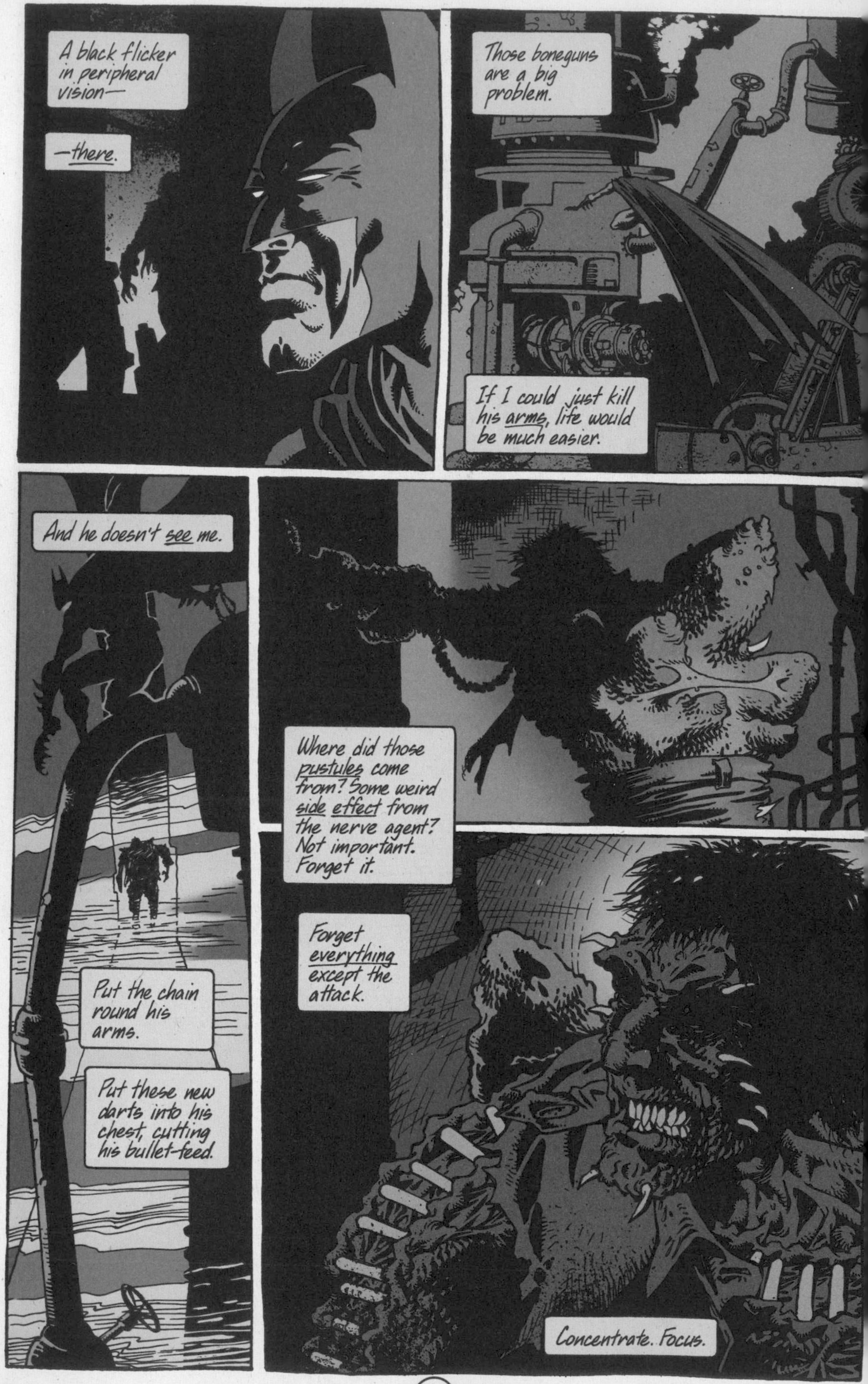
A black flicker in peripheral vision—
—there.
Those boneguns are a big problem.
If I could just kill his arms, life would be much easier.
And he doesn't see me.
Where did those pustules come from? Some weird side effect from the nerve agent? Not important. Forget it.
Forget everything except the attack.
Put the chain round his arms.
Put these new darts into his chest, cutting his bullet-feed.
Concentrate. Focus.

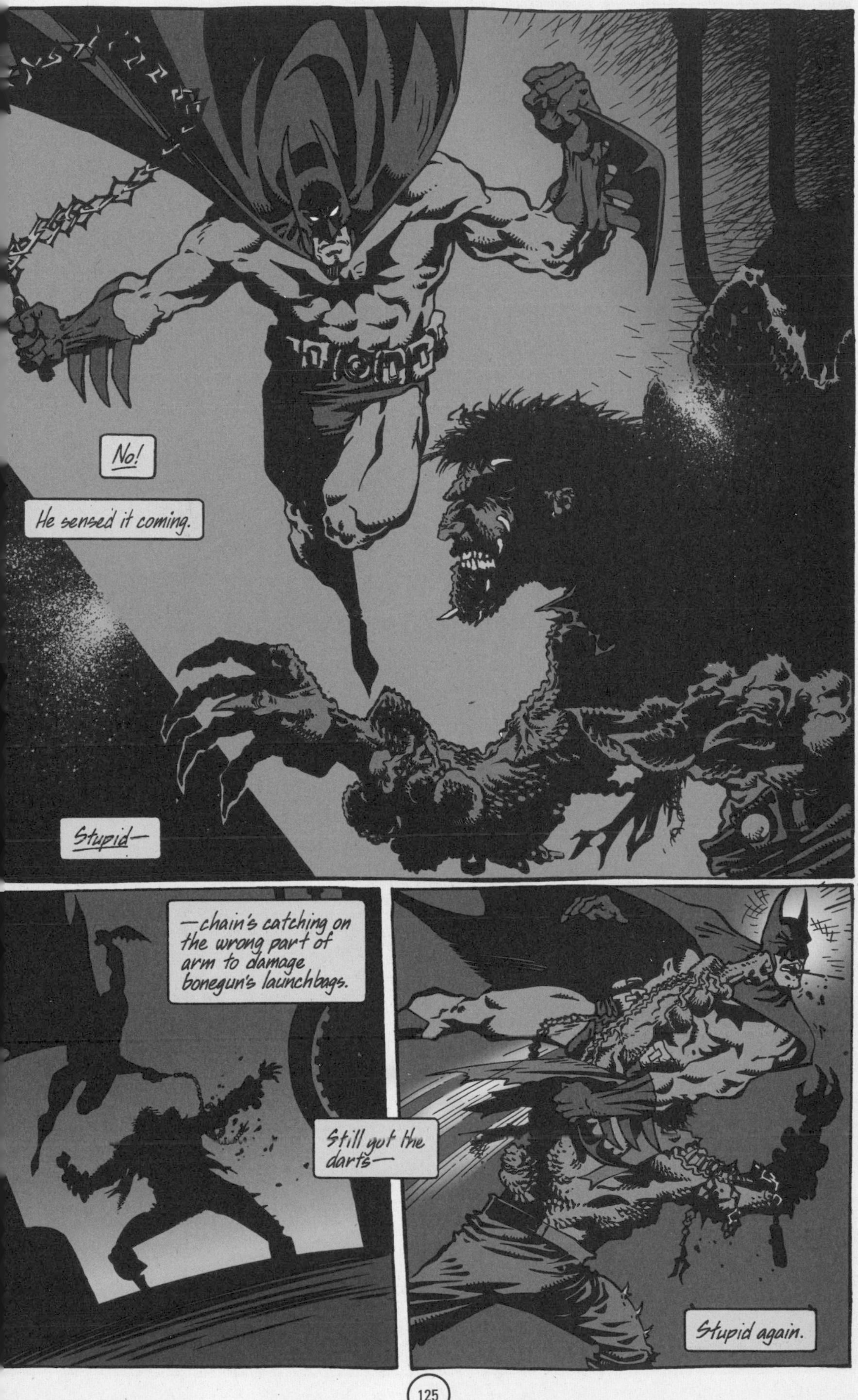
No!
He sensed it coming.
Stupid—
—chain's catching on the wrong part of arm to damage bonegun's launchbags.
Still got the darts—
Stupid again.

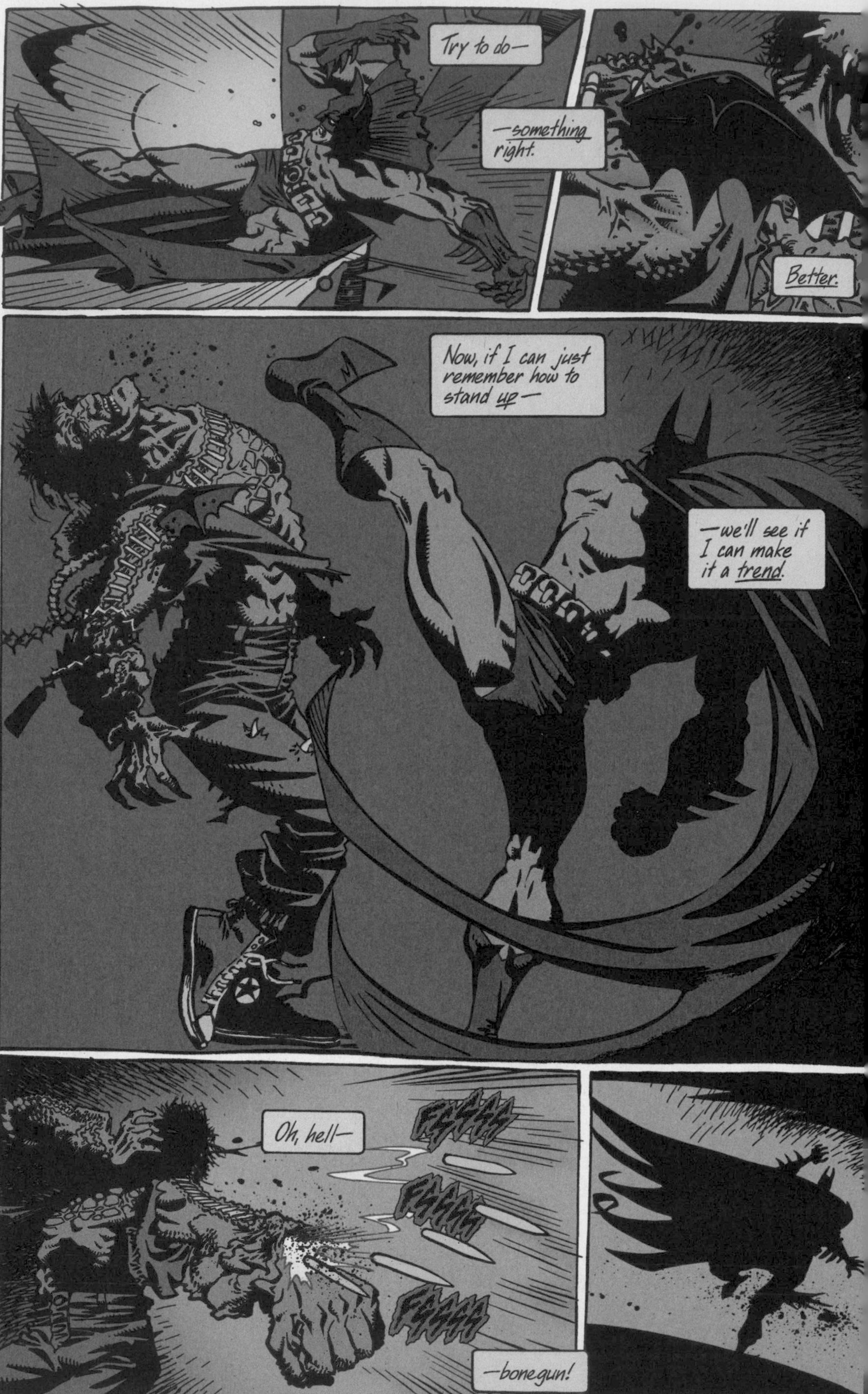

Try to do—
—something right.
Better.
Now, if I can just remember how to stand up—
—we'll see if I can make it a trend.
Oh, hell—
FSSSS
FSSSS
FSSSS
—bonegun!

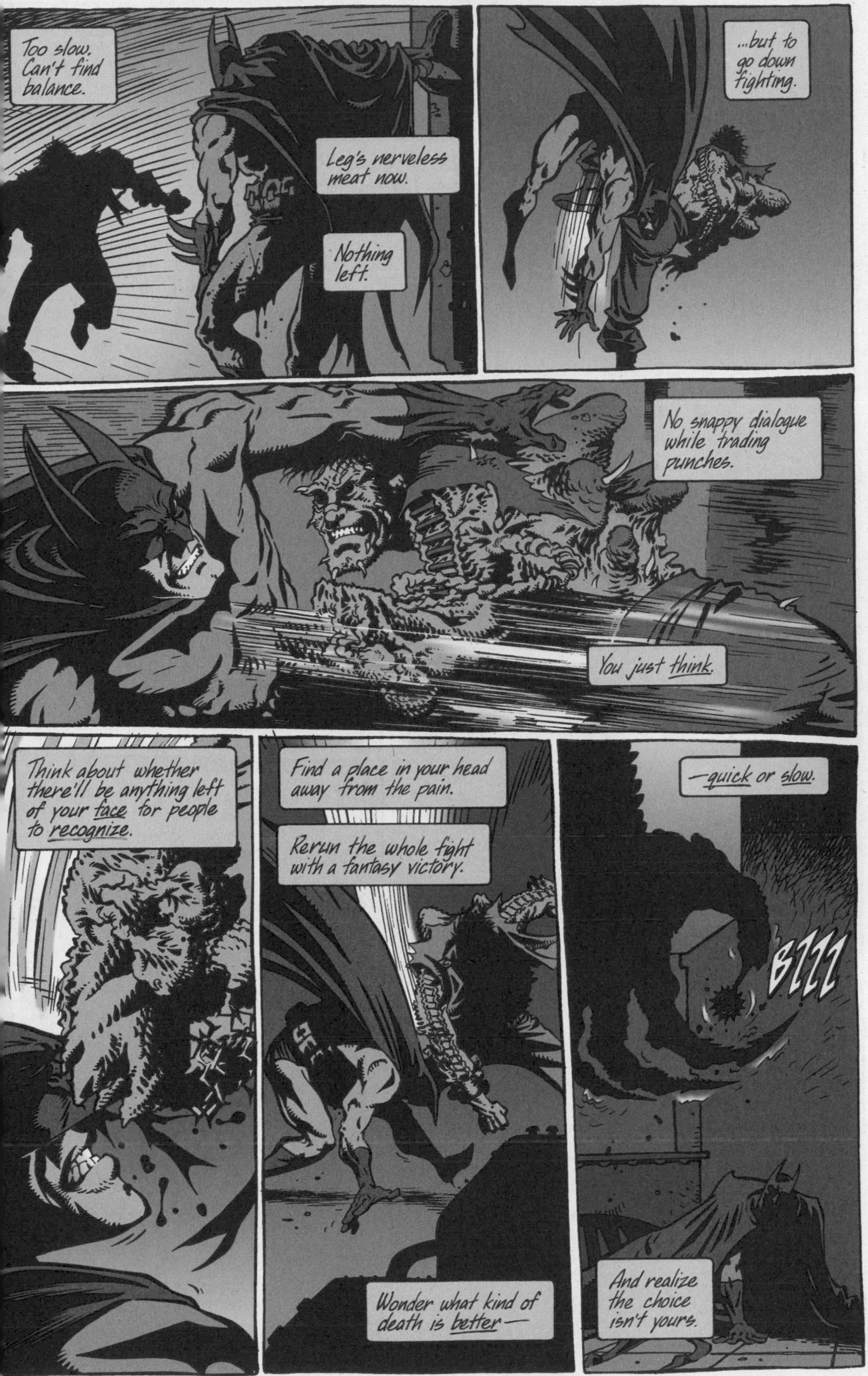
Too slow. Can't find balance.
Leg's nerveless meat now.
Nothing left.
...but to go down fighting.
No snappy dialogue while trading punches.
You just think.
Think about whether there'll be anything left of your face for people to recognize.
Find a place in your head away from the pain.
Rerun the whole fight with a fantasy victory.
Wonder what kind of death is better—
—quick or slow.
BZZZ
And realize the choice isn't yours.

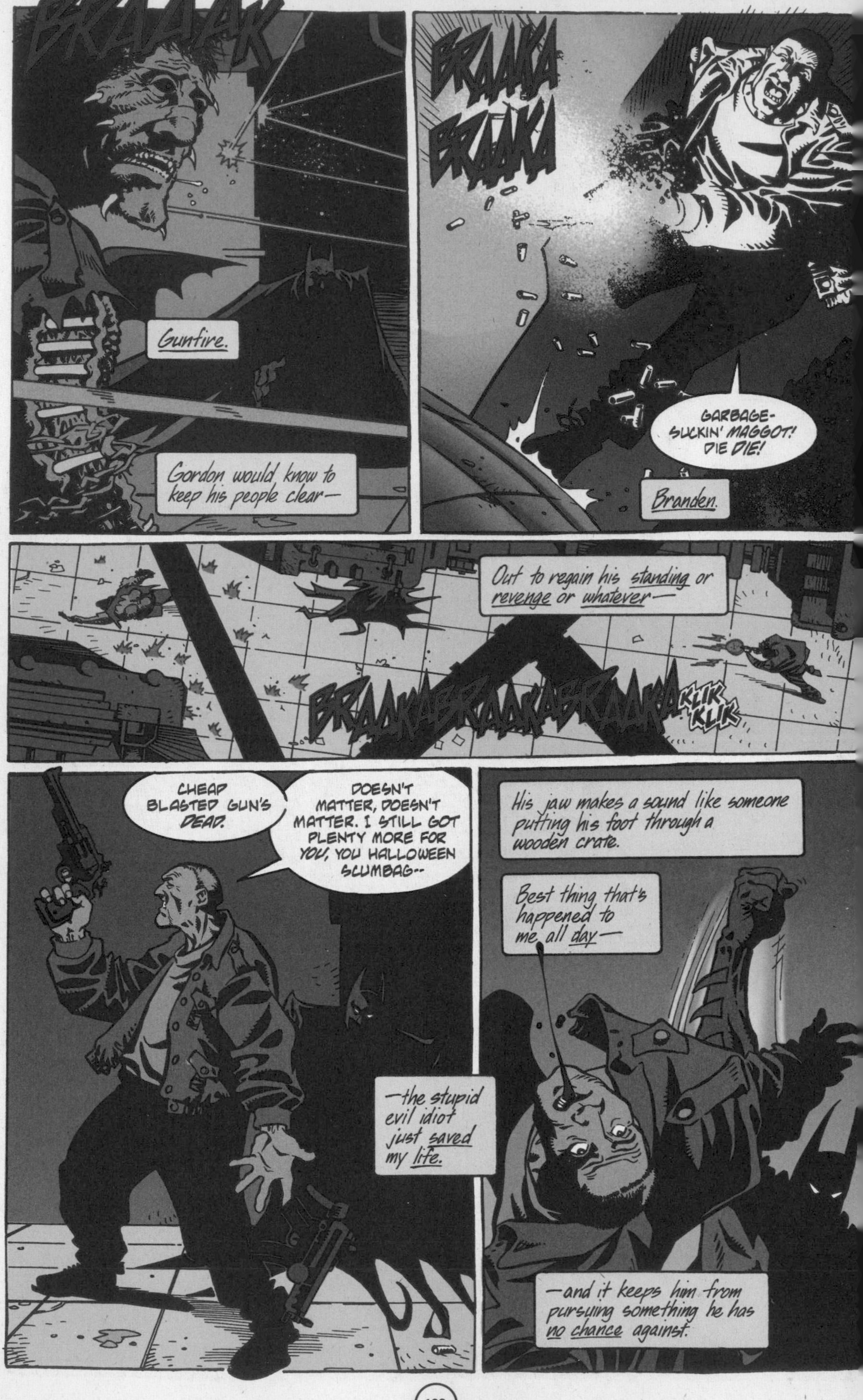

BRAAAK
Gunfire.
Gordon would know to keep his people clear—
BRAAKA BRAAKA
GARBAGE-SUCKIN' MAGGOT! DIE DIE!
Branden.
Out to regain his standing or revenge or whatever—
BRAAKABRAAKABRAAKA
KLIK KLIK
CHEAP BLASTED GUN'S DEAD.
DOESN'T MATTER, DOESN'T MATTER. I STILL GOT PLENTY MORE FOR YOU, YOU HALLOWEEN SCUMBAG--
—the stupid evil idiot just saved my life.
His jaw makes a sound like someone putting his foot through a wooden crate.
Best thing that's happened to me all day—
—and it keeps him from pursuing something he has no chance against.

Branden's surprise fire apparently drove my opponent out of the building.

Why not? He's neither stupid nor *bulletproof*.

And *I* have to stop thinking like he's *human*.

MASTER BRUCE. YOU'RE FADING *AWAY* AGAIN...

SORRY, ALFRED... GO ON...

THE COMPUTER SEARCH PROGRAM YOU INITIATED APPEARS TO HAVE *FOUND* SOMETHING.

A *BULLETIN BOARD* OPERATED BY *FREEDOM OF INFORMATION* ACTIVISTS...

THEY HAVE OBTAINED DOCUMENTS FROM THE SEVENTIES OF AN *ARTIFICIAL DISEASE* NAMED *VARIANT 66.*

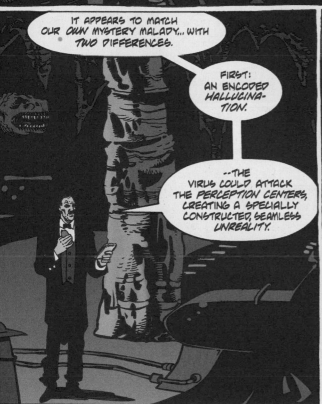

IT APPEARS TO MATCH OUR *OWN* MYSTERY MALADY... WITH *TWO DIFFERENCES.*

FIRST: AN ENCODED *HALLUCINA-TION.*

--THE VIRUS COULD ATTACK THE *PERCEPTION CENTERS,* CREATING A SPECIALLY CONSTRUCTED, *SEAMLESS UNREALITY.*

SECOND: THE VICTIMS WERE TO WORK IN *PAIRS.* IF ONE *DIED*--

--THE OTHER WOULD *REDEVELOP* THE DISEASE IN ITS *CONTAGIOUS* FORM.

OVER A MATTER OF *HOURS* THE SPORES WILL PRECIPITATE INTO *MEMBRANOUS SACS*--

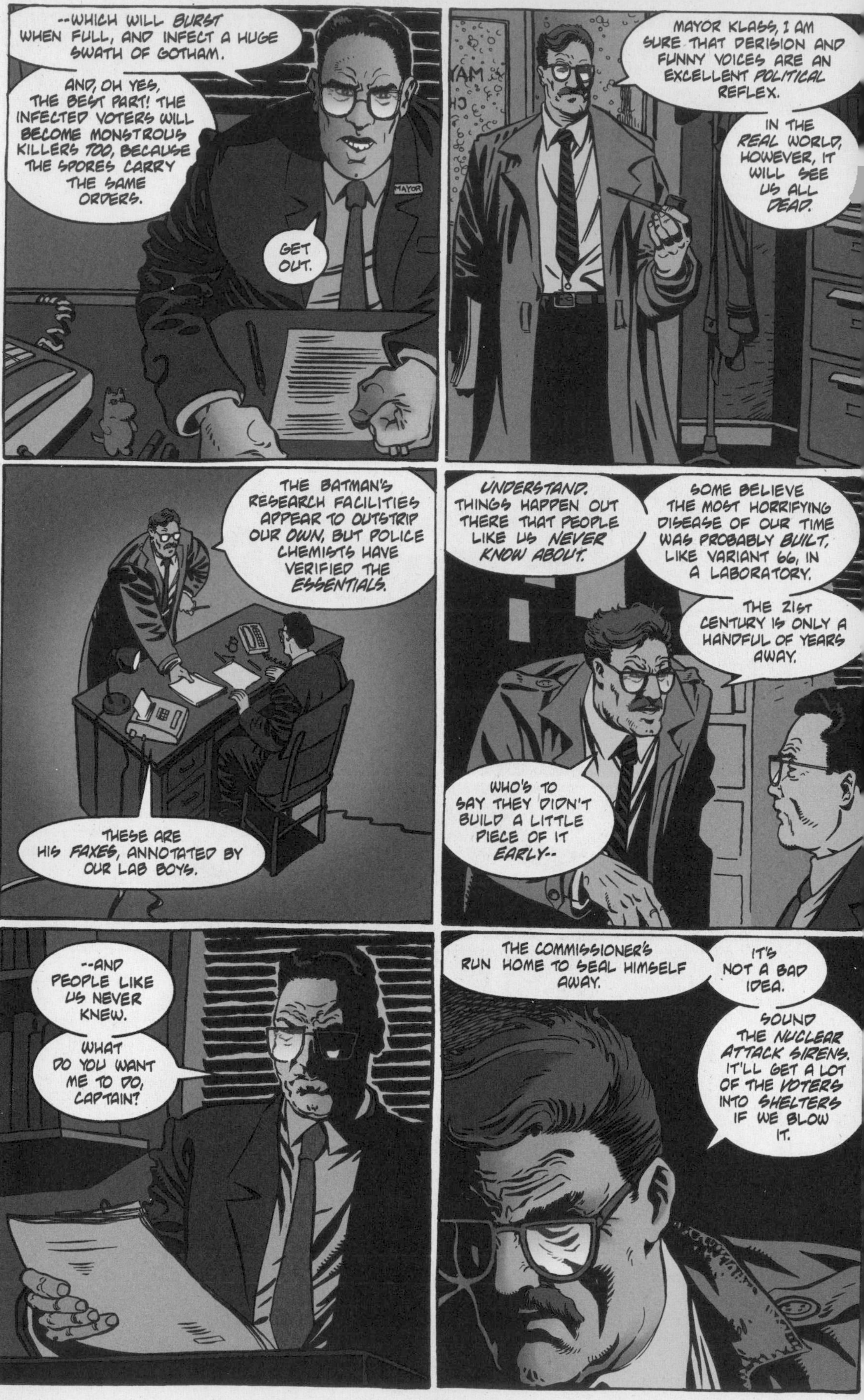
--WHICH WILL BURST WHEN FULL, AND INFECT A HUGE SWATH OF GOTHAM.
AND, OH YES, THE BEST PART! THE INFECTED VOTERS WILL BECOME MONSTROUS KILLERS TOO, BECAUSE THE SPORES CARRY THE SAME ORDERS.
MAYOR
GET OUT.
MAYOR KLASS, I AM SURE THAT DERISION AND FUNNY VOICES ARE AN EXCELLENT POLITICAL REFLEX.
IN THE REAL WORLD, HOWEVER, IT WILL SEE US ALL DEAD.
THE BATMAN'S RESEARCH FACILITIES APPEAR TO OUTSTRIP OUR OWN, BUT POLICE CHEMISTS HAVE VERIFIED THE ESSENTIALS.
THESE ARE HIS FAXES, ANNOTATED BY OUR LAB BOYS.
UNDERSTAND. THINGS HAPPEN OUT THERE THAT PEOPLE LIKE US NEVER KNOW ABOUT.
SOME BELIEVE THE MOST HORRIFYING DISEASE OF OUR TIME WAS PROBABLY BUILT, LIKE VARIANT 66, IN A LABORATORY.
THE 21ST CENTURY IS ONLY A HANDFUL OF YEARS AWAY.
WHO'S TO SAY THEY DIDN'T BUILD A LITTLE PIECE OF IT EARLY--
--AND PEOPLE LIKE US NEVER KNEW.
WHAT DO YOU WANT ME TO DO, CAPTAIN?
THE COMMISSIONER'S RUN HOME TO SEAL HIMSELF AWAY.
IT'S NOT A BAD IDEA.
SOUND THE NUCLEAR ATTACK SIRENS. IT'LL GET A LOT OF THE VOTERS INTO SHELTERS IF WE BLOW IT.

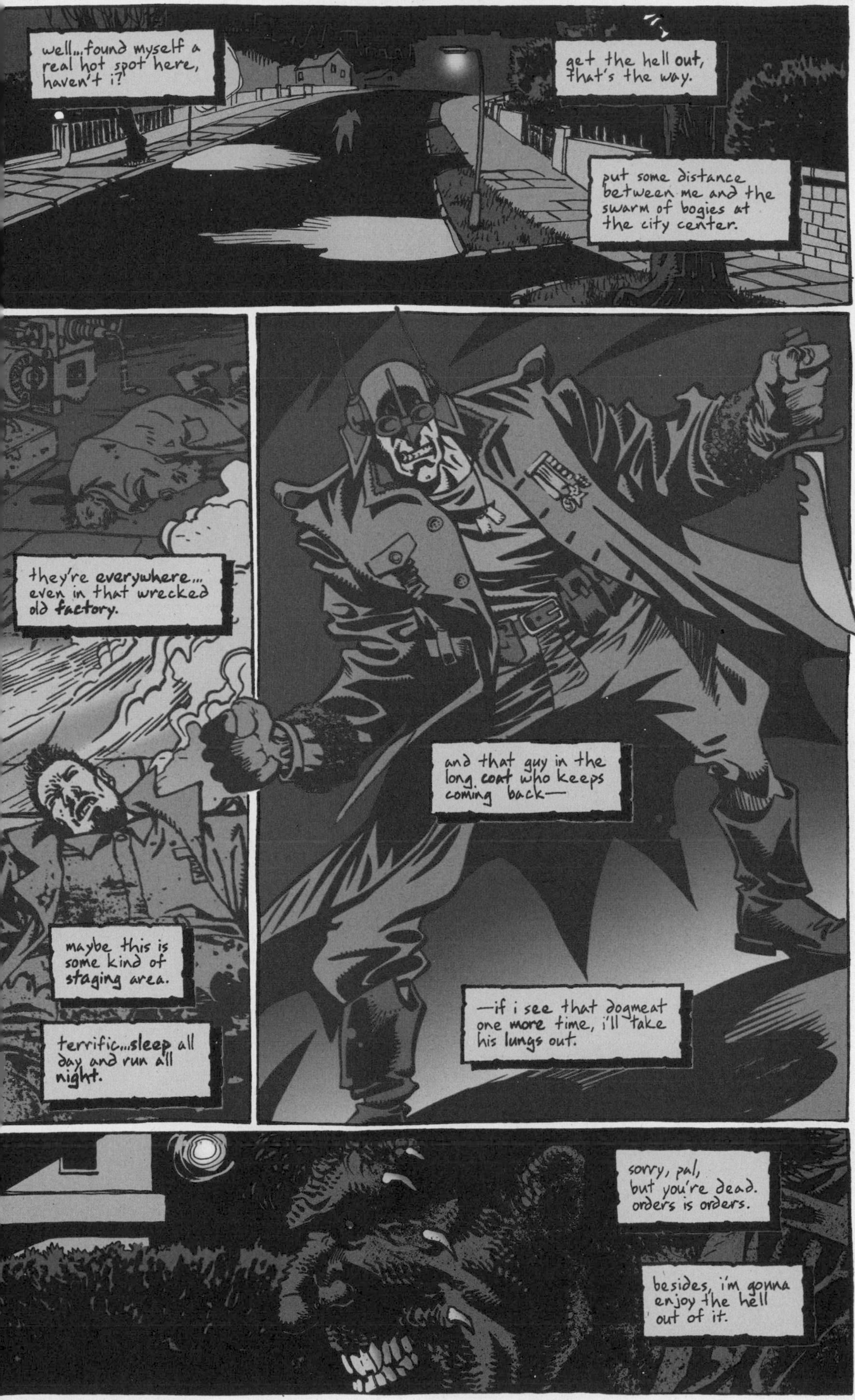

well...found myself a real hot spot here, haven't i?
get the hell out, that's the way.
put some distance between me and the swarm of bogies at the city center.
they're everywhere... even in that wrecked old factory.
maybe this is some kind of staging area.
terrific...sleep all day and run all night.
and that guy in the long coat who keeps coming back—
—if i see that dogmeat one more time, i'll take his lungs out.
sorry, pal, but you're dead. orders is orders.
besides, i'm gonna enjoy the hell out of it.

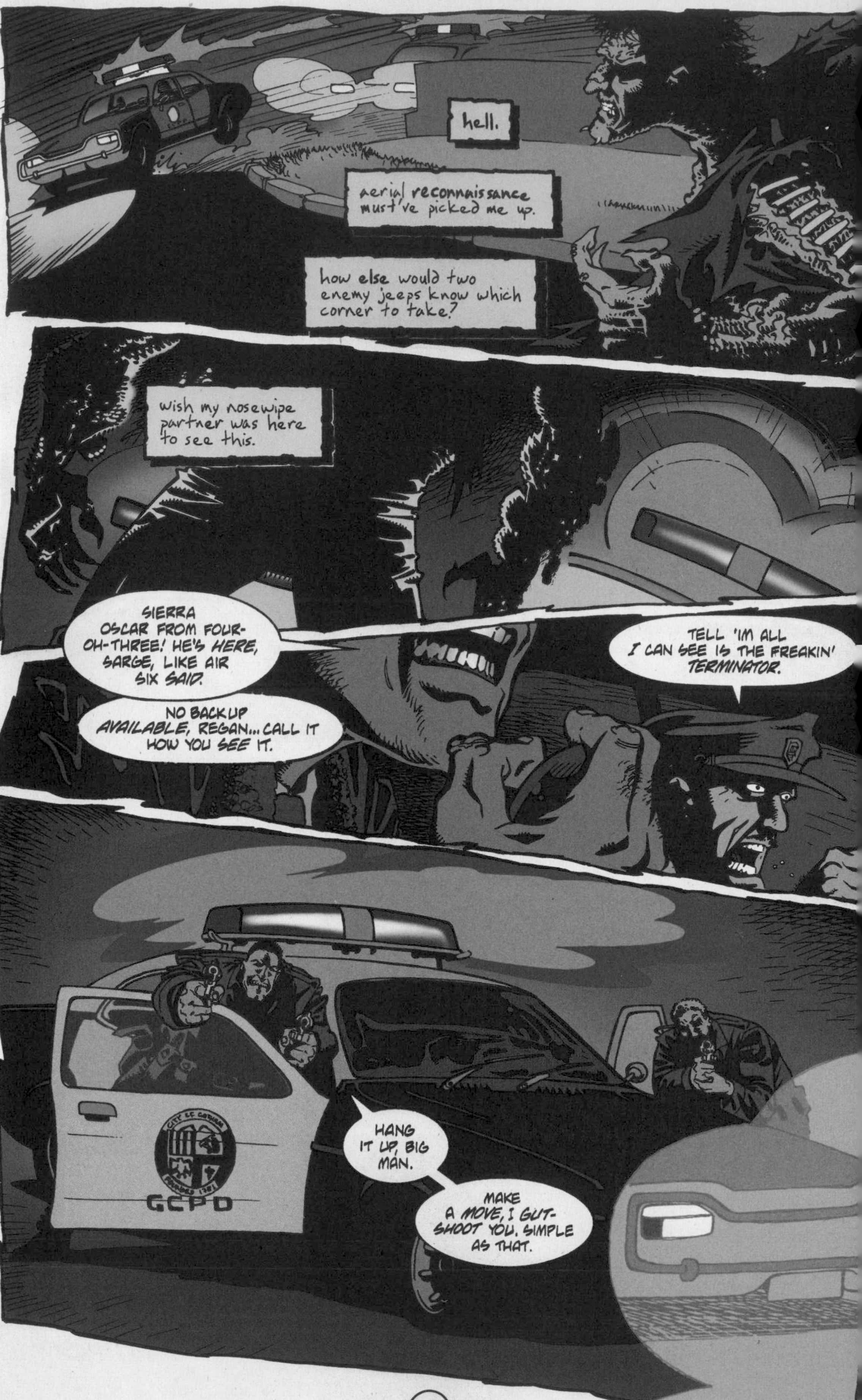
hell.
aerial reconnaissance must've picked me up.
how else would two enemy jeeps know which corner to take?
wish my nosewipe partner was here to see this.
SIERRA OSCAR FROM FOUR-OH-THREE! HE'S *HERE*, SARGE, LIKE AIR SIX *SAID*.
NO BACKUP *AVAILABLE*, REGAN... CALL IT HOW YOU *SEE* IT.
TELL 'IM ALL *I* CAN SEE IS THE FREAKIN' *TERMINATOR*.
GCPD
HANG IT UP, BIG MAN.
MAKE A *MOVE*, I GUT-*SHOOT* YOU. SIMPLE AS THAT.

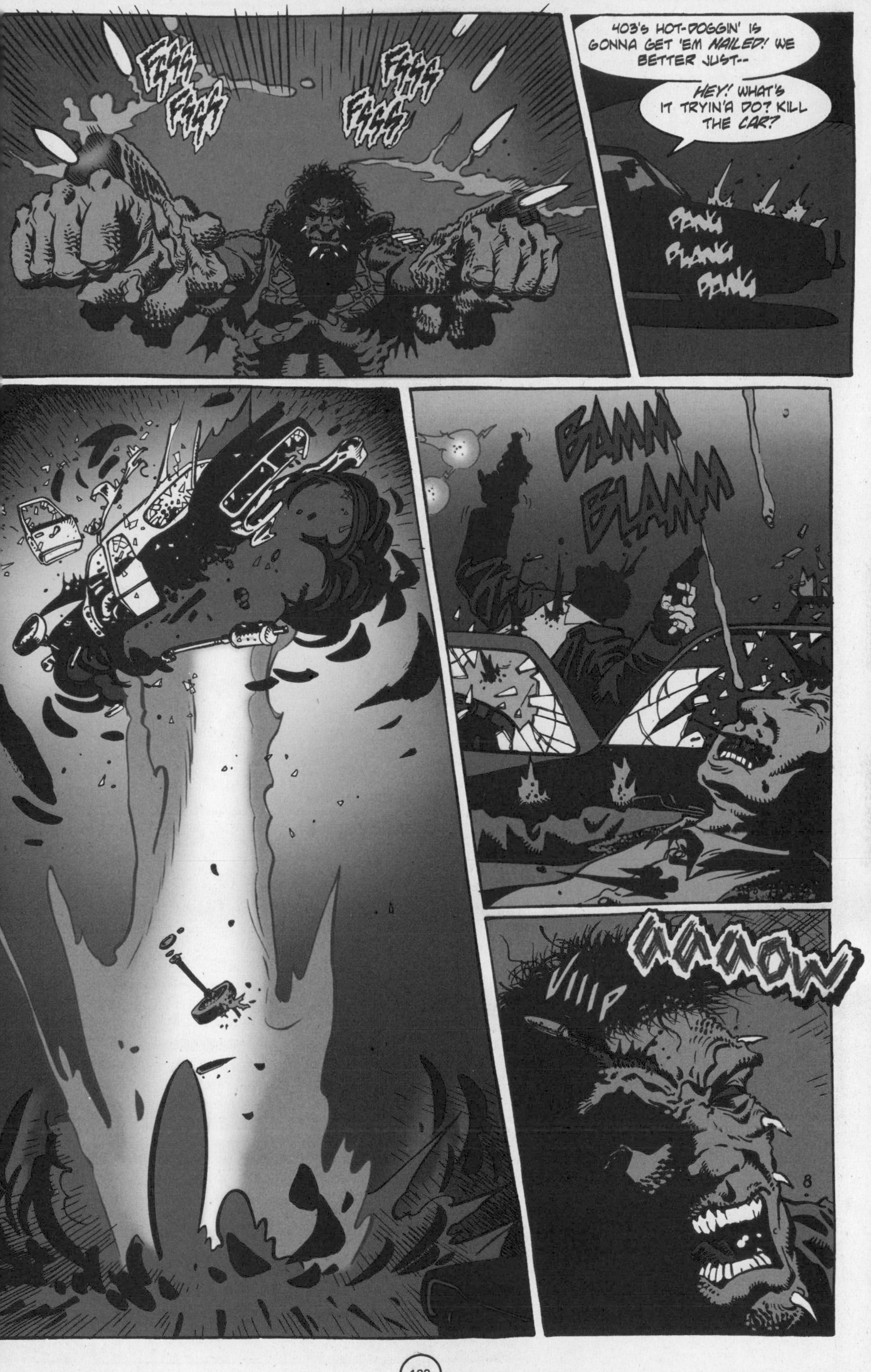
FSSS
FSSS
FSSS
FSSS
403's HOT-DOGGIN' IS GONNA GET 'EM NAILED! WE BETTER JUST--
HEY! WHAT'S IT TRYIN'A DO? KILL THE CAR?
PANG
PLANG
PANG
BAMM
BLAMM
VIIIP
AAAAOW

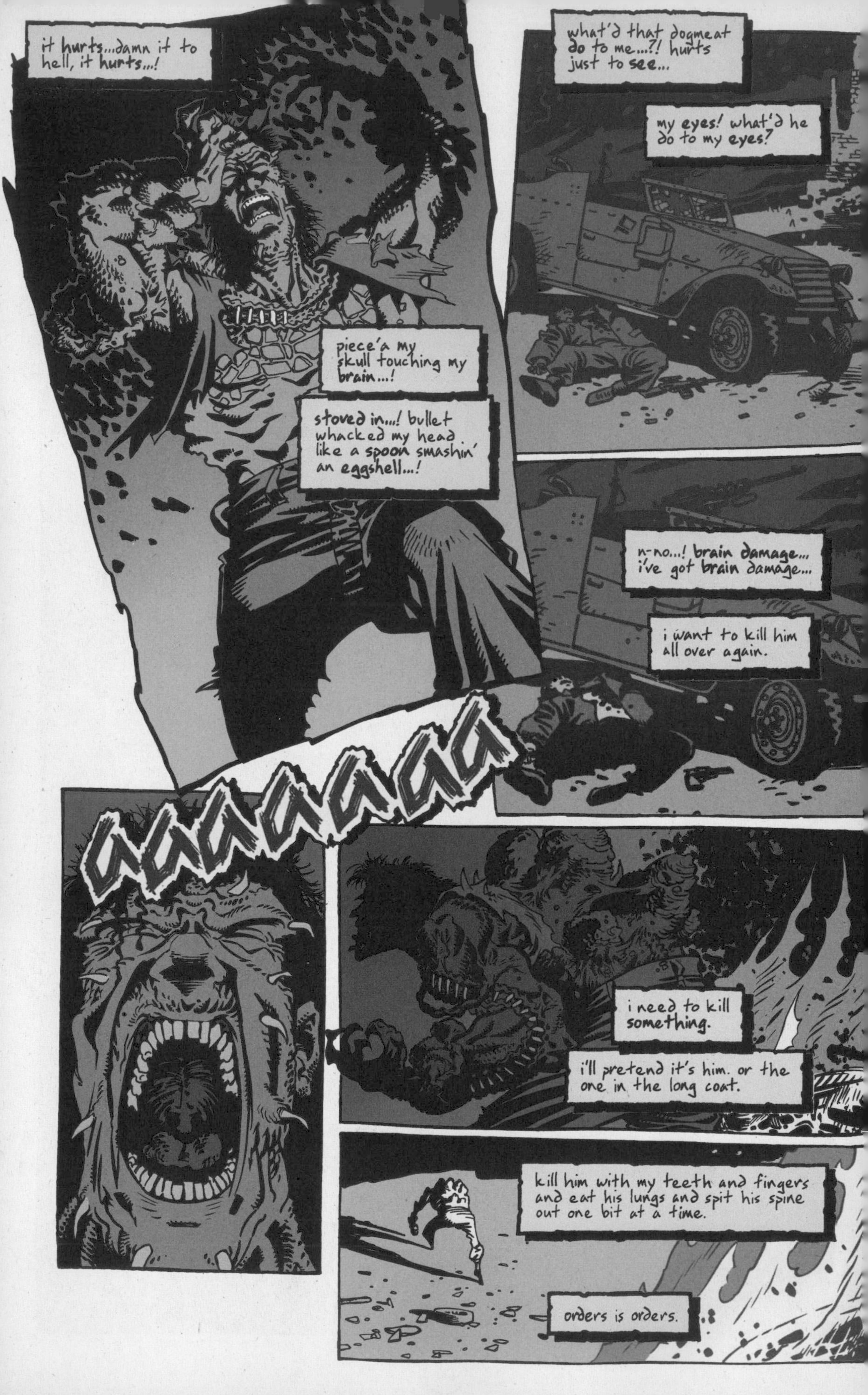
it hurts...damn it to hell, it hurts...!
piece'a my skull touching my brain...!
stoved in...! bullet whacked my head like a spoon smashin' an eggshell...!
what'd that dogmeat do to me...?! hurts just to see...
my eyes! what'd he do to my eyes?
n-no...! brain damage... i've got brain damage...
i want to kill him all over again.
aaaaaaaa
i need to kill something.
i'll pretend it's him. or the one in the long coat.
kill him with my teeth and fingers and eat his lungs and spit his spine out one bit at a time.
orders is orders.

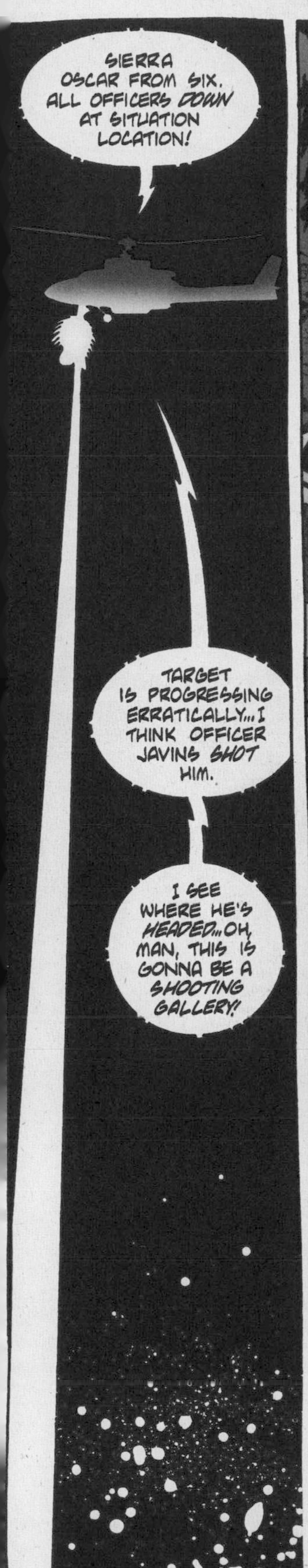
SIERRA OSCAR FROM SIX. ALL OFFICERS DOWN AT SITUATION LOCATION!
TARGET IS PROGRESSING ERRATICALLY...I THINK OFFICER JAVINS SHOT HIM.
I SEE WHERE HE'S HEADED...OH, MAN, THIS IS GONNA BE A SHOOTING GALLERY!

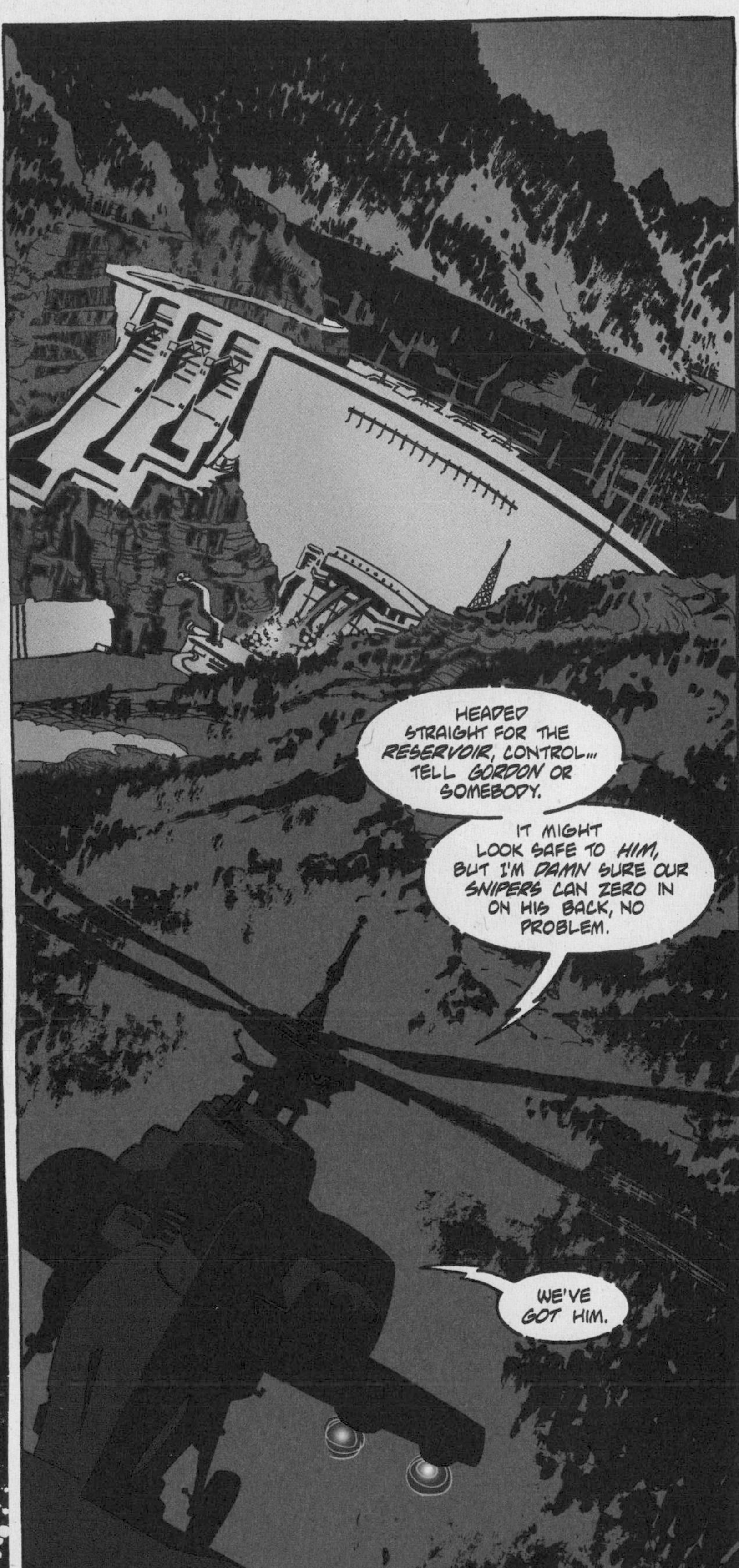
HEADED STRAIGHT FOR THE RESERVOIR, CONTROL... TELL GORDON OR SOMEBODY.
IT MIGHT LOOK SAFE TO HIM, BUT I'M DAMN SURE OUR SNIPERS CAN ZERO IN ON HIS BACK, NO PROBLEM.
WE'VE GOT HIM.

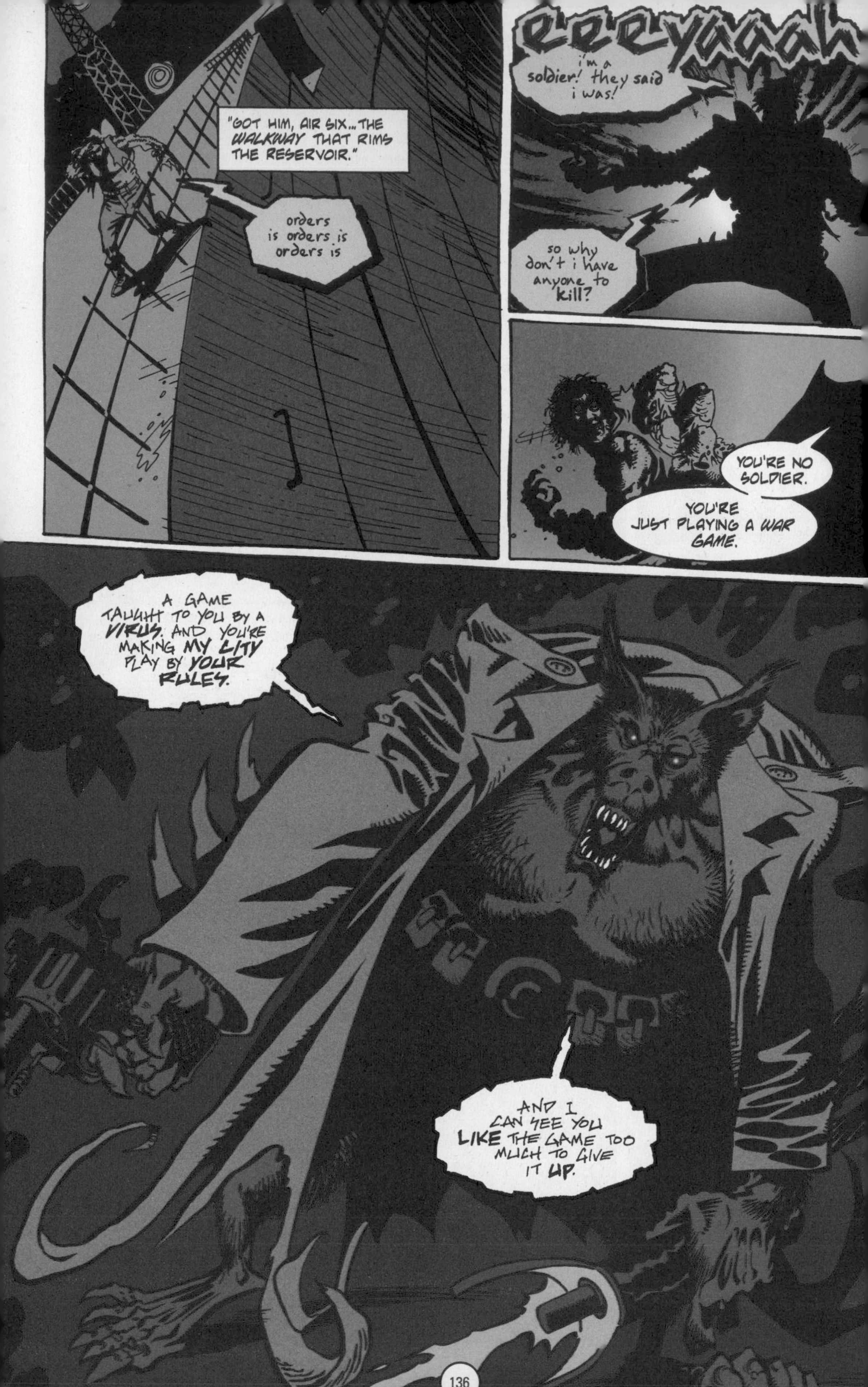

"GOT HIM, AIR SIX... THE WALKWAY THAT RIMS THE RESERVOIR."
orders is orders is orders is
EEEYAAAH
i'm a soldier! they said i was!
so why don't i have anyone to kill?
YOU'RE NO SOLDIER.
YOU'RE JUST PLAYING A WAR GAME.
A GAME TAUGHT TO YOU BY A VIRUS. AND YOU'RE MAKING MY CITY PLAY BY YOUR RULES.
AND I CAN SEE YOU LIKE THE GAME TOO MUCH TO GIVE IT UP.

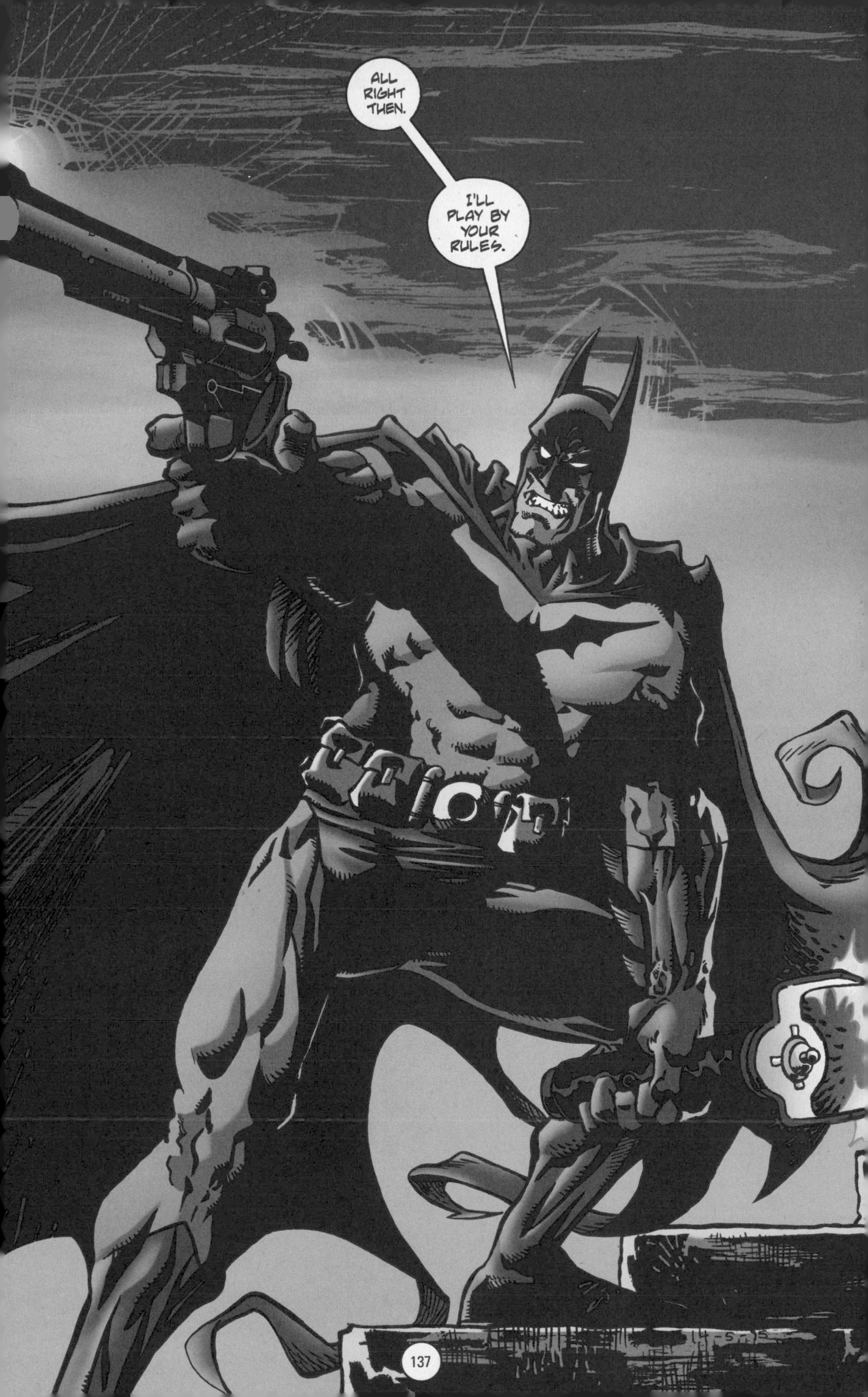
ALL RIGHT THEN.
I'LL PLAY BY YOUR RULES.

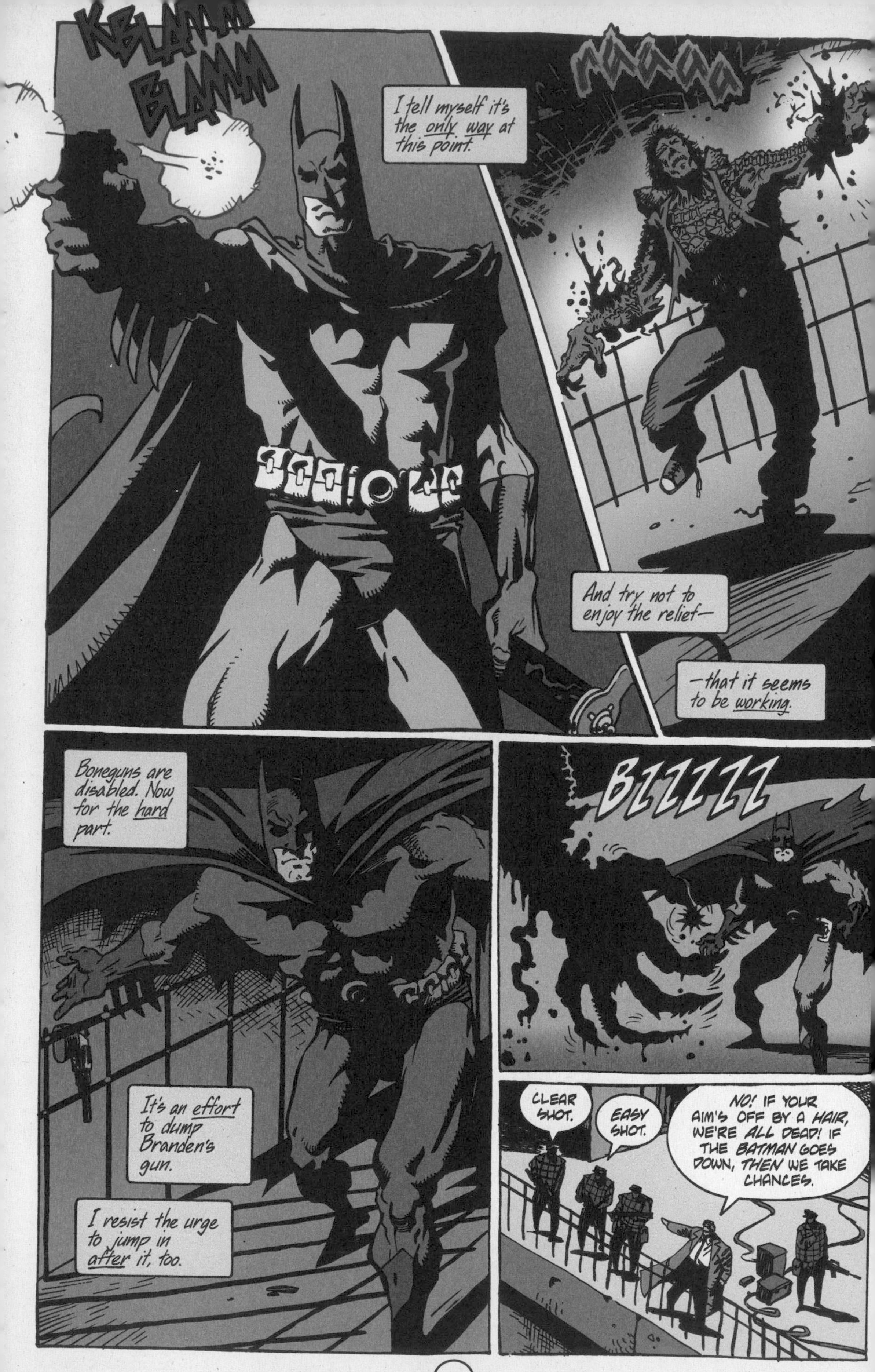
KBLAMM BLAMM
I tell myself it's the only way at this point.
AAAAAA
And try not to enjoy the relief—
—that it seems to be working.
Boneguns are disabled. Now for the hard part.
It's an effort to dump Branden's gun.
I resist the urge to jump in after it, too.
BZZZZZ
CLEAR SHOT.
EASY SHOT.
NO! IF YOUR AIM'S OFF BY A HAIR, WE'RE ALL DEAD! IF THE BATMAN GOES DOWN, THEN WE TAKE CHANCES.

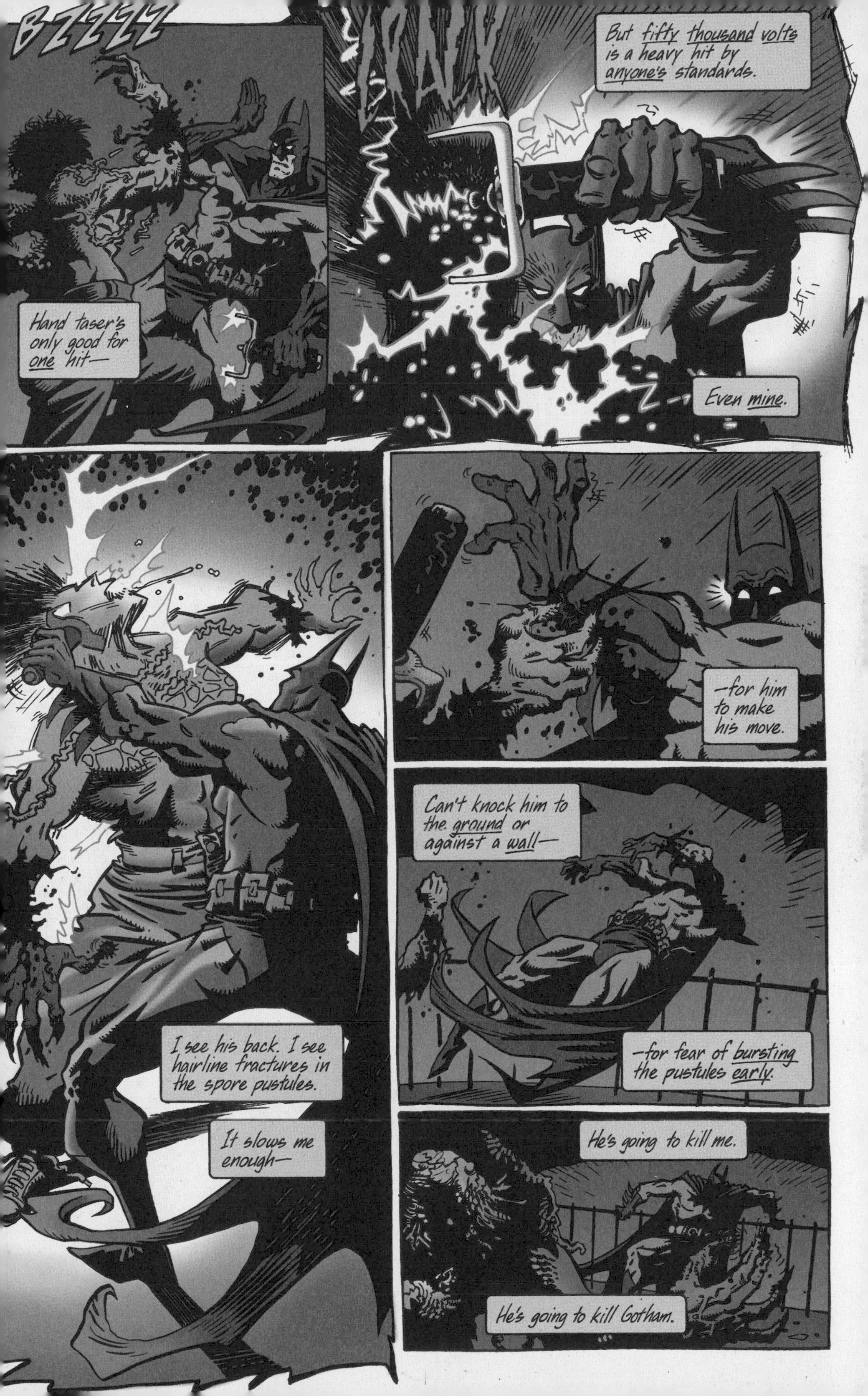
BZZZZ
Hand taser's only good for one hit—
But fifty thousand volts is a heavy hit by anyone's standards.
Even mine.
I see his back. I see hairline fractures in the spore pustules.
It slows me enough—
—for him to make his move.
Can't knock him to the ground or against a wall—
—for fear of bursting the pustules early.
He's going to kill me.
He's going to kill Gotham.

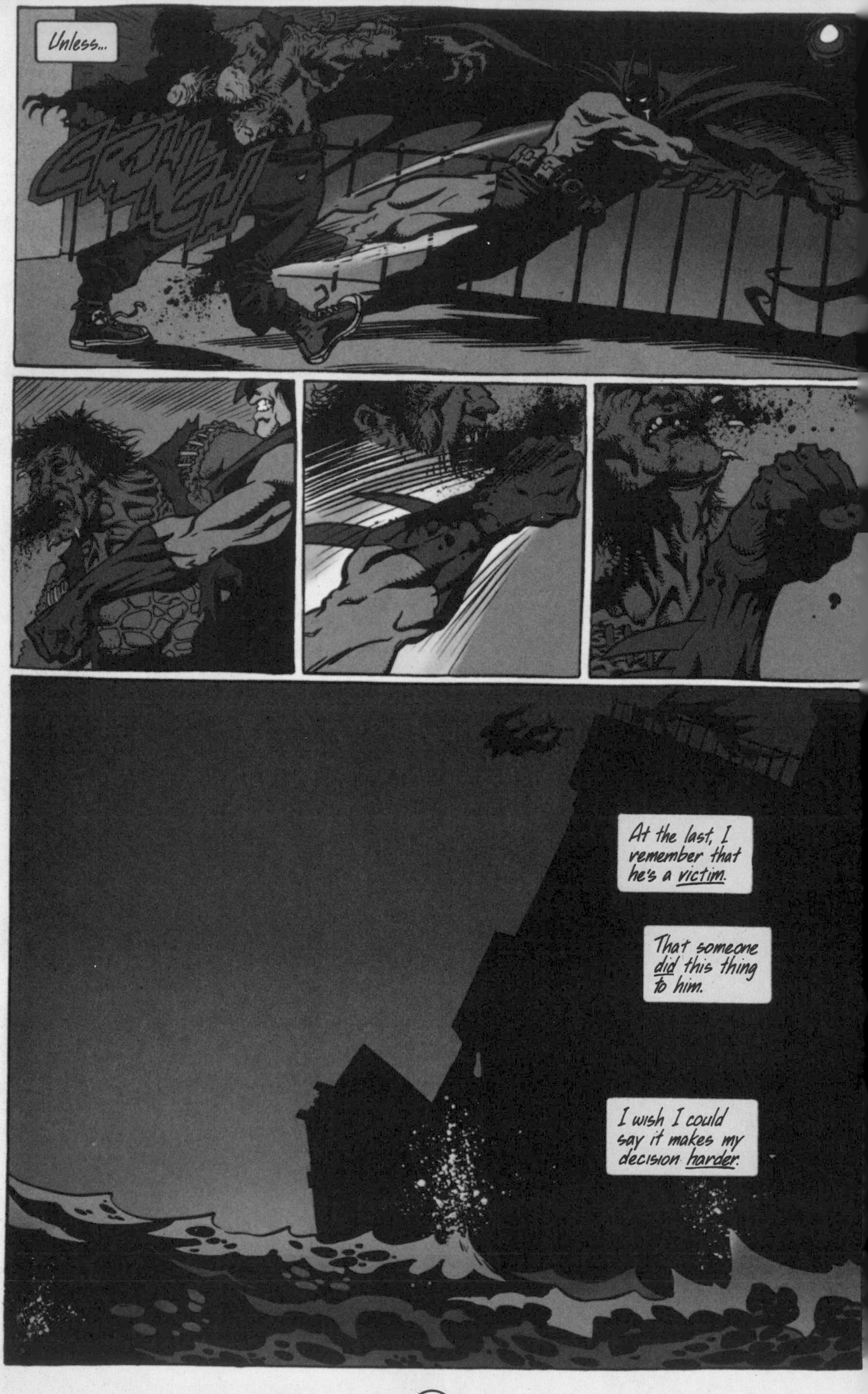
Unless...
At the last, I remember that he's a victim.
That someone did this thing to him.
I wish I could say it makes my decision harder.

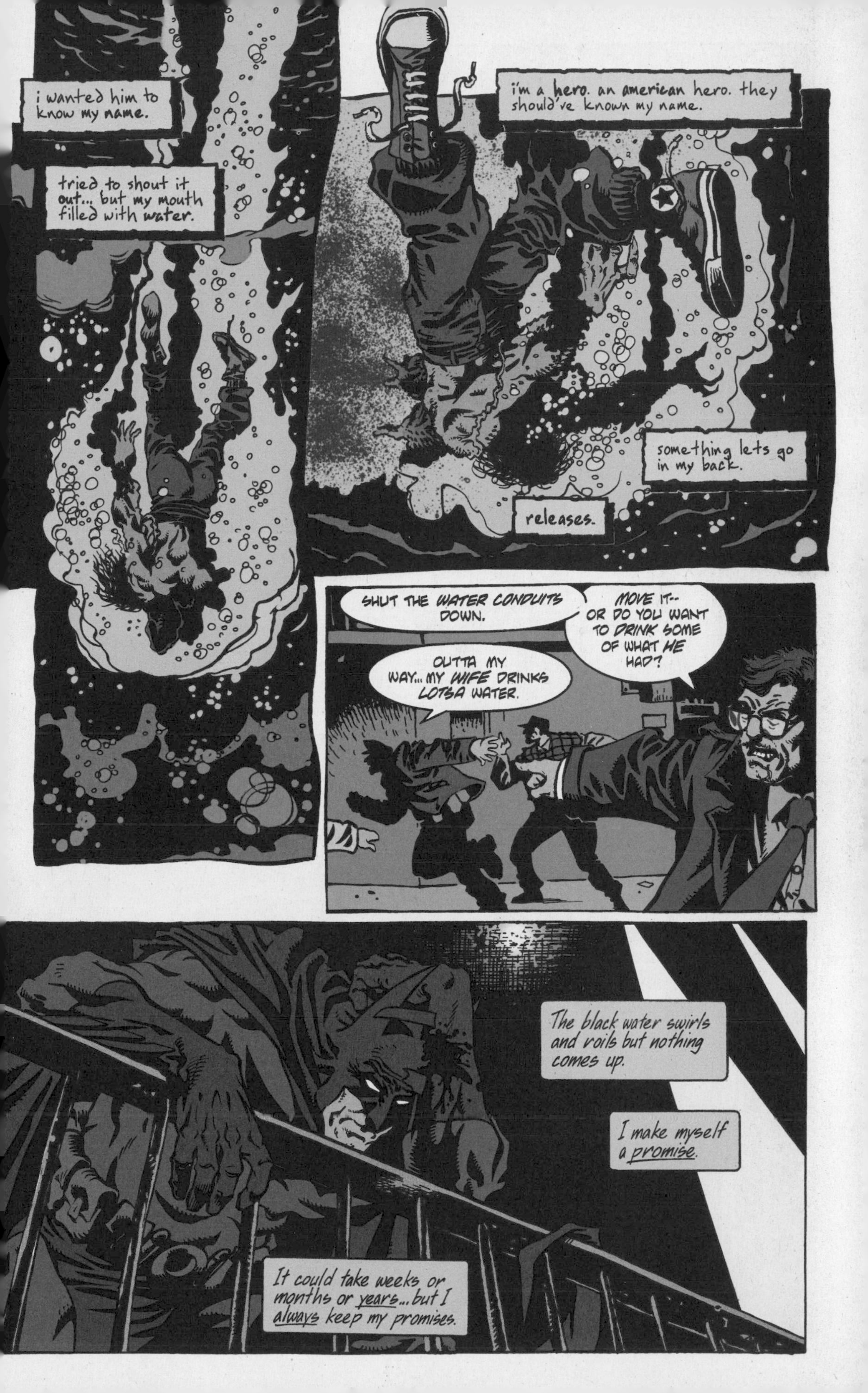
i wanted him to know my name.
tried to shout it out... but my mouth filled with water.
i'm a hero. an american hero. they should've known my name.
something lets go in my back.
releases.
SHUT THE WATER CONDUITS DOWN.
MOVE IT-- OR DO YOU WANT TO DRINK SOME OF WHAT HE HAD?
OUTTA MY WAY... MY WIFE DRINKS LOTSA WATER.
The black water swirls and roils but nothing comes up.
I make myself a promise.
It could take weeks or months or years... but I always keep my promises.

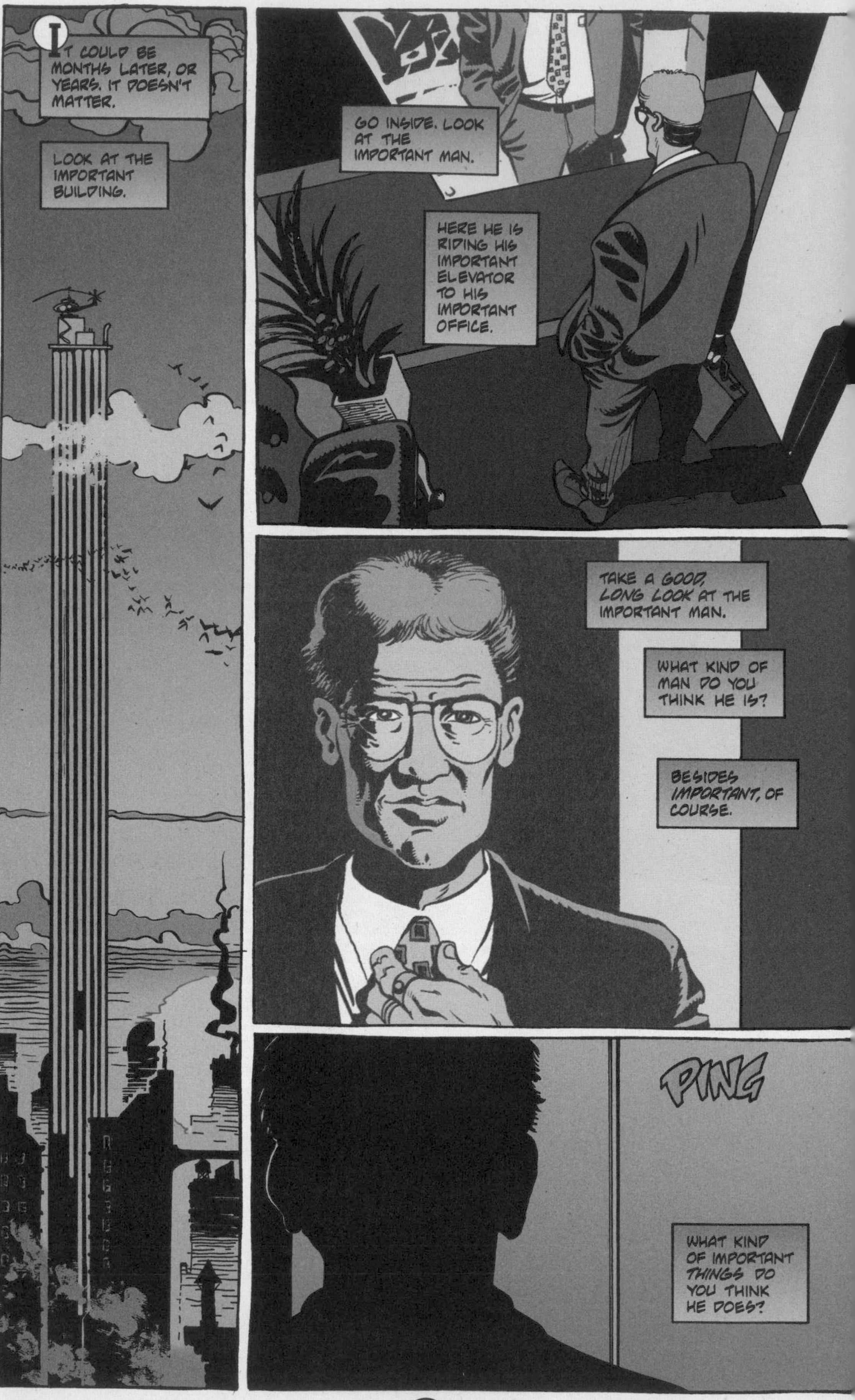
IT COULD BE MONTHS LATER, OR YEARS. IT DOESN'T MATTER.
LOOK AT THE IMPORTANT BUILDING.
GO INSIDE. LOOK AT THE IMPORTANT MAN.
HERE HE IS RIDING HIS IMPORTANT ELEVATOR TO HIS IMPORTANT OFFICE.
TAKE A GOOD, LONG LOOK AT THE IMPORTANT MAN.
WHAT KIND OF MAN DO YOU THINK HE IS?
BESIDES IMPORTANT, OF COURSE.
PING
WHAT KIND OF IMPORTANT THINGS DO YOU THINK HE DOES?

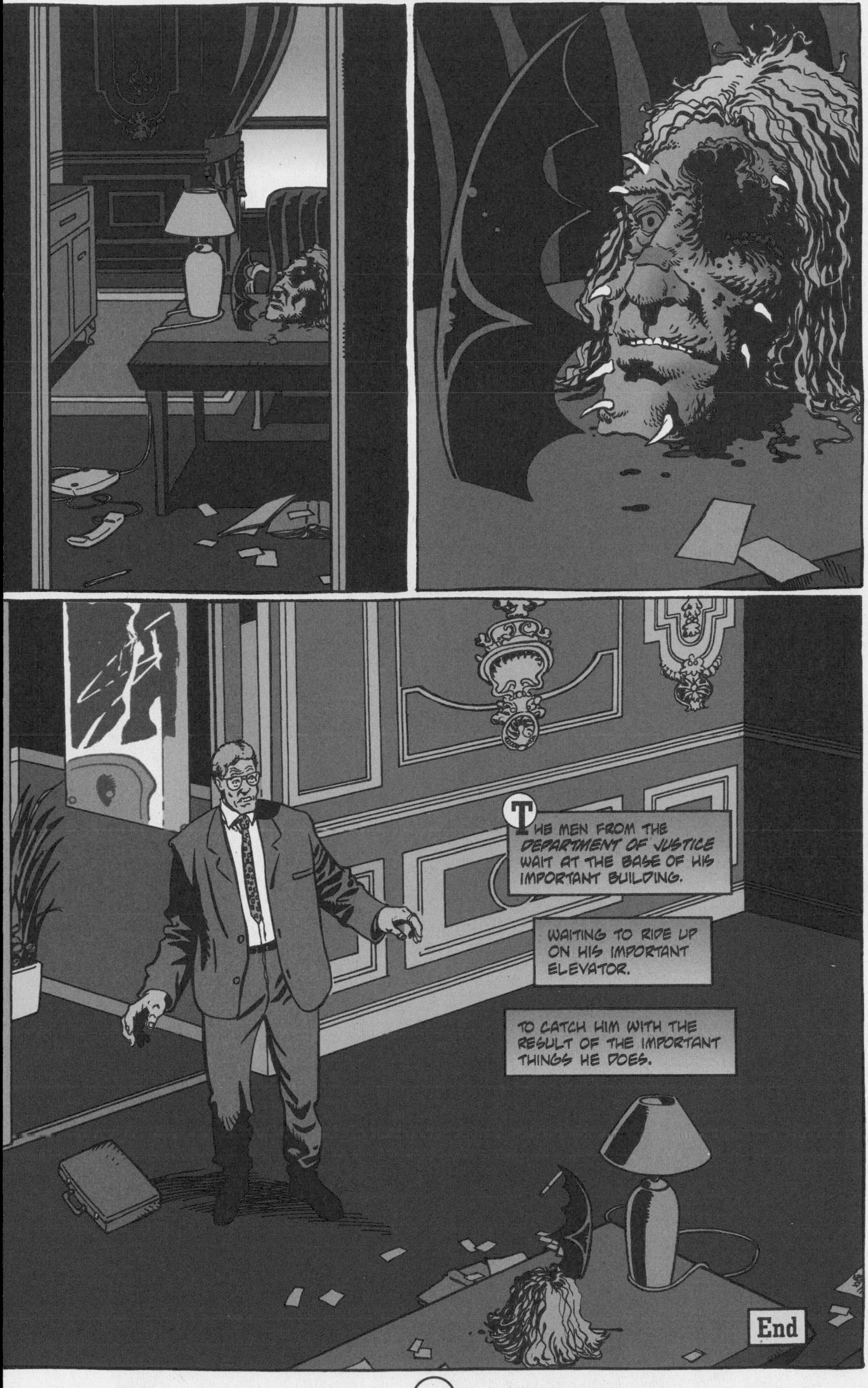
THE MEN FROM THE DEPARTMENT OF JUSTICE WAIT AT THE BASE OF HIS IMPORTANT BUILDING.
WAITING TO RIDE UP ON HIS IMPORTANT ELEVATOR.
TO CATCH HIM WITH THE RESULT OF THE IMPORTANT THINGS HE DOES.
End

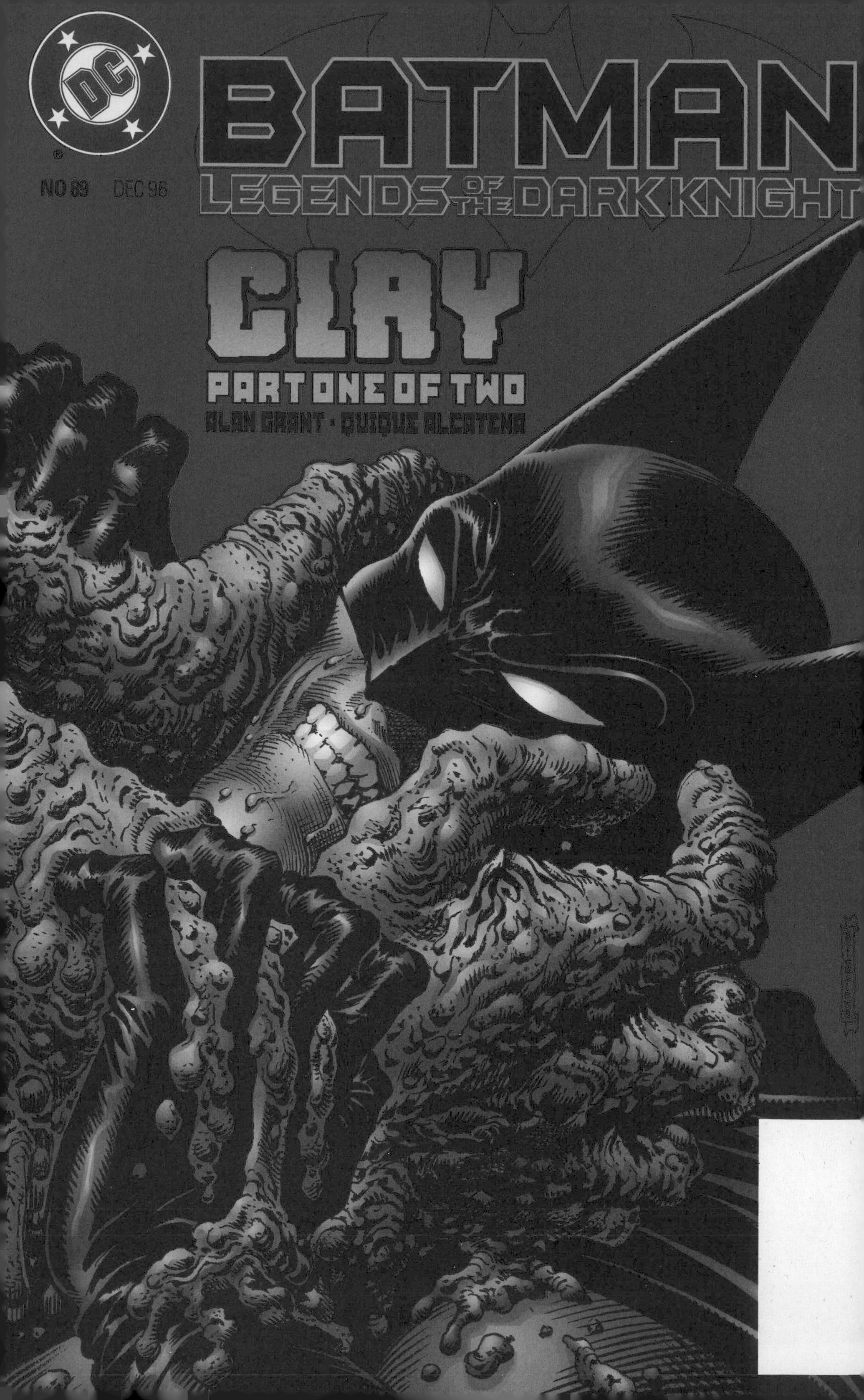
DC
BATMAN
NO 89 DEC 96
LEGENDS OF THE DARK KNIGHT
CLAY
PART ONE OF TWO
ALAN GRANT · QUIQUE ALCATENA

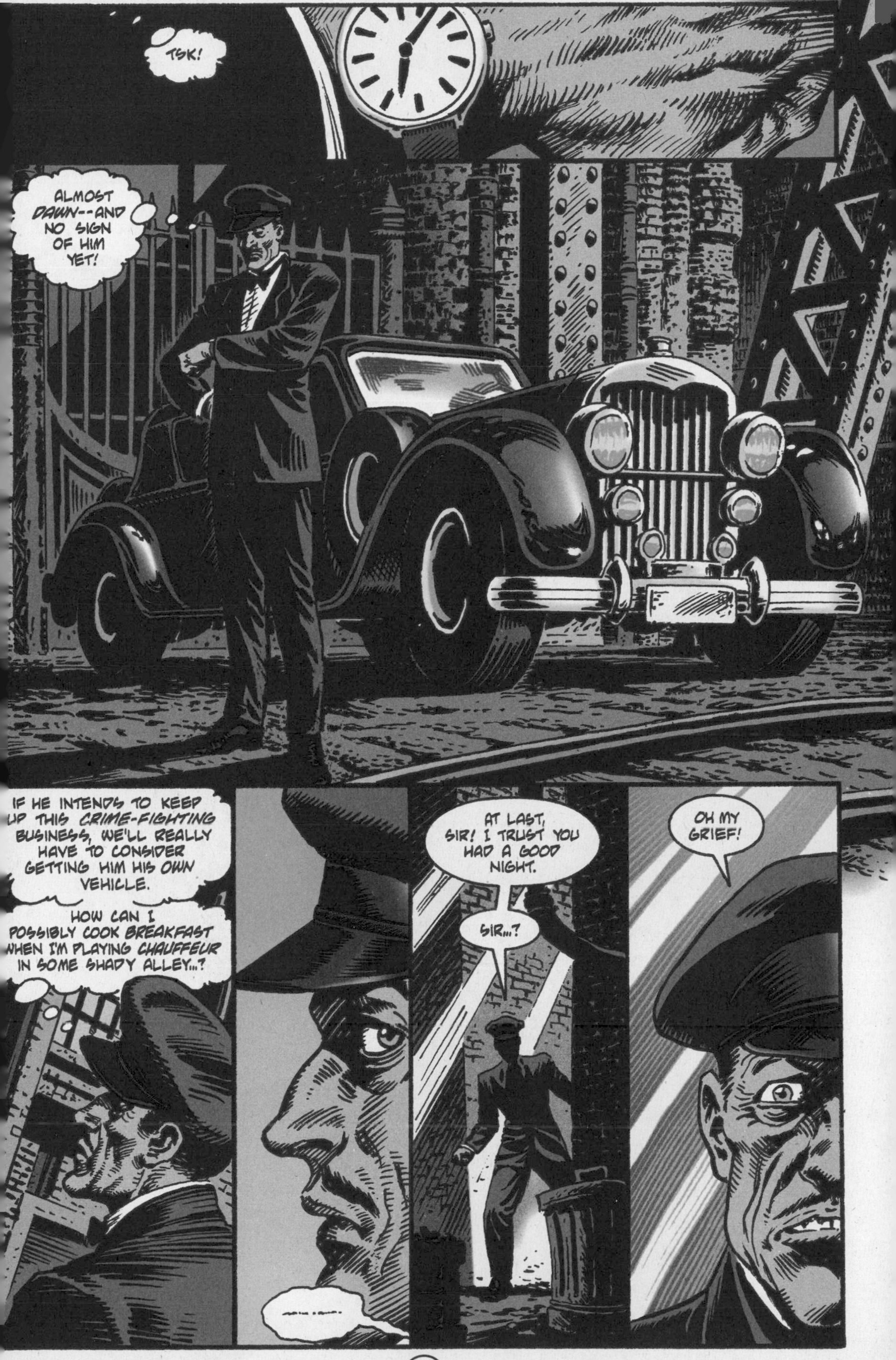
TSK!
ALMOST DAWN--AND NO SIGN OF HIM YET!
IF HE INTENDS TO KEEP UP THIS *CRIME-FIGHTING* BUSINESS, WE'LL REALLY HAVE TO CONSIDER GETTING HIM HIS OWN VEHICLE.
HOW CAN I POSSIBLY COOK BREAKFAST WHEN I'M PLAYING CHAUFFEUR IN SOME SHADY ALLEY...?
AT LAST, SIR! I TRUST YOU HAD A GOOD NIGHT.
SIR...?
OH MY GRIEF!

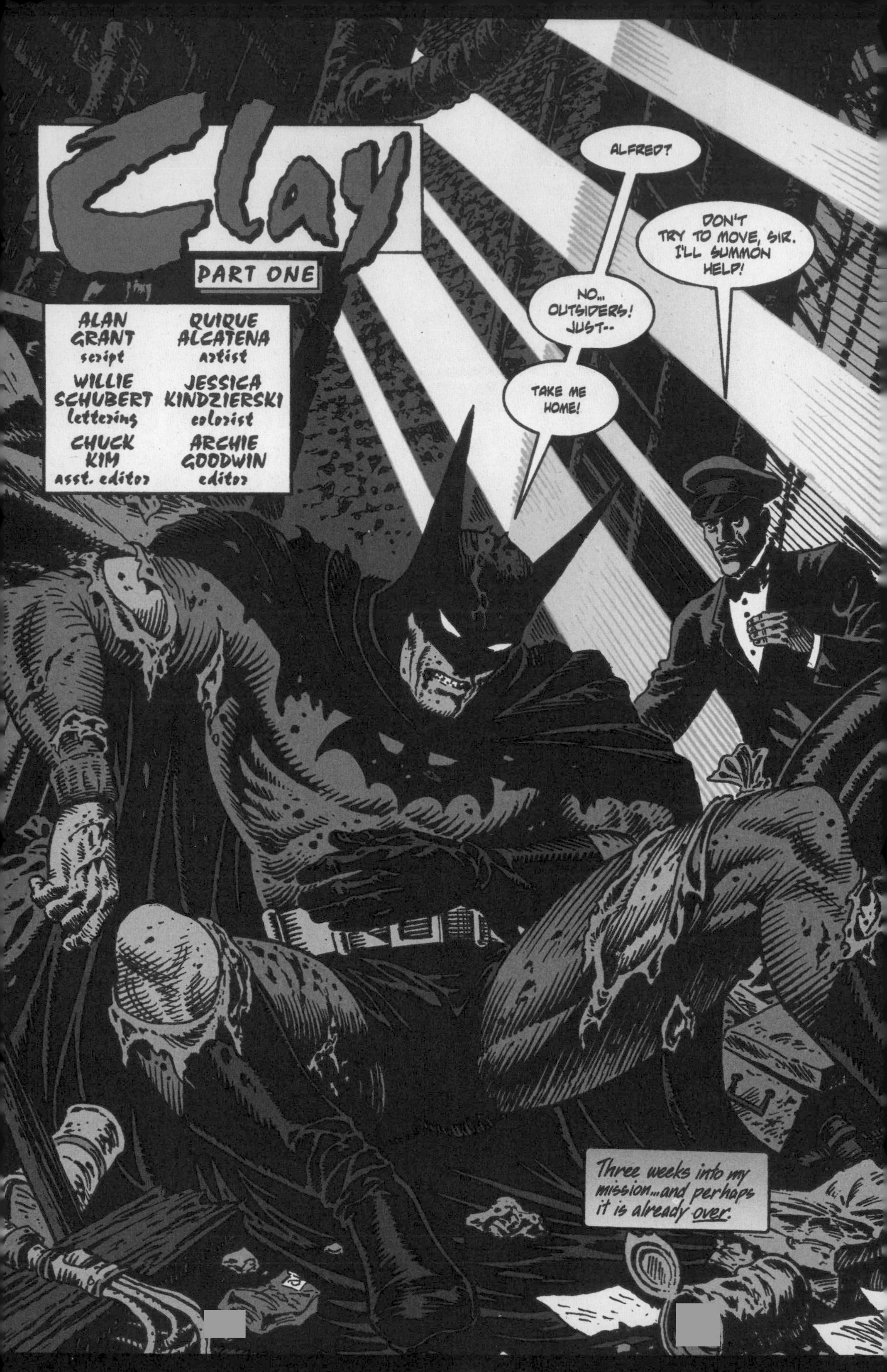
Clay
PART ONE
ALAN GRANT script
QUIQUE ALCATENA artist
WILLIE SCHUBERT lettering
JESSICA KINDZIERSKI colorist
CHUCK KIM asst. editor
ARCHIE GOODWIN editor
ALFRED?
DON'T TRY TO MOVE, SIR. I'LL SUMMON HELP!
NO... OUTSIDERS! JUST--
TAKE ME HOME!
Three weeks into my mission...and perhaps it is already over.

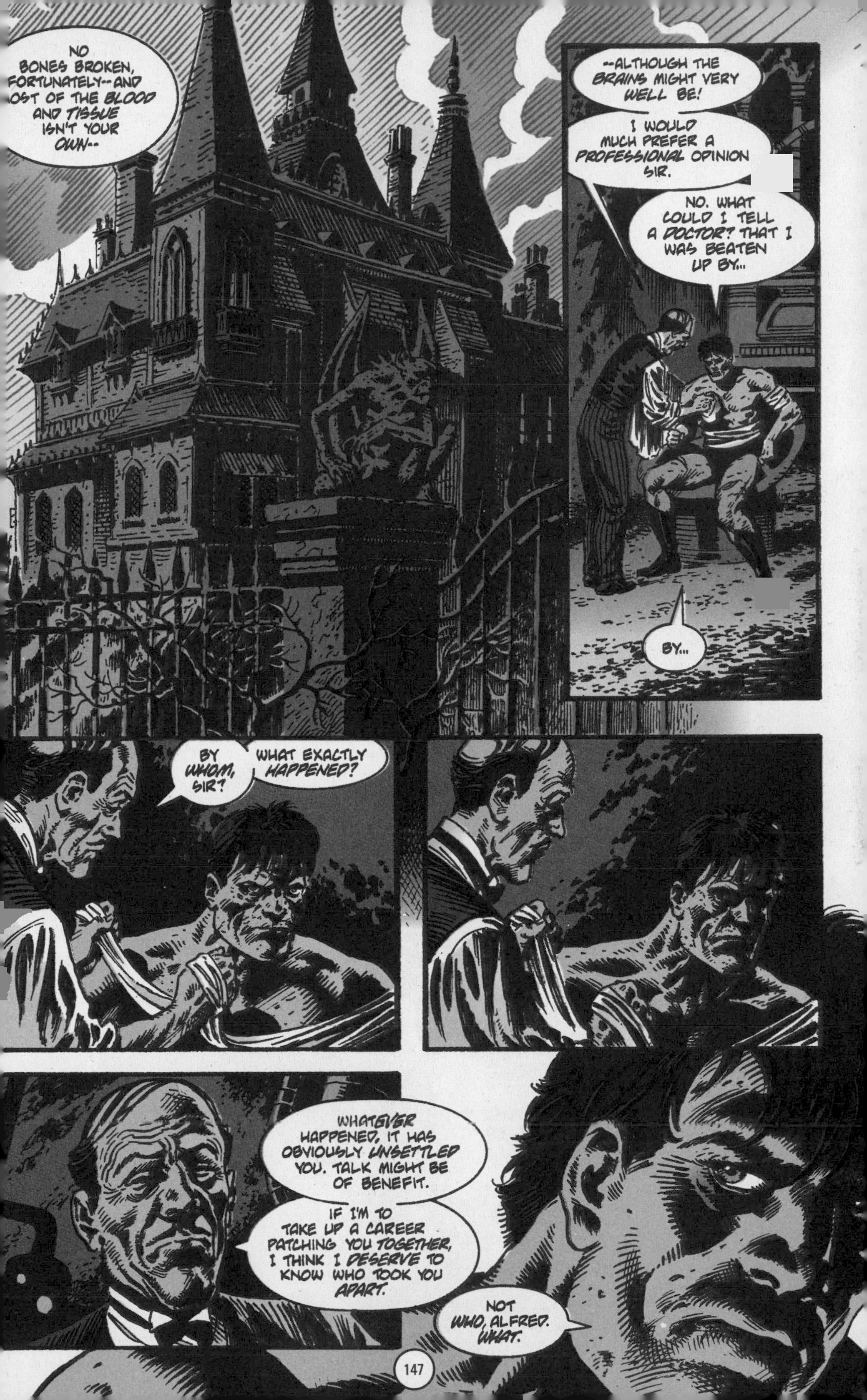
NO BONES BROKEN, FORTUNATELY--AND MOST OF THE BLOOD AND TISSUE ISN'T YOUR OWN--
--ALTHOUGH THE BRAINS MIGHT VERY WELL BE!
I WOULD MUCH PREFER A PROFESSIONAL OPINION SIR.
NO. WHAT COULD I TELL A DOCTOR? THAT I WAS BEATEN UP BY...
BY...
BY WHOM, SIR?
WHAT EXACTLY HAPPENED?
WHATEVER HAPPENED, IT HAS OBVIOUSLY UNSETTLED YOU. TALK MIGHT BE OF BENEFIT.
IF I'M TO TAKE UP A CAREER PATCHING YOU TOGETHER, I THINK I DESERVE TO KNOW WHO TOOK YOU APART.
NOT WHO, ALFRED. WHAT.

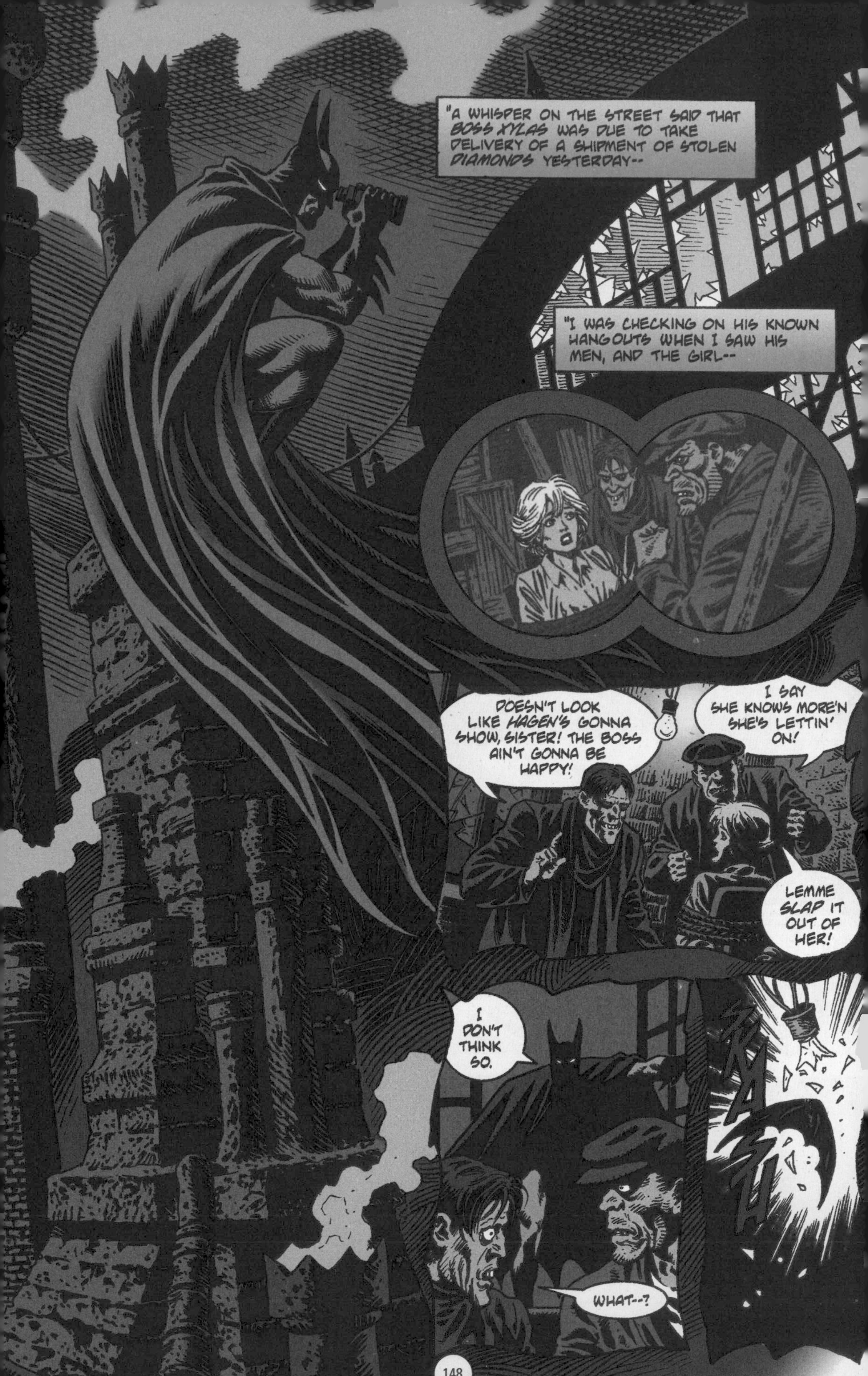
"A WHISPER ON THE STREET SAID THAT BOSS XYLAS WAS DUE TO TAKE DELIVERY OF A SHIPMENT OF STOLEN DIAMONDS YESTERDAY--
"I WAS CHECKING ON HIS KNOWN HANGOUTS WHEN I SAW HIS MEN, AND THE GIRL--
DOESN'T LOOK LIKE HAGEN'S GONNA SHOW, SISTER! THE BOSS AIN'T GONNA BE HAPPY!
I SAY SHE KNOWS MORE'N SHE'S LETTIN' ON!
LEMME SLAP IT OUT OF HER!
I DON'T THINK SO.
KRASH
WHAT--?

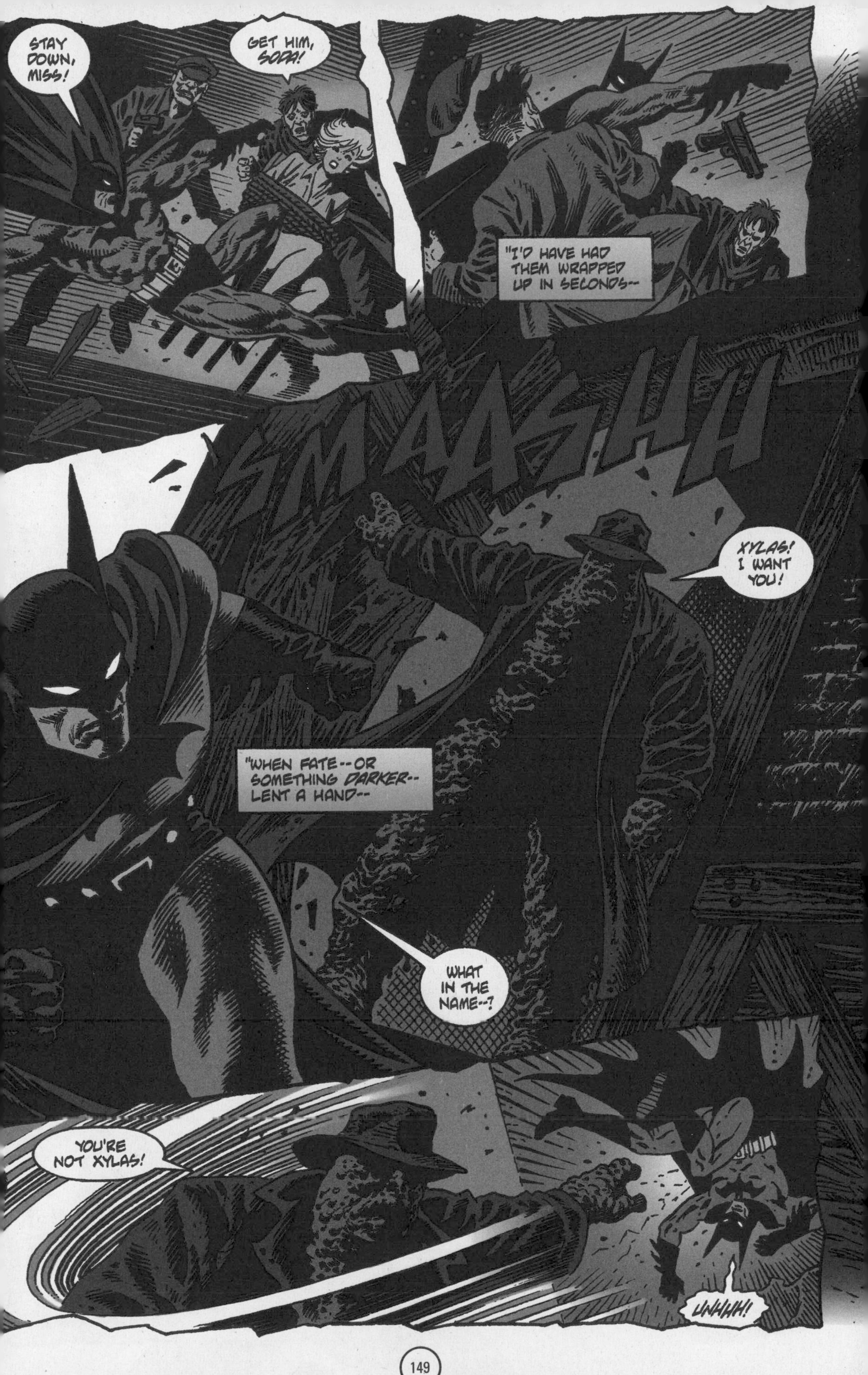
STAY DOWN, MISS!
GET HIM, SODA!
"I'D HAVE HAD THEM WRAPPED UP IN SECONDS--
SMAASHH
XYLAS! I WANT YOU!
"WHEN FATE--OR SOMETHING DARKER--LENT A HAND--
WHAT IN THE NAME--?
YOU'RE NOT XYLAS!
UNHHH!

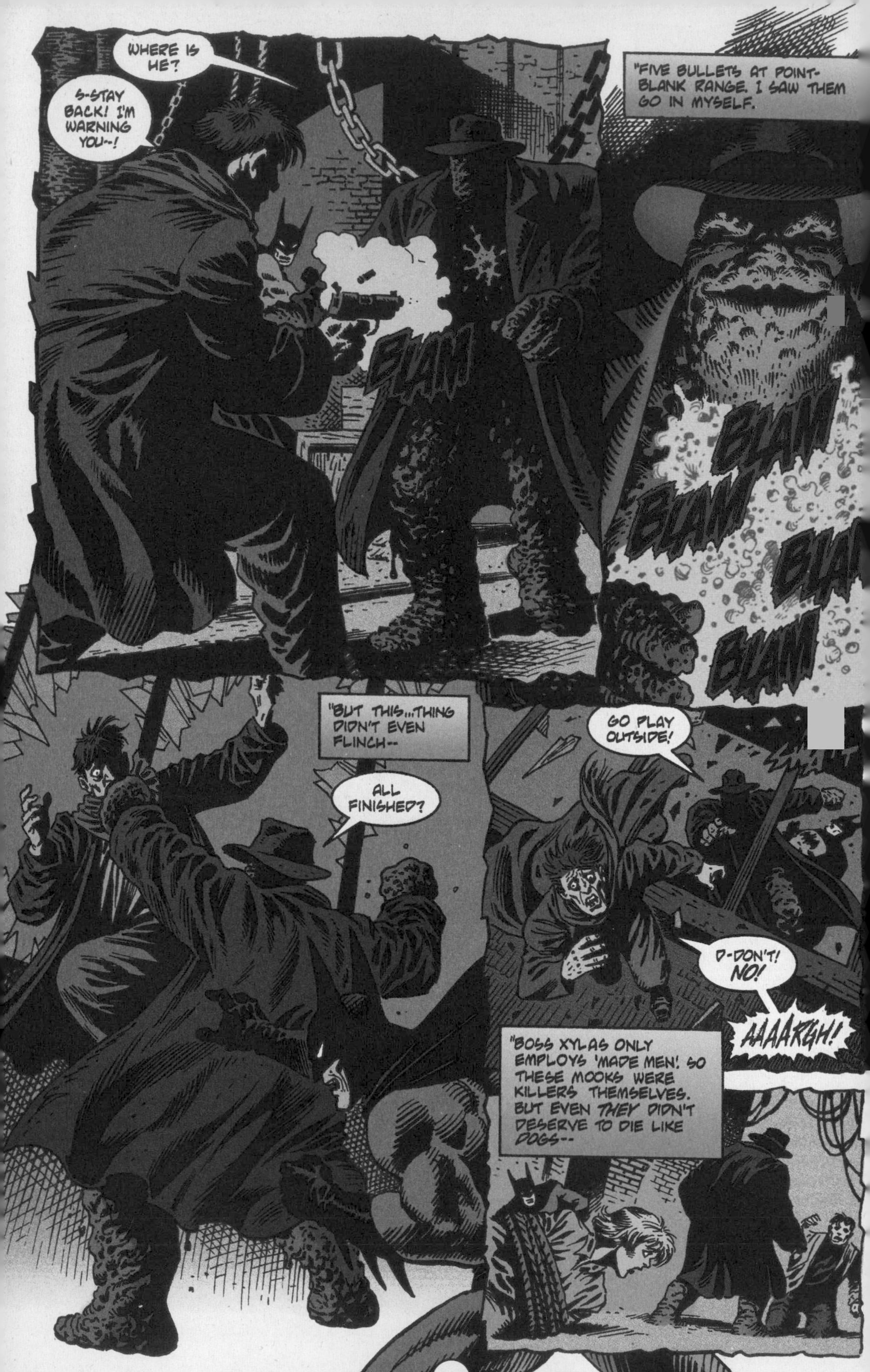
WHERE IS HE?
S-STAY BACK! I'M WARNING YOU--!
BLAM
"FIVE BULLETS AT POINT-BLANK RANGE. I SAW THEM GO IN MYSELF.
BLAM
BLAM
BLAM
BLAM
"BUT THIS...THING DIDN'T EVEN FLINCH--
ALL FINISHED?
GO PLAY OUTSIDE!
D-DON'T! NO!
AAAARGH!
"BOSS XYLAS ONLY EMPLOYS 'MADE MEN'. SO THESE MOOKS WERE KILLERS THEMSELVES. BUT EVEN THEY DIDN'T DESERVE TO DIE LIKE DOGS--

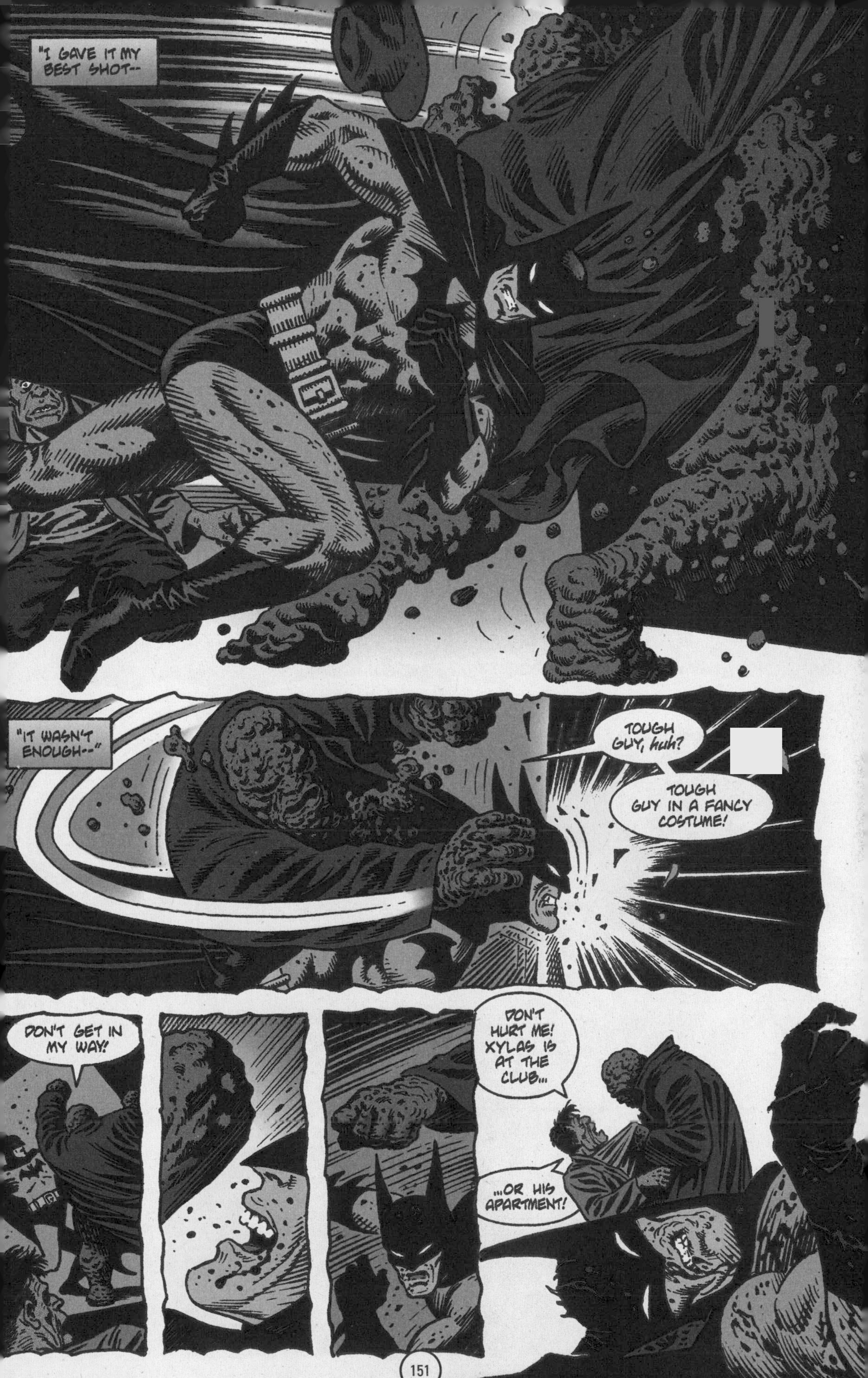
"I GAVE IT MY BEST SHOT--
"IT WASN'T ENOUGH--"
TOUGH GUY, huh?
TOUGH GUY IN A FANCY COSTUME!
DON'T GET IN MY WAY!
DON'T HURT ME! XYLAS IS AT THE CLUB...
...OR HIS APARTMENT!

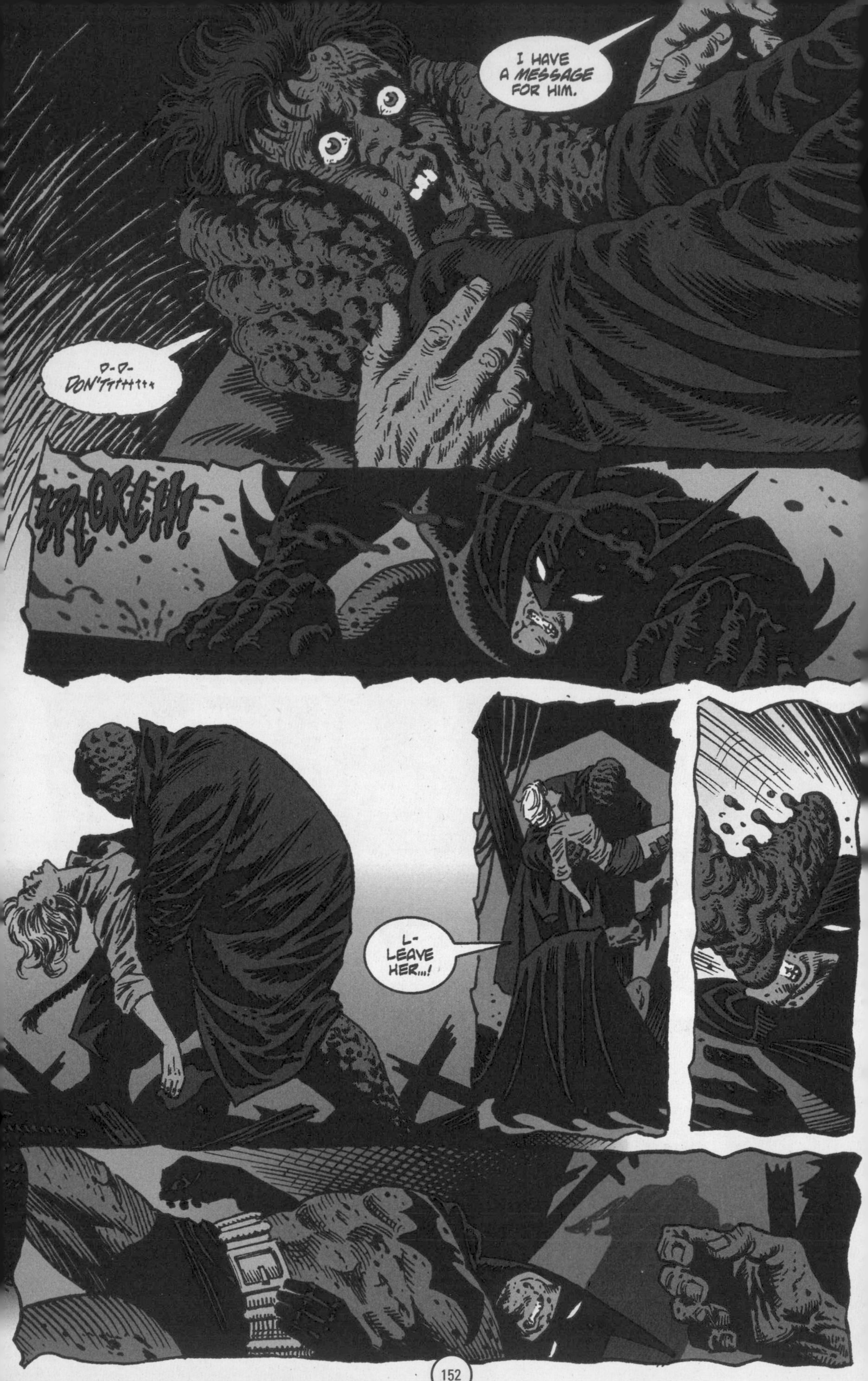

I HAVE A MESSAGE FOR HIM.
D-D-DON'Tttttttt
SPLORCH!
L-LEAVE HER...!

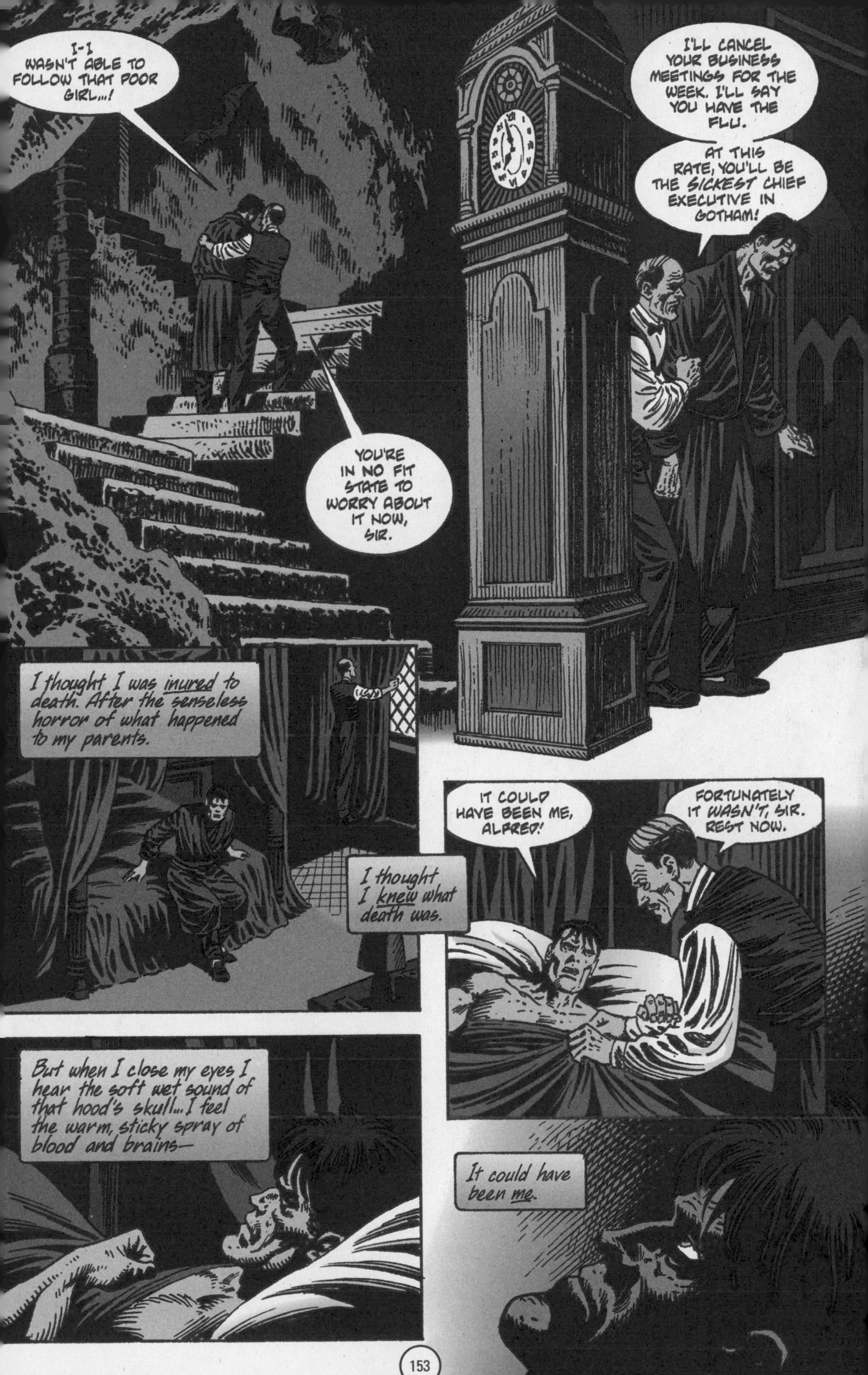
I-I WASN'T ABLE TO FOLLOW THAT POOR GIRL...!
YOU'RE IN NO FIT STATE TO WORRY ABOUT IT NOW, SIR.
I'LL CANCEL YOUR BUSINESS MEETINGS FOR THE WEEK. I'LL SAY YOU HAVE THE FLU.
AT THIS RATE, YOU'LL BE THE SICKEST CHIEF EXECUTIVE IN GOTHAM!
I thought I was inured to death. After the senseless horror of what happened to my parents.
I thought I knew what death was.
IT COULD HAVE BEEN ME, ALFRED!
FORTUNATELY IT WASN'T, SIR. REST NOW.
But when I close my eyes I hear the soft wet sound of that hood's skull... I feel the warm, sticky spray of blood and brains—
It could have been me.

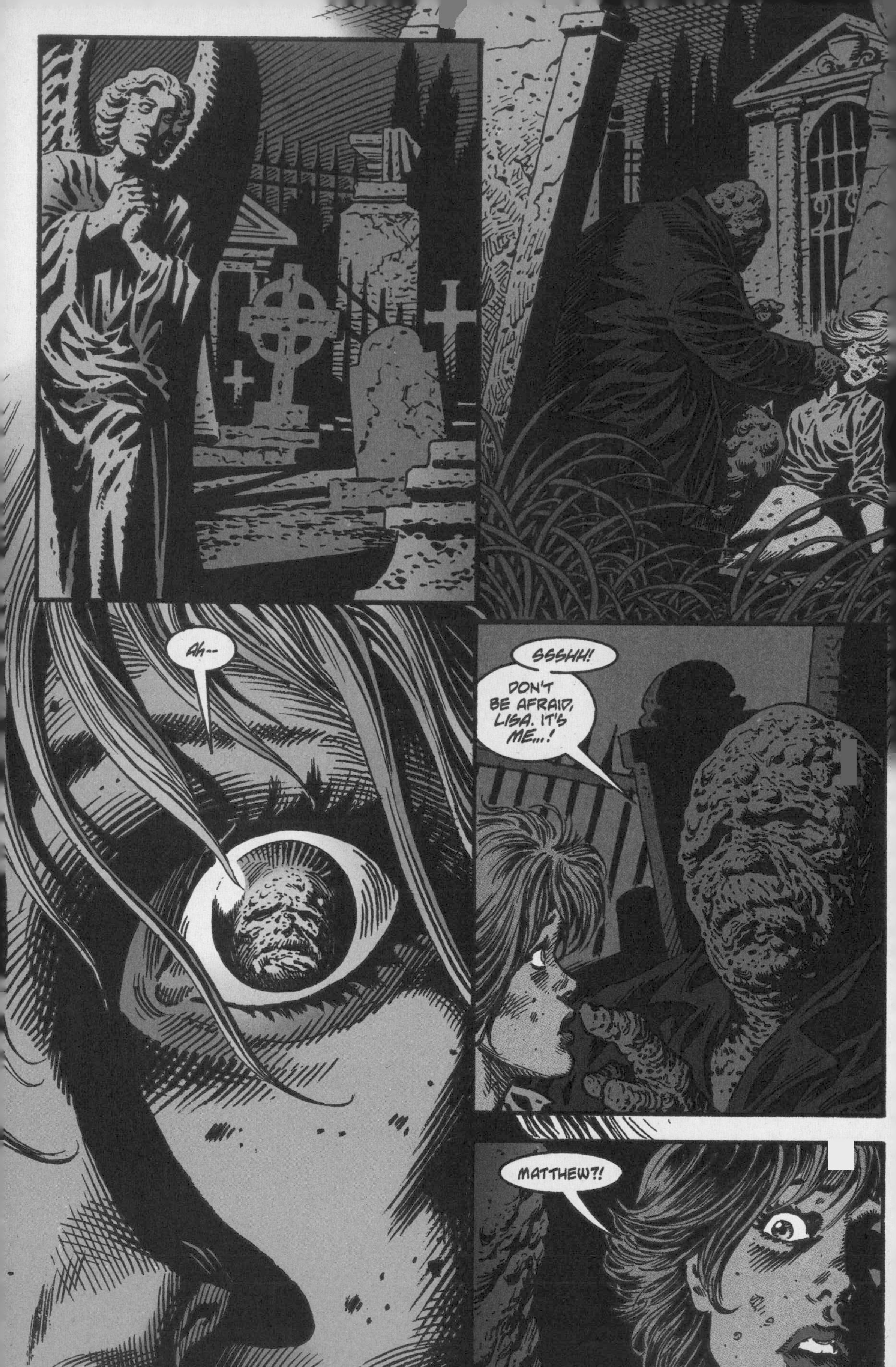
AH--
SSSHH!
DON'T BE AFRAID, LISA. IT'S ME...!
MATTHEW?!

In the dream, I'm terrified, running through a city of dead men and burst skulls.

All of them, good and bad, had laughed and cried. They loved and they hated. They succeeded and they failed.

Now, nothing. Death—the Great Leveller—strips away all meaning.

I chose the way of the warrior.

I knew Death would walk one pace behind me.

IT'S ONLY ME.

YOU CALLED OUT. YOU'RE FEVERED.

I'VE BEEN THINKING. CALL MY ATTORNEY.

Then why am I so afraid?

MAKE SURE MY WILL IS BROUGHT UP TO DATE.

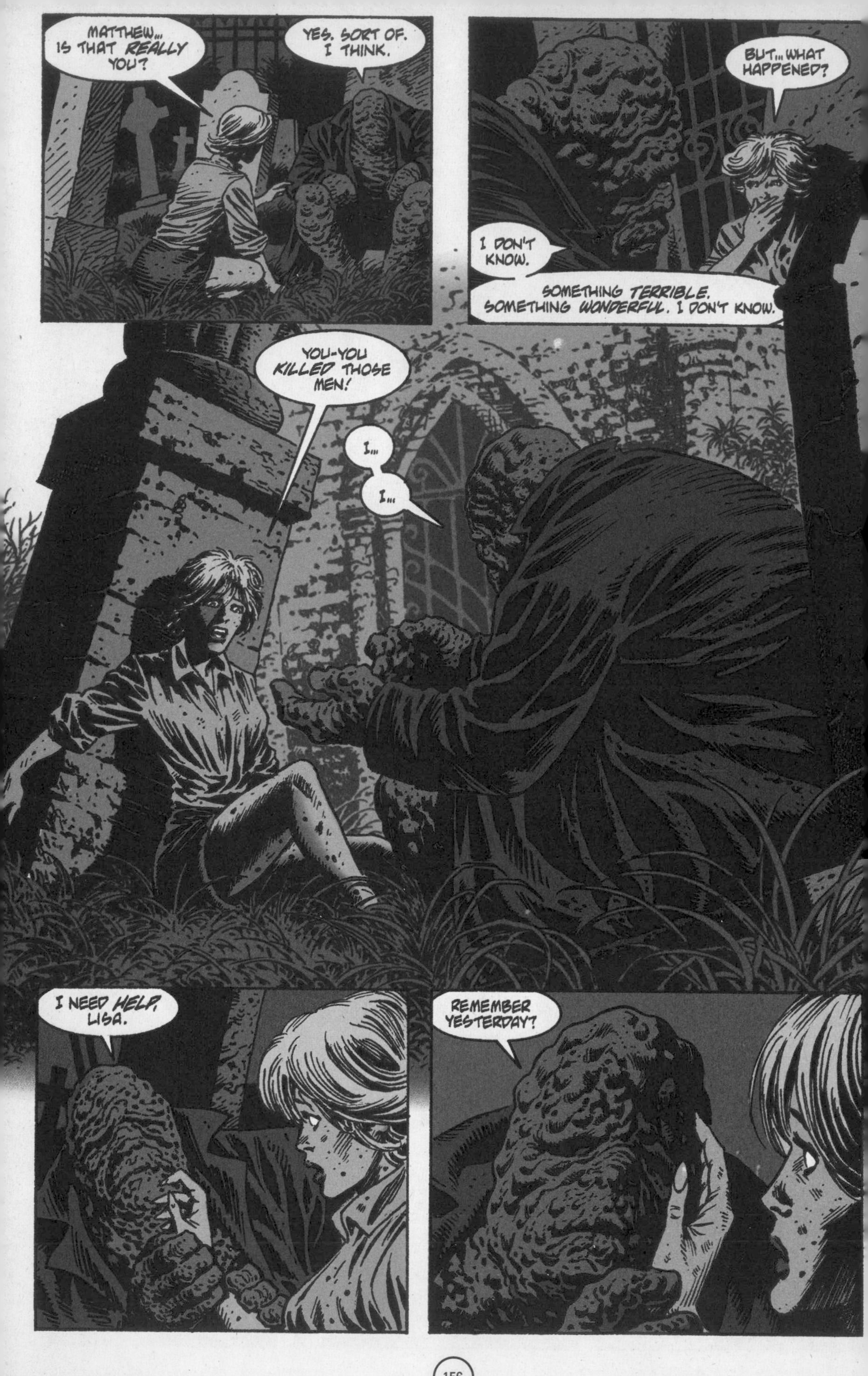
MATTHEW... IS THAT REALLY YOU?
YES. SORT OF. I THINK.
BUT... WHAT HAPPENED?
I DON'T KNOW.
SOMETHING TERRIBLE. SOMETHING WONDERFUL. I DON'T KNOW.
YOU-YOU KILLED THOSE MEN!
I...
I...
I NEED HELP, LISA.
REMEMBER YESTERDAY?

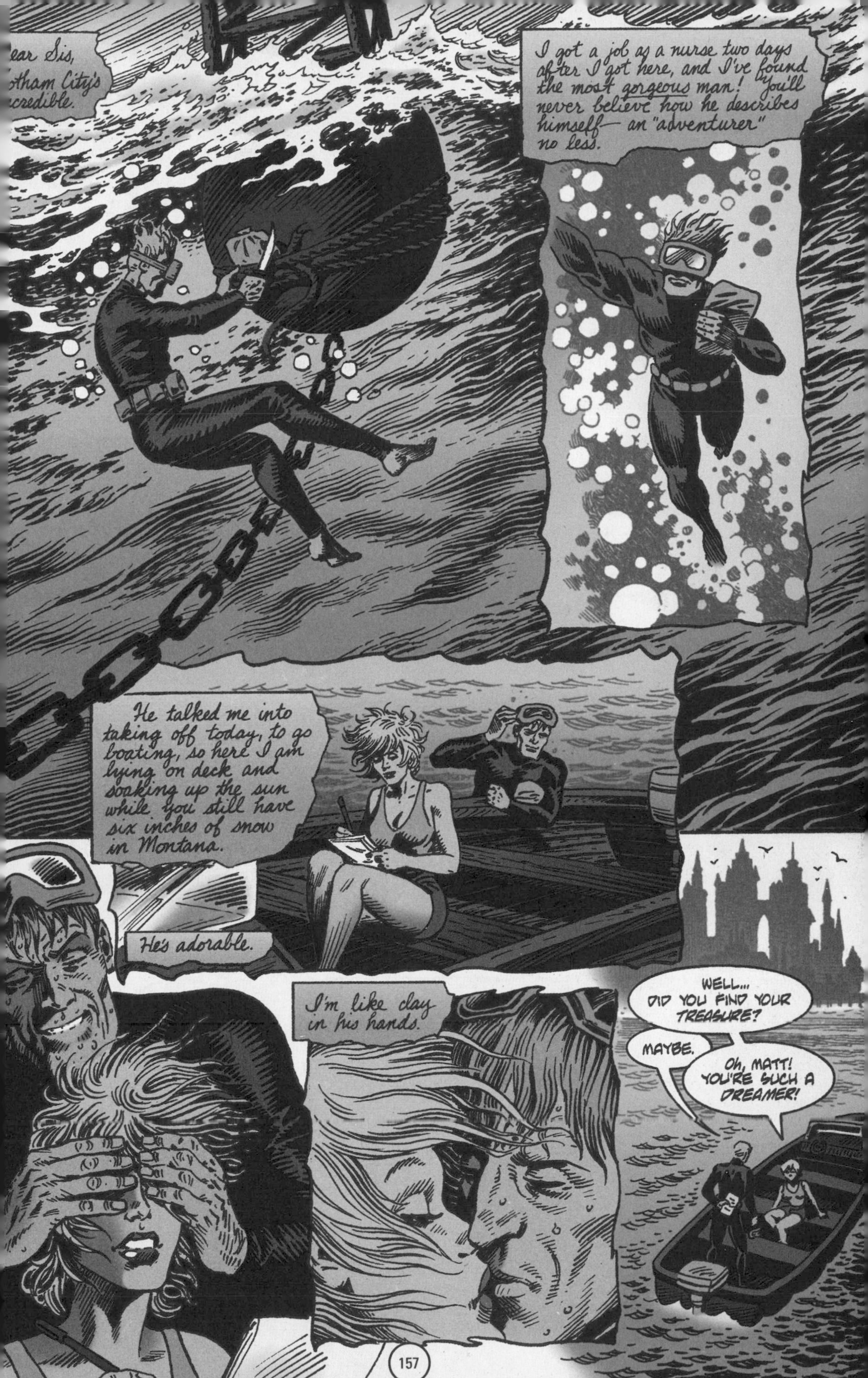
ear Sis,
otham City's
credible.
I got a job as a nurse two days after I got here, and I've found the most gorgeous man! You'll never believe how he describes himself— an "adventurer" no less.
He talked me into taking off today, to go boating, so here I am lying on deck and soaking up the sun while you still have six inches of snow in Montana.
He's adorable.
I'm like clay in his hands.
WELL... DID YOU FIND YOUR TREASURE?
MAYBE.
OH, MATT! YOU'RE SUCH A DREAMER!

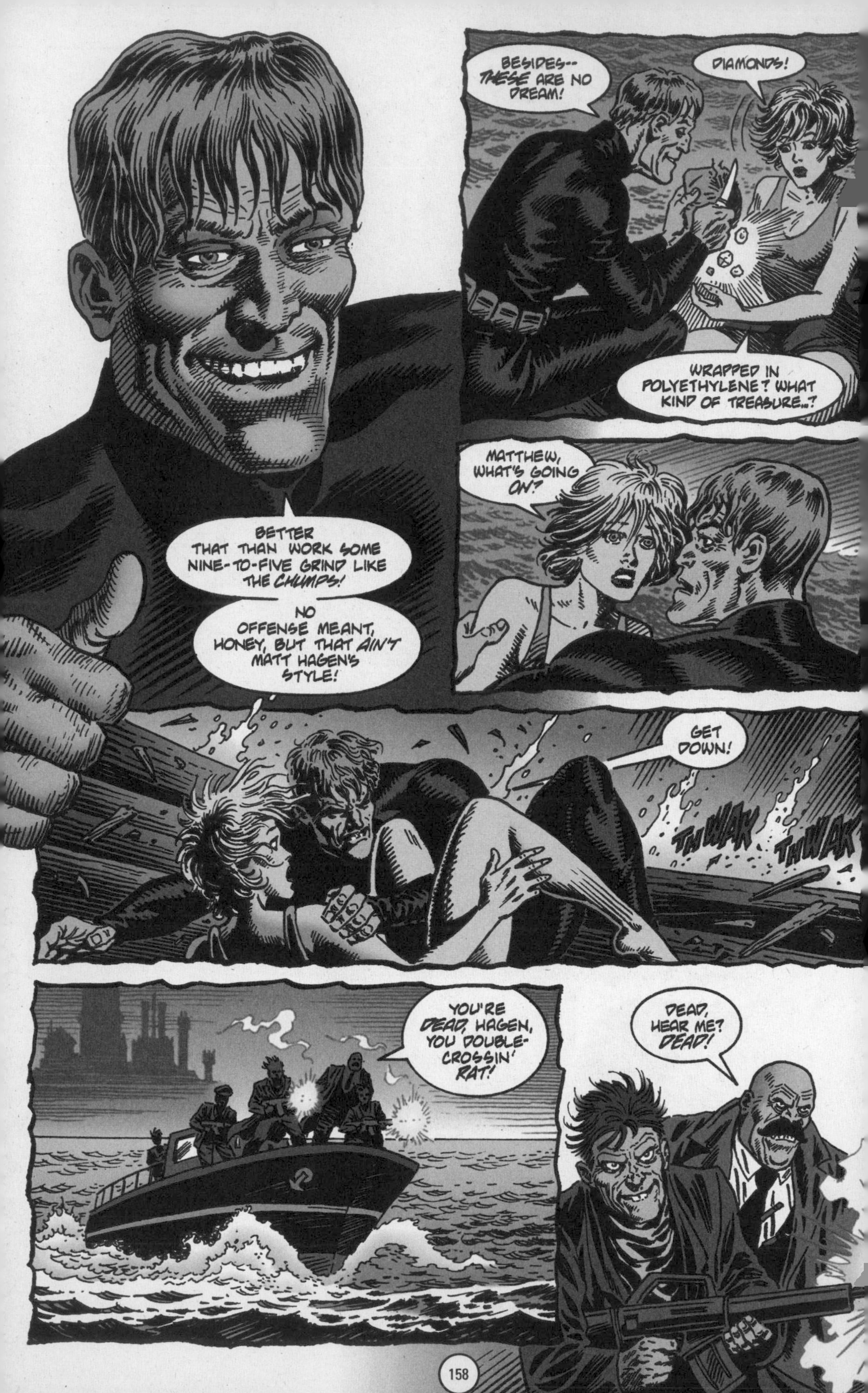
BETTER THAN THAN WORK SOME NINE-TO-FIVE GRIND LIKE THE CHUMPS!
NO OFFENSE MEANT, HONEY, BUT THAT AIN'T MATT HAGEN'S STYLE!
BESIDES-- THESE ARE NO DREAM!
DIAMONDS!
WRAPPED IN POLYETHYLENE? WHAT KIND OF TREASURE..?
MATTHEW, WHAT'S GOING ON?
GET DOWN!
THWAK
THWAK
YOU'RE DEAD, HAGEN, YOU DOUBLE-CROSSIN' RAT!
DEAD, HEAR ME? DEAD!

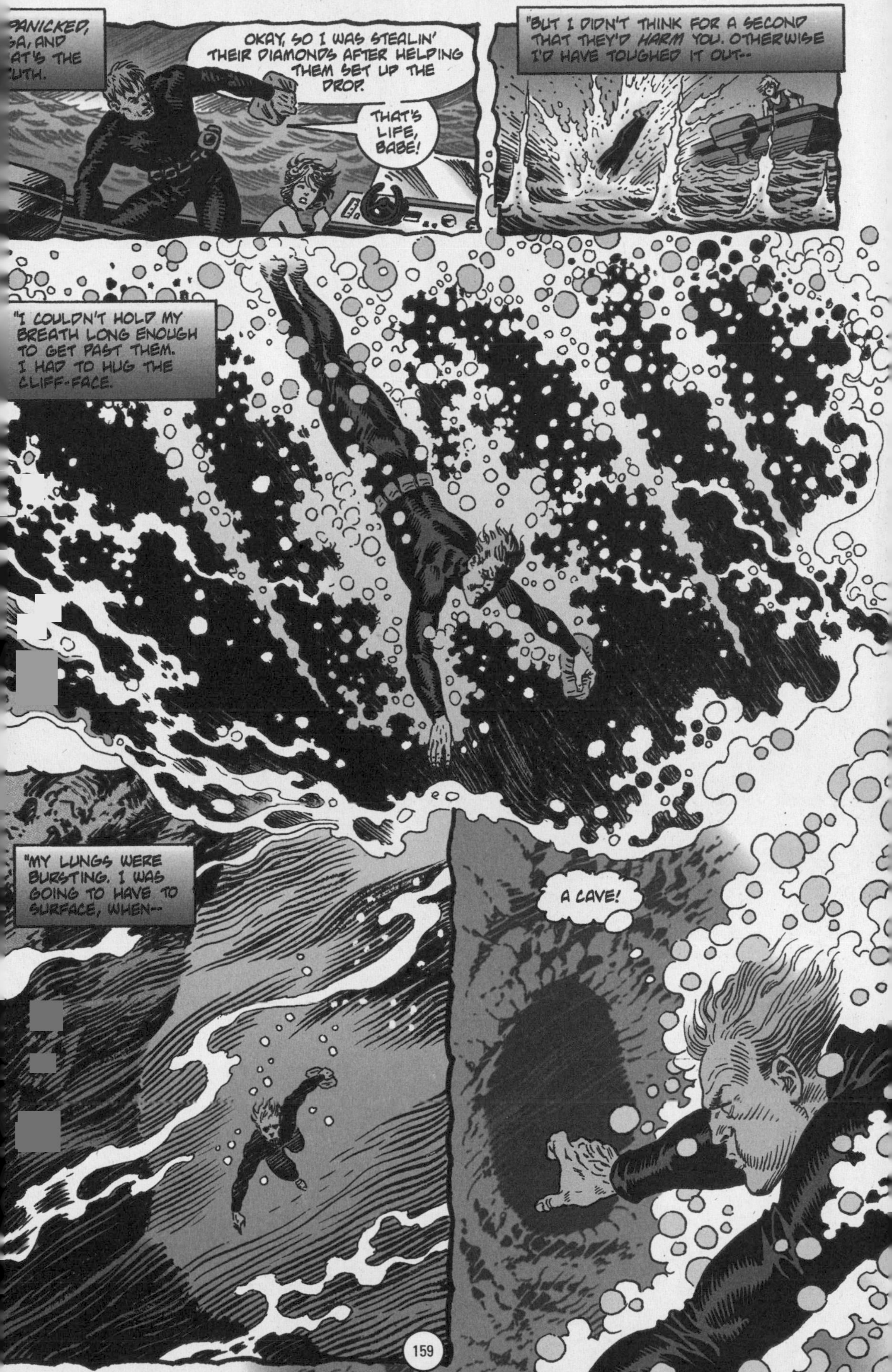
PANICKED,
SA, AND
AT'S THE
UTH.
OKAY, SO I WAS STEALIN' THEIR DIAMONDS AFTER HELPING THEM SET UP THE DROP.
THAT'S LIFE, BABE!
"BUT I DIDN'T THINK FOR A SECOND THAT THEY'D HARM YOU. OTHERWISE I'D HAVE TOUGHED IT OUT--
"I COULDN'T HOLD MY BREATH LONG ENOUGH TO GET PAST THEM. I HAD TO HUG THE CLIFF-FACE.
"MY LUNGS WERE BURSTING. I WAS GOING TO HAVE TO SURFACE, WHEN--
A CAVE!

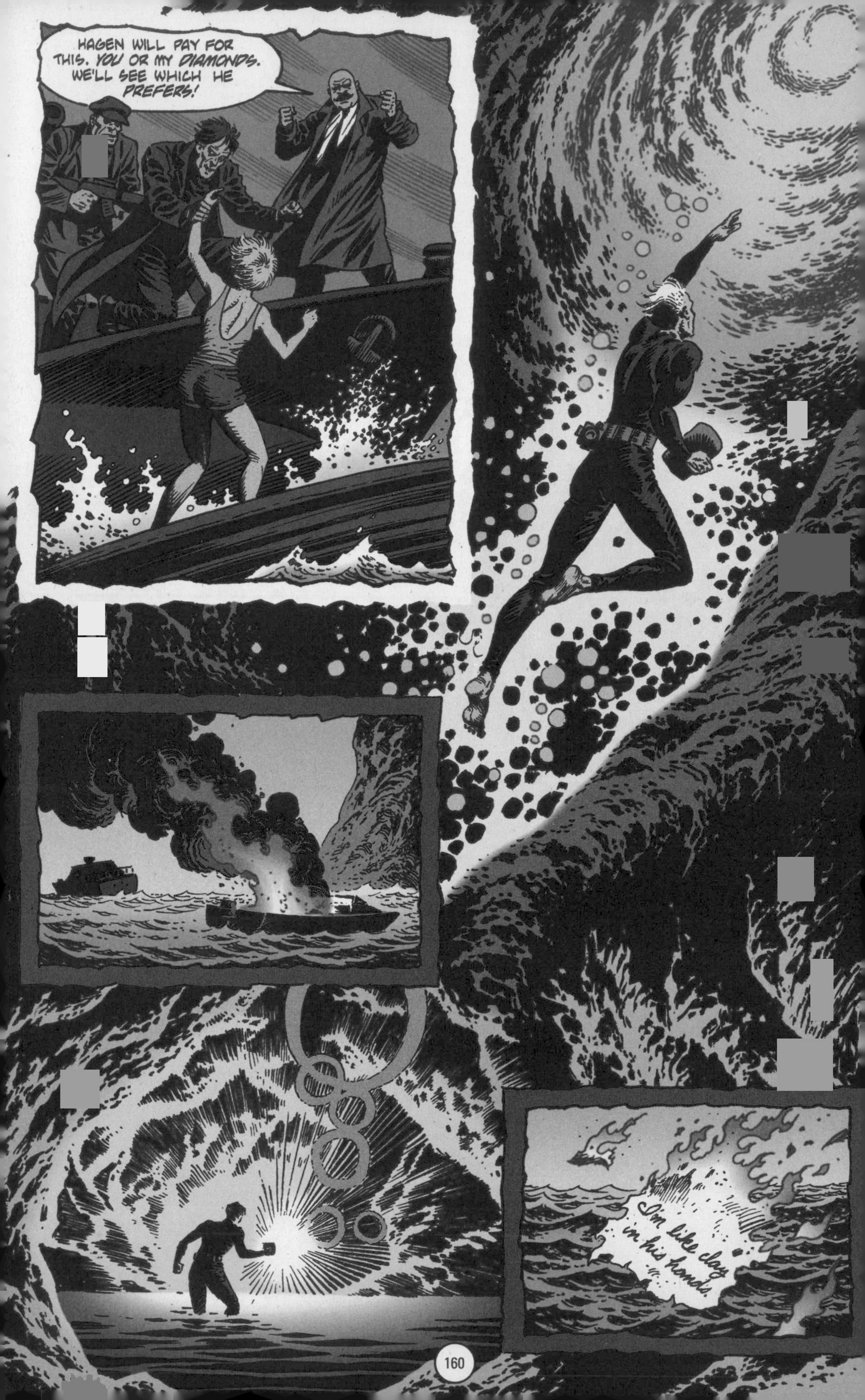
HAGEN WILL PAY FOR THIS. YOU OR MY DIAMONDS. WE'LL SEE WHICH HE PREFERS!
I'm like clay in his hands.

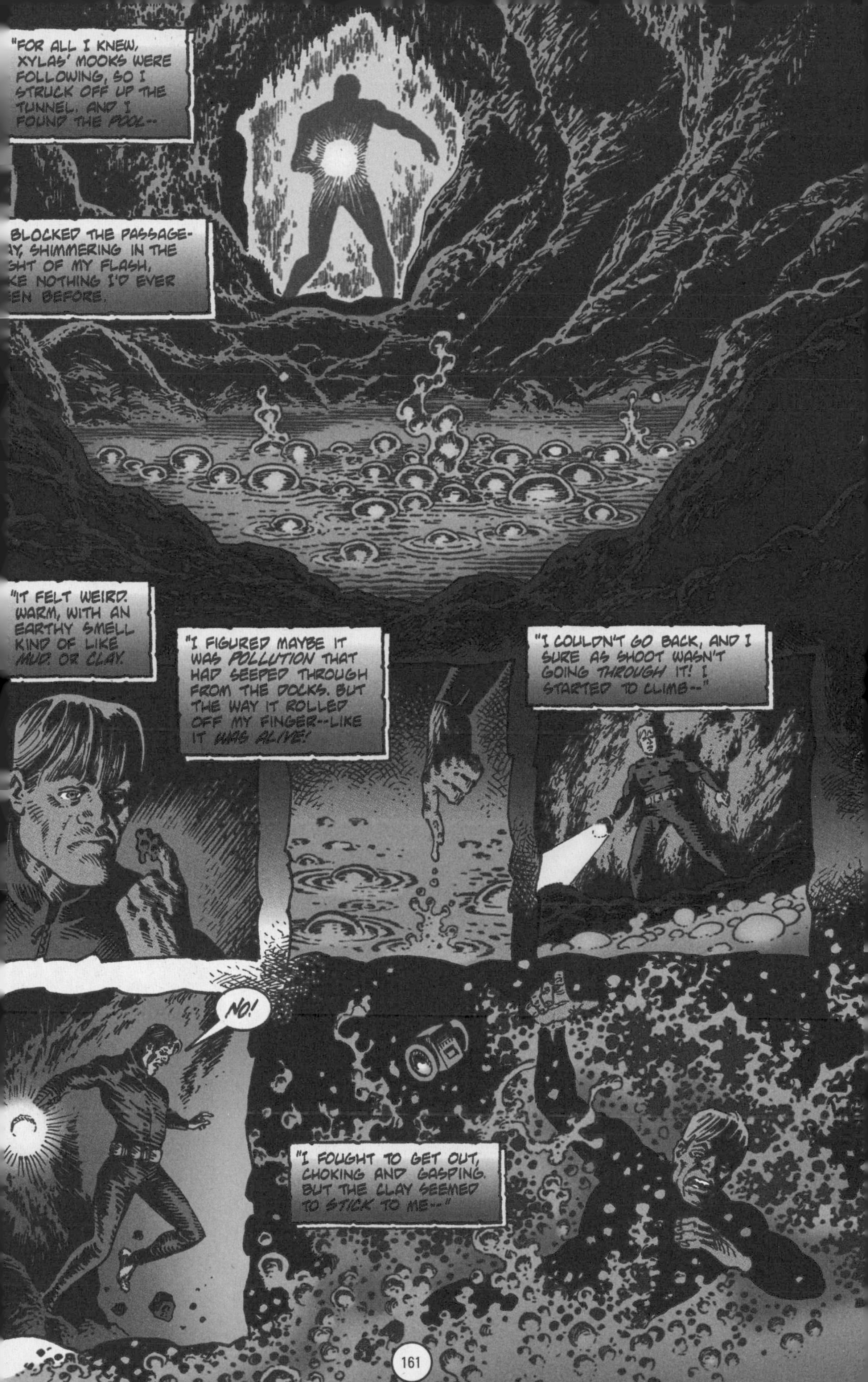
"FOR ALL I KNEW, XYLAS' MOOKS WERE FOLLOWING, SO I STRUCK OFF UP THE TUNNEL, AND I FOUND THE POOL--
BLOCKED THE PASSAGE- AY, SHIMMERING IN THE GHT OF MY FLASH, KE NOTHING I'D EVER EEN BEFORE.
"IT FELT WEIRD. WARM, WITH AN EARTHY SMELL KIND OF LIKE MUD. OR CLAY.
"I FIGURED MAYBE IT WAS POLLUTION THAT HAD SEEPED THROUGH FROM THE DOCKS. BUT THE WAY IT ROLLED OFF MY FINGER--LIKE IT WAS ALIVE!
"I COULDN'T GO BACK, AND I SURE AS SHOOT WASN'T GOING THROUGH IT! I STARTED TO CLIMB--"
NO!
"I FOUGHT TO GET OUT, CHOKING AND GASPING. BUT THE CLAY SEEMED TO STICK TO ME--"

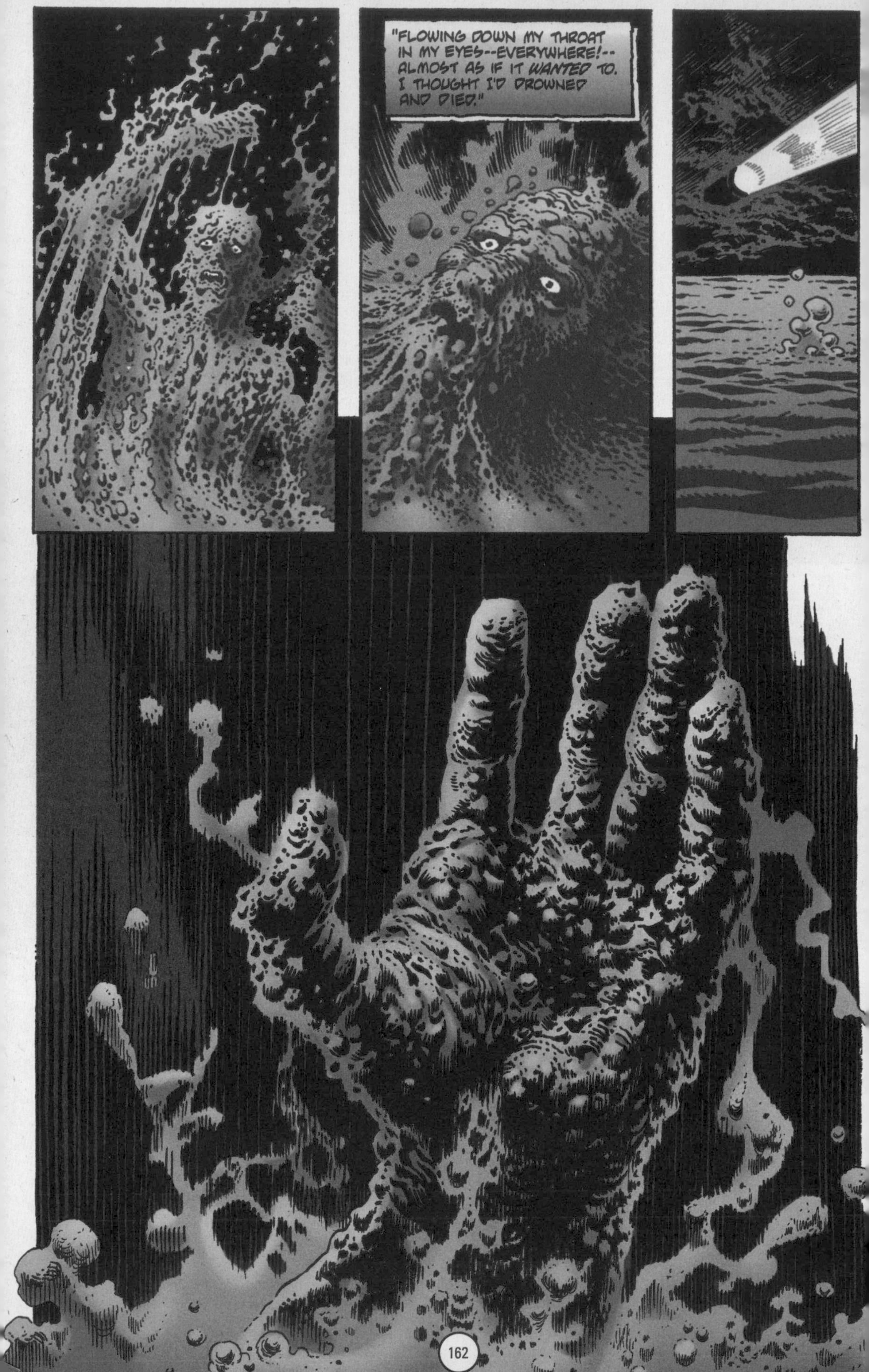
"FLOWING DOWN MY THROAT IN MY EYES--EVERYWHERE!--ALMOST AS IF IT WANTED TO. I THOUGHT I'D DROWNED AND DIED."

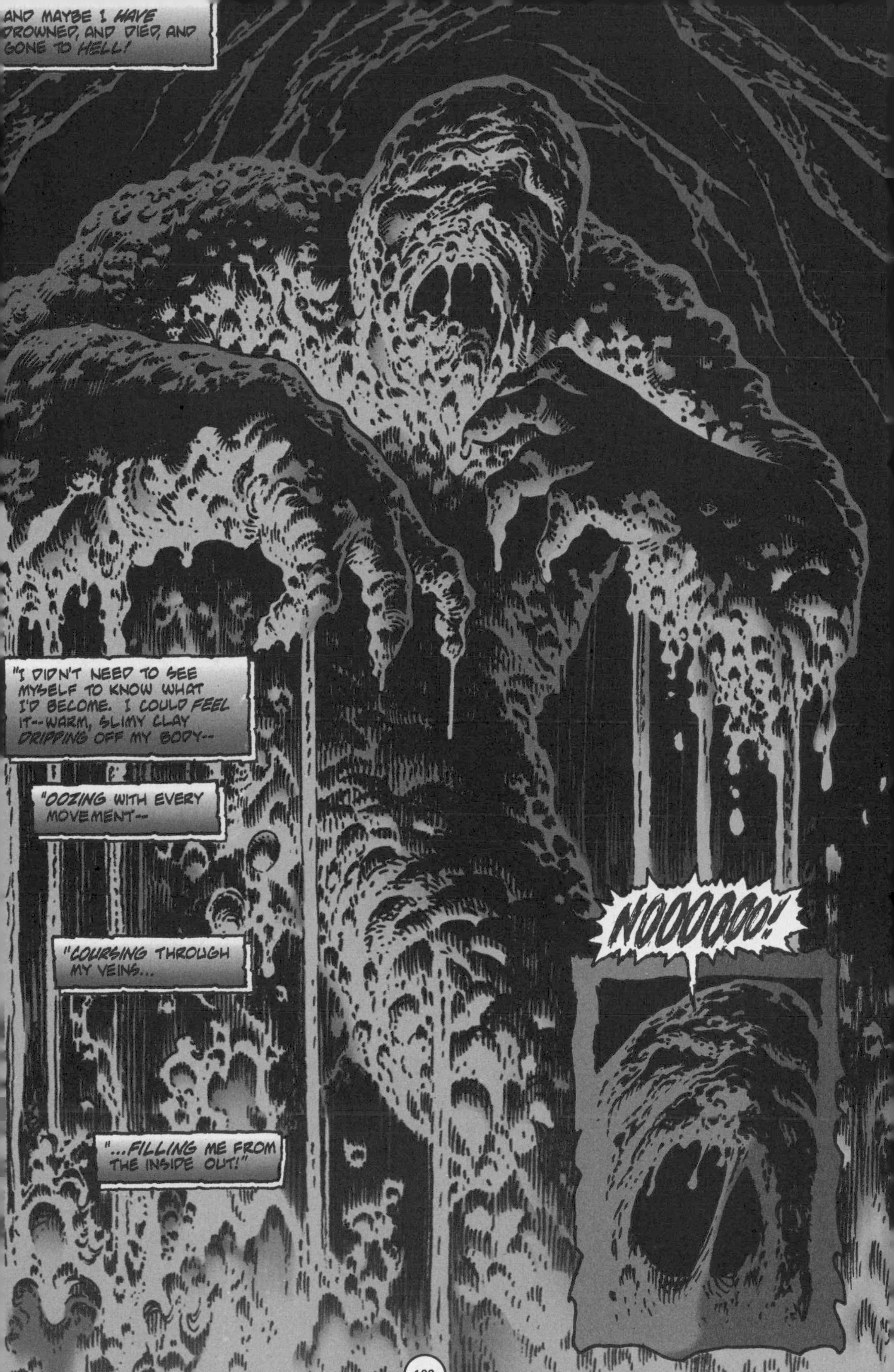
AND MAYBE I HAVE DROWNED, AND DIED, AND GONE TO HELL!
"I DIDN'T NEED TO SEE MYSELF TO KNOW WHAT I'D BECOME. I COULD FEEL IT--WARM, SLIMY CLAY DRIPPING OFF MY BODY--
"OOZING WITH EVERY MOVEMENT--
"COURSING THROUGH MY VEINS...
"...FILLING ME FROM THE INSIDE OUT!"
NOOOOOOO!

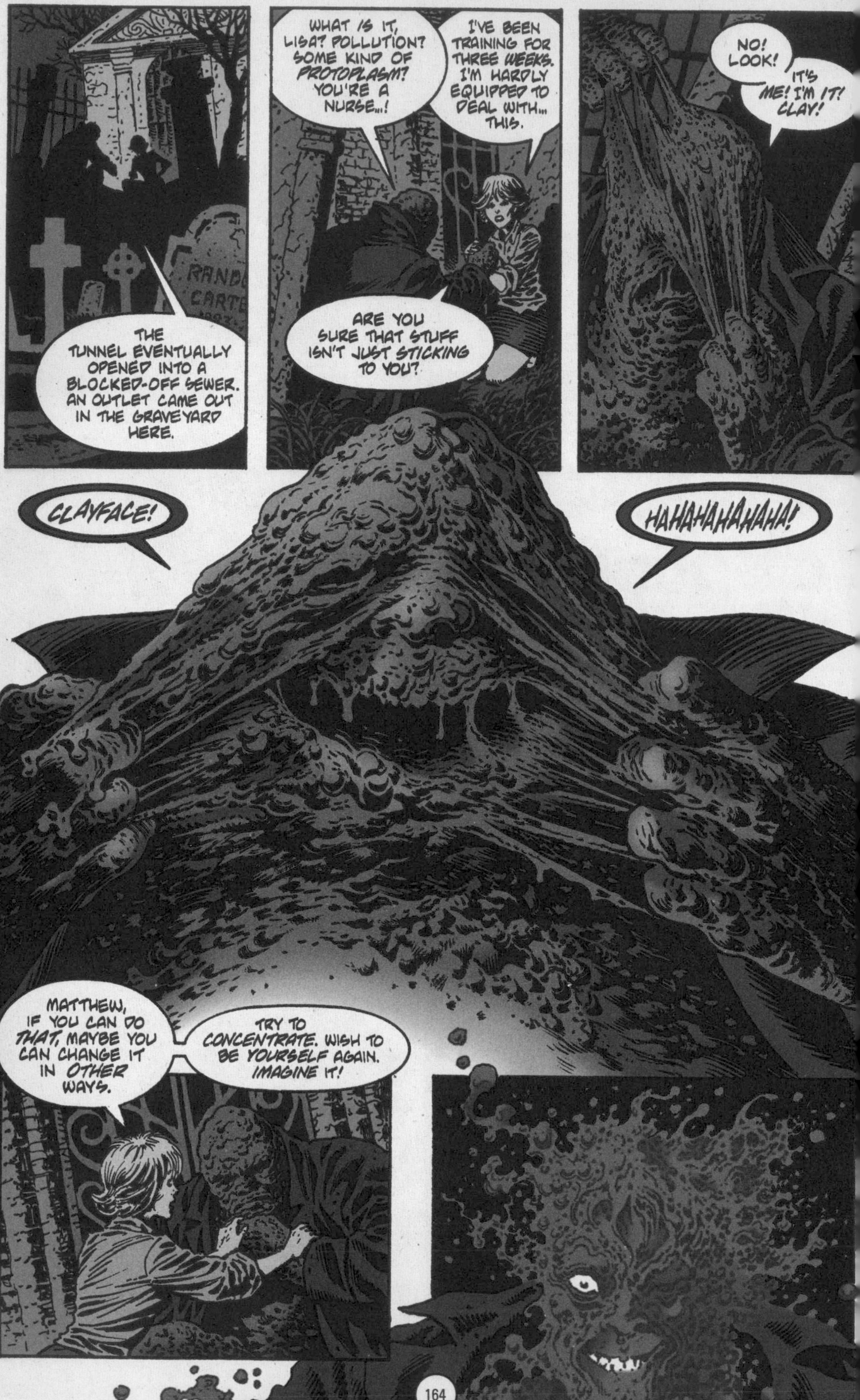
THE TUNNEL EVENTUALLY OPENED INTO A BLOCKED-OFF SEWER. AN OUTLET CAME OUT IN THE GRAVEYARD HERE.
WHAT IS IT, LISA? POLLUTION? SOME KIND OF PROTOPLASM? YOU'RE A NURSE...!
I'VE BEEN TRAINING FOR THREE WEEKS. I'M HARDLY EQUIPPED TO DEAL WITH... THIS.
ARE YOU SURE THAT STUFF ISN'T JUST STICKING TO YOU?
NO! LOOK!
IT'S ME! I'M IT! CLAY!
CLAYFACE!
HAHAHAHAHAHAHA!
MATTHEW, IF YOU CAN DO THAT, MAYBE YOU CAN CHANGE IT IN OTHER WAYS.
TRY TO CONCENTRATE. WISH TO BE YOURSELF AGAIN. IMAGINE IT!

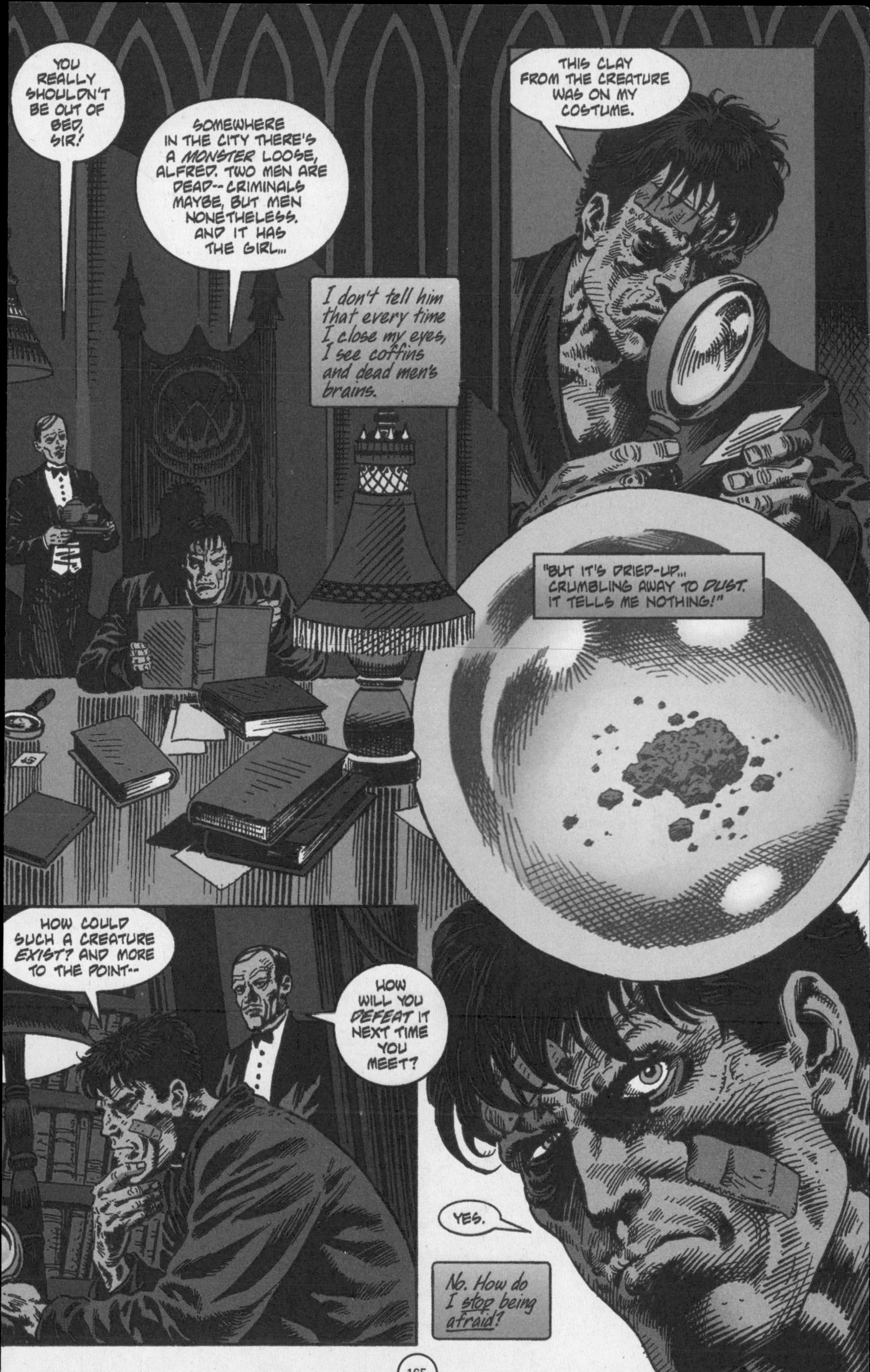
YOU REALLY SHOULDN'T BE OUT OF BED, SIR!
SOMEWHERE IN THE CITY THERE'S A MONSTER LOOSE, ALFRED. TWO MEN ARE DEAD--CRIMINALS MAYBE, BUT MEN NONETHELESS. AND IT HAS THE GIRL...
I don't tell him that every time I close my eyes, I see coffins and dead men's brains.
THIS CLAY FROM THE CREATURE WAS ON MY COSTUME.
"BUT IT'S DRIED-UP... CRUMBLING AWAY TO DUST. IT TELLS ME NOTHING!"
HOW COULD SUCH A CREATURE EXIST? AND MORE TO THE POINT--
HOW WILL YOU DEFEAT IT NEXT TIME YOU MEET?
YES.
No. How do I stop being afraid?

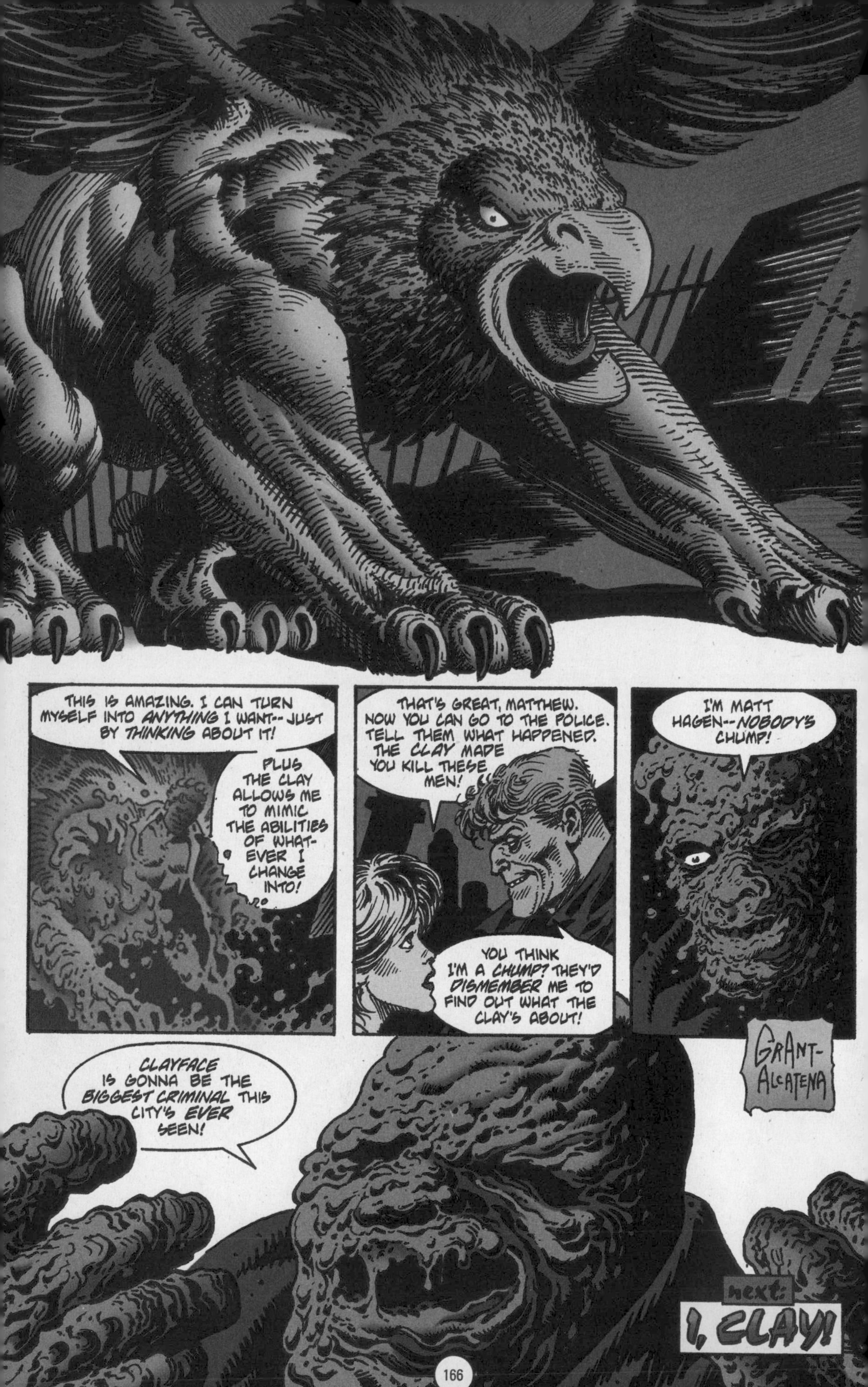

THIS IS AMAZING. I CAN TURN MYSELF INTO ANYTHING I WANT-- JUST BY THINKING ABOUT IT!
PLUS THE CLAY ALLOWS ME TO MIMIC THE ABILITIES OF WHAT-EVER I CHANGE INTO!
THAT'S GREAT, MATTHEW. NOW YOU CAN GO TO THE POLICE. TELL THEM WHAT HAPPENED. THE CLAY MADE YOU KILL THESE MEN!
YOU THINK I'M A CHUMP? THEY'D DISMEMBER ME TO FIND OUT WHAT THE CLAY'S ABOUT!
I'M MATT HAGEN--NOBODY'S CHUMP!
GRANT-ALCATENA
CLAYFACE IS GONNA BE THE BIGGEST CRIMINAL THIS CITY'S EVER SEEN!
next:
I, CLAY!

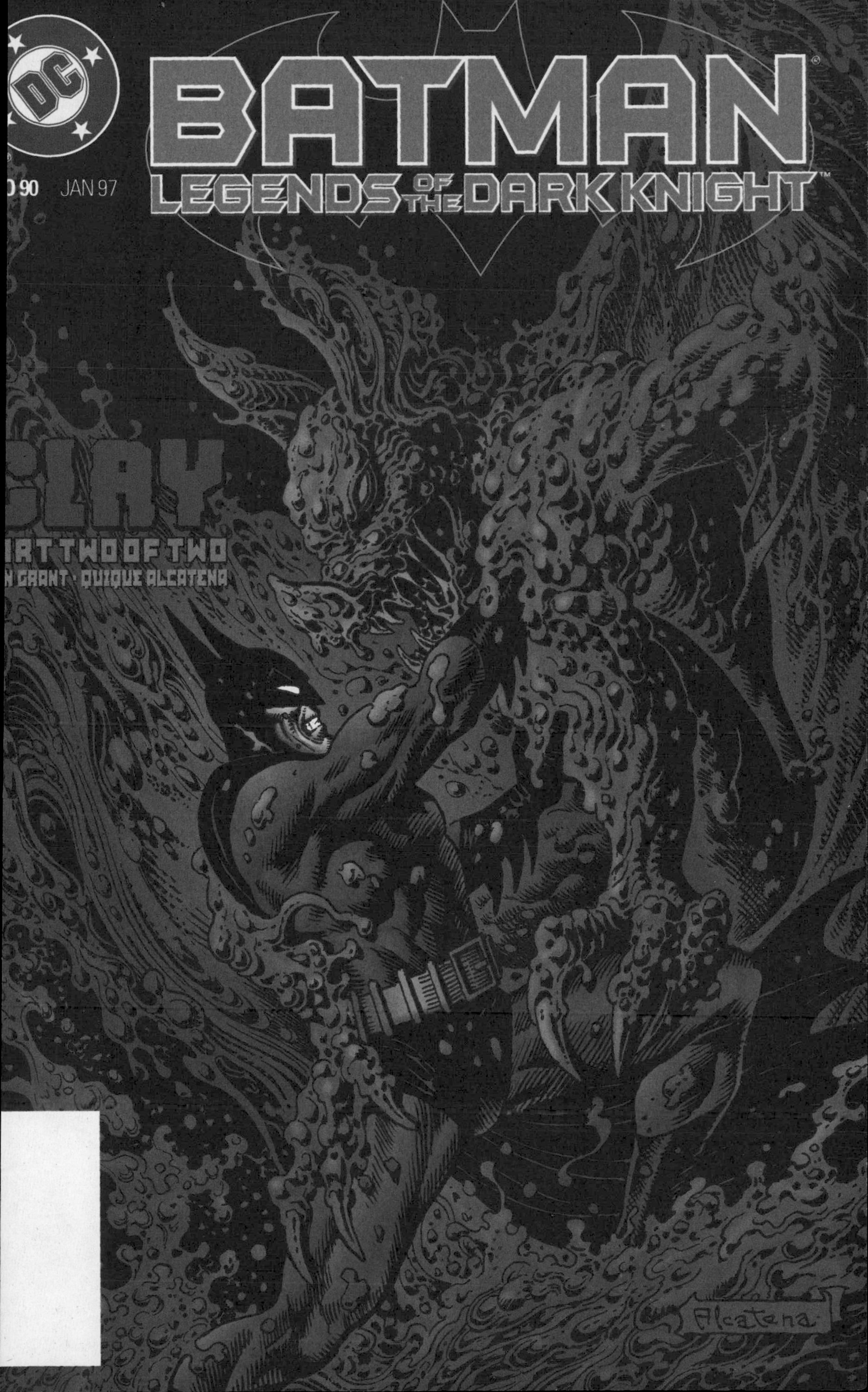
BATMAN
0 90 JAN 97
LEGENDS OF THE DARK KNIGHT
CLAY
RT TWO OF TWO
N GRANT · QUIQUE ALCATENA
Alcatena

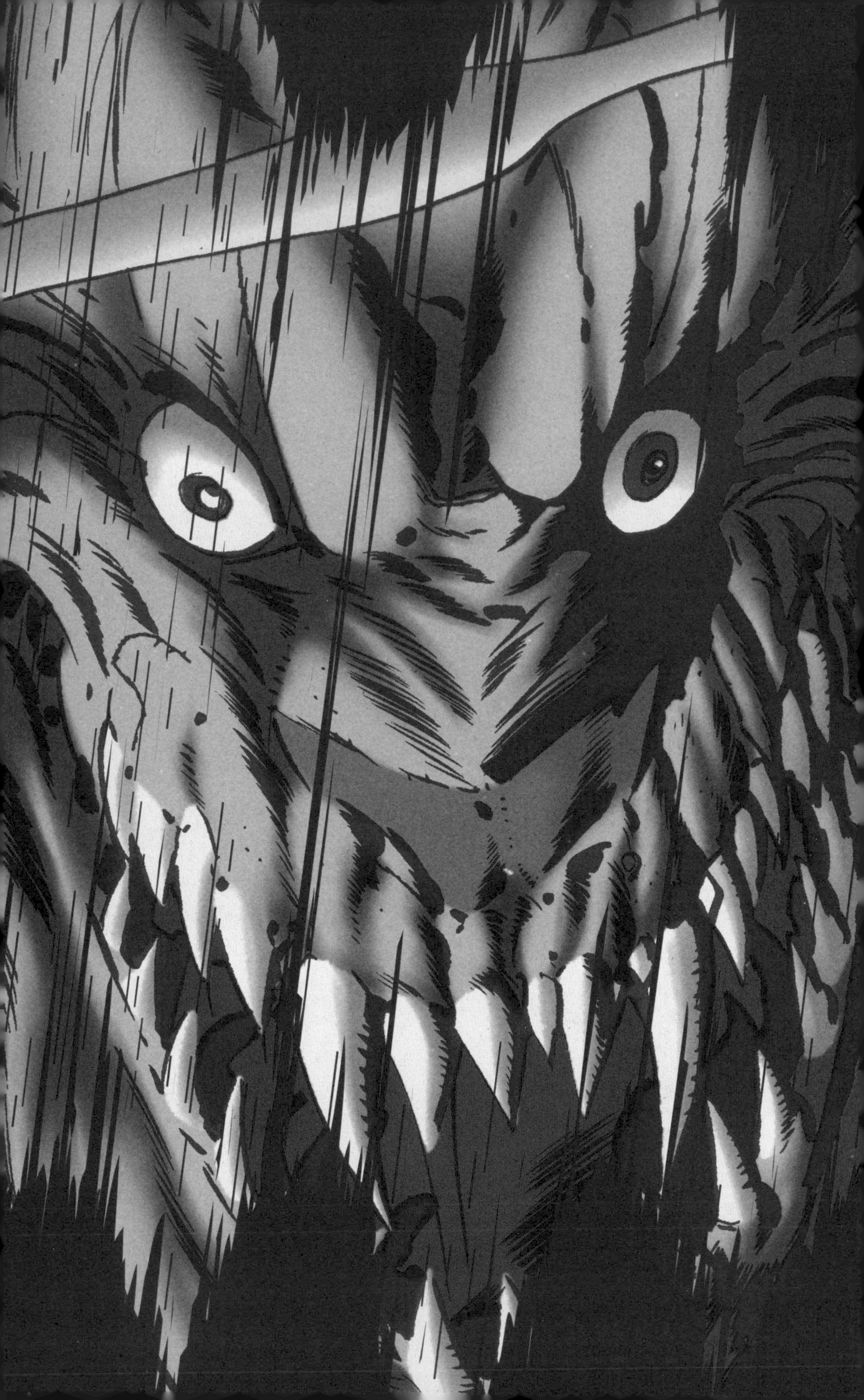

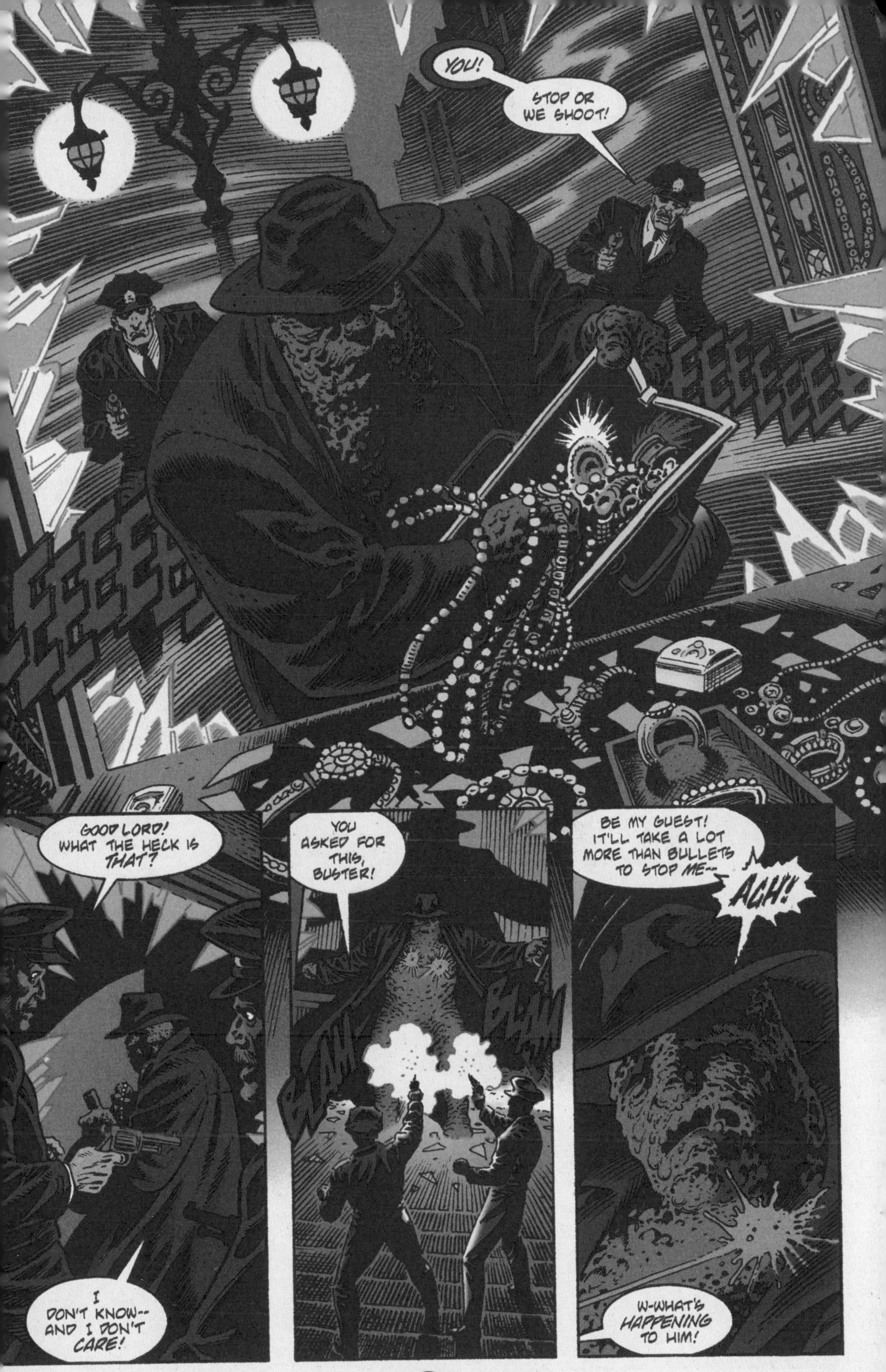
YOU!
STOP OR WE SHOOT!
GOOD LORD! WHAT THE HECK IS THAT?
I DON'T KNOW-- AND I DON'T CARE!
YOU ASKED FOR THIS, BUSTER!
BLAM
BLAM
BE MY GUEST! IT'LL TAKE A LOT MORE THAN BULLETS TO STOP ME--
AGH!
W-WHAT'S HAPPENING TO HIM!

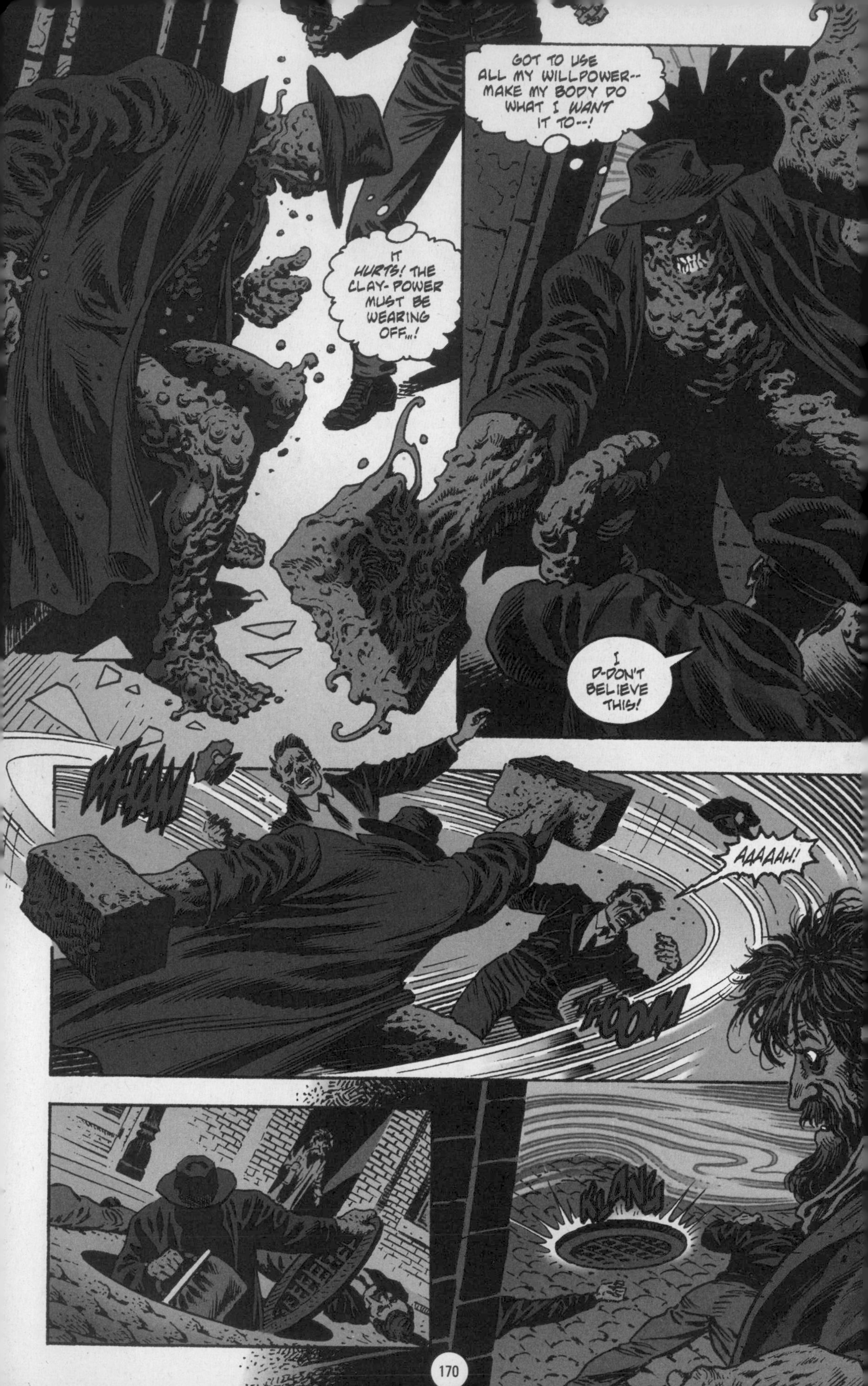

GOT TO USE ALL MY WILLPOWER-- MAKE MY BODY DO WHAT I WANT IT TO--!
IT HURTS! THE CLAY-POWER MUST BE WEARING OFF...!
I D-DON'T BELIEVE THIS!
WHAAM
AAAAAH!
THOOM
KLANG

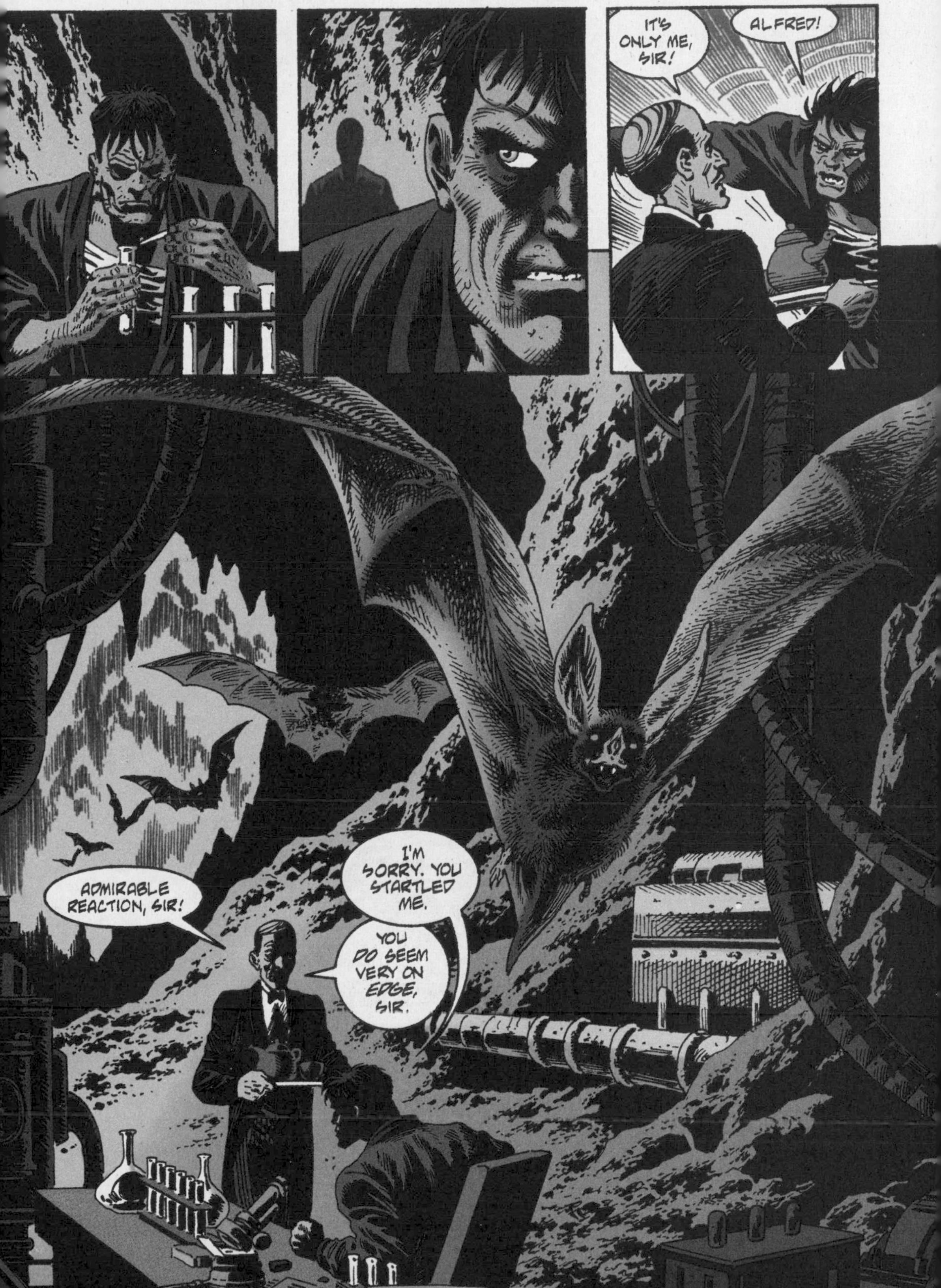

IT'S ONLY ME, SIR!
ALFRED!
ADMIRABLE REACTION, SIR!
I'M SORRY. YOU STARTLED ME.
YOU DO SEEM VERY ON EDGE, SIR.

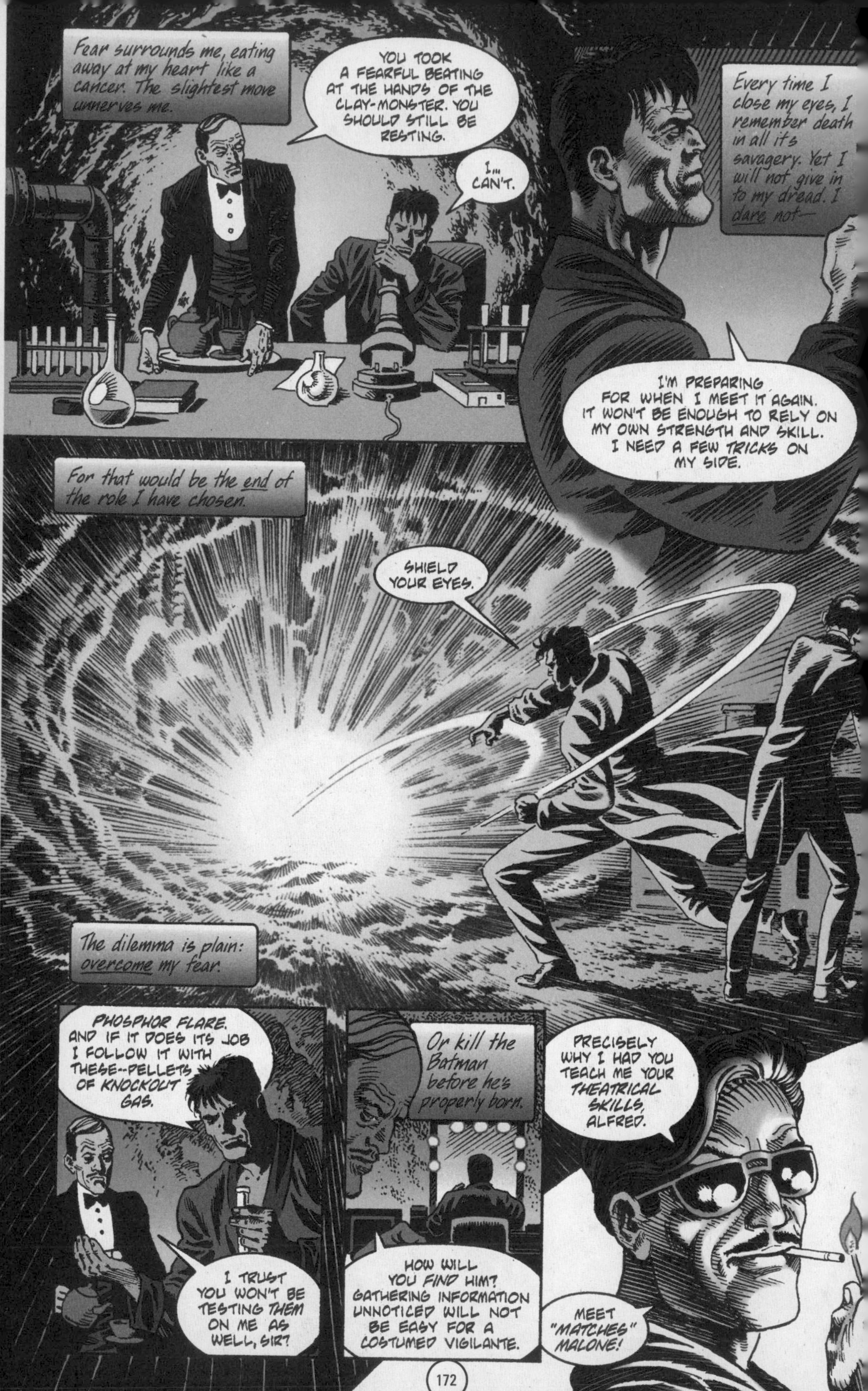

Fear surrounds me, eating away at my heart like a cancer. The slightest move unnerves me.
YOU TOOK A FEARFUL BEATING AT THE HANDS OF THE CLAY-MONSTER. YOU SHOULD STILL BE RESTING.
I... CAN'T.
Every time I close my eyes, I remember death in all its savagery. Yet I will not give in to my dread. I dare not—
I'M PREPARING FOR WHEN I MEET IT AGAIN. IT WON'T BE ENOUGH TO RELY ON MY OWN STRENGTH AND SKILL. I NEED A FEW TRICKS ON MY SIDE.
For that would be the end of the role I have chosen.
SHIELD YOUR EYES.
The dilemma is plain: overcome my fear.
PHOSPHOR FLARE. AND IF IT DOES ITS JOB I FOLLOW IT WITH THESE--PELLETS OF KNOCKOUT GAS.
I TRUST YOU WON'T BE TESTING THEM ON ME AS WELL, SIR?
Or kill the Batman before he's properly born.
HOW WILL YOU FIND HIM? GATHERING INFORMATION UNNOTICED WILL NOT BE EASY FOR A COSTUMED VIGILANTE.
PRECISELY WHY I HAD YOU TEACH ME YOUR THEATRICAL SKILLS, ALFRED.
MEET "MATCHES" MALONE!

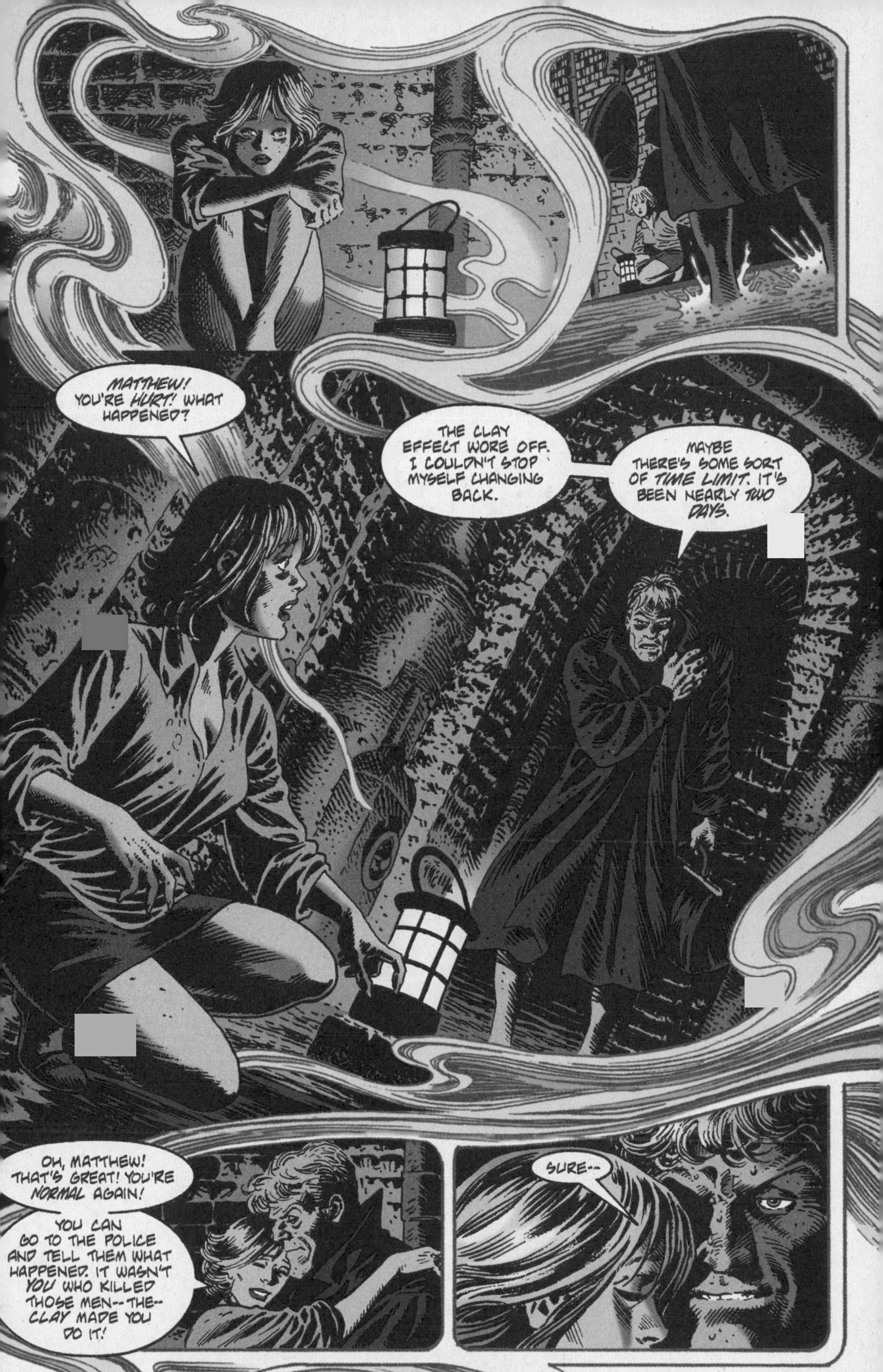
MATTHEW! YOU'RE HURT! WHAT HAPPENED?
THE CLAY EFFECT WORE OFF. I COULDN'T STOP MYSELF CHANGING BACK.
MAYBE THERE'S SOME SORT OF TIME LIMIT. IT'S BEEN NEARLY TWO DAYS.
OH, MATTHEW! THAT'S GREAT! YOU'RE NORMAL AGAIN!
YOU CAN GO TO THE POLICE AND TELL THEM WHAT HAPPENED. IT WASN'T YOU WHO KILLED THOSE MEN--THE--CLAY MADE YOU DO IT!
SURE--

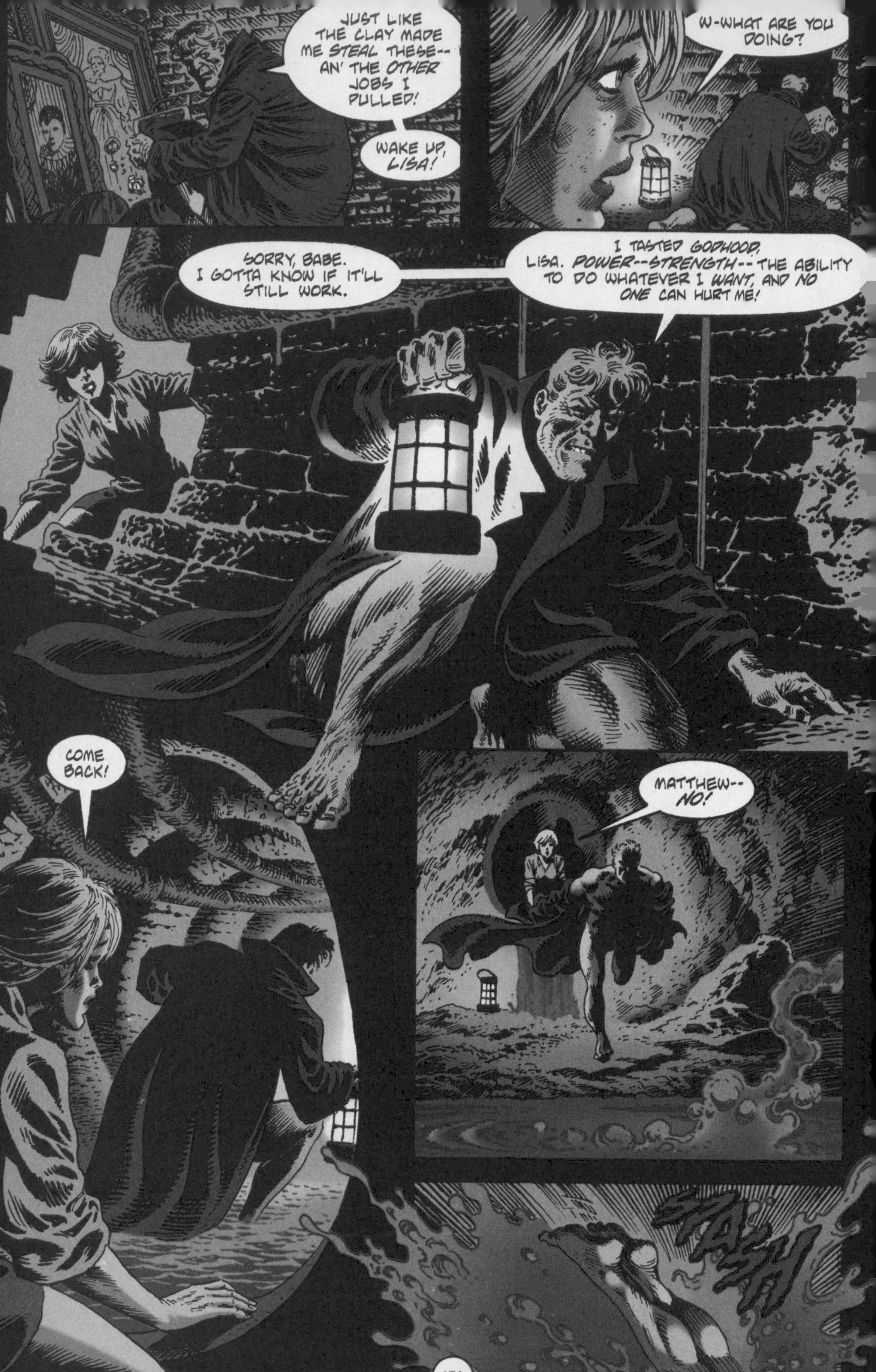
JUST LIKE THE CLAY MADE ME STEAL THESE--AN' THE OTHER JOBS I PULLED!
WAKE UP, LISA!
W-WHAT ARE YOU DOING?
SORRY, BABE. I GOTTA KNOW IF IT'LL STILL WORK.
I TASTED GODHOOD, LISA. POWER--STRENGTH--THE ABILITY TO DO WHATEVER I WANT, AND NO ONE CAN HURT ME!
COME BACK!
MATTHEW--NO!
SPLASH

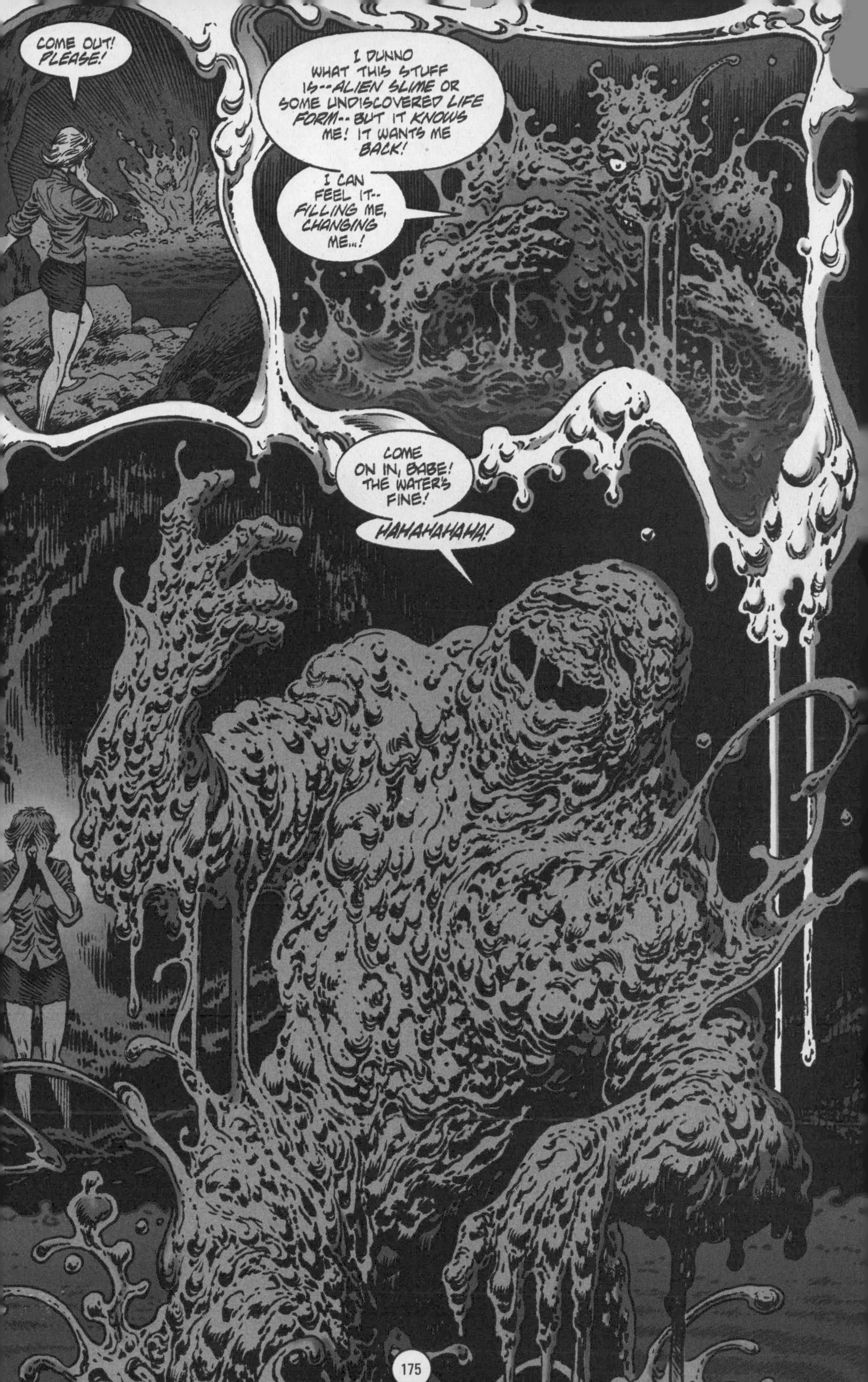
COME OUT! PLEASE!
I DUNNO WHAT THIS STUFF IS--ALIEN SLIME OR SOME UNDISCOVERED LIFE FORM--BUT IT KNOWS ME! IT WANTS ME BACK!
I CAN FEEL IT-- FILLING ME, CHANGING ME...!
COME ON IN, BABE! THE WATER'S FINE!
HAHAHAHAHA!

GOTHAM GAZETTE

MONSTER ON THE LOOSE?

Jeweler Robbed; One Guard Slain, One in Hospital

Link With Death of Local Hoodlums?

...mi-coherent statements made by injured securit... ...ard Ronald Rolfe (41) refer to a "man-like monster...

MONSTER MY EYE! WHAT WOULD A MONSTER WANT WITH A BAG OF JEWELS? WHY WOULD A MONSTER KILL DILL AND SODA AND RESCUE HAGEN'S CHICK?

DONN BOSS XYL...

BECAUSE IT'S NO MONSTER, THAT'S WHY! IT'S MATT STINKIN' HAGEN! MY DIAMONDS WEREN'T ENOUGH FOR HIM-- NOW HE'S GOIN' ON SOME KIND OF SPREE!

I'LL BE THE LAUGHIN' STOCK OF GOTHAM ONCE IT GETS ROUND HOW HE RIPPED ME OFF!

WE HIT HIS PLACE, BOSS.

AND HIS GIRLFRIEND'S. THEY AIN'T THERE.

AND WHEN YOU DO--

CHOWFF!

AN' YOU WON'T FIND THEM SITTIN' PLAYIN' CARDS! HIT EVERY BAR, EVERY HOTEL, EVERY FLOPHOUSE. FIND THEM!

GOTHAM

Jeweler Robbed; One Guard Slain, One in Hospital

...t With Death of Local Hood... ...herent statements made by... ...eald Rolfe (41) refer to by...

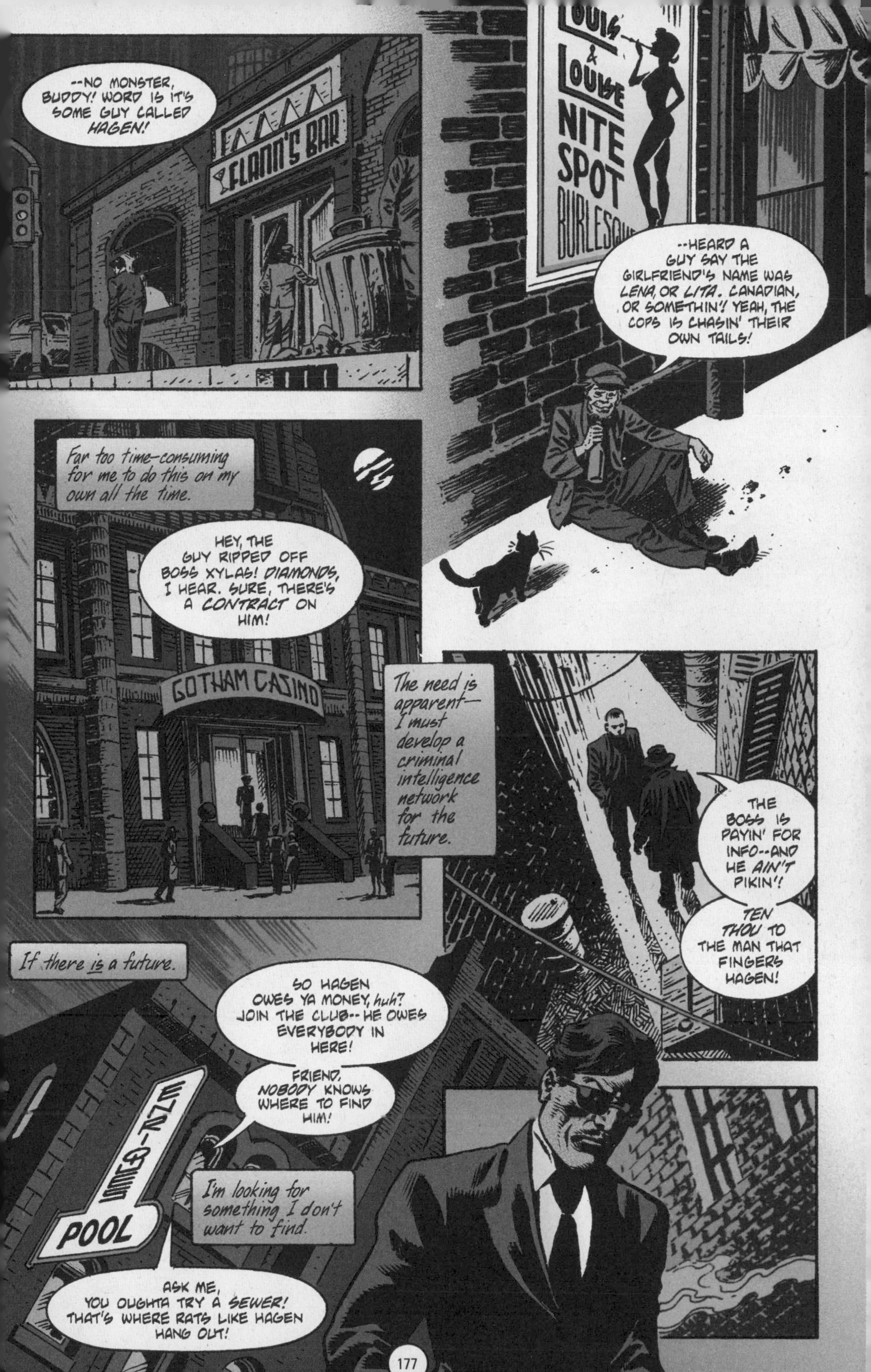
--NO MONSTER, BUDDY! WORD IS IT'S SOME GUY CALLED HAGEN!
FLANN'S BAR
LOUIS & LOUISE NITE SPOT BURLESQUE
--HEARD A GUY SAY THE GIRLFRIEND'S NAME WAS LENA, OR LITA. CANADIAN, OR SOMETHIN'! YEAH, THE COPS IS CHASIN' THEIR OWN TAILS!
Far too time-consuming for me to do this on my own all the time.
HEY, THE GUY RIPPED OFF BOSS XYLAS! DIAMONDS, I HEAR. SURE, THERE'S A CONTRACT ON HIM!
GOTHAM CASINO
The need is apparent— I must develop a criminal intelligence network for the future.
THE BOSS IS PAYIN' FOR INFO--AND HE AIN'T PIKIN'!
TEN THOU TO THE MAN THAT FINGERS HAGEN!
If there is a future.
SO HAGEN OWES YA MONEY, huh? JOIN THE CLUB--HE OWES EVERYBODY IN HERE!
FRIEND, NOBODY KNOWS WHERE TO FIND HIM!
I'm looking for something I don't want to find.
POOL
ASK ME, YOU OUGHTA TRY A SEWER! THAT'S WHERE RATS LIKE HAGEN HANG OUT!

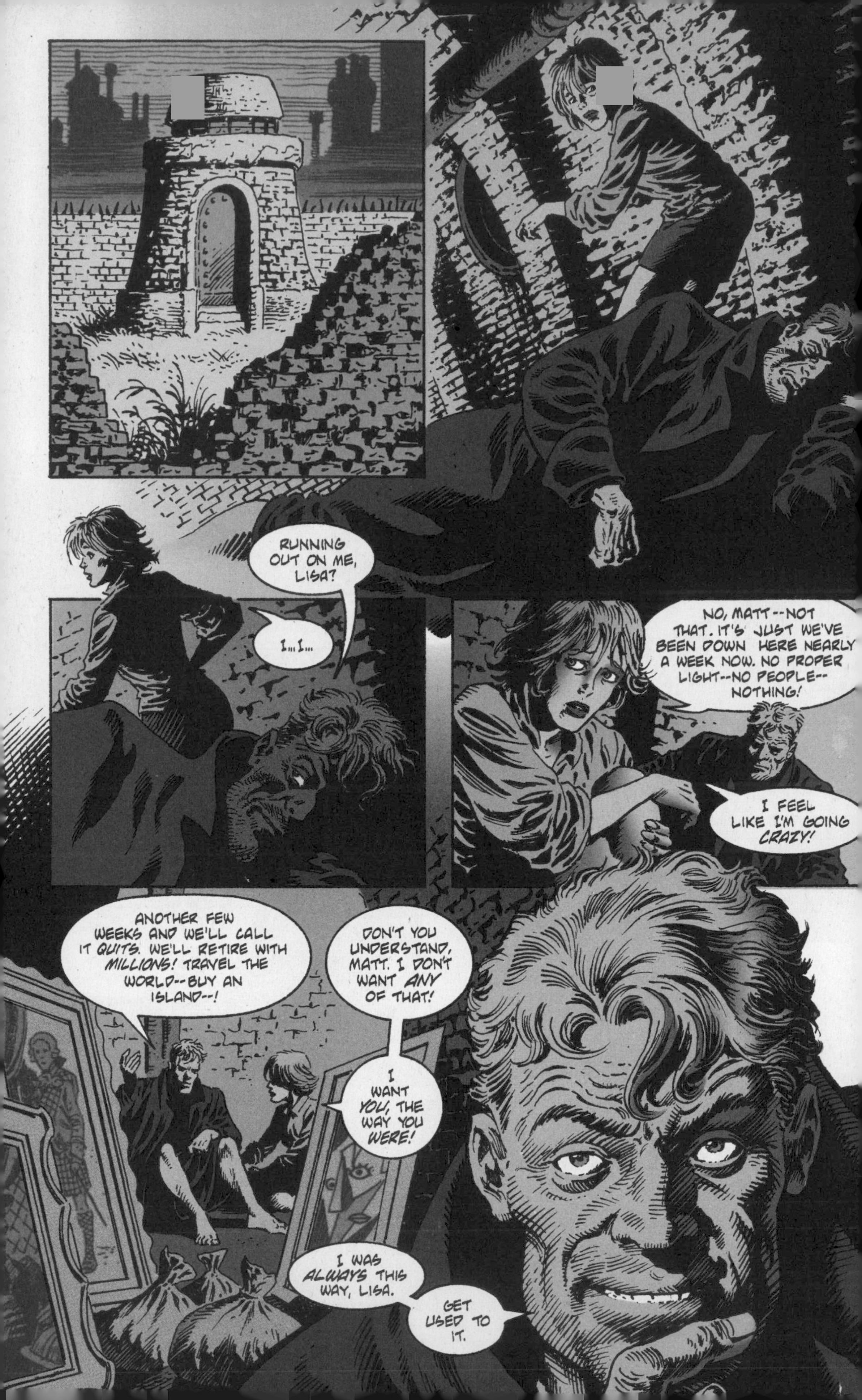
RUNNING OUT ON ME, LISA?
I...I...
NO, MATT--NOT THAT. IT'S JUST WE'VE BEEN DOWN HERE NEARLY A WEEK NOW. NO PROPER LIGHT--NO PEOPLE--NOTHING!
I FEEL LIKE I'M GOING *CRAZY!*
ANOTHER FEW WEEKS AND WE'LL CALL IT *QUITS.* WE'LL RETIRE WITH *MILLIONS!* TRAVEL THE WORLD--BUY AN ISLAND--!
DON'T YOU UNDERSTAND, MATT. I DON'T WANT *ANY* OF THAT!
I WANT *YOU,* THE WAY YOU *WERE!*
I WAS *ALWAYS* THIS WAY, LISA.
GET USED TO IT.

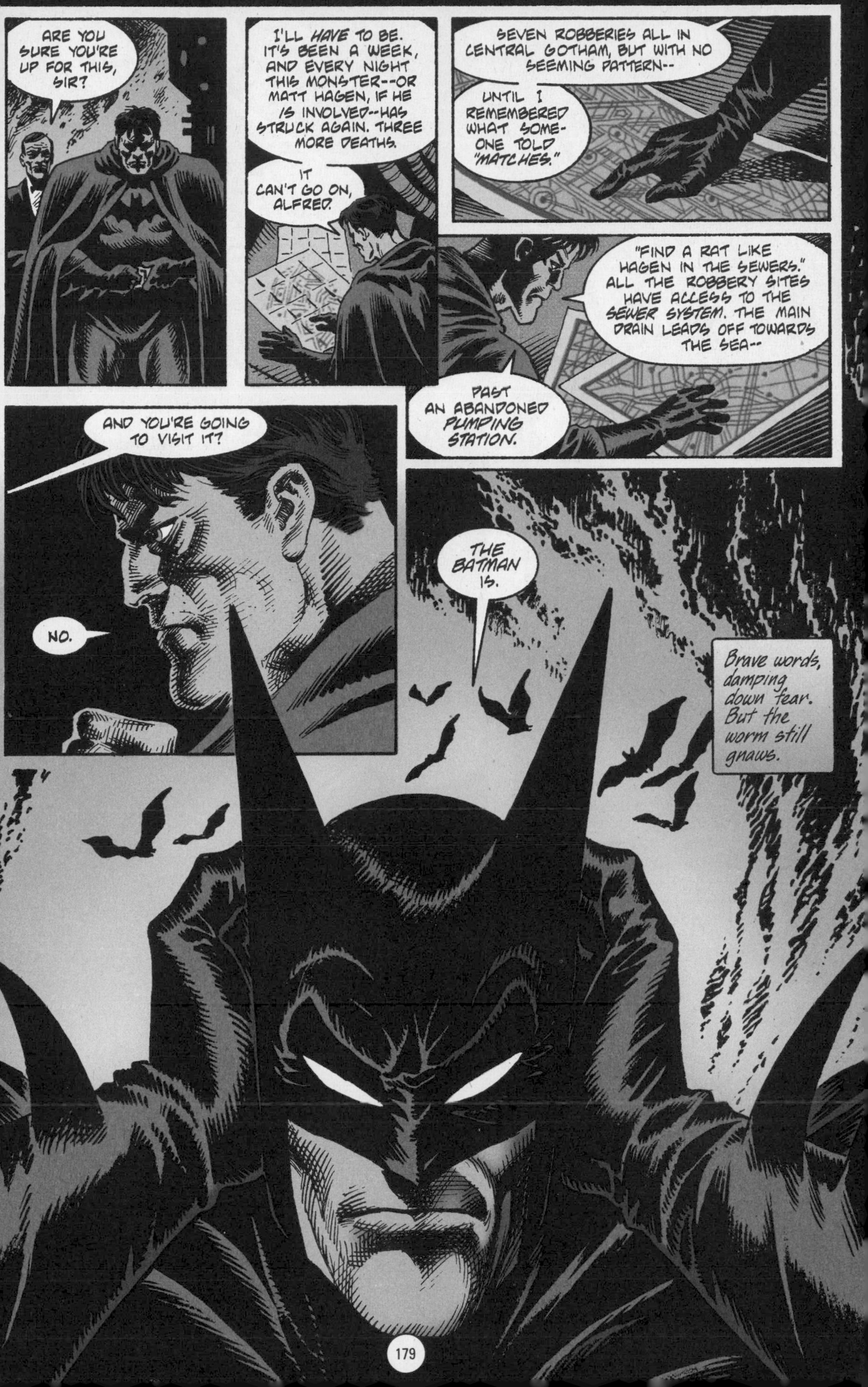
ARE YOU SURE YOU'RE UP FOR THIS, SIR?
I'LL HAVE TO BE. IT'S BEEN A WEEK, AND EVERY NIGHT THIS MONSTER--OR MATT HAGEN, IF HE IS INVOLVED--HAS STRUCK AGAIN. THREE MORE DEATHS.
IT CAN'T GO ON, ALFRED.
SEVEN ROBBERIES ALL IN CENTRAL GOTHAM, BUT WITH NO SEEMING PATTERN--
UNTIL I REMEMBERED WHAT SOMEONE TOLD "MATCHES."
"FIND A RAT LIKE HAGEN IN THE SEWERS." ALL THE ROBBERY SITES HAVE ACCESS TO THE SEWER SYSTEM. THE MAIN DRAIN LEADS OFF TOWARDS THE SEA--
PAST AN ABANDONED PUMPING STATION.
AND YOU'RE GOING TO VISIT IT?
NO.
THE BATMAN IS.
Brave words, damping down fear. But the worm still gnaws.

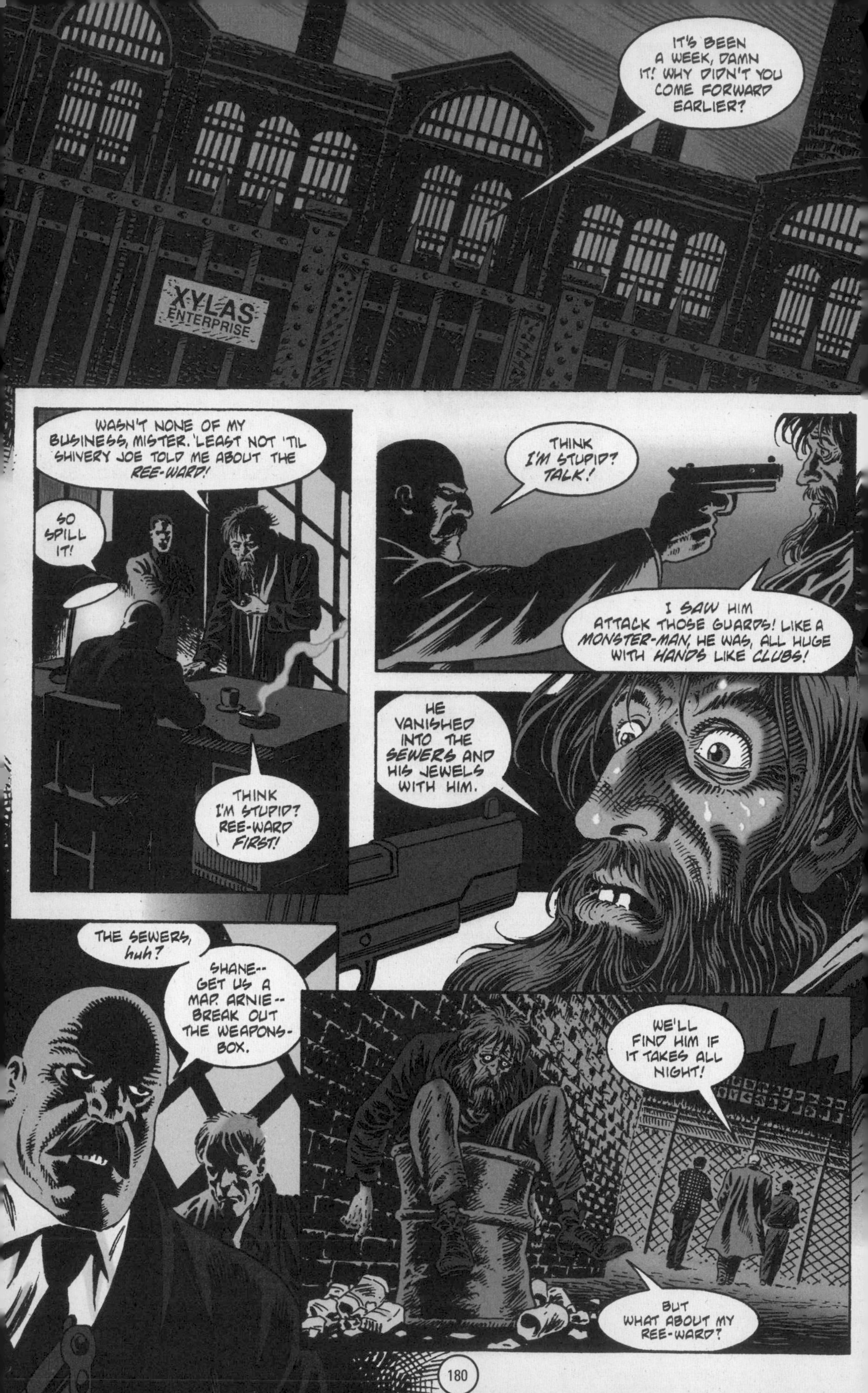

XYLAS ENTERPRISE
IT'S BEEN A WEEK, DAMN IT! WHY DIDN'T YOU COME FORWARD EARLIER?
WASN'T NONE OF MY BUSINESS, MISTER. 'LEAST NOT 'TIL SHIVERY JOE TOLD ME ABOUT THE REE-WARD!
SO SPILL IT!
THINK I'M STUPID? REE-WARD FIRST!
THINK I'M STUPID? TALK!
I SAW HIM ATTACK THOSE GUARDS! LIKE A MONSTER-MAN, HE WAS, ALL HUGE WITH HANDS LIKE CLUBS!
HE VANISHED INTO THE SEWERS AND HIS JEWELS WITH HIM.
THE SEWERS, huh?
SHANE-- GET US A MAP. ARNIE-- BREAK OUT THE WEAPONS-BOX.
WE'LL FIND HIM IF IT TAKES ALL NIGHT!
BUT WHAT ABOUT MY REE-WARD?

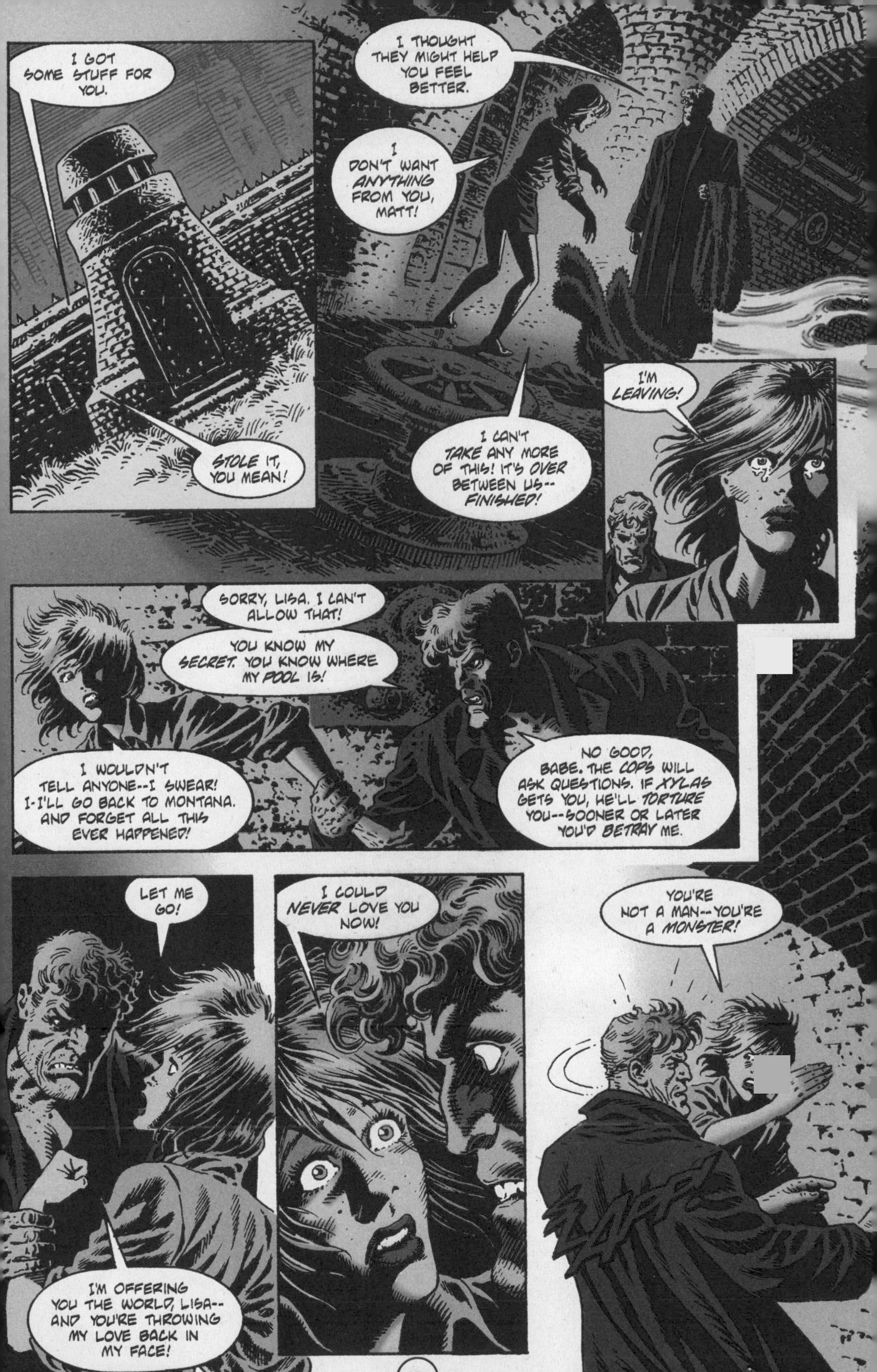
I GOT SOME STUFF FOR YOU.
STOLE IT, YOU MEAN!
I THOUGHT THEY MIGHT HELP YOU FEEL BETTER.
I DON'T WANT ANYTHING FROM YOU, MATT!
I CAN'T TAKE ANY MORE OF THIS! IT'S OVER BETWEEN US-- FINISHED!
I'M LEAVING!
SORRY, LISA. I CAN'T ALLOW THAT!
YOU KNOW MY SECRET. YOU KNOW WHERE MY POOL IS!
I WOULDN'T TELL ANYONE--I SWEAR! I-I'LL GO BACK TO MONTANA. AND FORGET ALL THIS EVER HAPPENED!
NO GOOD, BABE. THE COPS WILL ASK QUESTIONS. IF XYLAS GETS YOU, HE'LL TORTURE YOU--SOONER OR LATER YOU'D BETRAY ME.
LET ME GO!
I'M OFFERING YOU THE WORLD, LISA-- AND YOU'RE THROWING MY LOVE BACK IN MY FACE!
I COULD NEVER LOVE YOU NOW!
YOU'RE NOT A MAN--YOU'RE A MONSTER!

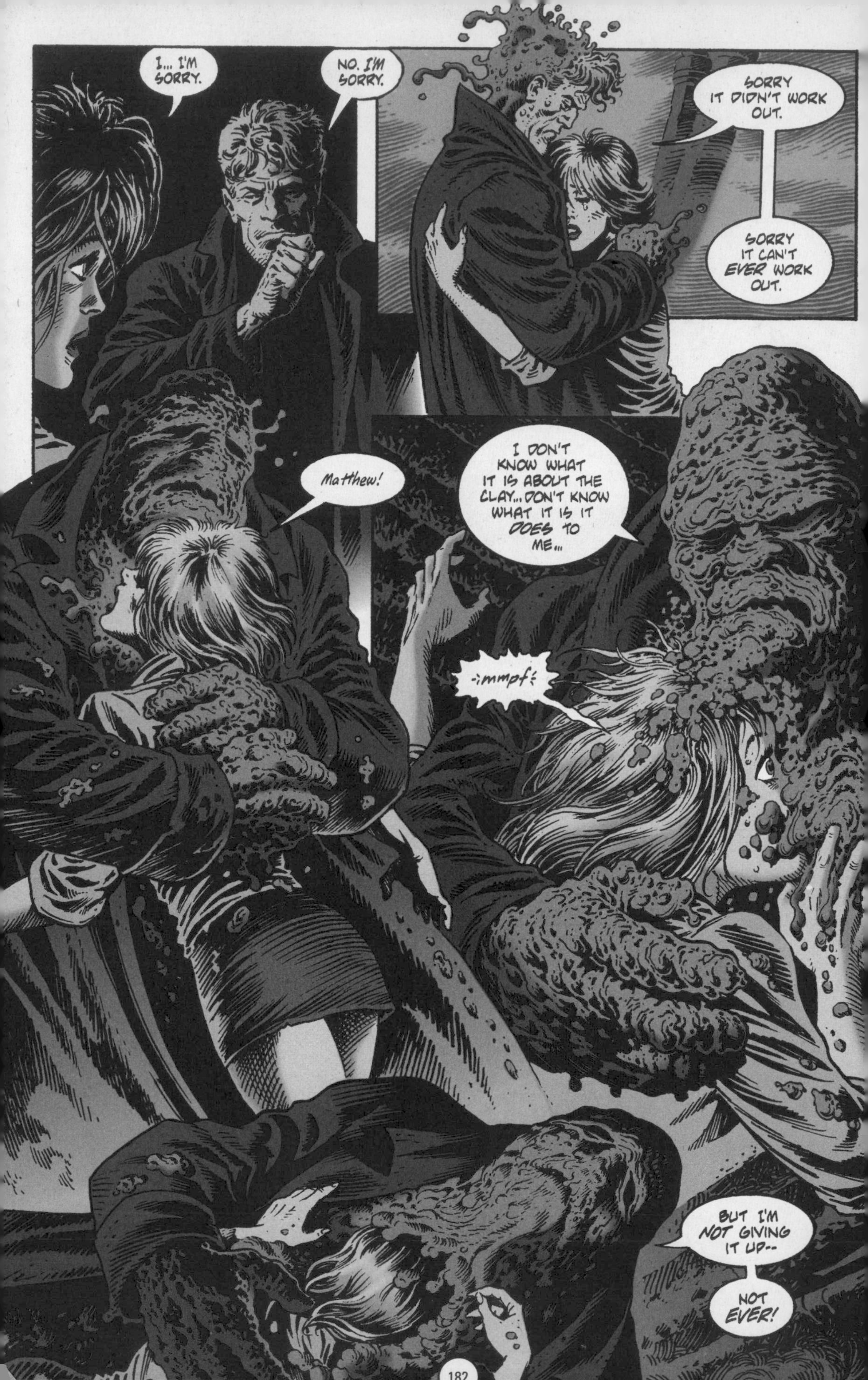
I... I'M SORRY.
NO. I'M SORRY.
SORRY IT DIDN'T WORK OUT.
SORRY IT CAN'T EVER WORK OUT.
Matthew!
I DON'T KNOW WHAT IT IS ABOUT THE CLAY... DON'T KNOW WHAT IT IS IT DOES TO ME...
mmpf
BUT I'M NOT GIVING IT UP--
NOT EVER!

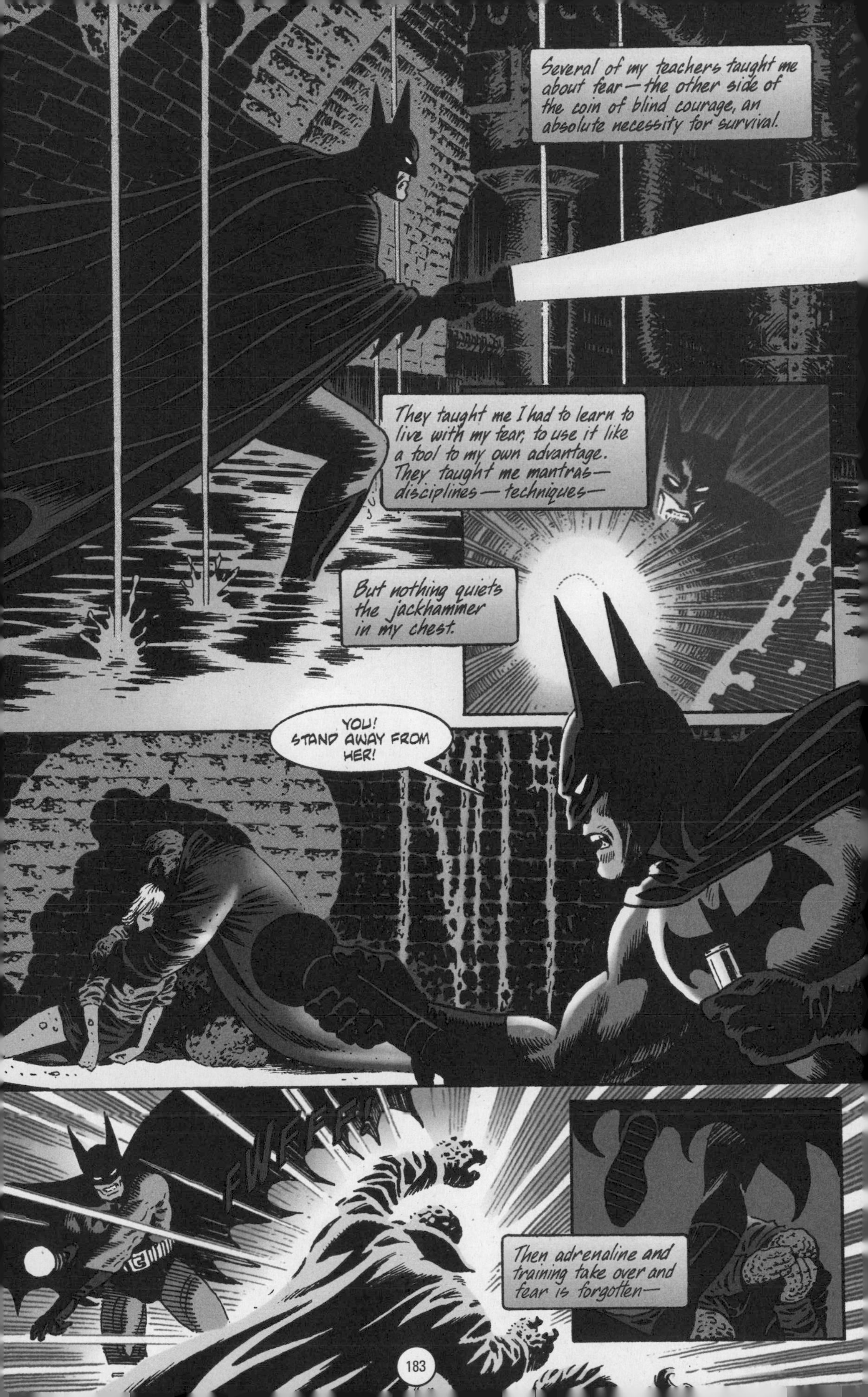
Several of my teachers taught me about fear—the other side of the coin of blind courage, an absolute necessity for survival.
They taught me I had to learn to live with my fear, to use it like a tool to my own advantage. They taught me mantras—disciplines—techniques—
But nothing quiets the jackhammer in my chest.
YOU! STAND AWAY FROM HER!
FWFFF!
Then adrenaline and training take over and fear is forgotten—

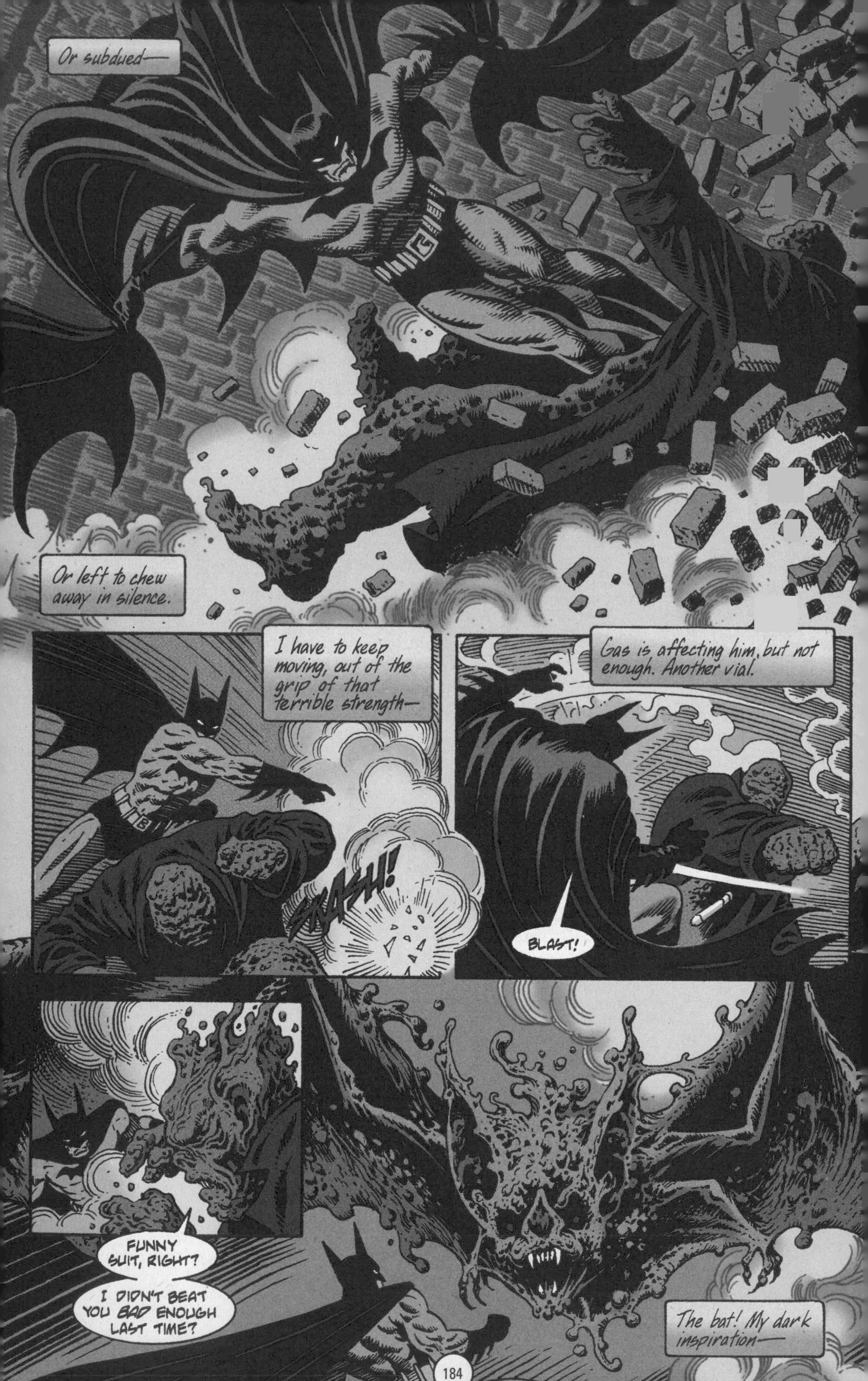

Or subdued—
Or left to chew away in silence.
I have to keep moving, out of the grip of that terrible strength—
SMASH!
Gas is affecting him, but not enough. Another vial.
BLAST!
FUNNY SUIT, RIGHT?
I DIDN'T BEAT YOU BAD ENOUGH LAST TIME?
The bat! My dark inspiration—

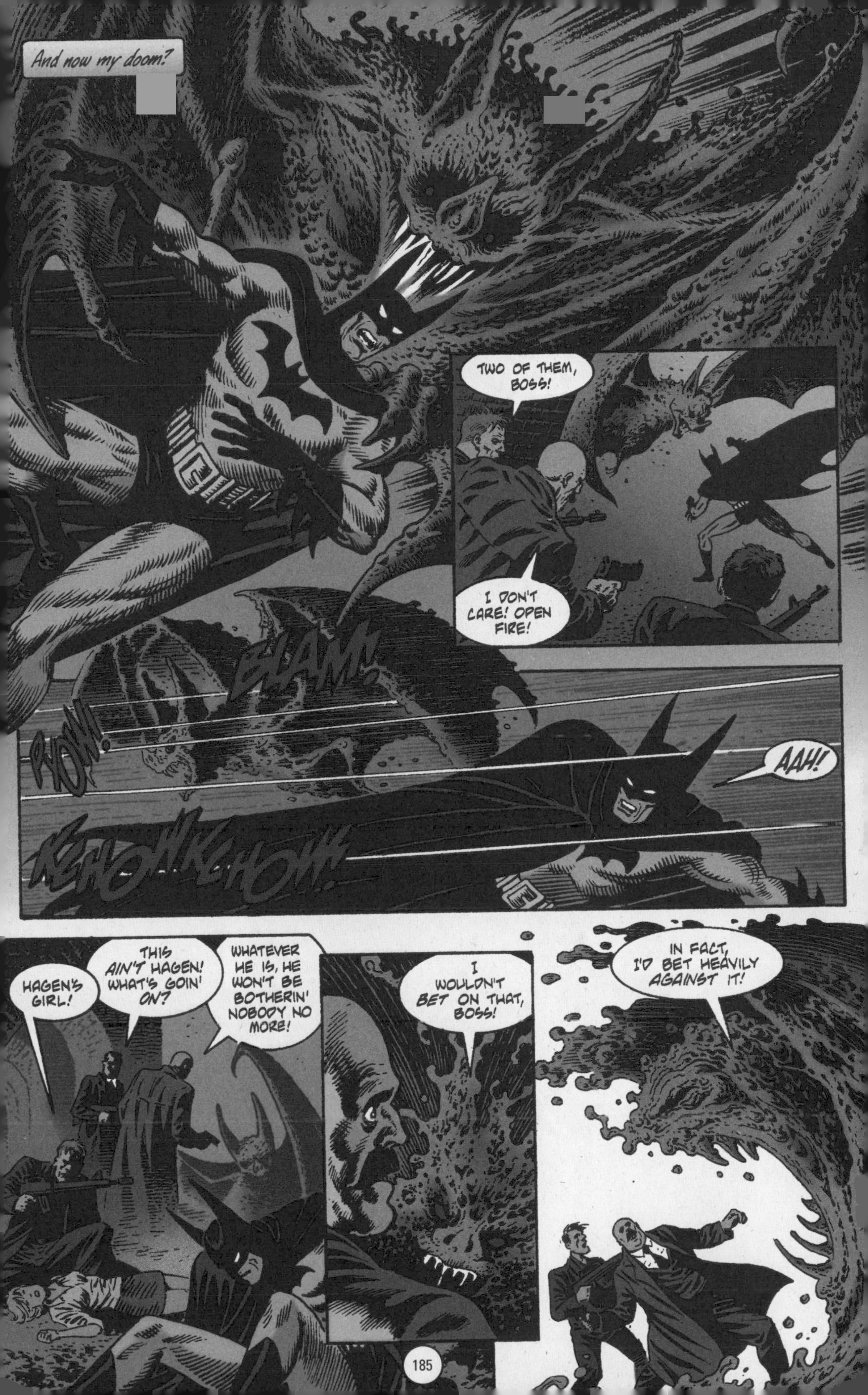
And now my doom?
TWO OF THEM, BOSS!
I DON'T CARE! OPEN FIRE!
BLAM!
PYOW!
KCHOW! KCHOW!
AAH!
HAGEN'S GIRL!
THIS AIN'T HAGEN! WHAT'S GOIN' ON?
WHATEVER HE IS, HE WON'T BE BOTHERIN' NOBODY NO MORE!
I WOULDN'T BET ON THAT, BOSS!
IN FACT, I'D BET HEAVILY AGAINST IT!

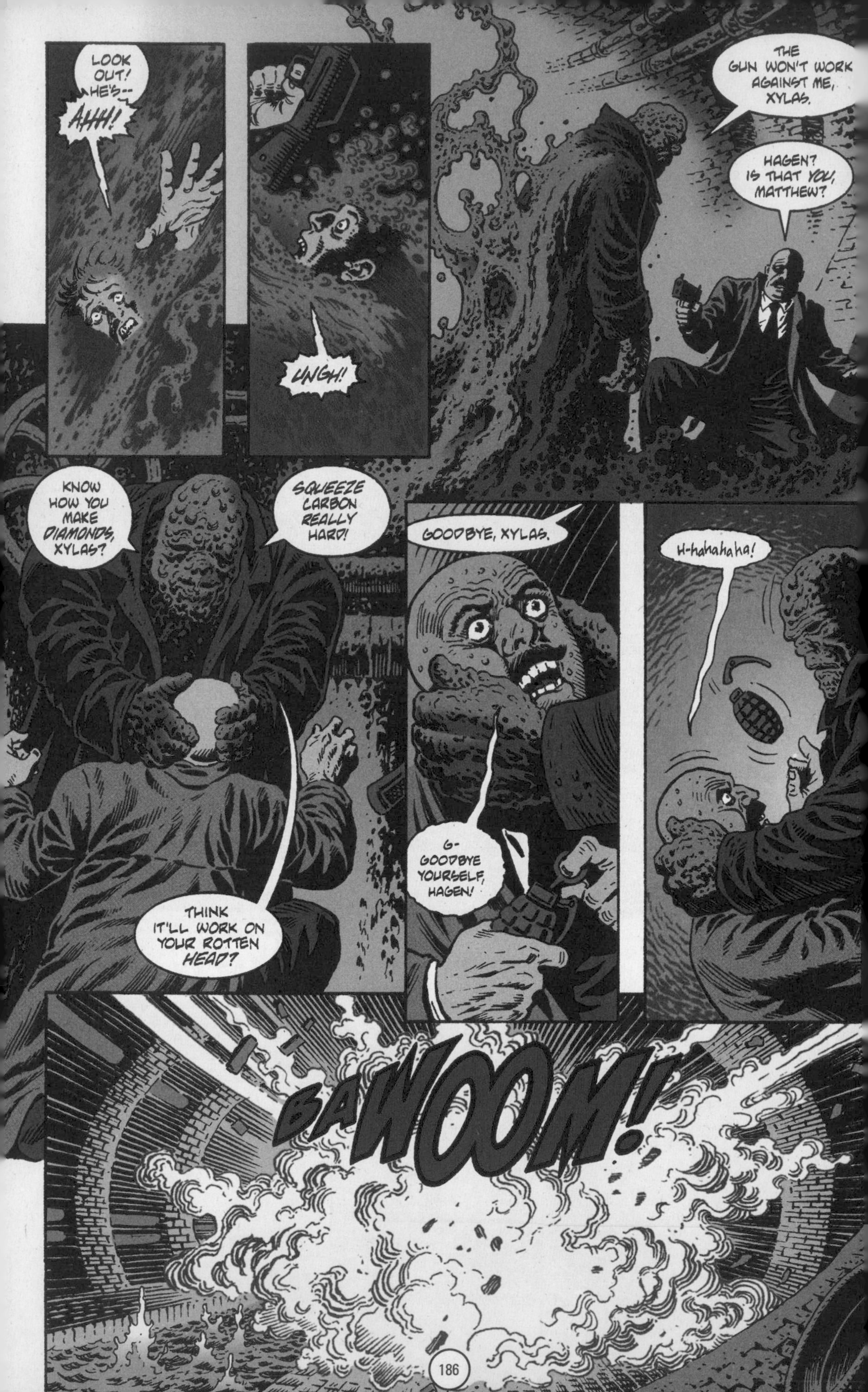

LOOK OUT! HE'S-- AHHH!
UNGH!
THE GUN WON'T WORK AGAINST ME, XYLAS.
HAGEN? IS THAT YOU, MATTHEW?
KNOW HOW YOU MAKE DIAMONDS, XYLAS?
SQUEEZE CARBON REALLY HARD!
THINK IT'LL WORK ON YOUR ROTTEN HEAD?
GOODBYE, XYLAS.
G-GOODBYE YOURSELF, HAGEN!
H-hahahaha!
BA WOOM!

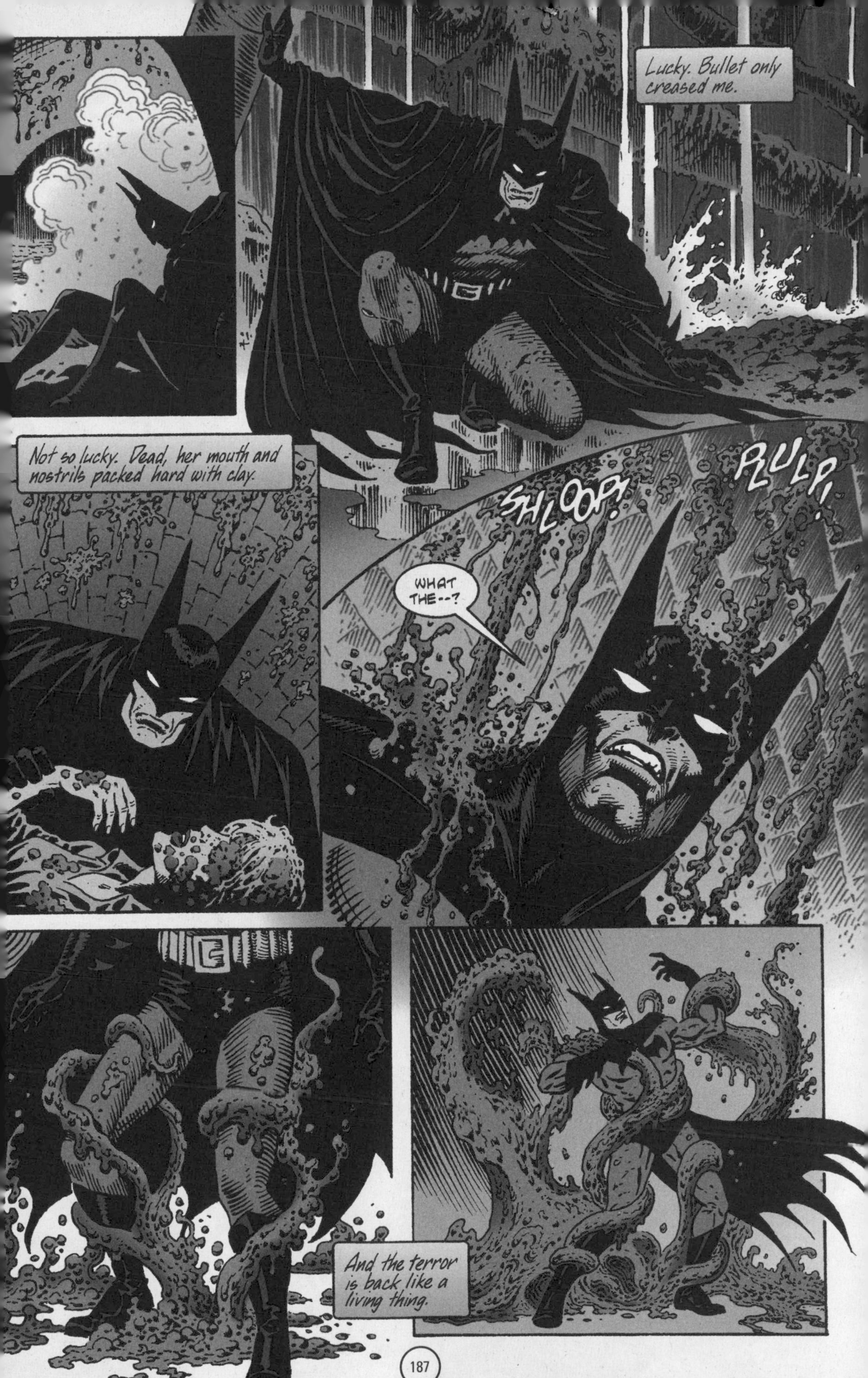
Lucky. Bullet only creased me.
Not so lucky. Dead, her mouth and nostrils packed hard with clay.
SHLOOP!
PLULP!
WHAT THE--?
And the terror is back like a living thing.

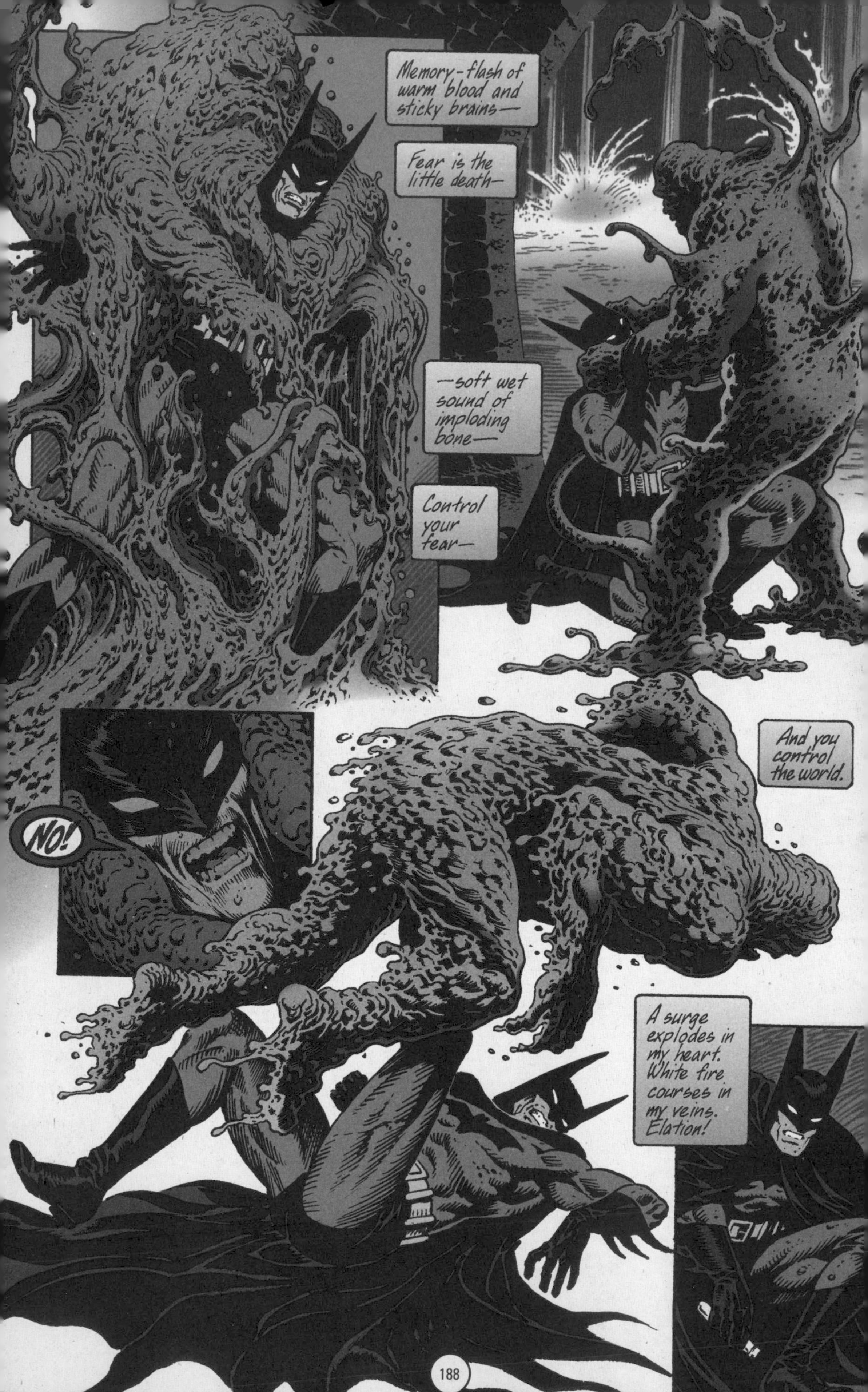
Memory-flash of warm blood and sticky brains—
Fear is the little death—
—soft wet sound of imploding bone—
Control your fear—
NO!
And you control the world.
A surge explodes in my heart. White fire courses in my veins. Elation!

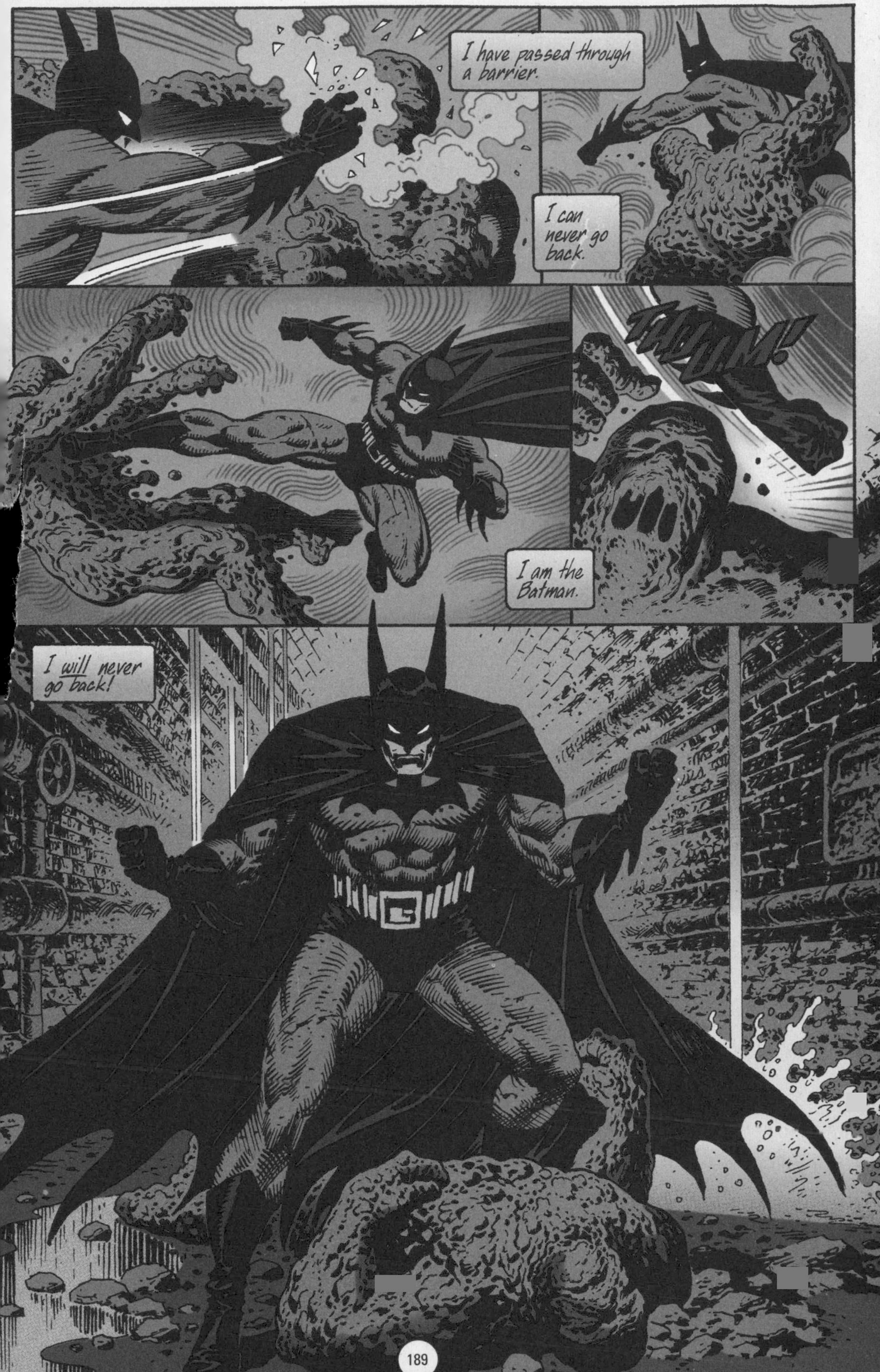
I have passed through a barrier.
I can never go back.
THOOM!
I am the Batman.
I will never go back!

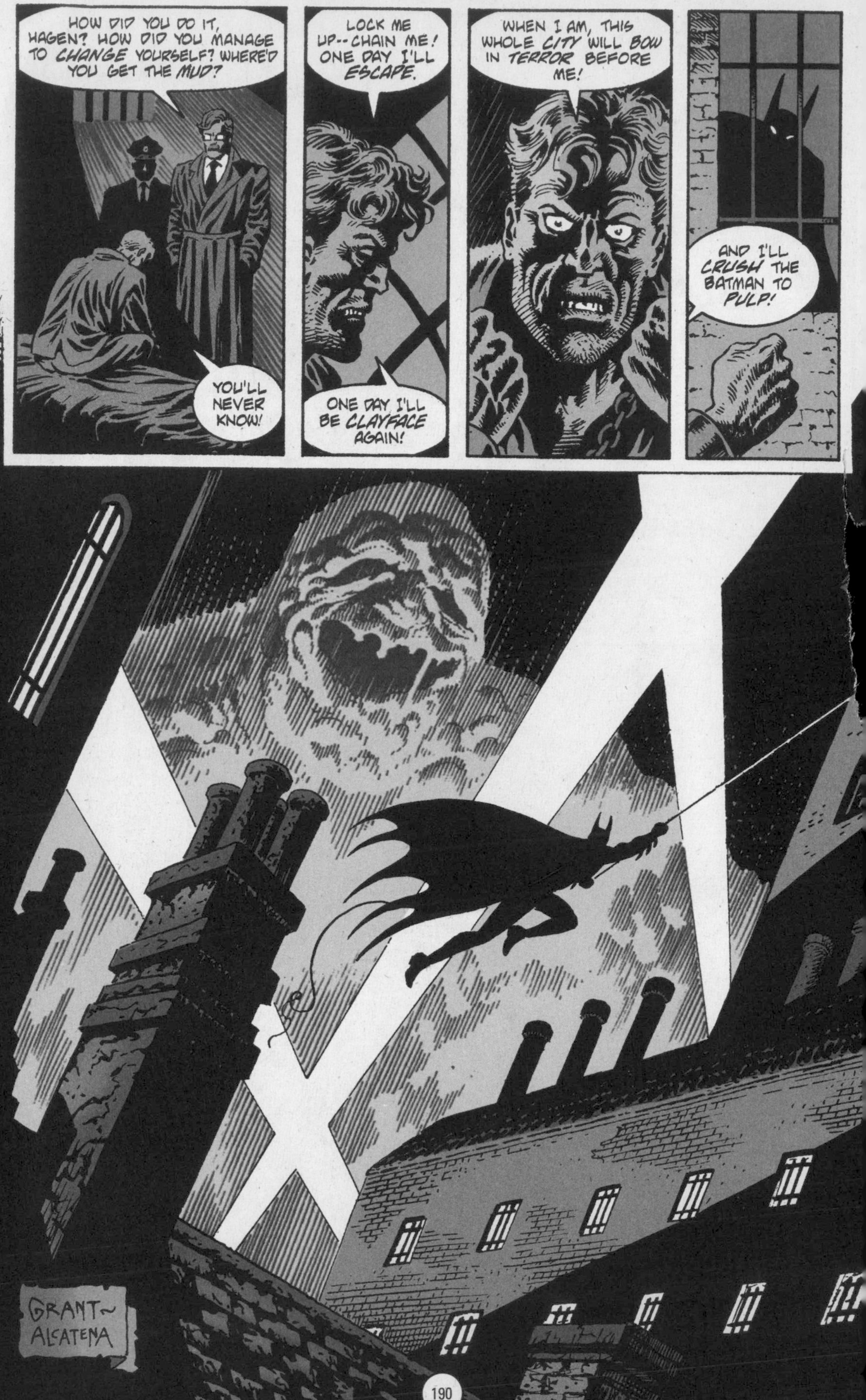
HOW DID YOU DO IT, HAGEN? HOW DID YOU MANAGE TO CHANGE YOURSELF? WHERE'D YOU GET THE MUD?
YOU'LL NEVER KNOW!
LOCK ME UP--CHAIN ME! ONE DAY I'LL ESCAPE.
ONE DAY I'LL BE CLAYFACE AGAIN!
WHEN I AM, THIS WHOLE CITY WILL BOW IN TERROR BEFORE ME!
AND I'LL CRUSH THE BATMAN TO PULP!
GRANT~ ALCATENA

MORE CLASSIC TALES OF THE DARK KNIGHT

BATMAN: HUSH
VOLUME TWO

BATMAN:
THE LONG HALLOWEEN

**JEPH LOEB
JIM LEE**

**JEPH LOEB
JIM LEE**

**JEPH LOEB
TIM SALE**

BATMAN:
DARK VICTORY

BATMAN:
HAUNTED KNIGHT

BATMAN:
YEAR 100

**JEPH LOEB
TIM SALE**

**JEPH LOEB
TIM SALE**

PAUL POPE

SEARCH THE GRAPHIC NOVELS SECTION OF
DCCOMICS.COM
FOR ART AND INFORMATION ON ALL OF OUR BOOKS!